Mark Durman's first career was as a British army officer, leaving as a brigadier. His second was as director of security for a US company. In both jobs, he lived in and/or regularly visited many countries throughout Europe, Africa, the Middle East and Asia and was deeply exposed to all the main religions of the world, to the arguments of believers in faiths, of non-believers and of those who still remained undecided. Mark has four previously published books, each set in different parts of the world. After retirement, he divides his time between Alicante, Spain and Paris.

Why? One Man's Journey

Mark Durman

Why? One Man's Journey

Vanguard Press

VANGUARD PAPERBACK

A CIP catalogue record for this title is available from the British Library.

ISBN 978-1-83794-367-8

Vanguard Press is an imprint of
Pegasus Elliot Mackenzie Publishers Ltd.
www.pegasuspublishers.com

First Published in 2025

Vanguard Press

Sheraton House Castle Park
Cambridge England

Printed & Bound in Great Britain

Dedication

To my sons, Anthony and William.

Acknowledgements

In writing this book, I had to delve back into a lifetime of experiences. I would particularly like to thank the following:

Claire Davies, editor of “OElink”, the magazine of King Edwards School, Bath. Claire’s support for my articles and for organising social events at the school rekindled so many adolescent memories.

Ian Cooling, former branch secretary of the Intelligence Corps Association and Hazel Donald ICA HQ Support Manager for keeping me in touch with the Corps.

Jim Knox for bringing us “old and bold” back together at Sandhurst in June 2023 to commemorate our time together at the Army Staff College, Camberley.

Timmy Henry, Clive O’Flynn, Sven Vermeulen, Jerome De Paepe, Sara Victoria Sandberg (née Eden) and many others working for Brink’s EMEA throughout Europe, Israel and South Africa, who gave me terrific support and friendship during my “second career”.

Paul Wood, Anna, Ben and Nelly and all our many friends and colleagues from the Walkers International Group, Torrevieja, Spain who have helped to keep me fit during the past ten years.

Thomas Forster for his computer expertise in sorting out my laptop every time it “froze”, a not infrequent occurrence!

Above all, I would like to thank Danièle Gourdon, herself a very successful author, for her patience, understanding and continued support. Researching and writing books can be a long and wearying business. It helps so much when we are both stressing at the same time.

Also by Mark Durman

Cash in Transit
The Warehouse
Verification
Adsum: Mission and Passion

Table of Contents

Part Three

Reflections

Part Four

Conclusions

Why? One Man's Journey

Preamble

"*The universe is a pretty big place. If it's just us, seems like an awful waste of space.*" – Carl Sagan

We're born, we live, we die. That's the fate of every human and of all other species on Planet Earth. The Christian Bible reminds us that we all have an appointment with death (Hebrews 9:27) which comes to the rich and poor alike. Death is no respecter of persons or families. Why do we exist, what is the point of us, what is the meaning of life and what happens when we die? There have been thousands of attempts to answer these questions but there's still no agreed solution. This book has another go.

The lives of homo sapiens have infinite variations such as place and date of birth, race, skin colour, social culture, religious upbringing, political pressures, birth sign. Some humans are born into prosperous families, live long, healthy lives and die in old age. Others are born into poverty, are ravaged by disease and die young. Some are born into families with strong religious influences and/or become believers in a faith: Christian, Muslim, Buddhist, Hindu or one of the many other faiths and sects. Some believe, are even convinced through their faith, they know what will happen to them when they die. The lives of some are dominated by political structures – democratic, fascist, communist. Some people are agnostic, some are atheist, have no religious beliefs but support Darwinian principles of evolution by natural selection. Do we go to heaven, hell or some other place or state or do we just cease to exist with no afterlife, no reincarnation, nothing, nada?

Throughout the ages, many theologians, philosophers, and other influencers have tackled this subject. Examples are:

. The Greek philosophers, for example, Socrates, Plato and Aristotle, who had a major influence on man's thinking for over a thousand years. They still do!

. The Christian "Holy Bible" which remains top of the book best-selling list. The Guinness Book of World Records estimates that more than five billion copies have been printed.

. The Qur'an (or Quran or Koran): the central religious text of Islam, believed by Muslims to be a revelation from God.

. The Hindu "Vedas": believed by Hindus to be the very breath of the supreme Brahman.

. The Buddhist Holy book "Tipitaka": believed to be the earliest collection of Buddhist writings.

. Theologians, philosophers and scientists such as Thomas Aquinas, Dante Alighieri, Baruch Spinoza, Voltaire, Sigmund Freud, Immanuel Kant, Friedrich Nietzsche, Charles Darwin, Bertrand Russell, Albert Einstein, Billy Graham, Martin Luther King, Stephen Hawking, Richard Dawkins and many, many more.

The works of these learned experts and religious texts reflect a wide spectrum of man's understanding of our world. I marvel at the vision and academic excellence of so many of these works. But I have a problem. Apart from the wide diversity of opinion whether or not there is a god, a creator, so many works fail to relate to the widely differing characteristics of the human being and to the mundane lives that many of us lead. We stumble along through life, sometimes learning from the many mistakes we make, sometimes not, sometimes leading inspiring lives which might be worthy of advancing to a higher after-life state, sometimes messing up either by intent or circumstance; and sometimes just drifting along. I believe that a principal purpose of religion and philosophy is to understand and relate to the life of the human being. Not some universal, mono-person but real living, breathing, frail, error prone human beings with all our emotions and individual personalities.

I have studied the works of many brilliant academics with professorships and other distinguished degrees awarded by various universities or establishments of spiritual learning. Many live, or have lived in the rarefied world of their university or church environment, mixed mainly with other academics or clerics and spent much of their time lecturing or preaching to others. Their lives had the advantage of living and working at a high academic level; but they often failed to relate fully to the challenges faced by many of us simple mortals; and there are a lot of us around. The most recent estimate puts the world's population as eight billion with India's population (1.429 billion) just surpassing that of China (1.426) billion. (The Times 2022).

There's another thing. Why do so many of the "meaning of life" books, especially those written by theologians lack the human emotion of humour? In my research, I found the odd reference to "joy" but usually in a constrained, prim and thin-lipped manner. Life doesn't have to be too serious, it can be funny especially when we laugh at our own stupidity!

Part One of this book reviews the main religions of the world. Christianity, Islam and Judaism share some common characteristics that distinguish them from other of the world's religions: belief in one god and in a sacred scripture – "the book". They share many similar concepts: one god made the universe and one god will end it. Each human has a soul and at his death, the soul separates from the body and goes into another dimension. There is a judgment to be made concerning the moral worthiness of each human at death for an eternal reward or punishment. Time is linear and there is only one period of existence for individuals and the entire universe. I examine what different faiths mean by saying "I believe." I look at how the Christian faith has been challenged and modified during its two-thousand-year history. I show how the Muslim faith is interpreted in different national cultures and outline the main beliefs of the Jewish, Hindu, Buddhist and other world religions. I also explore the effect that science has had particularly regarding the evolution and convictions of those who do not believe there is such a being as a god or a creator.

I examine what each of the above categories conclude regarding the meaning of our one time on planet earth; or more if we're reincarnated! I also look at some other factors which have profound influences on us humans. Why, for example, is music so universally popular? Why do some songs endure and are continuously repeated over the years, by all age groups and social backgrounds? Why does sport have such a major influence on people's lives? Football has billions of followers world-wide. From supporters of local clubs to the devoted fans of today's top national teams, sport enthrals and probably has far more influence on people's lives today than do most politicians, religious leaders or philosophers.

In Part Two of this book, I follow the detailed life of one human being, when and where it occurred, how it evolved and matured, what personal, social, professional and political influences it was exposed to and what were the effects, how it transitioned from childhood into old age via all the variants, stages, pressures, thoughts, desires, drives, likes, loves, hates, deceits, dreams, ambitions, disappointments, successes, failures along the way.

I searched for a suitable candidate, male or female, as a model or test benchmark. I considered such religious leaders as Jesus Christ or Muhammad bin Abdullah, or political icons such as Abraham Lincoln, Theodore Roosevelt, Martin Luther King, Winston Churchill or Margaret Thatcher. Then I considered choosing the life of a famous sportsman or woman, or of an author or film star or singer; but there is only so much of the lives of any of these eminent people which is known. For example, although there have been many biographies written about Winston Churchill and he also wrote his own very comprehensive memoirs; yet even with all this available information, there are still major gaps; how did his thoughts evolve from his childhood, what self-doubts did he feel, what jealousies, inner desires, feelings of guilt? Did he have dreams, if so, what about? And what might these feelings and emotions have had on his understanding of the meaning of his life? Such minute details about

Churchill, or any of the other candidates that I considered, are not available and yet without a fully comprehensive understanding of the full range of thoughts and emotions, any study of the life of a sample human being is incomplete.

There is only one model life that I know intimately – and that's my own, already into its ninth decade; longevity has its uses as the mind is a wonderful storehouse of experience. My life has not been extraordinary but nor has it been straightforward. During my lifetime, I have lived and worked in every continent of the world, have been directly exposed to all the world's main religions, have been with soldiers and others when they died and have many times been close to death myself. At times, my personal and domestic life has been a real mess, often through my own self-inflicted mistakes. I doubt if many of our leading spiritualists or philosophers have had such a wide range of personal experiences. I also doubt that they made as many mistakes as I have. Or if they did, I wonder if they would be prepared to admit them!

In Part Three, I summarise the main points made in Parts One and Two and examine how my personal life's experiences relate both to the main established religions and to other major influences. I then attempt in Part Four to draw some conclusions about what all the above means and what seem to work best, at least for me!

Part One: Religions: Believers and Non-Believers

Introduction

In this section I highlight some of the leading individuals who influenced religious thinking, particularly of the Christian faith, and record how religious faiths interact, sometimes reinforcing but often clashing. I have included examples of the works of many outstanding philosophers who have contributed to the eternal quest to understand the meaning of life and what may happen when we die. I have also included sections on: agnosticism, atheism, evolution, reincarnation, near death experiences, child prodigies, the interpretation of dreams and the power and influence of music and sport.

Chapter One

Christianity: The Challenge to Catholicism

"*Religion is excellent stuff for keeping people quiet.*" – Napoléon.

"*I am a deeply religious nonbeliever – this is a somewhat new kind of religion.*" – Albert Einstein

For over one thousand years, the Roman Catholic church was almost unchallenged as the Christian theological consensus. Key influencers whose ideas gradually led to divergence from the traditional Catholic church, and the emergence of the numerous variants of the Christian faith included some remarkable and brilliant individuals. Some leading examples are listed below.

Thomas Aquinas (1225–1274)

Aquinas, (real name San Tommaso d'Aquino) was an Italian Dominican priest whose work stands between antiquity and modernity. He has been referred to as "the greatest figure in thirteenth century Europe." As a student, he studied the texts of ancient Greek and Roman authors and their relationship to the Christian faith. He is widely admired for his arguments for reconciling faith with reason. He believed that in Western European civilisation, any human being, not only Christians, could have access to "great truths" whenever they made use of God's greatest gift – reason. He produced a comprehensive synthesis of Christian theology and Aristotelian philosophy that has influenced Roman Catholic doctrine for centuries. Aquinas argued that faith and science operate on two levels, having religious ethical laws and secular natural laws. After his death at the early age of forty-nine, he was canonised by the Church. His work has had many devotees through the centuries including until today. He was a prolific writer, producing many books during his short lifetime. His most acclaimed works include; Summa Theologica and Treatise on Happiness. He is attributed of having advised "Do unto others as you would have them do unto you" – a saying which has been a cornerstone of moral principles in most societies. More on this later!

Dante Alighieri (1265–1321)

Dante, an Italian poet, political and language theorist has influenced our culture and society since his composition of the three part "The Divine Comedy" – Hell, Purgatory, Heaven. This work has been inspirational to succeeding generations through to today. Although there appears to be no evidence that Dante was not a Christian, he was powerfully critical of many aspects of Roman Catholicism, for example he deplored the Church's sale of indulgencies. The Divine Comedy is a powerful and epic literary work; more than the authors of the Bible itself. Dante provided his readers with his vision of Hell that itself has inspired painters (e.g. Botticelli, Blake and Salvador Dali) and even today is the source of film makers, science fiction and computer games. T S Eliot described his influence; "Dante and Shakespeare divide the world between them. There is no third".

Comment: I include a third – the Russian Fyodor Dostoevsky (1821–1881) as both his *The Brothers Karamazov* and *Crime and Punishment* are in my view, sensationally deep and monumental books.

Dante's Divine Comedy mixes Christian theology with Greco-Roman myth as if both are equally true and can coexist together. He had the presumption to fill in what the Bible leaves out. His picture of Hell draws from Aristotle's view that reason is the most important thing in life (as Aquinas also concluded) – which later led to the idea in Protestantism that "an individual's reason is their path to salvation".

The Divine Comedy has been described as "a fulcrum in Western history" as it brings together literary and theological expression, pagan and Christian. His vision of the Afterlife influenced the Reformation, the

Renaissance and ignited much of the religious and philosophical thinking of the modern world.

The Reformation

This revolution in Christian thinking took place in the sixteenth century. Until this period, the Roman Catholic church had become deeply involved in the political life of western Europe. The resulting intrigues and political manipulations, combined with the church's increasing power and wealth contributed to the mounting criticism of the church as a spiritual force. Abuses such as the sale of indulgencies (or spiritual privileges) and other practices of corruption undermined the church's spiritual authority. Despite this, for most people, the church continued to offer spiritual comfort and was largely unchallenged as the accepted explanation of how the world had been created and was the morale authority of how people should live their lives.

John Wycliffe (1328–1384)

An early sceptic and critique of Roman Catholicism was this English scholastic philosopher and theologian. Wycliffe is widely considered one of the medieval forerunners of the protestant reformation. His criticism of the practices and beliefs of the Roman church preceded those of later reformers. Wycliffe also directed a translation of the Bible into English.

Desiderius Erasmus (1469–1536)

Another early reformer was the Dutchman Erasmus, known as Erasmus of Rotterdam and revered as "the Prince of the Humanists" for his influential scholarships and writings. A man of great intellect, Erasmus rose from humble origins to become one of Europe's greatest thinkers. His translation to Greek of the New Testament heralded a theological revolution at the forefront of which were Martin Luther and John Calvin.

Although the Reformation period marked the start of new variants of the Christian faith, the main players still retained their basic belief in Christianity and of Jesus Christ as being the son of God, the creator.

Martin Luther (1483–1546)

Luther was a German monk who was one of the most controversial figures in the history of Christianity. Luther called into question some of the basic tenets of Roman Catholicism and his followers split from the Roman Catholic Church to begin the protestant tradition. A prominent theologian, Luther's desire for people to feel closer to God led him to translate the Bible into a language of the people, radically changing the relationship between church leaders and their followers.

Luther's initial degree (University of Erfurt) was in grammar, logic, rhetoric and metaphysics and his intention was to become a lawyer. However, in 1505, he had a life changing experience that set him on a new course to becoming a monk. Caught in a horrific thunderstorm where he feared for his life, Luther cried out to St Anne, the patron saint of miners, his family's background: "Save me St Anne, and I'll become a monk!" The storm subsided and he was saved. It is not clear whether this was a spontaneous act or the idea was already in his mind as he was also driven by fears of Hell and God's wrath and felt that life in a monastery would help him find salvation.

Aged twenty-seven, Luther was appointed a delegate to a Catholic church conference in Rome. At this, he became disillusioned by what he thought was the immorality and corruption he witnessed there among the Catholic priests. After returning to Germany, Luther enrolled in the University of Wittenberg where he excelled in his studies, received a doctorate, becoming a professor of theology. During his lectures, he came to realise that the key to spiritual salvation was not to fear God or be enslaved by religious dogma but to believe that faith alone would bring salvation. This period marked a major change in his life and set the Reformation in motion.

On 31 October 1517, Luther, angry with Pope Leo X's new round of indulgencies to raise public funds to build St Peter's Basilica, nailed a sheet of paper with his "95 Theses" on the University of Wittenberg's chapel door. Though Luther had intended these to be discussion points, the 95 theses laid out a devastating critique of the indulgences – good works which often involved monetary donations, that popes could grant to people to cancel out penance for sins. Luther was famously quoted as saying "Why does not the Pope, whose wealth today is greater than the wealth of the richest Crassus, build the basilica of St Peter with his own money rather than the money of poor believers? (Note: The reference to Crassus presumably relates to Marcus Licinius Crassus – a Roman general and statesman reputed to be "the richest man in Rome.") Luther also sent a copy of his 95 theses to Archbishop Albert Albrecht of Mainz and further copies, aided by the use of a newly invented printing press, spread throughout Germany and Europe. The Church eventually moved to stop Luther's "act of defiance" and, by the authority of the Pope, he was ordered to recant his 95 theses. Luther refused, stating that he didn't consider the papacy had the authority to interpret scripture. In 1520 his defiance led to him being excommunicated from the Roman Catholic Church. He reportedly said: "Here I stand. I can do no other. God help me. Amen". The following year, Luther was summoned before the "Diet of Worms", a general assembly of secular authorities. After their hearing, and Luther's continued refusal to recant his Theses, he was declared a "convicted heretic".

Luther was not to be denied. With the aid of his allies, he hid out for a time in Wartberg Castle where he translated the New Testament into the German language, to give the ordinary people the opportunity to read God's word. He gained many followers and organised a new church, Lutheranism, which gained considerable support and patronage from German princes.

Later, Luther served as dean of theology at Wittenberg University from 1533 until his death in 1546. During this time, he suffered from several severe illnesses which may have affected the emphasis of his writings which included strident language aimed against Jews and, to a lesser extent, against Muslims. (Note: I have not found an explanation for his anti-Semitic views.)

To summarise, Luther's writings, teachings and translations radically affected Christian theology as his Lutherian message spread through Europe and the developing world.

Huldrych Zwingli (1484–1531)

Zwingli, a Swiss national, was educated in Vienna and Basil. He founded the Swiss Reformed Church and was an important figure in the broader Reformed tradition. Like Martin Luther, he accepted the supreme authority of the Scriptures but applied it more rigorously and comprehensively to all doctrines and practices. He believed that the state governed with divine sanction and that both the church and the state are placed under the sovereign rule of God. Where he differed from Luther was principally concerning the nature of the sacraments of baptism and the Eucharist (Lord's supper).

Zwingli was an admirer of Erasmus, and began preaching reformist ideas in Zurich where he challenged the ritualism, decadence and hierarchy of the Roman Catholic Church. He wrote his *67 Articles*, (doctrinal challenges, or debating points), to be presented at the First Disputation in Zurich in 1523 when he defended his beliefs against accusations of heresy by the Catholic Church. These Articles were adopted by most priests in Zurich at that time. As his movement spread, he rejected a number of the basic teachings of the church, declaring that Jesus alone was the head of the church, that the Mass was an affront to Christ and that there was no biblical foundation for the intercession of the dead or for purgatory. He also rejected the notions of priest celibacy and his teachings on the sacrament brought him into conflict with those of both Luther and the Catholic Church.

John Calvin (1509–1564)

The French theologian John Calvin is recognised as one of the most influential reformers. The five principles of Calvinism (as formulated by the Synod of Dordt in the Netherlands) are summarised by the acronym “tulip” standing for: total depravity, unconditional election, limited atonement, irresistibility of grace and the final perseverance of the saints. Calvin embraced Protestant beliefs following those already preached by Huldrych Zwingli. The movement was first called Calvinism in the early 1550s by Lutherans who opposed it. It was also called Reformed Tradition, Reformed Protestantism or Reformed Christianity. It emphasizes the sovereignty of God and the authority of the Bible. Calvinism became increasingly popular as a means of distinguishing Calvinists from Lutherans and the newer Protestant branches that emerged later. The majority of churches that trace their history back to Calvin (including Presbyterians, Congregationalists and other Calvinist churches) prefer to use the term “reformed” or “renewed” with the true order of the gospel.

xxx

Chapter Two

Christianity: Reformation/Enlightenment

The Reformation's roots in England were both political and religious. King Henry VIII, incensed by Pope Clement VII's refusal to grant him an annulment of his marriage, repudiated papal authority and in 1534 established the Anglican church with the king as supreme head of state. In spite of its political implications, the reorganisation of the church permitted the beginning of religious change in England, which included the preparation of a liturgy in English, the Book of Common Prayer. In Scotland, John Knox (1514–1572) was the foremost leader of the Protestant reformation and established the Presbyterian Church of Scotland.

All the reformers in the sixteenth century have one major thing in common; a continued belief in a God and the basic tenets of the Christian faith. They all had problems with the Roman Catholic Church, not because of its main beliefs but because of its corruption and its undistributed wealth. None queried the fundamentals of the faith – that there is a God, who created the world, and that Jesus Christ was his son, the virgin birth and the main teachings of the Bible. The first stirrings of questioning the very concept of the existence of a God was yet to emerge.

William Shakespeare (1564–1616)

There is some evidence of disbelief in the works of William Shakespeare, the greatest writer in the English language (in my opinion and that of very many others!), though there appear to be no accusatory letters or suspicions of disbelief against him. He has been called everything from a closet Catholic to an apologist for the Protestant religion, to being a pagan, to abandoning religion altogether. The subject of Shakespeare's religious beliefs is still hotly debated to this day. There appears to be no firm agreement and the jury is still out.

Shakespeare lived at a time of religious battles between Catholicism and Protestantism, of a period of necessary pretence. By the laws of the time, he had to conform to the newly established Christian Church of England, to attend church regularly as not attending could result in severe punishment. As Stephen Greenblatt wrote in *How Shakespeare Became Shakespeare*; "It seems likely that to infer the duplicity, disguises and things seeming other than they are and the intrigue within Shakespeare's plays was enhanced by a society that had to manoeuvre with daring, playful and clever wit in order to keep their heads on their shoulders." Greenblatt continued. "Shakespeare had a sympathetic audience not by vague chance but by intention. He needed to hook his audience and hold them in his thrall. His main audience was royalty; first Queen Elizabeth (Anglican Protestant) and then King James the First of England and Sixth of Scotland (Catholic) who was fascinated with witches. King James also wrote a book on the subject, "The Demonology". So, *Macbeth* was written, witches and all to pander to the desires and fears of King James."

Evidence that Shakespeare was a churchgoer can be found in the numerous references to concepts from sermons, which would have been delivered from the pulpit, and his many references to biblical texts. However, though he weaved these references into his plays, there is no evidence as to what he personally believed.

Many researchers turn to *Hamlet* which, perhaps of all his plays, seems best to reflect his personal views. Marcus Geduld asks whether Shakespeare could have had Catholic sympathies when he introduces his ghost figure who claims to be in Purgatory:

I am thy father's spirit,
Doom'd for a certain term to walk the night,
And for the day to fast in fires,
Till the foul crimes done in my days of nature
Are burnt and purged away

Geduld points out that British people at that time were supposed to deny the existence of Purgatory. So a ghost reference could be only one of two things; a hallucination or the devil. But as others see the ghost it cannot be a hallucination. Prince Hamlet considers the second possibility:

The spirit that I have seen
May be the devil: and the devil hath power
To assume a pleasing shape: yea, and perhaps
Out of my weakness and my melancholy,
As he is very potent with such spirits,
Abuses me to damn me

After his further conversation with Horatio it seems clear that the ghost is indeed Hamlet's dead father in Purgatory. Yet what Hamlet does not make clear is whether the ghost is a soul in Purgatory (the Catholic concept) or is the devil (the Protestant view). To muddy the waters even further, the ghost asks Hamlet to:

Revenge my foul and most unnatural murder.

Yet Catholics asked for prayers not revenge as it was only through prayer that souls could escape Purgatory and ascend to heaven. Crying for revenge is more a pagan than a catholic concept.

So, as Geduld points out, in this one play, there is a muddle of Protestant, Catholic and pagan doctrine. Such was the intrigue of this play and Shakespeare's wit.

Sticking with Hamlet, one of Shakespeare's most iconic speeches searches the idea of whether or not there is indeed an afterlife. Was he after all introducing an atheist concept?
Comment: this gives me the excuse to copy out some of my favourite lines of all literature!

To die, to sleep;

To sleep: perchance to dream: ay, there's the rub;
For in that sleep of death what dreams may come
When we have shuffled off this mortal coil,
Must give us pause…
For who would bear the whips and scorns of time…
But that the dread of something after death,
The undiscover'd country from whose bourn
No traveller returns, puzzles the will
And makes us rather bear those ills we have
Than fly to others we know not of?

There are many other examples of where Shakespeare has tempted his audience to conclude he has one religious view or another or maybe none at all. Examples are taken from King Lear, Titus Andronicus and others. But that was the fascination of this brilliant playwright and poet. He still makes us wonder. His inner personal views on religion continue to be debated today.

John Donne (1572–1631)

John Donne is one of the most important poets, and in his later life, theologian, of the late Elizabethan and Jacobean periods. In many ways, what is now known as metaphysical poetry began with Donne and his innovative use of imagery. Key characteristics of metaphysical poetry include: complicated mental and emotional experiences and the idea that the physical and spiritual universes are connected.

Donne's early poems, circulated in manuscript in the 1590s when he was still a young man in his twenties just out of university, are love thymes which are disarmingly frank, direct and sexy: for example, lovers together in bed, a man imploring his mistress to undress for him.

But after his conversion from Catholicism to the Church of England, and his entry into the priesthood (Donne would eventually rise to become Dean of St Paul's Cathedral), Donne's poetry replaced his female lover with the figure of God as his subject and addressee. He wrote a series of "Holy Sonnets" which possess all of the directness of his earlier poems, and the same level of passion and fervour. In one poem, Donne calls upon God to "ravish" him. He is regarded as a key figure of the Elizabethan and Jacobean literary and theological world.

From the origins of his romantic and sexual poetry emerged several memorable poems reflecting a depth of feeling about Donne's visualisation of the afterlife. One renowned example is:

"Bring us, O Lord God, at our last awakening Into the house and gate of heaven
To enter that gate and dwell in that house, Where there shall be no darkness nor dazzling, but one equal light
No noise nor silence, but one equal music; No fears nor hopes, but one equal possession;
No ends nor beginnings, but one equal eternity;
In the habitation of thy glory and dominion,
World without end,
Amen."

Comment. This poem has a remarkable similarity with the experiences of those who have had near death experiences (NDEs) – covered in Chapter 11 below. I wonder if Donne himself had recovered from a major life-threatening accident himself or had met some other person who had.

The Puritans

One product of King Henry VIII's separation of the Church of England from the Roman Catholic was the birth of Puritanism, a religious movement which developed in the late sixteen and seventeenth centuries. The Puritans sought to "purify" the Church of England of the remnants of Roman Catholic "popery" that they claimed had been retained during the reign of Queen Elizabeth I (reigned 1558–1603). The Puritans were identified by their spirit of moral and religious earnestness that governed their whole way of life.

Their efforts to transform the English nation finally led to civil war (1642–1646), the execution of King Charles I in 1649 and the installation in 1653 of Oliver Cromwell (1599–1658), as Lord Protector of the Republican Commonwealth of England, Scotland and Ireland. The Puritan ideal of realising the "Holy Commonwealth" was by the establishment of a covenanted community which was carried to the American colony of Virginia.

Comment. The Puritan movement, its various factions and its rise and subsequent fall of political influence is a complex subject requiring a lengthy treatise to describe. That is not a subject for this book suffice to summarise that the Puritan movement was an early expression of division in Christian religious thought during this period of English history and of the early development of European settlements on the east coast of America. This seventeenth century period and the role of Puritanism is brilliantly covered in Robert Harris's *Act of Oblivion* (2022). Although a fictional novel, Harris' book is painstakingly researched and comprehensively describes the Puritan movement both in England and in America.

xxx

Many years passed before European politics, philosophy, science and communications were radically reoriented during the course of what has been described as the "long" eighteenth century (1685–1815) as part of a movement of the Age of Reason or The Enlightenment. In this "meantime" period there were two outstanding characters who left behind them a great contribution to the Christian religious debate.

René Descartes (1596–1650)

"*Je pense, donc je suis*" "I think therefore I am". Descartes was a French philosopher, mathematician, scientist and "lay" Catholic who invented analytic geometry, linking the previously separate fields of geometry and algebra. He has been called the father of modern philosophy. He laid the foundation for seventeenth century rationalism as a highly systematic school of philosophy in its own right for the first time in history, combining philosophy, mathematics and science. For Descartes, ethics was a science, which had its roots in metaphysics. He argued for the existence of God, investigated the place of man in nature, formulated the theory of mind-body dualism and defended free will. He was a convinced rationalist believing that reason is sufficient in the search for the goodness we should seek. Virtue consisted in the correct reasoning that should guide our actions.

Descartes described himself as a devout Catholic but there were those who challenged his concept of how he saw God even accusing him of atheism, though he is explicitly critical of atheism in his "Meditations".
Comment: For reasons I cannot find explained, his books were prohibited by the Catholic church.

To summarise, Descartes was an extraordinarily talented individual whose abilities spanned the different disciplines of philosophy, mathematics and science. I can't help wondering how he would have reacted concerning developing religious philosophy and thinking had he lived in the later years of the Enlightenment. We shall never know.

Baruch Spinoza (1632–1671)

In looking for the best summary available about this remarkable Dutch philosopher, I found a piece on the Internet produced by "The School of Life". It is so well written that I have reproduced it, with thanks to the authors, in its entirety here.

"Baruch Spinoza was a seventeenth-century Dutch Jewish philosopher who tried to reinvent religion – moving it away from something based on superstition and ideas of divine intervention to being a discipline that was far more impersonal, quasi-scientific and yet also, at all times, serenely consoling.

Baruch – the word means "Blessed" in Hebrew – was born in the Jewish quarter of Amsterdam in 1632, a thriving centre of Jewish commerce and thought. His ancestors were Sephardic Jews, who had fled the Iberian peninsula following the Catholic-inspired expulsion of 1492. Baruch, a studious highly intelligent child, received an intensely traditional Jewish education: he went to the local Jewish school, the yeshiva and followed all the Jewish High holidays and rituals.

Gradually, he began to distance himself from the faith of his ancestors: "although I have been educated from boyhood in the accepted beliefs concerning Scripture," he later wrote with characteristic caution, "I have felt bound in the end to embrace other views."

His fully fleshed out views were to be expressed in his great work, *Ethics*, written entirely in Latin and published in 1617. In Ethics, Spinoza directly challenged the main tenets of organised religion in general and Judaism in particular:

- God is not a person who stands outside of nature
- There is no one to hear our prayers
- Or to create miracles
- Or to punish us for misdeeds
- There is no afterlife
- Man is not God's chosen creature
- The Bible was only written by ordinary people
- God is not a craftsman or an architect. Nor is he a king who calls for believers to take up the Holy Sword. God does not see anything. He does not judge. He does not even reward the virtuous person with a life after death. Every representation of God as a person is a projection of the imagination.
- Everything in the traditional liturgical calendar is pure superstition and mumbo-jumbo.

However, despite all this, remarkably, Spinoza did not declare himself an atheist. He insisted that he remained a staunch defender of God.

God plays an absolutely central role in Spinoza's Ethics, but it isn't anything like the God who haunts the pages of the Old Testament.

Spinoza's God is wholly impersonal and indistinguishable from what we might call variously nature or existence or a world soul: God is the universe, and its laws; God is reason and truth; God is the animating force of everything that is and can be. God is the cause of everything, but he is the eternal cause. He doesn't participate in change. He is not in time. He cannot be individuated. Spinoza writes: "Whatever is, is in God, and nothing can exist or be conceived without God."

Throughout his text, Spinoza was keen to undermine the idea of prayer. In prayer, an individual appeals to God to change the way the universe works. But Spinoza argues that this is entirely the wrong way around. The task of human beings is to try to understand how and why things are the way they are – and then accept it, rather than protest at the workings of existence by sending little messages up into the sky.

As Spinoza put it, but rather caustically: "Whosoever loves God cannot strive that God should love him in return." In other words, only naïve (but perhaps rather touching) narcissism would lead someone at once to believe in a God who made the eternal laws of physics and then to imagine that this same God would take an interest in bending the rules of existence to improve his or her life in the same way.

Spinosa was deeply influenced by the philosophy of the Stoics of Ancient Greece and Rome. They had argued that wisdom lies not in protest against how things are, but in continuous attempts to understand the ways of the world – and then bow down peacefully to necessity.

Senaca, Spinosa's favourite philosopher, had compared human beings to dogs on a leash being led by the necessities of life in a range of directions. The more one pulls against what is necessary, the more one is strangled therefore the wise must always endeavour to understand ahead of time how things are – for example, what love is like or how politics works – and then change their direction accordingly so as not to be strangled unnecessarily. It is this kind of Stoic attitude that constantly pervades Spinoza's philosophy.

To understand God traditionally meant studying the Bible and other holy texts. But Spinosa now introduces another idea.

The best way to know God is to understand how life and the universe work: it is through a knowledge of psychology, philosophy and the natural sciences that one comes to understand God.

In traditional religion, believers will ask special favours of God. Spinoza proposes instead that we should understand what God wants and we can do in one way above all: by studying everything that is. By reasoning, we can accede to a divine eternal perspective.

Spinoza makes a famous distinction between two ways of looking at life, we either see it egoistically, from our limited point of view, as he put it:

Sub specie durationis – under the aspect of time

Or we can look at things globally and eternally:

Sub specie aeternitayis – under the aspect of eternity

Our nature means that we'll always be divided between the two. Sensual life pulls us towards a time bound partial view. But our reasoned intelligence can give us unique access to another perspective – it can quite literally allow us here Spinoza becomes beautifully lyrical – to participate in eternal totality.

Normally, we call "bad" whatever is bad for us, and "good" whatever increases our power and advantage, but to be truly ethical means rising above these local concerns. It might all sound forbidding, but Spinoza envisaged his philosophy as a route to a life based on freedom from guilt, from sorrow or from shame.

Happiness involves aligning our will to that of the universe. The universe – God – has its own projects and our task is to understand rather than rail against these. The free person is one conscious of the necessities that compel us all.

Spinoza writes, the wise man, the person who understands how and why things are, "possesses eternally true complacency (acquiescentia) of spirit."

Needless to say, these ideas got Spinoza into very deep trouble. He was excommunicated from the Jewish community of Amsterdam in 1656. The rabbis issued a writ known as a cherem against the philosopher:

"By the decree of the angels" it went… "and by the command of the holy men, we excommunicate, expel, curse and damn Baruch de Espinoza, with all the curses which are written in the book of the Law. Cursed be he by day and cursed be he by night: cursed be he when he lies down, and cursed be he when he rises up…"

Spinoza was forced to flee Amsterdam and eventually to settle in the Hague, where he lived quietly and peacefully as a lens grinder and private tutor till his death in 1677.

Spinoza's work was largely ignored. In the nineteenth century, Hegel took an interest as did Wittgenstein – and some twentieth century scholars.

But on the whole Spinoza offered a warning about the failures of much of religious philosophy at that time.

Ethics is one of the world's most beautiful books. It contains a calming, perspective-restoring take on life. It replaces the God of superstition with a wise and consoling pantheism.

And yet Spinoza's work failed utterly to convince any but a few to abandon traditional religion and to move towards a rationalist, wise system of belief. The reasons are in a way simple and banal. Spinoza failed to understand – like so many philosophers before and since – that what leads people to religion isn't just reason, but far more importantly, emotion, belief, fear and tradition. People stick to their beliefs because they like the rituals, the communal meals, the yearly traditions, the beautiful architecture, the music and the sonorous language read out in synagogue and church.

Spinoza's Ethics arguably contains more wisdom than the Bible – but because it comes without any of the Bible's supporting structure, it remains a marginal work, studied here and there in universities in the west – while the traditional religion that he thought outmoded in the 1670s continues to thrive and convince people.

If we're ever to replace traditional beliefs, we must remember just how much religion is helped along by ritual, tradition, art and a desire to belong: all things that Spinoza, despite his great wisdom, ignored at his peril in his bold attempt to replace the Bible.

Comment: Thank you "The School of Life" for this excellent piece on Baruch Spinoza! I found this compelling reading. My only critique is that Spinoza had more of a long-lasting influence on other philosophers and free thinkers than is suggested in the article. For example, he heavily influenced Goethe who in turn, had a major impact on nineteenth century religious thinking throughout Europe.

xxx

The period of the Enlightenment lasted from 1685 through to 1815, during which time, European politics, philosophy and communications were radically reoriented as thinkers emphasised "reason, individualism and scepticism". Of direct relevance to this book, this was the first time in European history when the very basis of the Christian religion was openly challenged by some thinkers who argued that the universe seemed to determine its own course without God's intervention. Some even disputed the very existence of a God. Key European contributors were: Gottfried Leibniz, Isaac Newton, John Locke, Voltaire, David Hume, Immanuel Kant, Johann Wolfgang von Goethe, Johann Christoph Friedrich von Schiller amongst many others.

Voltaire (1694–1778)

François-Marie Arouet (known by his pen name of Voltaire,) was a French philosopher who initially received a classical education under the Jesuits at

Lycée Louis-le-Grand in Paris but abandoned his studies to pursue his literary ambitions. Although Voltaire called his philosophy "Theism", he rejected many Christian doctrines such as the subject of "evil" which caused him to doubt God's attributes of goodness and benevolence and the idea of an afterlife. Above all, Voltaire believed in the efficacy of reason; that social progress could be achieved through reason and that no authority, religious or political, should be immune to the challenge of reason.

Calling the Christian faith the "infamous superstition", Voltaire rejected all miracles recorded in the Bible. While acknowledging Jesus as superior to all other religious leaders and accepting his moral teachings, Voltaire refashioned Christ to be a humanist and deist while rejecting his divinity.

Voltaire famously summed up his view of the Bible as "The Bible. That is what fools have written, what imbeciles commend, what rogues teach and young children are made to learn by heart:" Of God, he said, "If God did not exist, it would be necessary to invent him."

David Hume (1711–1776)

The Scottish philosopher David Hume is famous for his sceptical metaphysics. He has been referred to as "the most influential philosopher ever to write in the English language". Hume called into question a number of religious beliefs such as miracles and immortal life. Concerning belief in God, Hume challenges some of the arguments for the existence of God but in his writings, he repeatedly speculates about God's nature. Some of his researchers have concluded that many of Hume's affirmation passages in his writings are intended to be understood in their natural sense, that is, although he believes there is a God, he is more like the type of God described so eloquently by Baruch Spinoza. (see above). Among his contributions was the recognition of the difference between matters of fact and matters of value. He argues that moral judgements were matters of value because they were about sentiments and passions.

Immanuel Kant (1724–1804)

Kant set the terms for much of nineteenth and twentieth century philosophy, and continues to exercise a significant influence today in metaphysics, epistemology, ethics, political philosophy, aesthetics, and other fields. The fundamental idea of Kant's "critical philosophy" – especially in his three Critiques: the Critique of Pure Reason (1781, 1787), the Critique of Practical Reason (1788), and the Critique of the Power of Judgment (1790) – is human autonomy. He argues that human understanding is the source of the general laws of nature that structure all our experience; and that human reason gives itself the moral law, which is the basis for belief in God, freedom, and immortality. Therefore, scientific knowledge, morality, and religious belief are mutually consistent and secure because they all rest on the same foundation of human autonomy, which is also the final end of nature according to the teleological worldview of reflecting judgment. Kant introduced these concepts to unify the theoretical and practical parts of his philosophical system.

Johann Wolfgang von Goethe (1749–1832)

Goethe was a German free thinker who believed that one could be inwardly Christian without following any of the Christian churches, many of whose central teachings he opposed, sharply distinguishing between Christ and the tenets of Christian theology, and criticizing its history as a "hodgepodge of fallacy and violence" Goethe is quoted as describing himself as "not anti-Christian, nor un-Christian, but most decidedly non-Christian" and having listed the symbol of the cross among the four things he most disliked. (Comment: I couldn't find out what the other three things were!)

Goethe had a great effect on nineteenth century thinking and was the originator of many ideas which later became widespread. He produced volumes of poetry, essays, criticism, a theory of colours and works on evolution and linguistics.

xxx

Chapter Three

Christianity Today

Despite the works of some of the free thinkers of the Enlightenment period, there remained a general recognition that God existed: a God, not necessarily a Christian God as described in the Bible, but some sort of higher body who created our world and had some influence on our present and future existence. Even Spinoza believed in "a God" though his interpretation was far removed from that of his Jewish leaders of that time. For his pains, poor Spinoza was excommunicated by the Jewish hierarchy of Amsterdam in the most harsh and unforgiving terms.

It was not until the mid-nineteenth century, that some thinkers, particularly those who trained in the new sciences of the day, came to support the basic concept that there is no God, no creator, no higher authority at all. For that philosophy to be fully articulated, we had to wait until the publication of Darwin's *On the Origin of Species* in 1859, Thomas Henry Huxley's "invention" of the term "agnostic" and the arguments of Atheists, which are the subject of a later chapter of this book.

Christianity in its various forms has until today remained the religion of the majority of Europeans, the Americas and much of the rest of the non-Arabic, non-Asian world. Published statistics of present membership and active followers of the world's main religions are confusing, largely relying on self-reporting. Christianity has the alleged world's largest following (2.38 billion) some thirty-one per cent of all religions. The Roman Catholic church, based in the Vatican and led by the Pope, is the oldest and largest of all branches of Christianity – some fifty per cent, with about 1.3 billion followers worldwide.

In the United States, there are twenty-three listed different denominations of Christianity each with more than one million members – membership and congregation numbers varying widely. Denominations include such bodies as: American Catholic Church (declared membership of seventy-one million), Southern Baptist convention, The Fundamentalist Church of Latter-Day Saints, United Methodist Church, Assembles of God USA, Episcopal Church (US), Presbyterian Church, Pentecostal Assemblies of the World, Jehovah's Witnesses, Seventh Day Adventist Church and many more.

Roman Catholic scandals, US Southern Baptist Church cover ups are somewhat reminiscent of the rebellious factions during the reformation period. Here are some examples.

Roman Catholic

In recent years, there has been a flood of accusations of child abuse cases in the Roman Catholic church. These have ranged from cities across the US, to schools in Ireland to Australian country towns. From 2001 to 2010, the Holy See examined sex abuse cases involving about three thousand priests, some of which dated back fifty years. In a 2001 apology, John Paul II called sexual abuse within the church "a profound contradiction of the teaching and witness of Jesus Christ". In 2018, Pope Francis accused victims of fabricating allegations, but later apologised for his "tragic error" and expressed "shame and sorrow" for the tragic history of abuse. According to a BBC report in November 2021, high profile cases and harrowing testimony given to public enquiries have continued to keep the issue in the headlines. One damning enquiry found that some 216,000 children in France had been sexually abused by members of the clergy since 1950. Efforts by Pope Francis to address the problem have included an unprecedented summit on paedophilia in the church and changing its laws to explicitly criminalise sexual abuse. But alleged cover-ups continue to dog the Catholic Church and victim groups claim that the Vatican has not done nearly enough to rights its wrongs.

US Southern Baptist Church

A UK Times article (23 May 2022) highlighted a report by the Houston Chronicle and San Antonio Express that leaders of the US Southern Baptist Convention conspired for almost two decades to cover up sexual abuse and to smear victims. Survivors of assault by clergymen repeatedly shared allegations with the executive committee "only to be met, time and time again, with resistance, stonewalling and even outright hostility." Cover-ups and denials allowed "convicted molesters" to continue acting in trusted roles in the latest sex scandal to engulf the church.

xxx

Church of England

The Church of England still remains nominally the religion with the most followers in the UK but today it is not going well. According a Sunday Times report (29 May 2022), the peak for Church of England attendance was the year 1906. In 1958, there were 2.88 million people listed as members of local Anglican churches. By 2019, this had fallen to just 89300. Out of the C of E's sixteen thousand churches, four thousand have Sunday congregations of under fourteen while eight hundred have fewer than seven. At the 2021 annual General Synod, the Archbishop of York, Dr Cottrell, even concluded that the Church might be dying. The average age of regular church attendees seems to back up the Archbishop's comments. There has been a continuous decline. From the best available statistics I can find, less than two percent of the UK population are now regular attendees, stemming from the lack of young churchgoers to replace the old. The average age of a worshipper now is sixty-one. I am no expert on this subject but from what I have read, it seems that many UK churchgoers are neither convinced about the deity nor about some form of existence after death. Church leaders face a major problem. Can these endangered parishes be saved? Is reading from the Book of Common Prayer in a pew in a mediaeval building on a Sunday morning really where they think the future of the church lies? Is this what will draw in the young?

Despite this major decline in regular church attendance in UK, the death in September 2022 of Queen Elizabeth prompted a world-wide outpouring of emotion and respect for the queen's life and for all she had achieved during the seventy years of her reign – an emotion which combined both political and religious elements. As the monarch, Queen Elizabeth's titles included Defender of the Faith and Supreme Governor of the Church of England. She occupied a unique space among the world's religious leaders. When she met with popes, evangelists and other religious leaders, she was meeting them as the leader of the Church of England.

The late queen will be remembered for her steadfast faith in Christianity, for being a moral and religious leader, for her regular church attendance and for her quiet mourning as head of church and state at the death of her husband, Prince Philip. While not often spoken of as a religious leader, it is history that brought her to that moment at the death of her father, King George VI. Those who watched her state funeral couldn't help but recognise the influence of her deep Christian faith – a faith that she often referred to in her annual Christmas Day, televised, primetime message to the Commonwealth nations.

Queen Elizabeth didn't speak about her faith in abstract terms. She was specific. She spoke about Jesus and what his life meant to her personally. To quote directly a few of her own words: "God sent into the world a unique person – neither a philosopher nor a general, important though they are, but a Saviour, with the power to forgive. It is my prayer that… we might all find room in our lives for the… love of God through Christ our Lord." By her own words and public testimony, the late Queen Elizabeth was a devout follower of Jesus. These are the words of a monarch, the United Kingdom's head of state. But they are also the words of an evangelist.

The church played a prominent role throughout the ceremonies during the queen's funeral; the services in Scotland at Balmoral Castle, in Edinburgh at Holyrood Palace and St Giles cathedral, in London at the Palace of Westminster, the funeral service at Westminster abbey and later at Windsor

Castle. But it is debatable whether the outstandingly well organised programme of events will have any lasting influence on people's Christian faith. Apart from the participation of the Church dignitaries, the immense following and TV coverage of the ceremonies relayed around the world were due to the combination of British traditional assets such as: the bearing, discipline and precision of the military, the grandeur and pageantry of the state occasion (gun carriage, military bearer parties), the splendour of the architecture of the palaces and church buildings and the wonderful musical/choral arrangements played during the services.

xxx

Science versus Christian Religion

The advance of science has thrown into doubt the validity not only of the Christian faith but also general religious beliefs, in the existence of God or a god as having created our universe. But it has not been entirely a one-way traffic as, conversely, there are many respected academics including several scientists who at some time of their lives were agnostic or atheists but who subsequently became believers in Christianity. Examples are:

Albert Henry Ross, (1881–1950)

Published under the name Frank Morison. Ross doubted the life of Christ as written in the New Testament, particularly the references to the resurrection. Over a ten-year period, he investigated the origins of the gospels accounts. Despite his earlier misgivings, he eventually became convinced of the truth of Jesus' resurrection. He set out his findings and the rationale behind them in his book entitled *Who Moved the Stone?*

CS Lewis (1898–1963)

Lewis was a British writer and lay theologian and was regarded as one of the intellectual giants of the twentieth century. He was a Fellow and Tutor in English literature at Oxford University then in 1954 was elected to Chair of Medieval literature at Cambridge University. His best-known books are: *Mere Christianity*, *Out of the Silent Planet*, *The Great Divorce* and *The Screwtape Letters*. In 1929, he abandoned atheism and in 1931 was converted to Christianity. In 1941, he began his renowned war-time broadcast talks on Christianity and in 1946, he was awarded an Honorary Doctor of Divinity by St Andrews University.

Robert Sheldrake (born 1942)

Sheldrake is a biochemist researcher in parapsychology who has denounced the academic structure of science studies and, perhaps influenced by his work in India, changed from an atheist to being a Christian.

Alan Lightman (born 1948)

Lightman is an American physicist, writer and "social entrepreneur". He is professor of the practice of Humanities at the Massachusetts Institute of Technology (MIT). He is the author of many books, his first to find fame was *Einstein's Dreams*, which has been translated into more than thirty languages. Lightman is known for exploring the intersection of the sciences and the humanities, especially the dialogue between science, philosophy, religion and spirituality.

Lee Strobel (born 1952)

Strobel is an American who is an "atheist turned Christian". His influential books include; *The Case for Christ*, *The Case for Heaven*, *The Case for a Creator* and *The Case for Faith*.

Alistair McGrath (born 1953)

McGrath is a scientist who was originally a non-believer but who became a Christian. McGrath holds a doctoral degree in molecular biophysics. He has written many books including *The Twilight of Atheism* which examines the rise and fall of disbelief in the modern world. McGrath expresses his

Christian beliefs with great passion. He strongly challenges many of the atheist views of Richard Dawkins.

Comment. McGrath is a highly articulate speaker who has appeared in several interviews shown on YouTube. He is married to Joanne Collicut, herself a committed Christian. McGrath and Collicut co-wrote the book "The Dawkins Delusion.", a counter to Dawkins own "The God Delusion". I was impressed, but with many reservations, by the extended interview (Facing the Canon with Alistair McGrath) featured on YouTube (December 2021). In my view, he is a typical "seen the light" Christian – highly academically gifted but with little real-life experience. He is just too "over the top" in his passionate conviction that Jesus is his saviour. Perhaps he has lived too rarefied an existence among fellow academics.

Such is the complexity of this subject, there are some scholars whose beliefs changed in the opposite direction. One example is:

Bart D Ehrman (born 1955)

Ehrman was originally a member of the Episcopal Church of the United States and a "born again" evangelical but now describes himself as an "agnostic atheist". Ehrman criticises the New Testament, the historical Jesus and the development of early Christianity. He has written some thirty books which have sold two million copies and have been translated into twenty-seven languages.

xxx

Some great orators

Periodic high-level spikes in Christian conversions have occurred due to the power of oratory of some preachers whose followers were encouraged to embrace the Christian faith, not necessarily through true belief but by the fear of being "sinners and inciting the wrath of God". Many reasoned that it was a good life plan to be quiescent and follow the teaching of preachers as a life insurance policy to go to "heaven" after death.

Influential Christian orators during the last century include:

Billy Graham (1918–2018)

Graham, the American Evangelist and Southern Baptist Minister was an extraordinarily powerful "showman" orator who held audiences spellbound by his persuasive delivery. It is claimed that more than 3.2 million responded to his invitation to "accept Jesus Christ as their personal savour" and that he preached the gospel to more people in person than anyone else in the history of Christianity. I remember his visit to UK in 1956 when his "sermons" filled football stadiums of supporters. That year he had a much-publicised meeting with the young Queen Elizabeth, herself a devout Christian.

RC Sproul (1939–2017)

Sproul, an ordained pastor in the Presbyterian Church of America, was founder and chairman of the Ligonier Ministries. He made daily broadcasts in the US and internationally under the title of "Renewing Your Mind". He was a prolific writer whose books include: *The Holiness of God*, *What is Reformed Theology*? and *Chosen by God.*

John F MacArthur (b 1939)

MacArthur is a pastor/teacher from the Grace Community Church, Sun Valley, California. He is a popular syndicated Christian teacher and radio speaker under the banner: "Grace to you". His many books include: *The Heart of the Bible*, *Twelve Extraordinary Women*, and *Gospel according to Jesus.*

xxx

Chapter Four

Preaching Politics from the Pulpit

Several Christian leaders have combined their religious oratory with political involvement and influence. Billy Graham had close associations with Presidents Eisenhower, Lynden B Johnson and Richard Nixon. Other famous Christians who also influenced political events include:

Desmond Tutu (1931–2021)

Tutu, the South African Anglican bishop and theologian was also an anti-apartheid and human rights activist, confident of Nelson Mandela.

Michael Christodoulou Mouskos (1913–1977)

Mouskos was a Greek-Cypriot, ordained in the Greek orthodox church who took the title of Archbishop Makarios III. He became the first president of Cyprus in 1960 and is regarded by many Greek-Cypriots as the "Father of the nation". He was an active supporter of Enosis, the armed movement, which advocated the union of Greece with Cyprus.

Martin Luther King (1929–1968)

King, the American Baptist minister, became the most visible spokesman and leader of the US civil rights movement. His infectious speeches had a profound effect on the US national consciousness.

Ian Paisley (1926–2014)

Paisley was a Northern Ireland religious leader who also served as leader of the Democratic Unionist Party. He was First Minister of Northern Ireland from 2007 to 2008. His booming voice, strong Northern Irish (Ulster) accent and uncompromising attitude is a symbolic reminder of the days of the Northern Irish "troubles" prior to the Good Friday Agreement of 1998, which he opposed.

Russian/Ukrainian versions of their Orthodox Churches

Russia's invasion of Ukraine in 2022/23 has driven a wedge within the Orthodox Church. While the head of the Russian Orthodox Church, Patriarch Kirill, justified the war, it was condemned by the Ukrainian Orthodox churches, as well as some priests in Russia. According to Thomas Bremer, professor of ecumenical theology at the University of Münster, in keeping with Putin's line and in accordance with the President's initial ban on reporting on the war or even calling it as such, Patriarch Kirill has never used the word "war" for the invasion of Ukraine but instead has spoken of "events" and "military actions." While the Russian Orthodox Church is the primary church in Russia, Ukraine is characterised by religious diversity. Currently, two Orthodox churches exist in Ukraine – the independent Orthodox Church of Ukraine (OKU) and the Ukrainian Orthodox Church (UOK). Each of these churches has referred to the "war" by name and emphatically condemned it. According to Bremer, the Moscow patriarch's failure to speak out for peace has led to many bishops of the UOK in Ukraine to stop mentioning his name in prayer, as is customary. Bremer states, "This shows a great movement away from Moscow. The Moscow patriarch has lost the trust of his brethren in Ukraine. Professing to be part of the Orthodox Church in Russia can be both a religious as well as cultural affiliation. There are people in Russia who call themselves Orthodox but at the same time say they don't believe in God. This is a matter of identity."

Comment. Both Orthodox Churches (Russian and Ukraine) seem to believe that God is on their side. This is similar to the conflicting views during WWII when the allied powers prayed to God to help defeat the Nazis, while the Wehrmacht soldiers all went to war wearing their issued "Gottmituns" belts!

Justin Welby, (born 1956), Archbishop of Canterbury

The Most Revd Justin Welby was ordained in 1992 after an eleven-year career in the oil industry. He spent his first fifteen years serving in the Coventry diocese, often in places of significant deprivation. In 2002, he was made a Canon of Coventry Cathedral, where he jointly led its international reconciliation work. During this time he worked extensively in Africa and the Middle East. He has had a passion for reconciliation and peace-making ever since that period. He was Dean of Liverpool from 2007 to 2011, Bishop of Durham from 2011 to 2012, before being fast tracked to being appointed Archbishop of Canterbury in late 2012.

Welby gave his 2022 Easter sermon from the pulpit of Canterbury Cathedral at the height of the early days of the Russian invasion of Ukraine. He made passing reference to the greatest humanitarian crises since the end of WWII, merely calling for a cease fire. Instead, he chose to pontificate about the British Government's plan to deport "asylum seekers" to Rwanda as being an act "opposite of the nature of God". He made this assertion with limited supporting facts and with no suggestion of any alternative solution to the problem of dealing humanely with the thousands of mostly young, male, African individuals who daily were illegally attempting to cross the channel from France to UK, organised and exploited by criminal gangs. His comments prompted a hard-hitting article in the UK Times which felt that Archbishop Welby's message went too far in its critique of government migration policy. The Times article said that the archbishop is fully entitled to comment on political matters, "He is an important religious voice in debates on public policy and welfare but he is not more than that. In declaring that a particular government scheme is "ungodly" and to use his sermon to convey that sentiment to the congregation of Canterbury Cathedral is beyond the archbishop's reach. Where the archbishop went wrong was not in his theological reflection, but in implying God favours or disfavours particular policies.

Referring to the same issue, Simon Jenkins, writing in the Guardian (May 2022), called the Rwanda plan "shocking and bizarre but that, when a state-established church summons God to condemn an evil policy, it merely confuses the forces that need mustering against it." The same paper stated that Jenkins is right. It continued, "Asylum policy isn't a religious matter. Dragging religion into an already highly charged debate is unlikely to enhance the discussion. Political decisions should be based on reasoned arguments that stand or fall on their own merits. Religious leaders are as entitled as anyone else to speak out on political issues. They should not, however, be given a privileged platform to do so and their voice shouldn't be louder than anyone else's."

As this issue progressed further, the entire senior leadership of the Church of England, with the Most Reverend Stephen Cottrell, Archbishop of York at the fore, denounced the Rwanda migrant flights and stated: "Whether or not the deportation flights leave Britain, this policy should shame us as a nation". Their letter also added that "the shame is our own, because our Christian heritage should inspire us to treat asylum seekers with compassion, fairness and justice, as we have for centuries".

The bishops' letter, printed in The Times newspaper, provoked a lively response from readers. Typical of these included:

"The Church has no understanding of this issue whatsoever, and offers zero solutions. This kind of ivory tower liberal vanity and clueless do-gooding can cause enormous harm."

And

"The Church makes no reference to, or perhaps just doesn't understand, the totally different situations of genuine asylum seekers and economic immigrants. The vast majority of those attempting the crossing, organised by criminal gangs, are from the latter category."

And

"I believe the figure for small boat crossings in 2021 was over twenty-one thousand raising to over forty-seven thousand in 2022. If thirty-thousand young men (conservative assumption of "young men only" – the actual figure appears to be closely guarded), came ashore in landing craft, armed, we would rightly call it an invasion. What is taking place – and has been for years – is an invasion by stealth. There are completely legal routes for immigration with very many visas being issued, for example, to Nigerians, Indians plus the government's offer of relocation for millions of Hong Kong citizens."

In June 2022, the Right Reverend Nick Baines, Bishop of Leeds proclaimed that Russia should keep Ukraine's Dombas region in order to achieve peace. As expected, his remarks produced a howl of protest from bloggers in the UK Times (24 June 2022) who without exception accused the bishop of interfering in matters beyond his remit.

Welby was at it again when speaking at a gathering of Anglican leaders on 7 August 2022. (Report in The Times of 8 August 2022 by Kaya Burgess, Religious Affairs correspondent). He proclaimed that climate change was the result of wealthier countries having declared war on God's creation and now want to cling to their wealth rather than help poorer nations. He also said that "The Church of England had historically enjoyed too cosy a relationship with state power."

Of the eighty-two comments submitted in The Times about Welby's remarks about climate change, everyone was negative. The most used word was "hypocritical". Perhaps these comments were best summed up by one from Neil Woodcock who wrote "Unctuous hypocritical cant. I guess that means he will be shutting down most of the rooms in Lambeth Palace and walking to Canterbury."

Part of the problem is that twenty-six Church of England bishops continue to have automatic reserved places as "Lords Spiritual" in our British House of Lords, an allocation dating back to the fourteenth century. These bishops don't even begin to represent the spread of today's public opinion. Whatever their stated views, they can hardly provide spiritual insight for the UK's diverse population representing Catholics, Muslims, Jews, Rastafarians, Humanists or the many other beliefs.

Of note also is the connection between Welby (born 1965) and Nicky Gumbel (born 1967), both of whom went to Eton College and studied at Trinity College, Cambridge. Welby has regularly described himself as being on the evangelical wing of Christianity and has associated himself with the Alpha course established by the ex-barrister, Gumbel, at the Holy Trinity Brompton – abbreviated to HTB. Andrew Atherstone, himself a committed Christian, has recently written a book "*Repackaging Christianity: Alpha and the building of Global Brand*." The Alpha course, described as a "Discipleship course for new Christians", was established in the 1970s and claims to have twenty-nine million participants from one hundred countries. When I learnt that the course deals with the questions, "Why am I here? Who is Jesus, Questions of life." I thought I'd better pay close attention considering I am addressing similar issues! I haven't personally attended an Alpha course but have read much of the feedback from those who have. They described the videos that are shown, many of which I have watched on You Tube. Though I have read some criticism about brainwashing in the Alpha course, it appears merely to be a basic introduction to what Christianity is all about and is not a secretive cult. Good luck to all those involved but, to me, it in no way deals with the meaning of life (unless of you believe in the Christian faith!) nor does it answer the "why" questions that are the subject of this book! How many of the Alpha course attendees actually converted to Christianity and have since remained believers is unknown. Of interest is that Welby was selected to be Archbishop of Canterbury, the Head of the Church of England in late 2012 by the then British Prime Minister, David Cameron (born 1966), who also went to Eton College at the same time as Welby and Gumbel. The Church of England is registered as a charity and pays no tax! This mix of evangelicalism and the present leadership of the Church of England has sardonically been described as "a potent combination of posh people finding Jesus, meaning and the Holy Spirit."

Welby had his moment on the world stage when he preached the sermon at the funeral of Queen Elizabeth on 19 September 2022. He paid homage to the queen's life of servitude. His excellent well-crafted sermon was widely praised by the national and international press. His words included:

We pray especially for all her family, grieving as every family at a funeral – including so many families round the world who have themselves lost someone recently – but in this family's case doing so in the brightest spotlight. May God heal their sorrow, may the gap left in their lives be marked with memories of joy and life.

Her Late Majesty's broadcast during Covid lockdown ended with: "We will meet again", words of hope from a song of Vera Lynn. Christian hope means certain expectation of something not yet seen." The above were conciliatory words of homage to his monarch. However, his introductory words, made before the gathering of some five-hundred world leaders, dignitaries and gathered royalty and a TV audience of an estimated 4.1 billion people were more questionable. These were:
"The pattern for many leaders is to be exalted in life and forgotten after death. The pattern for all who serve God – famous or obscure, respected or ignored – is that death is the door to glory." I wonder how many of the world leaders present, many who had non-Christian faiths, took Welby's words to heart and felt duly chastened. Or perhaps many felt irritated by being lectured to by an unelected Christian leader from a country where only an estimated two percent regularly go the church!

In December 2022, Welby paid a short visit to Ukraine where he pontificated to the Press about his views on Russia's invasion, saying, among several other political comments, that the war could drag on for decades like the Israel-Palestine conflict. He was again widely criticised for his remarks, many suggesting that, if he really wanted to contribute usefully, he might be better advised to go to Moscow to speak to his fellow Christian, Patriarch Kirill, head of the Russian Orthodox Church. Kirill has been reported as justifying the war and even blessing bullets as they were loaded for use in Ukraine. The many comments about Welby's visit that were sent to The Times (2 December 2022) were all highly critical. To quote from one: "His words are no doubt inspired by the "Church of England War Studies Institute! The Oracle speaks as his flock diminishes!"

Another example of Welby's political comments was to Beth Rigby (Sky News Jan 2023) when he proposed that higher taxes should be used to pay for more social welfare.

In May 2023, Justin Welby again took centre stage during the coronation of King Charles, an event which was also attended by the world's royalty and major political Heads of State. He played such a prominent role in the service that one could be excused for wondering if we were going to end up with King Justin rather than King Charles!

On subjects which are within Welby's remit to give spiritual leadership, his most quoted comments (2022/3) are: a highly challenged proposal to spend one hundred million pounds on "reparations for slavery in the eighteenth century" and a "measly compromise" (Alice Thomson, The Times, 25 Jan 2023) on the subject of whether or not gay marriages should be blessed in church. Welby favours lecturing politicians about doing the right thing while declining to show the spiritual leadership his appointment of leader of the Anglican church requires.

Perhaps my comments on Welby are too harsh but I feel them to be justified due to his habit of pretending that he has some sort of personal communication line to his version of God. This is at odds with his quoted comments that he, at times, doubts the very existence of God, yet he is certain about Jesus, not just as a historical person around whom the Jesus myth coalesced but a real divine Jesus. (BBC Bristol interview September 2014). As the American philosopher Delos McKnown remarked, "The invisible and the non-existent look very much alike!"

Post Script. Welby resigned as Archbishop of Canterbury in November 2024!

XXX

Chapter Five

Islam

Islam is the fastest growing religion with an alleged 1.6 to 1.9 billion followers, accounting for some twenty-five per cent of the world's religious followers. Its core principle is for its followers to submit their will to that of God and to recognise that there is only one divine God (Allah). The religion is based in belief of the five pillars: Belief in Allah (Tawheed), Prayer, Zakat (purifying your wealth by donating to charity), Fasting and Pilgrimage to Mecca (Hajj). Muslims believe that the Qur'an is the literal word of God which was revealed to God's messenger Muhammad to bring humankind out of the darkness of polytheism and ignorance and into the light of Islam.

The Qur'an became "the book of guidance for all mankind". It abrogates all scriptures before it and contains signs of God's greatness, miracles, parables and lessons. It explains the names and attributes of God and His creation. It calls followers to believe in God, his angels, his messengers, the Last Day, and in fate and the divine decree.

After the holy Qur'an, the sayings of the Prophet (hadith) and the description of his way of life (sunna) are the most important Muslim texts.

Sunni and Shi'a

The principle ideological difference between Sunni and Shi'a relate to the dispute about religious authority and the overall leadership of all Muslims following the death of Muhammad, the Prophet. Those who followed the Prophet's closest companion (Abu Bakr) became known as Sunni (the followers of the Prophets example – Sunnah). Those who followed the Prophet's cousin and son-in-law (Ali) became known as Shi'a (the followers of the Party of Ali-Shi'atu Ali). Sunnis focus on following the Prophet's example while Shi'a focus on the lineage of Muhammad's family through a series of Imams.

Sunni and Shi'a communities have more in common in their beliefs and practices than they have differences. Both believe and share: the centrality of the Qur'an, Hadith (Book of sayings) and the Five Pillars of Islam, as described above.

For centuries Sunni and Shi'a communities have lived and coexisted peacefully in many parts of the world and have even intermarried. Since the Iranian Revolution in 1979, there has been tension between Sunnis and Shi'as throughout the middle east. Iran saw the rise of a Shi'a theocracy which has supported Shi'as in Iraq, Saudi Arabia, Bahrain, the Syrian regime of Bashar al-Assad and the Hezbollah and Hamas movements in Lebanon and Gaza. Shi'as comprise some ten per cent of the global Muslim followers and form a majority in five countries: Azerbaijan, Bahrain, Lebanon, Iran and Iraq.

Reza Asian (b 1972). Asian is an Iranian-American scholar of sociology of religion who has written four acclaimed books including "*No God but God*". As a youth, he converted from an upbringing in Shi'a Islam to evangelical Christianity but later reverted back to Islam. He is currently professor at the University of California, Riverside. In his documentary series for CNN, called "Believer", Asian explored the relationship between the terms "faith" and "religion". He recalls how he recognised the power of religion and, in many senses, the languages used in different religions are in reality often saying much the same. I found his books and lectures very useful in understanding many of the complexities of the Muslim religion.

There is often also an intermingling of politics and religion within the countries where the Muslim faith is predominant. A prime example is Iran, which since the Shah was overthrown in the 1979 revolution, is now officially known as The Islamic Republic of Iran. Islam is also the dominant political force throughout the Middle East. Other countries which have majority Muslim followers, for example Indonesia and Malaysia, manage (at present!) to keep a balance between political democratic practises and individual freedoms to practice any faith or none.

I have restricted this chapter to describing merely the basics of the Islamic faith as I deal in more detail in Part Two where I cover my personal interaction with Islam during my years spent in Brunei, The Gulf states, Turkey and Indonesia.

XXX

Chapter Six

Judaism

Judaism is the oldest of the Abrahamic monotheistic religions, (the other two being Christianity and Islam), dating back some four thousand years. There are an alleged fourteen million Jews worldwide, most living in the US and Israel. Traditionally, an individual is considered Jewish if his or her mother is Jewish.

Followers believe in a single God, who created the universe. The Jewish sacred text is the Tanakh, the "Hebrew Bible" which includes the same books as the Old Testament of the Christian Bible. The first five books, known as the Torah, describe the laws that Jews are to follow. Jewish people believe there's only one God who has established a special agreement with them (a covenant), communicating through prophets. Good deeds are rewarded and those that are evil are punished. According to the text of the Torah, God first revealed himself to Abraham, a Hebrew, who became known as the founder of Judaism. Abraham and his descendants were chosen people. More than a thousand years later, God revealed his laws to the Jewish prophet, Moses at Mount Sinai.

The Commandments, as written in the Torah are:

1. Worship no other God but Me.
2. Do not make images to worship
3. Do not misuse the name of God. Observe the Sabbath Day (Saturday)
4. Keep it Holy.
5. Honour and respect your father and mother
6. Do not murder.
7. Do not commit adultery.
8. Do not steal.

9. Do not accuse anyone falsely. Do not tell lies about other people
10. Do not envy other's possessions.

In the US, there are some six million Jews, around 2.4% of the population. They have become the richest religious group in American society; twenty-five percent of the four hundred wealthiest American are Jewish. Some explanations made for their financial prowess are that they allegedly embrace entrepreneurship, study more, have quick perception, know how to seize opportunities and have good networking skills!

During and after the Holocaust, many Jews returned to their traditional homeland, the region of Palestine and embraced Zionism, a movement advocating the creation of a Jewish state. In 1948, Israel was formally recognised as an independent nation.

As with my foreshortened chapter on Islam, to avoid duplication, I also cover this subject in more detail in Parts Two and Three.

xxx

Chapter Seven

Hinduism, Buddhism, Taoism

Hindu is the world's third largest religion with more than 1.2 billion followers worldwide. Historically, the term has been used as a geographical, cultural and religious identifier for people living in the Indian sub-continent. Today, Hindu is the main religion of India and Nepal but also has strong following in many other countries throughout Asia and beyond.

Hinduism is a heterogeneous religion and consists of many schools of thought. Hinduism has no traditional ecclesiastical order, no centralised religious authorities, no governing body and no prophets. Hindus can choose to be polytheistic, monotheistic, pantheistic, monistic, agnostic, humanist or atheistic. Estimates of Hinduism by country reflect this diversity of thought and way of life.

Hindus believe in a God who has many manifestations, deities and images. They believe that existence is a cycle of birth, death and rebirth, governed by Karma – a complex belief in cause and effect. Hindu philosophy traditionally observes four stages of life; Brahmacharya – the "student" stage which lays the foundation for spiritual practice; Grihastha – the "householder" stage when the individual maintains a home, and a family and is a supportive and productive member of society; Vanaprashta – a stage of devotion to spiritual practice and service; Sannyasa – a stage of renunciation where, having fulfilled all prior obligations, a person is free to devote themselves entirely to spiritual growth.

xxx

Buddhism (meaning "enlightenment") has an alleged three hundred seventy-six million followers worldwide, seven per cent of the world's population. It is a spiritual tradition that focuses on personal development and the attainment of a deep insight into the true nature of life. Buddhists seek to reach a state of nirvana, following the path of the Buddha, Siddhartha Gautama, who went on a quest for Enlightenment around the sixth century BC.

There is no belief in a personal god. Buddhists believe that nothing is fixed or permanent and that change is always possible. The path to Enlightenment is through the practice and development of morality, meditation and wisdom.

Buddhists believe that life is both endless and subject to impermanence, suffering and uncertainty. These states are called the tilakhana, or the three signs of existence. Existence is endless because individuals are reincarnated over and over again, experiencing suffering throughout many lives. It is impermanent because no state, good or bad, lasts forever. Our mistaken belief that things can last is a chief cause of suffering.

Both Hindu and Buddhist religions believe in reincarnation and both believe in Karma. There are also some differences between these two religions including: Hinduism accepts the caste system while Buddha taught against it. Hinduism has thousands of gods while Buddhism does not have a god.

Karma

Karma, a Sanskrit word that roughly translates to "action, work or deed", is a core concept in several Asian religions, including Hinduism and Buddhism. Though its specifics are different depending on the religion, karma generally denotes the cycle of cause and effect – actions have consequences, each action a person takes will affect him or her at some time in the future. This rule also applies to a person's thoughts and words, and the actions other people take under that individual's instructions. Today, some people use the word karma in ways that are not consistent with its traditional meaning. For example, karma is often misused to denote luck, destiny or fate. Karma is also misused as a way to explain sudden hardships. Everything is energy, including your thoughts and emotions, which are energy in motion. In essence, everything you do creates a corresponding energy that comes back to you in some form. Everything you do creates either a positive or negative consequence. Using karma as a set of powerful guidelines for your life can incentivise you to be more mindful of your thoughts, actions, and deeds before you make decisions.

The twelve Laws of Karma are:

1. The Great Law (of cause and effect). You reap what you sow! Whatever you put into the universe is what comes back to you.
2. Law of Creation. This law underscores the importance that life doesn't just happen. To make things happen in your life, you need to take action, instead of waiting for something to magically come your way.
3. Law of Humanity. This law is based on the principle that you must be humble enough to accept that your current reality is the result of your past actions. For example, if you're blaming your colleagues for your poor performance at work, you must accept that you created this reality by not performing as well as you could have.
4. Law of Growth. Wherever you go, there you are. Ultimately, you only have control of yourself. How you use this control, shapes how the universe responds to you.
5. Law of Responsibility. Take ownership of the good and bad things you create rather than looking outside yourself to find excuses.
6. Law of Connexion. This emphasises the interconnexion of the past, present and future.
7. Law of Focus. Concentrate on a single train of thought. If you have several goals, follow them in linear, ranked order rather than giving each goal only a fraction of your energy.
8. Law of Giving and Hospitality. This emphasises the link between belief and practice, and the importance of ensuring your actions reflect your deeper beliefs.
9. Law of Here and Now. Live in the present moment – it is all you really have. Looking backwards to examine what was, prevents us from being totally in the here and now.

10. Law of Change. According to this principle, history will continue to repeat itself until you learn from the experience and take steps to do something differently to stop the cycle. Change gives you a new path so that you can create a new future and a better version of yourself, free from the patterns of the past.

11. Law of Patience and Reward. All your greatest successes require consistent hard work. True joy follows what you're supposed to be doing and waiting for the reward to come in its own time

12. Law of Significance and Inspiration. You get back from something whatever you have put into it. Every personal contribution is a contribution to the whole. This gives your life a motivational boost. Without your presence and contribution, the energy of the universe would be reduced.

Buddhism also has is critics. In an article in May 2022, the Sunday Times quoted Sanitsuda Ekachai, a leading Thai Buddhist commentator and critic of the ecclesiastic establishment, as saying, "The clerical system is rotten, run by old men who have lost touch with the world, clinging to feudal hierarchy and power. Sex scandals and corruption will never cease when temple money is up for grabs. Reforms are urgently needed, but I have no confidence in the projects for change. In this autocratic deferential system, even asking questions of these holy men, never mind changing them, is seen as unacceptable disrespect."

I have no idea how much support there is for Sanitsuda Ekachai's criticism. I much prefer to quote from Matthieu Ricard's superb book *L'infiniti dans la Paume de la Main*, p 17, "Wisdom, knowledge, kindness, nobility, rigour, honesty; the most important thing for everyone is to devote oneself to what you really want in life; it's about analysing your mind and thoughts, to recognise that it is most often under the sway of selfishness and that this selfishness tends to be the source of fundamental ignorance of our true nature and that of the world."

Matthieu Ricard (b 1946) is a French national, the son of the philosopher Jean-François Revel and artist Yahne le Toumelin. He has a PhD in molecular genetics. He became a Buddhist monk and resides at Shechen Tennyi Dargyeling Monastry in Nepal. Apart from *L'infiniti dans la paume* *de la main*, his many other fascinating and informative books include: *A Guide to Happiness, A Guide to Developing Life's Most Important Skills, In Search of Wisdom* and many more. Ricard has been called "The happiest man alive."

Comment. I have been fortunate to have spent some time in Yogyakarta (Java) and to have visited and studied both the amazing and majestic ninth century Buddhist temple of Borobudur, the largest Buddhist temple in the world and the Hindu Prambanan temple, the largest in Asia after Angkor Wat. These magnificent constructions helped me to appreciate the richness of both Hindu and Buddhist cultures and traditions and the power and yet the simplicity of the message of the Twelve Laws of Karma. It was noteworthy that both these religions stress the value of self-responsibility (you reap what you sow!) rather than the edicts sent down from above as described in the Christian Bible (ten commandments, the creed) and the Islamic Qur'an (five pillars). Also, both Hinduism and Buddhism believe in forms of reincarnation (cycle of rebirths) while Christianity and Islam do not.

I have also stayed several times with my younger son who lives and works in Bali, the one Indonesian island where Hinduism predominates. I have had the chance to experience the way of life of the Balinese people, their devotion of their many gods and images and the moving and emotional ceremonies such as Melasti. I found their way of life and their beliefs far more compelling and convincing than anything I have experienced in either the Christian or the Islamic religions. More on this later!

Tao Te Ching.

Many people today are looking for a form of spiritualism that allows them to think beyond just their own existence and to find peace and solace in a way of learning, thinking and acting which helps them to understand a life that does not involve a god, creator but nonetheless encourages the participant to understand better the meaning of life. According to Tom Butler-Brown, an LSE graduate and author of five best-selling books, "For some, the teachings of Tao has produced the answer. As a religion, Taoism emerged during the Hundred Schools of thought, a golden age in Chinese philosophy which also saw the rise of Confucianism. Yet this era also straddled the time of the Warring States, so both philosophies were a reaction to their era, attempting to identify the sources of order in times of turmoil.

Butler-Brown writes “Tao is very simply the timeless, changeless spirit that runs through all life and matter. The task of life, according to Lao Tzu, is to bring ourselves into attunement with the Te, so that we are always moving with the grain of the universe and not against it. Tao Te Ching sets out a set of some eighty short sayings and principles, designed to encourage the reader towards following a modest, pure life style.

Comment. I have no personal experience of this practice, having merely read Tom Butler-Brown’s book in which he introduces Tao Te Ching’s teachings and their background. I am impressed that this philosophy predates any other religion which suggest that the universe was created by a God and that, through him, we can achieve a peaceful after-life. I understand that there are numerous followers of this philosophy among today’s younger generation.

Ancient Chinese thinkers sought to understand the meaning of life. One example is the Mausoleum of Yangling, near Xi’an, which shows the influence that the First Emperor had on how death was understood at that time. Emperor Jing (188–141 BC) and Empress Wan copied the idea of Emperor Qin’s terracotta army. They were buried with an army of thousands of terracotta soldiers, eunuchs, musicians and acrobats as well as hundreds of animals, model weapons, chariots, tools and personal adornments. The burial site was discovered by chance during the discovery of a motorway. It demonstrates the legacy of Qin and Han, which, as in ancient Egypt, continued for centuries. (Quotes from the *Heritage of the Qin and Han Dynasties: The Xi’an Warriors* exhibition, MARQ, Alicante, Spain 2023)

XXX

Chapter Eight

The Agnostics, the "Not Quite Sure", the "Sitting on the Fence", the Atheists!

When I listed the number of "followers" of religions, I used the qualification "alleged" as there are so many shades of "believers" in religious faiths. At the one extreme there are those who fervently believe in their faith, who take the words of the scriptures literally, devoutly go regularly to their church, mosque or other place of worship, say their prayers as required and live the life dictated, as they believe it, by their God. This can lead to living a good, pure life but, conversely can have violent and negative effects, examples being Christians in the US who feel it their duty to blow up abortion clinics, suicide bombers, the 9/11 twin towers attack, Iran under the ayatollahs, or other harsh regimes in some Muslim countries, where females are not allowed to go to school, drive or travel without a male escort. At the other end of the spectrum, there are those whose parents had answered the required question "what religion" on their child's passport/identity document purely because they were required to write something but which had no true bearing on what either the parents or the child actually felt about religion. When the child grew up sufficiently to have their own opinion, many had no interest to change what their parents had written.

Between these extremes, there are some who follow a faith "in principle" because it has been the tradition of their family/race/nationality, some because they find comfort in religious customs and traditions, some because they feel that by following and practising a religion, they will have some sort of insurance policy to go to "heaven" when they die, some believe the main teachings of a particular religion but don't accept some of the details, for example, believe in the principles of Christianity, such as the Ten Commandments but can't accept that Christ was the son of God.

Then there are those who "sit on the fence", who don't not believe, but feel the need for some sort of proof about the veracity of religion before they commit themselves, who are doubtful or uncertain about the existence or demonstrability of God or other deity: These "doubters" are collectively referred to by the term "agnostics". Richard Dawkins in his book *The God Delusion* (p 69) quotes the preacher in his school chapel as describing agnostics as: "namby-pamby, mushy pap, weak tea, weedy, pallid fence-sitters." In the same paragraph, Dawkins quotes the Catholic historian Hugh Ross Williamson as saying; "He respected the committed religious believer and also the committed atheist but reserved his contempt for the wishy-washy boneless mediocrities who flapped around in the middle."

Much has been written by and about "agnostics", a term coined by the English biologist Thomas Henry Huxley in 1869 as part of his philosophy rejecting the validity of claims of spiritual knowledge, particularly in reference to the existence of a deity or deities. When researching material for this book, I found that the subject of being agnostic has been much written about, in addition to Huxley, particularly by philosophers, Christian theologians, scientists and "free thinkers". Dawkins then balances his earlier quote by agreeing that being agnostic is a reasonable position where we lack evidence one way or the other.

The mid nineteenth century marked the emphasis that theories and dogmas needed to be tested and proved before any theory can become an accepted fact. This period is renowned for the acceleration of technical innovation and of science, "pure and free, untrammelled by religious dogmas." (These words are from the influential "X" club members connected to the Royal Society.) Some of many, many examples of the advance of scientific and technical innovation during this period include: the typewriter, printing press, camera, electric battery/dynamo, telephone, telegraph, microphone, sewing machine, internal combustion engine/ steam powered locomotive, rotary washing machine, revolver/machine gun, dynamite.

Charles Darwin (1809–1882)

The same scientific approach was used by the British naturalist, geologist and biologist Charles Darwin, whose name will always be best known for his immense contribution to the study of evolution. He proposed the theory of biological evolution by natural selection and that all species of life have descended from common ancestry. This proposition is now widely accepted both as a fundamental concept in science but also is the starting point of argument for many of today's leading atheists such as Richard Dawkins. In 1858, Darwin received a manuscript from **Alfred Russel Wallace (1823–1913)** who, while exploring in Indonesia, had developed a theory of evolution similar to Darwin's. This led to Darwin and Wallace producing joint scientific journals and the publication of Darwin's world famous *On the Origin of Species.*

Darwin defined evolution as "descent with modification", the idea that species change over time, give rise to new species, and share a common ancestor. He proposed that the mechanism for evolution is natural selection. Because resources are limited in nature, organisms with heritable traits that favour survival and reproduction will tend to leave more offspring than their peers, causing the traits to increase in frequency over generations. Darwin argues that natural selection causes populations to become adapted, or increasingly well suited to their environments over time. Natural selections depend on the environment and requires heritable variation in a group. To this day the theory of evolution by natural selection is accepted by the scientific community as the best evidence-based explanation for the diversity and complexity of life on Earth.

Thomas Henry Huxley (1825–1895)
Huxley was one of the first supporters of Darwin's theory of evolution by natural selection and did more than anyone else to advance its acceptance among scientists and the public during the period. Huxley was a passionate defender of Darwin's theory – so passionate that he has been referred to as "Darwin's Bulldog". He was a leading biologist who carried out research in zoology and palaeontology. He was initially an opponent of evolutionary change but later came to accept these views. He is quoted as reacting to reading Darwin's *On the Origin of Species* by exclaiming "How stupid of me not to have thought of that!" Huxley's most famous work, published in 1863 is *Evidence of Man's Place in Nature* – a comprehensive review of

what was known at the time about primate and human palaeontology and ethology, a first attempt to apply evolution to the human race.
Darwin, Wallace, Huxley and others who shared their views were fiercely attacked by religious groups in the late nineteenth century as the theory of natural selection radically cut across traditional religious thought that God is the creator and Jesus Christ, or Mohammad, or other prophets are God's spokesmen. The period was characterised by much heated debate which also included efforts to define or redefine the words "agnostic" and "atheist". A classic quote from that period was that attributed to the Principle of King's College, London, the Reverend Dr Wace, who denounced Huxley's "cowardly agnosticism" pronouncing. "He may prefer to call himself agnostic; but his real name is an older one – he is an infidel, that is to say an unbeliever. The word infidel, perhaps, carries an unpleasant significance. Perhaps it is right that it should. It is, and it ought to be, an unpleasant thing for a man to have to say plainly that he does not believe in Jesus Christ."

When analysing differing opinions concerning God's existence or non-existence, Dawkins, in "The God Delusion", outlines the many shades of the spectrum ranging from the one extreme of total belief through a mid-way point of impartiality to the total opposite atheist views that there "definitely is no God"

Typical examples of the debate in the late nineteenth century/early twentieth were the conflicting pronouncements of Robert G Ingersoll and Bernard Iddings Bell.

Robert G Ingersoll (1833–1899)
Ingersoll was an American lawyer and orator who campaigned for his definition of agnosticism. He was particularly critical of much of the contents of the Bible and he popularised humanistic philosophy and scientific rationalism. He supported equality for African Americans, and women's suffrage. He was a prolific writer – with some thirty books published between 1879 and 1894, perhaps the best-known being *Why I am an Agnostic*, *Challenging the Bible*, *About the Holy Bible* and *Some mistakes of Moses*. Summarising quotes from *Why I am an Agnostic* are:

"I gave up on the Old Testament on account of its mistakes, its absurdities, its ignorance and its cruelty. I gave up on the New because it vouched for the truth of the Old. I gave it up on account of its miracles, its contradictions, because Christ and his disciples believed in the existence of devils – talked and made bargains with them, expelled them from people and animals. This, of itself, is enough. We know, if we know anything, that devils do not exist – that Christ never cast them out, and that if he pretended to, he was either ignorant, dishonest or insane. These stories about devils demonstrate the ignorant origin of the New Testament."

And

"Suppose we had a man in this country who could control the wind, the air and lightning and suppose we elected him to govern these things, and suppose he allowed whole States to dry and wither, and at the same time wasted the rain in the sea. Suppose that he allowed the winds to destroy whole cities and to crush to shapelessness thousands of men and women, and allowed the lightnings to strike the life out of mothers and babies. What would we say? What would we think of such a savage? And yet, according to the theologians, this is exactly the course pursued by God."

Comment: Phew, strong stuff!

Bernard Iddings Bell (1886–1958)

Bell was an American Christian author, Episcopal priest and leading educator, who held a number of religious posts in US universities and religious institutions including St John's Cathedral, Providence, Rhode Island and as chaplain to Episcopalians at the University of Chicago. He published over twenty books and numerous articles and sermons. His books included: *Beyond Agnosticism* (1930) and *The Church and Social Revolution* (1938).

Unlike Ingersoll, who was condemning of the Holy Bible and its teaching, Bell argued that although agnosticism was an important philosophical discipline, scientific data, observed by human senses and processed by human reason, it is insufficient for discovering the truth. To paraphrase Bell, he argued that beyond what can be measured by scientific tools, there are two other types of perception: one's ability to communicate inner truths through creative expression and one's ability to "read" another person and find harmony with them, which "we call love." One's love cannot be dissected and logged in a scientific journal… If one presupposes that God is in fact a knowable loving person, one's life becomes full, meaningful, and fearless in the face of death. It does not defy reason but exceeds it. Because God has been experienced through love, the orders of prayer, fellowship and devotion now matter. They create order in one's life, continually renewing the "missing piece" that had previously been lost. They empower one to be compassionate and humble, not small minded and arrogant.

Comment. The lives of these two outstanding Americans did not coincide in their maturity as Bell was only thirteen years old when Ingersoll died. Both were reputedly great orators. Their views appear to have been in total contradiction. How fascinating it would have been if the two had lived during the same timeframe and could have been persuaded to debate with each other!

xxx

Chapter Nine

Atheism

"*Atheism is the denial of God or the existence of any divine being.*" (Internet Encyclopaedia of Philosophy).

Bertrand Arthur William Russell (1872–1970)

No review of the works of great agnostics and atheists of the late nineteenth/early twentieth century would be complete without reference to Bertrand Russell who was the Nobel Prize winner (for literature) in 1950. Concerning religion he succinctly said "My own view on religion is that I regard it as a disease born of fear and a source of untold misery to the human race." According to Russell, not only are most religious beliefs intellectually and morally pernicious, but also the religious point of view itself "is a conception quite unworthy of free men."

Russell considered four categories of religion: his criticisms of arguments supporting the existence of God; his observation that religion has historically impeded the advancement of knowledge; his conclusion that religion has advanced theories of morality that are more harmful than good; and his analysis of religion being not simply a body of belief but as a mode of feeling.

Russell succeeded in breaking down many of the previous mystics and social taboos surrounding religion. His plain language approach encouraged people to view religion as a subject where personal beliefs and views could freely be discussed and developed, thus enabling the merits of religion to become a socially acceptable subject for debate and criticism. As the Nobel Prize committee noted, the 1950 award went to Russell "in recognition of his varied writings in which he champions humanitarian ideals and freedom of thought."

One of Russell's most telling arguments is his analysis of "*The Problem of Evil*". He wrote that the creation of a contingent world could never eliminate God's responsibility for the existence of evil. The world, so say Christians and other religions, was created by God who is both good and omnipotent. Before he created the world, he must surely have foreseen all the pain and misery it would contain. He is therefore responsible for all of it. It is "useless to argue that the pain in the world is due to sin. In the first place this is not true, it is not sin that causes rivers to overflow their banks or volcanos to erupt. But even if it were true, it would make no difference. If I were going to beget a child knowing that child was going to be a homicidal maniac, I should be responsible for his crimes. If God knew in advance the sins of which man would be guilty, He would clearly be responsible for all the consequences of those sins when he created man."
Comment. There is a similarity between this argument of Russell's to that of Robert G Ingersoll – Chapter 8 above.

Russell wrote equally plainly on the question of whether religion has impeded the advancement of knowledge and introduced harmful theories of morality. He wrote: "The objections to religion are of two sorts – intellectual and moral. The intellectual objection is that there is no reason to suppose any religion is true; the moral objection is that religious precepts date from a time when men were more cruel than they are (now), and therefore tend to perpetuate inhumanities that the moral conscience of the age would otherwise outgrow." Russell argues that the conclusion to be drawn is that religious faith has served as a shield against the advancement of knowledge both in ethics and in the sciences: "When two scientists disagree, they do not invoke the secular arm; they wait for further evidence to decide the issue, because, as men of science, they know that neither is infallible. But when two theologians differ, since there is no criteria to which either can appeal, there is nothing for it but mutual hatred and an open covert appeal to force."

The tortures of the Inquisition, the condoning of slavery in the Bible and the Qur'an, the burning of women and men for witchcraft, the coming together to pray for deliverance at times of plague (which only led to the further spread of disease), all resulted from religious beliefs and practices.

Russell says the conclusion is obvious: "the more intense has been the religion of any period and the more profound has been the dogmatic belief, the greater has been the cruelty and the worse has been the state of affairs." In 1947, Russell described himself as an agnostic, with the caveat: "Therefore, in regard to the Olympic Gods, speaking to a purely philosophical audience, I would say that I am an Agnostic. But speaking popularly, I think that all of us would say in regard to those gods that we are Atheists. In regard to the Christian God, I should, I think, take exactly the same line."

For most of his adult life, Russell maintained that religion was little more than superstition and, despite any positive effects, was largely harmful to people. He believed that religion and religious outlook served to impede knowledge, fostered fear and dependency, and was responsible for our world's wars, oppression and misery.

Comment. For years I had dismissed Bertrand Russell as a bit of a crank especially when I learned he went to prison during the WWI period for being a conscientious objector and for his strong support for nuclear disarmament. For me, as a soldier during the 1960s–90s, his pacifist views were totally contrary to my own. I had also read his argument against the existence of God by demonstrating his "parable of the celestial teapot." At the time I first read this, probably in my late teens, I dismissed the whole idea as ridiculously stupid. It was only much later, when reading more of Russell's work that I came to appreciate his brilliant mind and how multi-talented he was. I particularly learned to respect the clarity of both his thinking and writing.

Herbert George (H G) Wells (1866–1946)

H G Wells was a prolific writer, principally of science fiction (e.g. *The Time Machine, War of the World,*) but also wrote multiple non-fiction works on politics, religion and social commentary. Of Christianity, he wrote:

"It is not now true for me. Every believing Christian is, I am sure, my spiritual brother… But if systemically I called myself a Christian, I feel that to most men I should imply too much and so tell a lie." Of other world religions, he wrote: "All these religions are as true for me as Canterbury Cathedral is a true thing and as a Swiss chalet is a true thing. There they are, and they have served a purpose, they have worked. Only they are not true for me to live in them… They do not work for me".

In *The Fate of Homo Sapiens* (1939), Wells criticised almost all world religions and philosophies, stating "there is no creed, no way of living left in the world at all, that really meets the needs of the time… When we come to look at them coolly and dispassionately, all the main religions, patriotic, moral and customary systems in which human beings are sheltering today, appear to be in a state of jostling and mutually destructive movement, like the houses and palaces and other buildings of some vast, sprawling city overtaken by a landslide." Wells's opposition to organised religion reached a fever pitch in 1943 with publication of his book *Crux Ansata,* subtitled *An Indictment of the Roman Catholic Church.*

xxx

Atheism today

When considering today's non-believers or atheists, often referred to as "The new Atheists" my immediate point of reference is Richard Dawkins and his fellow "horsemen" – Daniel Dennett, Sam Harris and Christopher Hitchens as these four have been in the forefront of leading literature and promotion of both disproving either that there is a "god" or that there was a "creator" – a superior being who formed the universe and governed all that exists including mankind. Between 2004 and 2007, each of them published books critical of religion and promoting atheism. What set these books apart from others was that they were all published by major publishing companies and all received critical acclaim. Three of the books went on to make the New York Times Best Seller list

In 2007, the "four Horsemen" filmed a landmark discussion about modern atheism. This has become a classic on YouTube and viewed millions of times. During this discussion, the four give their personal slant on the fundamental questions of human existence while challenging the others to articulate their own stance on God and religion, cultural criticism, spirituality, debate with people of faith, and the components of a truly ethical life.

Richard Dawkins (b 1941)

Dawkins is a British evolutionary biologist and author. "He is emeritus fellow of New College, Oxford and was Professor of Public Understanding of Science in the University of Oxford from 1995 to 2008. An atheist, he is well known for his criticism of creationism and intelligent design." (extract from Wikipedia).

In 1976, he published his first book, *The Selfish Gene*, in which he tried to rectify what he maintained was a widespread misunderstanding of Darwinism. Dawkins argues that natural selection takes place at the genetic rather than species or individual level, as had often been assumed. Genes, he maintains, use the bodies of living things to further their own survival. The book is notable not merely for its content but it is written in a style which is easy to understand by the non-expert (like me, for example!) Dawkins followed up with a continuing series of books during the next thirty years which cemented his place as a major thought-provoking author who has kept alive the debate for asserting the supremacy of science over religion in explaining the world. In 2006, his book *The God Delusion* was published and has received world-wide acclaim. It is written in a clear and at times, amusing style, while relentlessly and systematically highlighting the fallacies in religious belief and ultimately concludes that the laws of probability preclude the existence of an omnipotent creator. Dawkins used *The God Delusion* as a platform to launch the Richard Dawkins Foundation for Reason and Science, an organisation seeking to foster the acceptance of atheism and to champion scientific answers to existential questions. The following year (2007), he launched the Out Campaign which encourages atheists to declare their beliefs.

Apart from his books, Dawkins is a highly experienced and popular lecturer. He has an engaging and easy style of delivery honed from his many years as an Oxford University Professor.

Daniel Dennett (b 1942)

"Dennett is an American philosopher, writer and cognitive scientist, whose research centres on the philosophy of mind, science and biology particularly as those fields relate to evolutionary biology and cognitive science. He is

co-director of the Centre of Cognitive Studies and the Austin B Fletcher Professor of Philosophy at Tufts University. Dennett is a member of the editorial board for the Rutherford Journal." (Extract from Wikipedia).
Dennett is a confirmed compatibilist on free will which he explains in his 1978 book *Brainstorms* and much of his more recent work which is concerned with fleshing out his previous ideas. He addresses this from an evolutionary standpoint, from what distinguishes human minds from animal minds and to outlining how free will is compatible with a naturalist view of the world.

In 1991, Dennett wrote *Consciousness Explained* in which he describes consciousness as something like the product of multiple layers of computer programmes running on the hardware of the brain. In his 2006 book, *Breaking the Spell: Religion as a Natural Phenomenon*, Dennett attempts to account for religious beliefs naturistically, explaining evolutionary reasons for the phenomenon of religious adherence. In his 2017 book, *From Bacteria to Bach and Back*, Dennett tells us "there is a winding path leading through a jungle of science and philosophy, from the bland assumption that we are physical objects, obeying the laws of physics, to an understanding of our conscious minds."
Comment. I like the way Joshua Rothman introduced an article about Dennett which was printed in The New Yorker in March 2017. He writes: "Four billion years ago, Earth was a lifeless place. Nothing struggled, thought or wanted. Slowly, that changed. Seawater leached chemicals from rocks; near thermal vents, those chemicals jostled and combined, some hit upon the trick of making copies of themselves that, in turn, made more copies. The replicating chains were caught in oily bubbles, which protected them and made replication easier; eventually, they began to venture out into the open sea. A new level of order had been achieved on Earth. Life had begun. The tree of life grew, its branches stretching towards complexity. Organisms developed systems, subsystems and sub-subsystems, layered in ever-deepening regression. They used these systems to anticipate their future and to change it. When they looked within, some found they had selves – constellations of memories, ideas, and purposes that emerged from the systems inside. They experienced being alive and had thoughts about

that experience. They developed language and used it to know themselves; they began to ask how they had been made.

This, to a first approximation, is the secular story of our creation. It has no single author; it has been written collaboratively by scientists over the past few centuries. If, however, it could be said to belong to any single person, that person might be Daniel Dennett. In the course of forty years, and more than a dozen books, Dennett has endeavoured to explain how a soulless world could have given rise to a soulful one. His special focus is the creation of the human mind. Into his own he has crammed nearly every related discipline: evolutionary biology, neuroscience, psychology, linguistics, artificial intelligence." (Joshua Rothman; March 2017).

Sam Harris (b 1967)

Harris is an American philosopher, author and podcast host. He sprung to prominence through his first book, *The End of Faith* (2004), which allegedly he started writing the day after the 9/11 (2001) New York Twin Towers/Pentagon bombings carried out by Al Qaeda. His book remained on The New York Times Best Seller list for thirty-three weeks. Since then he has written a further six books. His work had been translated into over twenty languages.

The End of Faith and Harris's follow up *Letter to a Christian Nation* contain plenty to outrage against just about everyone. Harris assails political correctness, evangelicals, liberals, right wingers and even Judaism. The one constant is his absolutism about reason. If an idea can't survive rigorous testing and scrutiny, Harris thinks it should be binned.

Harris is a quietly spoken but highly articulate orator who has debated with many prominent figures on the topics of God, religion and spirituality in general. He rarely comes off the worse in these debates though he has been accused of being too dogmatic in has condemnation of all religions. "I think this country needs a sophisticated attack on religion." Van Harvey, a retired professor of religious studies at Stanford University, is quoted as saying of Harris, "But pushing moderates into the same camp as fanatics, that seems like a very crude mistake." According to Van Harvey, "Not only has Harris picked a fight with those who could be on his side, but his solution – let's all ditch God – is laughable given the role that religion plays in so many lives. Others say he has taken these "Old Books" at their literal word, instead of the way that the faithful actually engage the scriptures. Put more simply, he doesn't know what he's talking about!"

Van Harvey's put-down critique of Harris has been echoed by other religious scholars who believe that Harris has grossly oversimplified scripture. They accuse him of drawing far-reaching conclusions based on the belief of radicals. His stand against organised religion is so unconditional that it's akin to the intolerance he claims he is fighting. If there is such a thing as a secular fundamentalist, they contend, Harris is it. Some even agree with his conclusions about the dangers of fanaticism but find his argument ham-fisted.

Miroslav Volf, a Yale professor of theology is quoted as saying: "All of reason is informed by faith, and there is no mature faith that hasn't been coupled with and enlightened by some reason. It's also wrong for Harris to assume that Christians consider the Bible the direct word of God. Most don't, so combing the scriptures for the fingerprints of fallible authors, so then declaring victory once you find them, is silly. Most Christians believe that while the Bible was inspired by God, it is not free-floating megaphone pronouncements out of nowhere by God. It was given through the medium of a culturally situated people, with the limitations of their knowledge at the time. And it's our task to ask, "What does this mean to me today?"
Comment. These "religious scholars" would say that, wouldn't they, after Harris has directly trashed their life's work!

Christopher Hitchens (1949–2011)
Hitchens was a British/American author, critic, and bon vivant whose outspoken views on politics and religion placed him at the forefront of public debate. He was a brilliant and much sought after orator in both the US and the UK. The son of a British naval commander, as a child he lived in Malta and Rosyth, Scotland before attending boarding school in UK and enrolling in Balliol College, Oxford. While at university he joined the group of International Socialists. He held strong left-wing views as a young man

but later moderated his political opinions while always continuing to embrace atheism. He migrated from the UK to the US in 1981 and became a much sought after speaker and debater in both countries. He died in 2011 of complications related to oesophageal cancer.

In his best-seller *God is not Great*, Hitchens lays out the case against religion which he expands to include all religions rarely criticized by Western secularists such as Buddhism. He claimed that organised religion was "the main source of hatred in the world", calling it "violent, irrational and hostile to free inquiry, contemptuous of women and coercive towards children." The book received mixed reviews ranging from praise in The New York Times for his "logical flourishes and conundrums" to accusations in the Financial Times of "intellectual and moral shabbiness". In 2007, Hitchens began a series of written debates on the question of "Is Christianity Good for the World?" with Christian theologian Douglas Wilson. This was published in Christianity Today magazine. One of his recurring explanations for religion was that it derived from a time when mankind had no knowledge of science, the formation of the earth or of medicine. It filled a need to find an explanation, the first attempt at philosophy and science, but based on a total myth and complete ignorance. In 2009, "Intelligence Squared" sponsored a debate with the question "Is the Catholic Church a force for good in the World?" John Onaiyekan, the Nigerian prelate of the Catholic Church and Ann Widdecombe argued that it was, while Hitchens joined Stephen Fry in arguing that it was not." The latter side won the debate, according to an audience poll.
Resulting from his books, speeches and debates, Hitchens became highly respected for his "persuasiveness, enthusiastic rhetoric, verbal barbs and linguistic dexterity".

xxx

Atheists can count many brilliant men as declared non-believers. These include: Steven Weinberg, (1933–2021), the US theoretical physicist (Nobel laureate in physics) and writer of, for example, *The First Three Minutes*, a view of the Origin of the universe, Brian Greene (b1963) whose books include *Until the End of Time* (2020) and Stephen Hawking (1942–

2018). In an interview published in The Guardian, Hawking regarded the brain as “a computer which will stop working when its components fail”, and the concept of an afterlife as a “fairy story for people afraid of the dark”. In 2011, narrating the first episode of an American television series Hawking declared: “We are each free to believe what we want and it is my view that the simplest explanation is there is no God. No one created the universe and no one directs our fate. This leads me to a profound realisation. There is probably no heaven, and no afterlife either. We have this one life to appreciate the grand design of the universe, and for that, I am extremely grateful.” Hawking’s association with atheism and freethinking was in evidence from his university years onwards, when he had been a member of Oxford University’ humanist group. He was later scheduled to appear as the keynote speaker at a 2017 Humanists UK conference. In an interview with El Mundo, he said: “Before we understand science, it is natural to believe that God created the universe. But now science offers a more convincing explanation. What I meant by ‘we would know the mind of God’ is, we would know everything that God would know, if there were a God, which there isn’t. I’m an atheist.” In addition, Hawking stated: “If you like, you can call the laws of science ‘God’, but it wouldn’t be a personal God that you would meet and put questions to.”

Peter Atkins (b 1940)

Atkins began his academic life at Leicester university where he gained his PhD. He later studied at the University of California, Los Angeles before returning to UK as Professor of chemistry at Lincoln College, Oxford. He has received honorary doctorates from universities in the Netherlands (Utrecht), Russia (Mendeleev, Moscow) and been visiting professor at universities in France, Japan, China, New Zealand and Israel.

Atkins research was in the application of quantum mechanics to chemical problems and theoretical aspects of magnetic resonance. He is a prolific writer, the best known of which is “*Physical Chemistry*”, now in its ninth edition, used throughout the world and translated into many languages.
A quote from Atkins is: “Scientific knowledge is the only way of acquiring knowledge because it is evidence based. Religious knowledge is probably

a paradigm of unreliability because it is based on sentiment, authority and wish-fulfilment."

The scientific community also have their defenders of Christianity. Prominent among these are: Miroslav Volf, a Yale professor of theology, Van Harvey, a retired professor of religious studies at Stanford University – (both referenced above as critics of Sam Harris) and:

John Lennox (b 1943)

Lennox is Professor of Mathematics (Emeritus) at Oxford University. He is Northern Irish, a mathematician, bioethicist and Christian apologist. He studied at Cambridge University, and was Senior Alexander Von Humboldt Fellow at the universities of Wurzburg and Freiburg. He has produced over seventy published mathematical papers and a number of books on the interface between science, philosophy and theology including: *Can Science Explain everything?* (2019) and *Cosmic Chemistry: Do God and Science Mix?* (2021).

Lennox has lectured extensively in North America, Eastern and Western Europe and has taken the pro-Christian line in debates with Richard Dawkins, Christopher Hitchens and other atheists.

XXX

Chapter Ten

Religion and Evolution

The Oxford dictionary gives two definitions of evolution: These are:
1. The process by which different kinds of living organism are believed to have developed from earlier forms during the history of the earth.
2. The gradual development of something.

The subject of "evolution" has brought out the widest division both between religious groups views and scientific evolutionary research. When considering evolution, some religions tend to refer merely to the development of the earth from its formation (e.g. "the big bang" theories) and neglect the evolution of the human species. For example, the rejection of evolution by most Christian evangelicals is largely mirrored by their church principles, such as the US Southern Baptist Church and the Lutheran Church-Missouri Synod which explicitly reject evolutionary theory as being in conflict with what they believe as being "biblical truth".

Where do we humans come from?

Our first known human ancestors appeared between five million and seven million years ago when some apelike creatures in Africa began to walk habitually on two legs. There were flaking crude stone tools by 2.5 million years ago. Some spread from Africa into Asia and Europe about two million years ago. (The New York Times 26 Feb 2002.) Most scientists currently recognize some fifteen to twenty different species of early humans. The oldest known evidence for anatomically modern humans are fossils found at Jebel Irhoud, Morocco.

One remarkable archaeological site is located in Atapuerca, near the city of Burgos, in northern Spain. The site contains a rich fossil record of the earliest human beings in Europe, from nearly one million years ago and extending into the Modern era (from seven thousand years ago). The site constitutes an exceptional and unique scientific reserve providing priceless information about the evolution, appearance and way of life of our remote human ancestors who have since disappeared.

The story of Atapuerca is brilliantly told in the Museum of Human Evolution, situated in the heart of Burgos city. The museum charts the first discovery of hominids over the last three million years and during the earth's varying eco and climatic systems. It describes the divergence between the human and chimpanzee lines which share several common characteristics and the evolution through the Australalopithecus genus to Homo Habilis and Rudolfensis, to Homo Georgicus, to Homos Antecessor and Heidelbergensis – leading to our Homo Sapiens' immediate predecessor, Homo Neandertal. The museum shows how Homo Sapiens, described as having had the "first anatomically modern" skeleton, when the line emerged in Africa about one hundred and fifty thousand years ago. It illustrates the archaeological work which continues at the Atapuerca site today and the scientific methodology used to ensure the accuracy of their conclusions.

This fascinating and important work enhances today's man's understanding of the nature of our origins and perhaps understands why many religions struggle to reconcile past religious beliefs with the discoveries of human archaeology. It is also somewhat symbolic (or ironic!) that the Museum of Human Evolution is located directly opposite the majestic Burgos Catholic Cathedral and on the route of the Saint James Way Christian pilgrimage route to Santiago de Compostela! It is difficult to reconcile the archaeological findings of human evolution such the physical discovery of fossils, bones, tools etc displayed in the Museum, with Christian concepts of God's divine creation of Adam and Eve in the garden of Eden!

Religious Group's views on evolution.

Catholic. The church generally accepts evolutionary theory as a scientific explanation for the development of all life. However, this acceptance comes with the caveat that natural selection is a God-directed mechanism of biological development and that man's soul is the divine creation of God. (Reference: Catechism of the Catholic church)

Church of England. The church is not known to take an official stance against Darwin's theories, though many senior Anglicans strongly denounced "The origins of species" when it was first published, arguing against it at public debates.

Judaism. While all of the major movements of US Judaism – including the Reconstructionist, Reform, Conservative and Orthodox branches – teach that God is the creator of the universe and all life, Jewish teachings generally do not find an inherent conflict between evolutionary theory and faith.
(Reference: Religious Action Centre of Reform Judaism – (Jewish Values and the Origin of Life.)

Islam. While the Qur'an teaches that Allah created human beings, Islamic scholars and followers are divided on the theory of evolution. Theologically conservative Muslims who ascribe to literal interpretations of the Qur'an generally denounce the evolutionary argument for natural selection, whereas many theologically liberal Muslims believe that while man is divinely created, evolution is not necessarily incompatible with Islamic principles. Sabboor Ahmad, a modern writer and podcaster, whose books include "*A failed Hypothesis*" asks "Can evolutionary theory in purely natural terms explain why we have the moral beliefs that we do?" Sabboor accepts Darwinism as a working model but not as a "fact". He states that God explains why, whereas science only gives us working models which can change.
(Reference: Pew Research Centre – updated February 2014)

Buddhism/Hinduism. Many Buddhists see no inherent conflict between their religious teachings and evolutionary theory. Indeed, according to some Buddhist thinkers, certain aspects of Darwin's theory are consistent with some of the religion's core teachings, such as the notion that all life is impermanent. While there is no single Hindu teaching on the origins of life, many Hindus believe that the universe is a manifestation of Brahman,

Hinduism's highest god and the force behind all creation. However, many Hindus today do not find their beliefs to be incompatible with the theory of evolution.

Comment. Much of Darwin's work in the 1850s was original and can correctly be described by religious bodies as "theories". However, the discoveries of fossils, bones and tools at archaeological sites such Atapuerca are factual not mere theories – all have been physically unearthed and aged by accepted aging methodology! Through my research for this book, I have appreciated the brilliance of some of the world's leading scientists and philosophers, including many who have declared themselves to be atheists stemming from their scientific backgrounds. Their work and the many "YouTube" recorded debates between prominent theologians and atheists have firmed up my agreement that the scientific principle of only accepting a truth if the evidence is there to support it against the acceptance by many theologians, especially Christians and Muslims, of the words of prophets which may or may not have been correctly interpreted and eventually written down. I found the works of Charles Darwin and other "evolutionists" compelling, this being the basis of so much further work into the whole principle of biological evolution by natural selection and its confirmation by archaeological discoveries.

I could now end this examination of "the meaning of life" right here and now and declare that I am on the side of the evolutionists. That's it – done, finished – my conclusion is… Ah, but! Or is it? As much as I identify with so much of the evolutionist conclusions, I feel there is more to it than that we've evolved over a vast stretch of time, that we have a certain life span then we die. Nothing more or less. Our genes will continue to evolve while the earth still exists but for the individual there is nothing there after the years of life.

I believe there is something lacking in this matter of fact, somewhat sterile, argument. It's not the logic that's missing, it's some other ingredient. It stems from human emotion – happiness, sadness, love, desire, pride, jealously, guilt, sexual drive, frustration, remorse, regret, mental distress, human suffering and tragedy. I read and heard very little of these emotions in the evolutionist determination. Current scientific techniques also have limitations. They cannot measure or demonstrate the content of consciousness. It is impossible to produce scientific evidence that someone is in love or why someone appreciates a certain piece of music or a particular painting. The things that can be measured are the chemical, electrical or magnetic changes in brain activity; the content of thought, feelings and emotions cannot be measured in a strictly scientific test. When we are in love, our world is beautiful yet when we are depressed that very same world can be a torment. In other words, the world is merely a picture constructed in our minds which can change according to our moods and emotions of the moment. Consciousness cannot be located or defined in a particular time or place.

When Atheists tell people that they lead meaningless lives in a meaningless universe, I believe they miss so much of the human emotional depth of life. Religion, whether its followers believe that The Bible or Qur'an are literally true or not, still provides a depository for asking fundamental questions such as; How are we to live? Is there a consciousness separate from the mind? Are we truly only accountable to ourselves? What about the phenomenon of near-death experiences (NDEs)? What about reincarnation? What about child prodigies? I searched for references to the above in the books, for example written by the "Four Horsemen". Zilch; at least I could find very little on these subjects. Or perhaps I've missed it among the vast bibliography I've been wading through. About the closest I could find are references in Dawkins *The God Delusion* to *Hallucinations* in Chapters Three *Arguments for God's Existence* and Chapter Ten *A Much Needed Gap*. In these references, Dawkins attempts to pass off unexplained or unexplainable phenomena as mere hallucinations which he argues have logical non spiritual sources. Perhaps he's right but my next section in this book shows that Dawkins and his fellow atheists might just be wrong.

xxx

Chapter Eleven

Near Death Experiences (NDEs)

Consciousness poses the most baffling problems in the science of the mind. There is nothing that we know more intimately than conscious experience, but nothing that is harder to explain." (David Chambers, philosopher).
The term "consciousness" has many differing interpretations, definitions and meanings – for example in English psychology and philosophy, in Hindi, Urdu, and in Arabic. In using the term in this section of my book I took the Cambridge dictionary as my guide. But even here, there are variants:

1. The state of understanding and realising something:
2. The state of being awake, aware of what is around you, and able to think:
3. The fact of noticing the existence of something:

A near death experience is (Wikipedia) "a profound personal experience associated with death which researchers claim share similar characteristics. When positive, such experiences may encompass a variety of sensations including detachment from the body, feelings of levitation, total serenity, security, warmth, the experience of absolute dissolution and the presence of a light. When negative, such experiences may include sensations of anguish and distress."

NDEs have been recorded since ancient times, by all civilisations, cultures and religions. The oldest recorded medical report of NDEs that I can find was produced by Pierre-Jean du Monchaux, an eighteenth century French military doctor who described such a case in his book *Anecdotes de Médecine*. The study of the phenomenon of NDEs has only been made possible by recent advances of medical science in treating patients, particularly those who have had cardiac arrests. Some believe that an NDE happens when your mind leaves this plane of consciousness, some that it involves communing with a higher being and others that it is simply a hallucination induced by the slow death of neurons."

As Tom Whipple, Science Editor of the Times writes (9 May 2022), "Until the 1960s if your heart stopped you would die, but that is no longer the case and millions of people have been brought back to life after cardiac arrest. Many of these survivors have consistently described an apparently universal and unique cognitive state. When brought back to life they consistently describe the same or very similar experiences."

NDEs are associated with changes in personality and outlook on life. Researchers have identified a consistent set of values and belief changes associated with individuals who have had NDEs. Among these changes, a greater appreciation of life has been noted, together with higher self-esteem, greater compassion for others, less concern for acquiring material wealth, a heightened sense of purpose and self-understanding and a greater ecological sensitivity. However not all after effects are beneficial and in some cases they have led to changes in attitude and behaviour leading to psychosocial and psychospiritual problems. Leaders in research into NDEs include: Professors Raymond Moody, Bruce Greyson, Peter Fenwick and Dr Pim van Lommel.

Raymond Moody (b 1944)

Moody is an American philosopher, psychiatrist and author who has been involved in researching NDEs for over forty years. His findings published in his book *God Is Bigger Than the Bible* is a summation of thousands of near-death experiencers, many of whom were profoundly affected by their encounter with a "divine" presence. Moody identified twelve different NDE elements but emphasised that most people experience only a few of these. Each NDE is unique and is experienced as a coherent episode rather than a series of clearly distinct episodes. The NDE and its effect on patients appeared to be essentially the same worldwide except for some religious/culture-specific differences in content and interpretation. Moody described the twelve NDE elements and the order in which they usually occurred as follows:

1. The ineffability of the experience. This refers to the fact that what happens in a life-threatening situation is usually totally unfamiliar and indescribable to the patient. It is not surprising that patients have difficulty in trying to put their experience into words. Some patients said that words couldn't do their experience justice – human language was woefully inadequate for conveying the full extent, the depth and the other dimensions they'd seen.

2. A feeling of peace and quiet; pain was gone.

3. The awareness of being dead.

4. An out-of-body experience (OBE); from a position outside and above their own physical bodies, people witness their own resuscitation or operation.

5. A dark space, experience by only 15 percent of people as frightening; people are pulled towards a small pinpoint of light in this dark space, which they describe as:

. A tunnel experience; they are drawn rapidly towards the light.

. A frightening NDE; approximately one to two percent of people linger in this dark space and experience their NDE as frightening (also known as a hell experience).

6. The perception of an unearthly environment, a dazzling landscape with beautiful colours, gorgeous flowers, and sometimes music.

7. Meeting and communicating with deceased persons, mostly relatives.

8. Seeing a brilliant light or a being of light; experiencing complete acceptance and unconditional love and gaining access to a deep knowledge and wisdom.

9. The panoramic life review, or review of life from birth; some people see their entire life flash before them; there appears to be no time or distance, everything happens at once, and people can talk for days about a life review that lasted only a few minutes.

10. The preview or flash forward; people have the impression that they are witness to part of the life that is yet to come; again, there is no time or distance.

11. The perception of a border; people are aware that if they cross this border or limit, they will never be able to return to their body.

12. The conscious return to the body, accompanied by great disappointment at having something so beautiful taken away.

Bruce Greyson (b 1946)

Greyson is Professor Emeritus of Psychiatry and Neurobehavioral Sciences at the University of Virginia. He is author of "*After: A Doctor Explores What Near-Death Experiences Reveal about Life and Beyond*". In this book, Greyson reveals his journey towards rethinking the nature of death, life and the continuity of consciousness. Cases of remarkable experiences on the threshold of death have been reported since ancient times, and are described today by ten percent of people whose hearts stop. For years, the medical world generally ignored these "near death experiences", dismissing them as "tricks of the brain" or wishful thinking. But after patients started describing events that he could not just sweep under the rug, Dr Greyson began to investigate. As a physician with no particular religious belief, he approached NDEs from purely a scientific perspective. In his book *After*, he shares the transformative lessons he learnt after some four decades of research. Our culture has tended to view dying as the end of consciousness, the end of our existence – a dreaded prospect that for many people evokes fear and anxiety. But Dr Greyson shows how scientific revelations about the dying process can support an alternative theory. Dying could be the threshold between one form of consciousness and another, not an ending but a transition. This new perspective of the nature of death can transform the fear of dying that pervades our culture into a healthy view of it as one more milestone in the course of our lives. Dr Greyson's book challenges us to open our minds to these experiences and to what they can teach us, and in so doing, expand our understanding of consciousness and of what it means to be human.

Comment. The above text was provided by the publisher of Dr Greyson's book. I include it in its entirety as it provides an excellent summary of advances made into the scientific study of NDEs in the US.

Peter Fenwick (b 1955)

Fenwick is a graduate of Trinity College, Cambridge where he studied Natural Science. He gained his clinical experience at St Thomas's Hospital. He is President of the Horizon Research Foundation, an organisation that supports research into end-of-life experiences and also President of the British branch of the International Association for Near-Death Studies. Fenwick's interest in NDEs was prompted by reading Raymond Moody's book *Life after Life*. He reassessed his own opinion after a discussion with one of his own patients, who described a near-death experience very similar to that of Moody's subjects. Since then, he has collected and analysed more than three hundred examples of NDEs. Fenwick has been criticised by some in the medical community for arguing that human consciousness can survive bodily death. He has argued that consciousness may be more than just a function of the brain.

Pim van Lommel (b 1943)

Van Lommel is a Dutch researcher and author in the field of NDEs. He studied medicine at Utrecht University, specialising in cardiology. He worked as cardiologist at the Rijnstate Hospital, Arnhem, for twenty-six years. His book *Consciousness beyond Life: The Science of the Near-Death Experience,* published in 2010 has been acclaimed by many but treated with reserve by some scientists and other medical specialists

Comment. I have taken many of the details below from Dr van Lommel's book either as short summaries or direct quotes.

The first coronary care units in Dutch hospitals opened in 1966, when massaging the heart, administering oxygen, and defibrillation were found to be effective in treating cardiac arrest patients. Cardiac arrest was and remains the most common cause of death for people with an acute myocardial infarction. Since the introduction of modern techniques of resuscitation and the establishment of coronary care units, mortality rates as a result of cardiac arrest have fallen sharply, and these days it is not uncommon for patients to survive cardiac arrest and be fully restored to good health.

While Dr van Lommel was working as a cardiologist, he was confronted with death on an almost daily basis. As a doctor, he was all but forced to reflect on the emotional, philosophical and physiological aspects of life and death. During his work he encountered several patients who had been resuscitated following cardiac arrests and who, according to accepted medical science, had been clinically dead. Clinical death is defined as a period of unconsciousness caused by a lack of oxygen to the brain because of the arrest of circulation, breathing or both following cardiac arrest in patients. If no resuscitation is started, the brain cells suffer irreparable damage and the patient dies.

Van Lommel's reflections were heightened by reading about American research into NDEs particularly by Raymond Moody's twelve NDE elements (details above). He wondered how patients could possibly experience consciousness during cardiac arrest and whether this was a common occurrence. As a result, he began systematically to ask all the patients at his outpatient clinic who had undergone resuscitation whether they had any NDEs. He recorded that in a two-year period there were twelve reports of NDEs having been experienced among just fifty cardiac arrest survivors. These reports aroused his curiosity further as, according to the current accepted medical knowledge, it was impossible to experience consciousness when the heart stopped beating. Lommel realised that Moody's twelve NDE elements classification was a useful starting point for examining the various elements, realising this is an artificial division as while these elements may be distinct, they cannot be isolated because the NDE constitutes a continuous experience. It is a practical division, however, because each of Moody's elements raises different questions about a possible scientific explanation for an NDE. How is it possible, van Lommel queried, for people to observe their own resuscitation from a position above their lifeless body? How can they have clear thoughts and retain their memories without a physical body? How is it possible to meet and recognise deceased relatives? How is it possible to experience a life review in mere minutes, as if time and distance do not exist in this other, unearthly realm?

During the period from1988 to 1992, Dr Lommel organised a detailed study in his own hospital and five nearby smaller hospitals with follow up interviews carried out eight years later of those who had reported having NDEs. All interviews were recorded on tape and transcribed. This allowed the researchers who conducted the eight years follow-up interviews to compare the content of the NDE with the experience as it had been reported in the hospital immediately after the cardiac arrest. Remarkably, after those eight years, patients related their NDE in almost the exact same wording down to the last detail. This was thought to be impossible if the patient had had a dream or invented their experience. All participants were also asked to complete an inventory which comprised thirty-four questions about self-image, compassion for others, material and social issues and attitude towards death. All findings underwent statistical analysis to identify differences. Within the four-year period, 344 patients who had had NDEs were involved. In 1992, the results of the study were published in The Lancet, the respected weekly peer-reviewed medical journal. This study not only made it onto the front pages of the major newspapers in Europe, the US, Canada and Australia but also in other countries such as Russia, China, India and Japan. Dr van Lommels's team also received hundreds of emails from other individuals from around the world who had experienced NDEs themselves and who felt supported and recognised by the study and its findings.

One US and two UK studies among cardiac arrest patients, with the same design as the Dutch study found near identical percentages of NDE after a successful resuscitation. None of these studies, comprising a total of 562 patients, could produce a definitive scientific explanation for the phenomenon.

Comments. I had only heard the term "Near Death Experience" before I began researching for this book and it had no particular significance to me. However, having since read the accounts from Messrs Moody, Greyson, Fenwick and particularly Pim van Lommel, this subject had considerable impact. I feel that van Lommel's studies were carried out with dedicated professionalism and his findings deserve the prominence given by the respected Lancet journal. Van Lommel has had to deal with several limiting factors such as a critical medical and scientific community. There has been professional opposition/resistance by some to the idea that consciousness can be a separate entity from the brain. Several patients who experienced NDEs found that they were not taken seriously by their doctors and nurses when they tried to describe their stories. Conventional medical training teaches that if all brain functions have ceased and the ECG has flatlined, the patient is dead. Many still query why, for instance, a serious oxygen shortage cannot explain an NDE and that we can be so certain of a loss of all brain function during a cardiac arrest. Dr van Lommel deals with such questions in detail in his book but scientists still look for objective rather than anecdotal evidence, no matter how well documented. The response of many doctors and other scientists can also be shaped by their religious or spiritual backgrounds or lack thereof.

Patients have often been reluctant to relate their experiences. For most of those who have had an NDE, it has been a dramatic event which they find difficult to explain, some have even stressed that there are not words in our languages that adequately explain their experiences. Some decide not to report their NDE for fear of not being believed or to be thought of as unbalanced. It is sometimes only years after the event, often stimulated by hearing of the experiences of others, that people decide to reveal their own. This reticence makes scientific studies of NDEs difficult.

There has also been over dramatizing by some US participants. I have watched and listened to many YouTube contributions featuring persons giving their NDE stories and how it has changed their lives. Some are filmed in a natural and convincing style e.g. by the German interviewer Werner Huemer who interviews his "NDE-ers" in a quiet, calm and undramatic way. Others are carried out accompanied by a fanfare of introduction and often accompanied by mood music and Hollywood style graphics. While I don't doubt the veracity of these stories, in my view this presentation style can detract from their authenticity. Near Death Experiences are dramatic enough without further embellishment. One example is the style of the American Eben Alexander. He has a fascinating tale to tell of his own NDE but in my opinion his speaking style is all too polished and bland, perhaps the result of his producer or the fact that he has repeated his story too many times. I don't doubt the full sincerity of his story but to me he comes across more like a slick commercial salesman than a sincere and humble NDE-er. Or perhaps it's just my old-fashioned Brit background which prefers simple to flash!

Overall I find that the NDE phenomenon to be very convincing but if it is to get a tick in the box from the scientific community, there needs to be a follow up to all the excellent work of Messrs Moody, Greyson, Fenwick and Van Lommel by producing firm objective evidence that can be tested or rejected under scientific scrutiny. As van Lommel himself writes; "We still lack the definitive answers to many important questions about consciousness and its relationship to the body." I wonder but somehow doubt that that will ever be achievable with NDE experiences, due to their essentially personal, individual and subjective character. Watch that space!

xxx

Chapter Twelve

Six Political Leaders

After reviewing the lives of many great religious leaders, other theologians, believers, non-believers, scientists and other academics, I wondered what some of the world's most inspirational and charismatic political leaders of recent times made of the same burning questions of the meaning of life and the afterlife. I chose six – all of whom rose from relatively humble origins to become leaders of their nations.

Napoléon Bonaparte (1769–1821) Napoléon was born in an obscure Corsican village, but became ruler over most of Europe. He rose to become commander of the French Grande Armée, when it was the most powerful force in Europe and North Africa, having gained major victories in battles in mid-Europe, the Iberian peninsula and Egypt. He was elected Emperor of the French in 1804. Yet only a few years later his armies suffered a retreat from Russia, then in 1815 were defeated at the Battle of Waterloo. Napoleon was sent in exile by the British where he died in 1821, still aged only fifty-two. What a life! In his few years on this earth, Napoleon experienced and achieved an amazing amount – born into a Catholic family, he shared Voltaire's belief (details in Chapter Two) that people needed "a religion" but he was indifferent to any particular denomination: in Egypt he had even said that he wanted to become a Muslim. He not merely excelled as a military commander but also immersed himself deeply in European politics. He considered that religious peace had to be restored to France. As early as 1796, when he was concluding the armistice in Italy with Pope Pius VI, he had tried unsuccessfully to persuade the pope to retract his briefs against the French priests who had accepted the Civil Constitution of the Clergy, which in practice nationalized the church. Pius VII, who succeeded Pius VI in March 1800, was more accommodating than his predecessor, and, ten months after negotiations were opened with him, the Concordat of

1801 was signed reconciling the church and the Revolution. The pope recognized the French republic and called for the resignation of all former bishops; new prelates were to be designated by the first consul and instituted by the pope; and the sale of the property of the clergy was officially recognized by Rome. The concordat, in fact, admitted freedom of worship and the lay character of the state, a legal position still adopted in France today.

One individual, especially one from such a humble origin, achieved so much in one short life time! We can now only wonder what Napoleon's conclusions were concerning the meaning of life, when he grew sick, was filled with depression and he knew his own death was approaching during his final years in isolation in St Helena! (Reference: Extracts taken from *Napoléon Bonaparte*, Larousse editions 2004/2008).

Kemal Mustafa Ataturk (1881–1938). Ataturk transformed Turkey from "the ashes of the six hundred year-long Ottoman Empire" into a modern twentieth century democracy, moved the capital city from Istanbul to Ankara, abolished the Caliphate and religious courts and schools, adopted western style clothes, instituted the emancipation of women, and reformed the civil, penal and commercial codes. Ataturk was a military genius, a charismatic leader and a comprehensive reformer. His own approach to religion was pragmatic. Some researchers claim he retained his Muslim beliefs. Others conclude he was a religious sceptic or was even agnostic. Andrew Mango *The Biography of the Founder of Modern Turkey* (2002) quotes him as saying:

"I have no religion, and at times I wish all religions at the bottom of the sea. He is a weak ruler who needs religion to uphold his government; it is as if he would catch his people in a trap. My people are going to learn the principles of democracy, the dictates of truth and the teachings of science. Superstition must go. Let them worship as they will; every man can follow his own conscience, provided it does not interfere with sane reason or bid him against the liberty of his fellow men.

We do not consider our principles as dogmas contained in books that are said to come from heaven. We derive our inspiration, not from heaven or from an unseen world, but directly from life."

Further details of his remarkable life and achievements are described in Part Two.

Soekarno (1901–1970). Soekarno was a man of considerable intellect who had emerged from a long period of oppression from the years of former colonial rule of Indonesia by the Dutch, the period of occupation by the Japanese during WWII, the subsequent jostling for power in the region by both the communist regimes of China and the Soviet Union on the one side and the US, UK and the Dutch on the other. Internally, he faced power struggles between those who sought an independent Indonesia with liberal values, those who wanted the emerging nation to be an Islamic state and those who advocated communism. Soekarno had the immense ability to achieve a balance between all these conflicting factors and to integrate a vast disparate archipelago into a cohesive nation which achieved independence (by declaration in 1945 and final transfer of sovereignty by the Netherlands in 1949). Soekarno was multi-lingual, helped by having a photographic memory. He despised traditional Javanese feudalism but pragmatically acquiesced to the Islamic culture, at times embracing communist values, was strongly opposed to the Malaysian federation yet generally maintained cordial relations with the west. His personal religious views remain ambiguous. (Details from *Sukarno. A political biography* (2007) by John D Legge)

Mahatma Gandhi (1869–1948). Gandhi was the primary leader of India's independence movement and also the architect of a form of non-violent civil disobedience that would influence the world. Until Gandhi was assassinated in 1948, his life and teachings inspired activists including Martin Luther King Jr. and Nelson Mandela.

Mohandas Karamchand Gandhi was born on October 2, 1869, at Porbandar, in the present-day Indian state of Gujarat. His father was the dewan (chief minister) of Porbandar; his deeply religious mother was a devoted practitioner of Vaishnavism (worship of the Hindu god Vishnu), influenced by Jainism, an ascetic religion governed by tenets of self-discipline and nonviolence. At the age of 19, Mohandas left home to study law in London at the Inner Temple, one of the city's four law colleges. Upon returning to India in mid-1891, he set up a law practice in Bombay, but met with little success. He soon accepted a position with an Indian firm that sent him to its office in South Africa. Along with his wife, Kasturbai, and their children, Gandhi remained in South Africa for nearly 20 years. In 1906 he first put into action satyagraha, his technique of nonviolent resistance. His success in South Africa gave him an international reputation, and in 1915 he returned to India and within a few years became the leader of a nationwide struggle for Indian home rule. He refashioned the Indian National Congress into an effective political instrument of Indian nationalism and undertook major campaigns of nonviolent resistance in 1920–22, 1930–34 (including his momentous march to the sea to collect salt to protest a government monopoly), and 1940–42. In the 1930s he also campaigned to end discrimination against India's lower-caste "untouchables" (Dalits; officially designated as Scheduled Castes) and concentrated on educating rural India and promoting cottage industry.

India achieved dominion status in 1947, but the partition of the subcontinent into India and Pakistan was a great disappointment to Gandhi, who had long worked for Hindu-Muslim unity. In September 1947 he ended rioting in Calcutta (Kolkata) by fasting. Known as the Mahatma ("Great-Souled"), Gandhi had won the affection and loyalty of millions. In January 1948 he was shot and killed by a young Hindu fanatic.

Gandhi was born a Hindu but his interpretation of Hinduism was his own. While keeping firm roots in ancient Hinduism, he welcomed contact with other religions, especially the Christian doctrines.

Nelson Mandela (1918–2013). Mandela was the son of a South African Xhosa chief. He studied law at the University of Witwatersrand and in 1944 joined the African National Congress (ANC). After the Sharpeville massacre (1960), he abandoned his nonviolent stance and helped found the "Spear of the Nation," the ANC's military wing. Arrested in 1962, he was sentenced to life imprisonment. He retained wide support among South Africa's black population and became an international cause célèbre. Released by President F.W. de Klerk in 1990, he replaced Oliver Tambo as president of the ANC in 1991. In 1993, Mandela and de Klerk were awarded the Nobel Peace Prize for their efforts to end apartheid and bring about the transition to non-racial democracy. In 1994, he was elected president in the country's first universal suffrage elections; by the time he stepped down in 1999, Mandela was the most universally respected figure of postcolonial Africa. History is still unsure of what Nelson Mandela's exact beliefs were regarding God and religion. He is known to have been a Christian, a Methodist (?). He rarely spoke or demonstrated any particular religious belief but recognised the power of all religions to influence people and to do good works.

Margaret Thatcher (1925–2013*)* Thatcher was a British conservative party politician who became Europe's first woman prime minister (1979–90) and was the only British prime minister in the twentieth century to win three consecutive terms. At the time of her resignation, she was Britain's longest continuously serving prime minister since 1827. She accelerated the evolution of the British economy from stateism to liberalism and became, by personality as much as achievement, the most renowned British political leader since Winston Churchill.

The daughter of Alfred Roberts, a grocer, Margaret Thatcher formed an early desire to be a politician. Her intellectual ability gained her a place in Oxford University, where she studied chemistry. She was active in politics, becoming one of the first woman presidents of the Oxford University Conservative Association. After graduating in 1947 she worked for four years as a research chemist, reading for "the bar" in her spare time, later practicing as a barrister, specializing in tax law. In 1951, she married a wealthy industrialist, Denis Thatcher who fully supported her political ambition. After Edward Heath lost two successive elections in 1974, Thatcher was the only minister prepared to challenge him for the party leadership. With the backing of the Conservative right wing, she was elected leader in February 1975 and thus began a fifteen-year ascendancy that would change the face of Britain.

Thatcher led the Conservatives to a decisive electoral victory in 1979 following a series of major strikes during the previous winter (the so-called "Winter of Discontent") under the Labour Party government of James Callaghan. She advocated greater independence of the individual from the state; an end to allegedly excessive government interference in the economy, including privatisation of state-owned enterprises and the sale of public housing to tenants; reductions in expenditures on social services such as health care, education, and housing; limitations on the printing of money in accord with the economic doctrine of moneterism; and legal restrictions on trade unions.

Thatcher embarked on an ambitious program of privatization of state-owned industries and public services, including aerospace, television and radio, gas and electricity, water, the state airline, and British Steel. By the end of the 1980s, the number of individual stockholders had tripled, and the government had sold 1.5 million publicly owned housing units to their tenants. Nonetheless, rising unemployment and social tensions during her first term made her deeply unpopular which could have caused her defeat in the general election of 1983 were it not for two factors: the The Falklands War (1982) between Britain and Argentina, over possession of a remote British dependency in the South Atlantic, and the deep divisions within the Labour Party, which contested the election on a radical manifesto that critics dubbed the "longest suicide note in history." Thatcher won election to a second term in a landslide.

During her eleven years as British Prime Minister, Margaret Thatcher held centre stage in World politics. She was a close ally of US President Ronald Reagan and was the first Western leader to form a cordial working relationship with Mikhail Gorbachev, then General Secretary of the Communist Party of the Soviet Union. Although her popularity varied from devotion by her supporters to intense dislike by her-detractors, the "iron lady" was a considerable political heavyweight of her era.

Her faith was Methodist Christian, she called her church "the most marvellous evangelical faith." Her father, a grocer, raised her in the church where he served as a lay preacher. She contrasted political and spiritual activity: "Nowhere in the Bible is the word democracy mentioned. Ideally, when Christians meet, as Christians, to take counsel together their purpose is not (or should not be) to ascertain what is the mind of the majority but what is the mind of the Holy Spirit – something which may be quite different." She also believed firmly in objective morality, coupled with humility: "To assert absolute moral values is not to claim perfection for ourselves. No true Christian could do that." She once told a journalist that she was "in politics because of the conflict between good and evil," and that she believed "in the end good will triumph."

xxx

After reviewing the lives of these brilliant individuals, I concluded that there was no common denominator concerning their views about religion. Although at one time, Napoléon professed to be considering becoming a Muslim, most of his recorded statements were generally hostile to any fixed religion as evidenced by his struggles to free France from the control of the Roman Catholic church. Though born and raised a Muslim, Ataturk's approach to religion was strictly pragmatic. Soekarno acknowledged Indonesia's strong ties to Islam while keeping his own personal beliefs ambiguous and encouraging respect for all faiths. Gandhi was born into a strong Hindu background but welcomed the content of other religions, including Christianity. Mandela was known to be a Christian but rarely showed strong conviction in that faith. By contrast, Margaret Thatcher was open in her devotion to the Methodist Christian faith.

To summarise, I could find no consensus concerning the meaning of life from any of these inspirational leaders.

xxx

Chapter Thirteen

Reincarnation – Child Prodigies

My searches on Google etc revealed that varying terms are used when referring to the concept of Reincarnation. The most used are: "The belief that a dead person's spirit returns to life in another body" or the concept that "the soul, or consciousness, is reborn into new lives". Many experts seem to have conflicting definitions for the terms: spirit, soul and consciousness. I shall use a simpler explanation of Reincarnation as "Leaving one life and going to another" which implies that the person's consciousness remains the same while occupying a new body.

There is a problem of separating the spiritual from the scientific when researching reincarnation as many scientists give little credence to reports of persons who claim to be reincarnated from another person, being suspicious of hearsay evidence unless it is supported by hard objective fact. For many scientists, reincarnation will always seem like a fantastical notion regardless of how much evidence is presented. Christopher French, a professor of psychology at Goldsmith's, University of London, who heads a unit that studies paranormal experiences, is quoted as saying. "I think it is far more likely that such apparent memories are, in fact, false memories rather than accurate memories of events that were experienced in a past life."

However, there is strong belief in the truth of Reincarnation among the main Eastern religions – e.g.: Hinduism, Jainism, Buddhism and Sikhism. The monotheisms, Christian, Muslim and Judaism all seem officially to reject the concept, yet in each of these religions, there are sects which continue to explore the concept.

Below, I have summarised extracts from a paper by Sarah Dowdey *How Reincarnation Works* (Updated: 16 April 2021) which gives an excellent description of how reincarnation is interpreted in the eastern religions.

"**Hinduism.** The Hindu religion is vast and varied. Its adherents worship an array of gods and celebrate diverse traditions. Reincarnation, to Hindus, is the religious or philosophical belief that the soul or spirit, after biological death, begins a new life in a new body that may be human, animal or spiritual depending on the moral quality of the previous life's actions. The entire universal process, that gives rise to the cycle of death and rebirth, governed by karma, is referred to as "Samsara", which may be good or bad. Based on the Karma one has followed, the subsequent birth is chosen. For example, if one has done a lot of divine service and has a desire to do more service at the time of death, his soul chooses a family that is supportive of his desire, for rebirth.

Jainism. Jainism is historically connected with the "samsara" tradition with which the earliest mentions of reincarnation are associated. Jain adherents believe the soul accumulates karma as an actual physical substance, unlike the Hindu idea of karmic law.

Buddhism. When Buddhism was established two thousand five hundred years ago, it incorporated the Hindu belief in reincarnation. Although Buddhism has two major subdivisions and countless variations in regional practices, most Buddhists believe in samsara or the cycle of rebirth. To Buddhists, Samsara is also governed by the laws of karma.

Sikhism. Sikhism also teaches reincarnation. Like Hinduism, the laws of Karma influence the quality of Sikh life. For Sikhs to exit the cycle of birth and rebirth, they must achieve "complete knowledge" and become one with God.
– Sarah Dowdey (2021)

The Ancient Western World. Although belief in reincarnation is a predominant element of many eastern religions, it was also taught in ancient

Greece and the Roman empire which influenced the philosophy of famous thinkers of the time, such as Plato.

Modern Western Scientific research. The main documented scientific work that has been carried out by researchers in the West relating to reincarnation has been by Professors Ian Stevenson and Jim Tucker.

Ian Pretyman Stevenson (1918–2007). Stevenson was a Canadian-born American, the founder and Director of Perceptual Studies at the University of Virginia School of Medicine (UVA), which studies and investigates the paranormal. Stevenson became famous for his research into cases he considered suggestive of reincarnation – the idea that emotions, memories and even bodily features can be passed on from one incarnation to another. His position was that certain phobias, unusual abilities and illnesses could not be fully explained by genetics or the environment. Stevenson's main emphasis was his meticulous studies of children's memories of previous lives. Stevenson travelled an average of fifty-five thousand miles every year, he lived as a "world citizen" for some forty years and collected, researched and documented nearly three thousand reincarnation type cases from different parts of the world. He published twelve books including "*Twenty Cases suggestive of Reincarnation*" and "*Where Reincarnation and Biology Intersect*." Most of his research was conducted with children who appeared to recall a past life. Typically, the child starts talking about a previous existence as soon as he or she can speak, and memories usually fade by the age of about eight. Most of these cases have the following pattern. A child, usually at the age of two or three, begins talking persistently of things, places and people about which the parents are thoroughly ignorant. The child may even behave quite differently from his brothers or sisters. This will appear very strange in terms of the circumstances of his upbringing. Finally, the child himself may relate all this to a previous life he claims to remember having led, sometimes in neighbouring places, in others in a distant place. All these cases have some common ingredients. There are repeated statements of a young child's identification with an earlier person. These children who remember lost lives give information about this person in the form of memories or people known to them. They ask to return to their previous homes and present familiar behaviour in the apparently strange environment. They address the alleged relatives with appropriate emotional responses. Most of these memories vanish between the ages of seven and nine.

Jim B Tucker (b 1959). Tucker is a child psychiatrist and Bonner-Lowry Professor of Psychiatry and Neurobehavioral Sciences at the University of Virginia School of Medicine (UVA). He is Director of the UVA Division of Perceptual Studies where he is continuing the work of Dr Ian Stevenson with children who report memories of previous lives, having previously worked with Dr Stevenson for several years.

Three "Reincarnation" examples. To give a flavour of the types of cases studied by Professors Stevenson and Tucker, below are just three of the many thousands of cases they researched and documented

Plane on Fire. Four-year-old James Leininger, whose parents lived in Louisiana, believed that he was once a WWII pilot who had been shot down over Iwo Jima. His parents, Bruce and Andrea first realised that James had these memories when he was two and woke up from a nightmare, yelling "Airplane crash! Plane on fire! Little man can't get out!" he also knew details about WWII aircraft that it would seem impossible for a child of that age to know. For instance, when Andrea referred to an object on the bottom of a toy plane as a bomb, James corrected her by saying it was a drop tank. Another time, he and his parents were watching a History Channel documentary, and the narrator called a Japanese plane a Zero, James insisted that it was a Tony. In both cases, James was correct.

The boy said that he had also been called James in his previous life and that he'd flown off a ship called "Natoma". His parents discovered a WWII aircraft carrier called "USS Natoma Bay". In its squadron was a pilot named James Hudson, who had been killed in action over the Pacific.

James talked incessantly about his plane crashing, and he was disturbed by nightmares a few times each week. His desperate mother contacted past-life therapist Carol Bowman for help. Bowman told Andrea not to dismiss what James was saying and to assure him that whatever happened had occurred in another life and that he was safe now. Andrea followed her advice and James's dreams diminished.

In Sri Lanka. A very young child, a girl, one day overheard her mother mentioning the name of an obscure town called "Kataragama" that the child had never been to. The girl informed her mother that she drowned there when her dumb (mentally retarded) brother pushed her in the river, that she had a bald father named "Herath" who sold flowers in the market near the Buddhist stupa, that she lived in a house that had a glass window in the roof, (a skylight), dogs in the backyard who were fed meat, that the house was next door to a big Hindu temple where devotees practised a religious ritual of smashing coconuts on the ground. The little girl did get a few items wrong. For instance, the dead girl's father wasn't bald (but the grandfather and uncle were) and his name wasn't "Herath" – that was the name of the dead girl's cousin. Otherwise, twenty-seven out of thirty idiosyncratic statements she made proved to be correct. The two families had never met, nor did they have friends, co-workers or other acquaintances in common.

Lizst. Vladimir Levinski, who was born David Secombe in England in the 1930s, had such an innate gift for playing the piano that he was able to teach himself to be a concert pianist – when asked about lessons he remarked, "I have no time for them, I have a technique of my own." So gifted was Levinski, and at a young age, that he came to recognise himself as the reincarnation of Franz Lizst, the German composer and pianist. By age twenty-one, he was performing for packed concert halls and known as the "Paganini of the Piano." Unfortunately, Levinski's interest in Lizst at times became an obsession such as when he was playing a concert in January 1952, he stopped playing halfway through to talk about Lizst. The audience was disappointed but Levinski felt the concert was a "tremendous success" in part because he experienced it as only the reincarnation of the renowned composer Lizst could (Article by Jacques-Louis David, 4 April 2019)

For most scientists, reincarnation will always be treated with reserve no matter how much evidence is presented as there is always the possibility of fraud in such cases. The parents of some of these children have been alleged to make money out of them. They train the child to enact the drama of reincarnation. But in many cases, there is sufficient evidence to rule out fraud. There is also the possibility of unconscious fraud. The child may be referring to someone he read or heard about, identifying himself with this person. The parents may have unconsciously added more to the tale as they retold it. For Dr Tucker, success doesn't mean persuading the doubters to accept the existence of reincarnation but rather encouraging people to consider the meaning of consciousness and how it might survive our deaths. To quote Dr Tucker, "I believe in the possibility of reincarnation, which is different from saying that I believe in reincarnation. I do think these cases require an explanation that that is out of the ordinary, although that certainly doesn't mean that we all reincarnate."

Comment. I have no particular opinion about this phenomenon as I have never personally met anyone who has claimed to be reincarnated and I read these "examples of reincarnation" with some reserve. Perhaps there will in future be some scientifically accepted methodology of researching the objective validity of reincarnation. In summary, Christian and Muslim religions do not believe in reincarnation but Eastern religions do. We can only read these fascinating examples, respect the strongly held convictions of these religions and keep an open mind.

xxx

Child Prodigies

Is there a connection between reincarnation and child prodigies? Wikipedia quotes psychology research literature as defining child prodigy as "a person under the age of ten who produces meaningful output in some domain to the level of an adult expert. The term "wunderkind" is sometimes used as a synonym for child prodigy, particularly in media accounts".

How is it possible for some very young children to acquire amazing ability in such complicated disciplines as music, literature, mathematics and visual arts? Could it be that they learnt these skills when living some former life?

Each child is different and develops in a unique way within limits of physical growth, social, emotional, behaviour, thinking and communication skills. All of these areas are linked, and each depends on and influences the others. Babies are born ready to learn, and their brains develop through use. In general, development happens in the same order in most children, but skills might develop at different ages or times.

There are some amazing exceptions. Some prodigies were born to parents who were themselves gifted in the same genre but many others had parents with no such skills or inclination. They come from diverse backgrounds, nationalities, sex and colour.

Here are some examples.

Music.

Russian Mysin Elisei played major piano works in concerts from the age of five. When he was six (or was it eight?), he stunned a major concert hall playing Mozart's Piano Concerto No 3 in D minor. He was so small, he couldn't reach the piano pedals, but he produced a polished and faultless performance with total poise and confidence.

YouTube shows a video of five-year-old Jonah Ho playing faultlessly Chopin's Fantasie in C-sharp Minor. Op 66.

Mysin, Jonah Ho and other child prodigies follow in the footsteps of some of the most famous classical composers of all time, such as:

. Mozart, who started composing from the age of four. Schubert, who wrote "Gretchen at the Spinning Wheel" age seventeen, which has been described as "a defining masterpiece of the Romantic Lieder tradition." Mendelssohn, who wrote numerous compositions during his boyhood, which included five operas and eleven symphonies for string orchestra, concerti, sonatas and fugues. Camille Saint-Saens, who produced his first composition at age three, debut concert aged five when he accompanied a Beethoven violin sonata on the piano.

. Bali-born Indonesian Joey Alexander learned to play jazz piano as a very young child. When he was eight years old, he performed for pianist Herbie Hancock at a UNESCO event in Jakarta. When he was only nine, he won the 2013 Master Jam Fest and has been hailed as "the greatest living jazz pianist".

. Stevie Wonder (born Steveland Judkins Morris), blind from birth and brought up in poverty, became a skilled musician in early childhood, learning to compose and play piano, organ and harmonica. He began playing and recording professionally from the age of twelve.

All the above are boys but there are also girl musical prodigies. Examples are:

. Umi Garret, known as the ten-year-old who played the piano upside down.

. Alma Deutscher, the girl prodigy composer of piano and violin sonatas and string quartets who, before the age of ten, wrote a full-length opera. Alma was interviewed by Clemency Burton-Hill in 2015 (BBC Culture: Counterpoint/Classical music 18 May 2015). She was quoted as saying "When I'm trying to do something else, when people are talking to me about something completely different, I get these beautiful melodies that play inside my mind. Sometimes it might be a human voice singing, sometimes a piano, sometimes a violin." At the age of eight, Alma recalled that, in the middle of the night, an entire set of piano variations in E-flat "announced itself to her subconscious". She said, "I woke up and didn't want to lose the melody so I took my notebook and wrote it all down which took me three hours."

. Emily Bear started to compose her own music aged three and by the age of eight had composed three hundred and fifty pieces. She had remarkable precocious talent and was invited to perform at the White House.

Mathematics.

. Greg Smith – b1989, skipped six grades at school due to his extraordinary ability studying mathematics, physics, calculous and French among other academic disciplines. When he was still a young child, he said he would gain three PhDs in unrelated disciplines before the end of his twenties. He is on track to achieve this.

. Blaise Pascal was a French mathematician, physicist, and religious philosopher who wrote a treatise on vibrating bodies at the age of nine; he wrote his first proof on a wall with a piece of coal, at the age of eleven years, and a theorem by the age of sixteen years. He is famous for Pascal's theorem and many other contributions in mathematics, philosophy, and physics.[

. John von Neuman, a Hungarian American, had extraordinary mental powers, speaking classical Greek by the age of six and as an adult, became a pre-eminent mathematician and expert in physics, economics and computer science.

. Yasha Asley, when just four years old, had a "math" age of fourteen, gained his "O" and "A" levels in math when aged eight and a first-class math degree at the age of fifteen.

. Luis, the little African American boy who regularly appeared on American TV shows demonstrating his amazing ability to solve arithmetical problems – additions, subtraction, equations. His adult interviewers/questioners were left far behind him even when they were using a calculator.

Art

There are many cases where children of very young ages produced acclaimed works of art that were exhibited in prestigious galleries around the world. Examples are:

. Hamzah Marbella from the Philippines who started painting aged two and won fifty awards by the age of eight.

. Wang Yani, from China whose work when she was still an infant was exhibited in exhibitions in China, UK, US and Germany.

. Alexandra Nachite, born in Romania, became known as “Petite Picasso” started drawing aged two, watercolours at five and oil/acrylic paintings aged seven.

. Aelita Andre’s first exhibition was when she was just two. “Autumn de Forest” (compared to Andy Warhol)

There are many others.

Comment. I’ve tried to make some sense of this subject by doing some serious “Googling” and found an amazing divergence of opinion. In summary, there is no clear objective explanation. Is this something to do with reincarnation? No one knows. No one can prove how or why these wunderkind children came by such extraordinary skills and knowledge.

xxx

Chapter Fourteen

Dreams

Considering that most of us spend about one third of our lives asleep, it would be remiss not to include a section about dreams in trying to fathom out The Meaning of Life. The available search engines are prolific in material about dreams but so much is contradictory or wrapped up in spiritual interpretations.

Wikipedia describes a dream as "a succession of images, ideas, emotions and sensations that usually occur in the mind during certain stages of sleep. Humans spend about two hours dreaming per night and each dream lasts around five to twenty minutes, although the dreamer may perceive the dream as being much longer than this." This subject has been important to humans since the early civilizations of Mesopotamia and Ancient Egypt and has inspired generations of both religious and scientific researchers to interpret their meaning and significance to our lives, often with great divergence of opinion.

Dreams and sleep are intertwined. It seems to be generally accepted that dreams occur mainly in the rapid-eye movement (REM) stage of sleep – brain activity is high and resembles that of being awake. To be studied, a dream must first be reduced to a verbal report, which is an account of the subject's memory of a dream, not the subject's dream experience itself.
In 1899, *The Interpretation of Dreams* by Sigmund Freud, (1856–1939), the "founder of psychoanalysis", was published. In this classic book, the author introduces his theory of the unconscious with respect to dream interpretation, and discusses what would later become the theory of the Oedipus complex. Freud described dreams as "the royal road" to the unconscious and suggested that by studying the obvious content of dreams, we could bring to light the hidden and unconscious desires that lead to

neurosis. Freud's research was probably the first serious attempt by a western academic to interpret the meaning of dreams. Subsequently his work was developed by the psychoanalyst Carl Jung (1875–1961) and many others. Dream interpretations are important as they are a reflection of one's physiological and psychological activities, thus producing important information about the person's thoughts and emotional state. Psychoanalysts can then use the person's dreams to understand better what is going on in their mind, perhaps on an unconscious level. Despite the best efforts to interpret dreams objectively, there can be no certainty due to the subjective account given by the dreamer after he/she has woken up.

In trying to learn more about this subject I searched through Google and other search engines. I found that many sites were written by Christian organisations and individuals all claiming to define dreams as having relevance to God and the Bible. Perhaps they are right but perhaps not! Examples are:

"Bibleword" – Does God speak through dreams?

"Crosswalk.com", "*God Does Talk to Us Through Our Dreams, The Spiritual Views and Meaning of Dreams* by Heather Riggleman (Jan 2021). God used dreams for three reasons – for encouragement, to reveal prophecy, to reveal a warning.

"universeofsymbolism.com" This site claims that dreams reveal the path that is meant for your highest goals, the path that you need to change or avoid and dreams that can reveal a future event.

"Soul shepherding." A site where Bill Gaultiere expresses his views relating to dreams, God and the Bible

"Eckankov.org". Spiritual interpretation of dreams relating to God

"dougaddison.com". Seven common spiritual dream meanings (April 2014)

All the above may be making valid points but the problem is that the dreams are very subjective, unique and highly personal. They also rely on the dreamer to remember them accurately. This very element raises doubt about the validity of many of these Christian interpretations. I decided to concentrate more on non-religious approaches and went with Kendra Cherry's paper entitled *Nine Common Dream Interpretations* (via Verywellmind.com, update February 2022). Cherry writes that analysing dream symbols and ascribing meaning to them has become a source of both entertainment and self-reflection in popular culture. Do dreams really have hidden meanings? Can you learn your unconscious wishes and desires by interpreting your dreams?

Cherry examines nine of the most common dreams and describes what dream interpretation "experts" have to say about them. Her first example is: Dreams about "Falling." According to many dream interpreters, "falling" dreams are a sign that something in your life isn't going well. It might suggest that you may need to rethink a choice, for instance, or consider a new direction of your life. "Dreaming of falling is very common. It is a symbol of fear in real life – perhaps of failing at work or in your love life. Falling often expresses a need to let yourself go more and enjoy life." says Russel Grant, author of *The Illustrated Dream Dictionary*.

The other eight dream types that Cherry reviews are: being naked in public, being chased, losing teeth, dying, taking a test, infidelity, flying, pregnancy.

Without reviewing interpretations, Cherry also lists some other common dream subjects. These are: discovering new rooms or passages, being dressed inappropriately, being unable to find a toilet, arriving somewhere late and having a massive wave approaching you.

I favoured Kendra Cherry's article as it was very well researched and listed some twenty-seven sources to support the facts used. The site used, "Verywell Mind", stresses that their articles are fact-checked to keep the content accurate, reliable and trustworthy.

Comment. I still don't know whether the interpretation of dreams really contribute to furthering knowledge of the meaning of life but I do believe it is a subject that must be included. My personal, often recurring, dream themes are "struggling to arrive on time and to find the right destination" and "being inappropriately dressed", each version with totally different situations, places and people but still so often about those two themes. To my mind, they are reminders of my awake desire both always to be punctual and to wear the right clothes (the latter probably as a result of years of having to wear a correct military uniform). I can see absolutely no connection with God, the Bible or any religious message. But there again, what do I know about that? One thing I am very sure about is that I'm very likely to dream after eating cheese for supper – especially Roquefort!

xxx

Chapter Fifteen

The Power and Influence of Music and Sport

Music

Music is one of the greatest of mankind's inventions. There is something phenomenal, powerful, majestic, deep, enigmatic and incomprehensible about music. Music has the power to establish a profound connection to the spiritual nature of life and to form a bond between fellow worshippers. Music has the ability to transform the most challenging situations and the most routine things into something deeply emotional, meaningful and spiritually powerful.

Music can relieve stress, it can boost self-confidence and act as divine therapy, having the ability to transport a person's thoughts to another place or dimension. This was recognised by ancient Greek philosophers and from the early days of the Christian faith. This explains why music is a central pillar used in religious services as it has the power to influence and lift a person's spirit.

There is no better recent example than the music that accompanied the various services relating to the funeral of Queen Elizabeth in September 2022, particularly the hymns, anthems and psalms sung by the choristers of the choir of Westminster Abbey and the State Trumpeters of the Household Cavalry.

William Henry Harris (1883–1973) was a renowned organist. He was professor of organ and harmony at the Royal School of Church Music and was involved in the musical education of the teenage Princess Elizabeth. He was best remembered for his Anglican church music and it was fitting that one of his anthems for unaccompanied double choirs, John Donne's poem "Bring us, O lord God", (details in Part Two below) was performed at the committal service of the queen at St George's Chapel, Windsor Castle.

Music can be in the form of Georgian chant, Vedic mantras, or devotional songs. It also forms the basis of gospel hymns, classical symphonies, indigenous drumming and the modern genres of electronic dance music (EDM), rock, hip-hop, and metal. Music helps to establish a connection to our divine and inner nature. It can be regarded as the sound of a person's spirit and a universal expression of spirituality. There are varying definitions of spirituality but many have a correlation to music which creates an ambiance of the key elements of love, emotion and passion. There is no other medium, which can transport humans to a level of their existence, which is beyond their physical body and intellect.

Lyrics also have a major impact on the power, emotion and lasting quality of music, never more so than today. Words, like thoughts, harmonies and melodies, can deeply affect us. When combined with music, words and the energy they carry, can resonate even more deeply. I wonder what are the priorities of many church attendee today. Is it to listen to the preacher or to engage with the hymn singing? Perhaps the brilliant Spinoza dipped out and failed to convince the existing church of his day because his teachings failed to incorporate the accompaniment of music!

Adding music (melody and accompaniment) to a lyrical statement or message activates more areas of the human brain than the words alone and can trigger emotions and memory. Words can be simple but still carry an important and evocative message. Add engaging images to this mix and there is what our churches have known for thousands of years as the ultimate power over the people, perhaps in a good way for the Christian faith, or a bad way, for example, the anthems used by the Nazis in the 1930s/40s to unite the masses behind Hitler.

For me, the key is simplicity and connecting harmony – the simple juxtaposing of lyrics and music. Four young men emerged out of the club scene in Liverpool in the 1960s and became legends in the field of lyrics/music which told simple but meaningful stories. The "Beatles" hit emotional points which are still revered today. An example of their work which is still very popular is John Lennon's (and now officially accepted as co-written by Yoko Ono) *Imagine* Written in 1971. It has been credited by various polls as "the greatest number one single of all time." Variously the words have been described as anti-religious, anti-war, anti-nationalist, anti-conventional, anti-capitalist – words that can inspire or irritate. Still performed worldwide, sometimes even associated with national anthems, *Imagine* still continues to split opinion. For some it's a moving peace anthem, for others, it is described as being corny, mushy and over sentimental. The words of this ballad are essentially raw, clear, simple and uncomplicated but, for me, they explain as much about the meaning of life as many deep philosophical tombs – maybe more!

Note: Due to concerns about Copyright issues, I have not included the full lyric wording of this song and those l refer to later in this chapter. I suspect most readers already knows them by heart!

Another classic example is *My Way* immortalised by Frank Sinatra, and copied by a million imitators. It tells the story which so many of us "oldies" can completely identify with and relate to. This song was originally composed by Frenchman Jean Revaux and songwriter/singer Claude Francois and released as "*Comme d'habitude*" in 1968. The following year it was reworked and released in English by Paul Anka and entitled "My Way". Paul released his own singing version but deferred to Sinatra's masterly interpretation. Great stuff as a commentary on life but it still does not answer the "what then" question that my book is seeking! Few karaoke exponents worth their salt don't at some time have a go at this iconic song.

I wonder why many theologians and philosophers haven't picked up on and incorporated into their research the amazing power of music, particularly when accompanied by emotional matching lyrics which, particularly for younger people, send a far more compelling message than religious services. The popularity numbers of pop music speak for themselves. There are at least six hundred music festivals held around the world each year of which the most famous are Woodstock in the US and Glastonbury in the UK. At Woodstock in 1969, one million people arrived but, due to absolute capacity limits, only five hundred thousand were able to get in. At "Glasto

2023" an estimated two hundred and ten thousand attended the five-day round the clock event which is held in a farmer's field. None were sleeping while they celebrated Sir Elton John's "final" UK performance. Nearly every country holds music festivals at least once every year – the US, Canada, South America, all European countries, Korea, Japan. Attendances have been problematical to calculate accurately but average attendances are estimated at twenty-five thousand. A conservative estimate of annual attendances at music festivals world-wide therefore is fifteen million (600 x 25,000). This compares with the Muslim pilgrimage to Mecca, one of the largest annual gathering in the world of religious pilgrims which is two and a half million. This is outnumbered by the up to nine million Hindu pilgrims at Kumb Mela but this is not held annually and is split into four river bank sites. The Christian pilgrimage to Compostela de Santiago attracts a mere two hundred thousand annually.

xxx

Sport and Music

In terms of support, influence and passion, sport also now far outperforms religion. The once every four-year Olympic games (for example the 2020 Tokyo games held while still under major COVID restrictions) was watched by more than three billion people worldwide. But the influence of football is second to none. According to Sortageous.com "statistics have shown that half the world's population watches football every week. That's around 3.5 billion people – of all nationalities, all religious backgrounds, all races, all cultures. No other sport even comes close. For example, the UK Champions League final is watched by more than three hundred and fifty-nine million people and the last World Cup (2022) held in Doha, Qatar has been described as "the most watched event on the world" with an estimated five billion viewers.

The attendance figures quoted above are staggering. If accurate, it could be said they reflect that the world's population has united behind a physical activity (principally football) at the expense of religion, politics and nationalism. Some supporters can passionately shape their lives around their favourite team. For example, Liverpool football club has managed to harness together both the game and an iconic theme tune of "You'll never walk alone." In the 1960s, Liverpool's Anfield Stadium was one of the first football grounds in the UK to have a Public Address system, and the Top Ten in the pop music charts would be played over the speakers before the match as a form of early pre-match entertainment. This was the time when "Merseybeat" bands like The Beatles and Gerry And The Pacemakers dominated the charts, so the fans would have heard a lot of their local heroes over the tannoy. "You'll Never Walk Alone" stayed at No. 1 in the charts for about four weeks in 1963, by which time it had become Liverpool FC's signature tune. The song was originally written by Oscar Hammerstein and composed by Richard Rodgers for the musical "Carousel" in 1945. The song's simple message has given the fans of Liverpool hope through some very tough times – both on and off the field.

In the finals of the 2005 UEFA Champions League Final in Istanbul, Liverpool were losing 0-3 to AC Milan. Legend has it that the motivating effect of the fans singing "You'll Never Walk Alone" gave the players hope when all seemed lost. This small act of defiance in the face of adversity galvanised the Liverpool team, and they managed to pull back and win the match on penalties, crowning them European Cup Champions.

Later, Carlo Ancelotti, then coach of AC Milan was asked which club had the best fans…
"In my opinion Liverpool fans. When they sing a song, they… I don't *know in English, but your skin is…" (flutters his fingers up and down his arm to explain). Many religious preachers can inspire but not many can provoke goose-bumps like "You'll never walk alone" sung by emotional Liverpool football fans!*

The song took on a much deeper and more tragic meaning after the Hillsborough disaster of 1989, when a human crush at the stadium in Sheffield injured hundreds and ninety-six fans lost their lives. There followed a twenty-five-year legal battle before the courts ruled that the victims were unlawfully killed and that a catalogue of failings by police and the ambulance services contributed to their deaths. Throughout the painful process, the lyrics and themes of "*You'll Never Walk Alone*" were prominent. On the day after the tragedy at Hillsborough, thirteen thousand people gathered at Liverpool's Roman Catholic Cathedral; five thousand in the church, and a further eight thousand spilling into the streets outside. "You'll Never Walk Alone" was sung by a lone choir boy, offering both comfort, hope and a meaning of life to a city in mourning.

The power of music and its combination with sports wins hands down over support for any particular religion. To many, it is this combination that reveals the true meaning of life!

xxx

Part Two
One Man's Journey

Introduction

In this part, I describe the events of one man's life. I explained in Part One why I have decided to use my own life's journey rather than trying to theorise about the detailed thoughts and actions of some other individual! I try to write it "warts and all" – feelings, ambitions, actions, relationships, responsibilities, achievements, failures, selfishness, weaknesses, mistakes, unfaithfulness, overindulgences – the mix that makes up the totality of life's experiences – at least mine! I reasoned that this section of the book needs to include enough detail to record how a life evolves and how and why some decisions were made when faced with particular situations. Anything less would read like an extract from Wikipedia, giving merely the bare facts of a life without explaining the deeper emotions and complexities that lay beneath individual actions. I write in descriptive narrative style, at times commenting on how social values and norms have changed, in some cases radically, during my long lifetime. I describe in some detail the work experiences during years in the British Army Intelligence Corps and later civilian employment. At times I digress to relate some vignettes which highlight how personal experiences including making some crazy mistakes can change or mould an individual's decisions and directions. I describe the political background to the timeframes and geographical regions involved. I found this detail to be a necessary and practical tool to help to clarify many aspects relating to the meaning of life. I had another purpose. I found so many books on this subject, particularly those written by some "ivory tower" clerics and academics were too serious, (and dare one say?) even at times, boring. I hope my interspersed digressions add colour and even some frivolity to this profound subject!

Chapter Sixteen

The Cradle

I was born in Somerset, England in 1939, a few months before the start of the second world war. My parents were poor and we lived in a small house in the village of Saltford, between the cities of Bath and Bristol. At some stage, my father was conscripted into the army and I have no recollection of seeing him until the end of the war in 1945. My only war memories were of often hearing the wailing of air raid sirens, the thunderous sound of planes overhead and of being taken by my mother into a little iron cage structure in her bedroom. I would sleep through the night cuddled up to my mother and my sister. The cage was supposed to protect us if a German bomb landed on top of our house. Fortunately, it was never put to the test. Apparently, the main German targets were the munitions and aircraft factories in nearby Bristol.

As a very young child, I lived through the war years being blissfully unaware of their significance and of the horrors and sacrifices endured by so many millions during that bleak period of history.

What if I hadn't been born in 1939 but, say, twenty years earlier? Then I would have been required to serve my country and to have experienced the death and destruction of that war. If I had survived, the rest of my life could have been shaped in a completely different way to that of a child born in 1939. Or what if I had been born in 1939 but not to a family living in Somerset, England? Suppose I had been born a German, or Jewish, and lived, for example, in Leipzig or Berlin. Then, my chances of survival through to 1945 would have been very slim. Or what if I had been born with a coloured rather than white skin? My life's experiences, perspectives and future would have been very different. However, the reality was what it was. I had no influence on the where or when or the colour of my skin. Life is a lottery at the time and place of our birth. As we grow up and come under influences of our family, our culture, our nationality, we make choices and develop as individuals.

During my early years, I was a happy child and a lucky one. I don't remember much detail except that my parents had to rely on ration cards for the first few years after the war. I was about ten when I first saw a strange looking yellow fruit. It was called a banana. I had good friends in the village and much of my free time was spent with them, learning to ride a bike, to swim and to indulge in all those hobbies that young boys enjoy if their environment permits.

My father was an artist and was often away from home for long periods with his easel and paints. My early world at home revolved around my mother who was always there for me – caring, loving, ensuring that my sister and I were brought up to be tidy, to have good manners and a positive attitude to life. My natural instinct was to be involved in outdoor pursuits rather than books and schoolwork but my mother was always strict in ensuring I did my homework and paid proper attention to getting good marks at school. Her conscientiousness paid off. The "big deal" for children then was the "eleven plus" exam. Rightly or wrongly, it was the method by which children were segregated between attending a grammar or a "secondary modern" school. My memories of that dreaded exam are still very clear. All the children in my village, at age eleven, had to take the exam on the same day in our local school – an old building in the middle of Saltford. The main classroom wasn't big enough for all of us, so we spilled over into two separate rooms. I remember being crammed behind a small desk with other children all around, each of us struggling for enough space to read the question paper and attempt our answers. I've no idea now what the questions were, or what answers I gave, but some days later my mother received a letter telling her I had passed the written exam and was required to attend an interview a few days later.

Writing was one thing, talking to grown-ups was quite another because by this age I was becoming acutely aware of my speech stammer. The idea of being interviewed by grown-ups I didn't know was really daunting. I will never forget this momentous episode in my life. The interviews were conducted in an old building in Keynsham, a village about two miles from Saltford. I remember waiting nervously outside the interview room as other children took their turns. Eventually from behind a closed door I heard my name being called. I opened the door to the room which had a highly polished floor. I was confronted by a group of, to me, elderly people sitting behind a large imposing desk. In my nervousness, my feet caught on a mat and I was propelled forward on the polished surface of the floor as the mat slid towards the desk, dumping me half under it. I found myself staring up from under the desk at the stout stockinged thigh of the lady president. I struggled to my feet, spluttering my apologies in my stammering voice. I think the interviewing panel must have been amused and understanding. I do recall they were very kind to me but I have no recollection of their questions. Afterwards, I told my mother I was sure I had failed but, astonishingly, my mother received a letter telling her that I had passed. I'm sure it must have been a sympathy vote! Success in the eleven plus exam turned out to be the first major positive milestone in my life. My parents could never have afforded to send me to a private school and if I had failed the "eleven plus", I would have been sent to the local secondary modern school in Bath which at that time produced poor academic results. Instead, this is what happened. King Edward's school for boys in Bath was then categorised as a "direct grant school". It had a great reputation for enabling its pupils to gain good exam results, usually leading to university places. It was principally fee paying but each year, two free scholarships were awarded to boys living in the city of Bath, two to boys living in the county of Somerset and two to boys from Wiltshire county. By some incredible twist of fortune, I was awarded one of the places for Somerset boys. What luck then to grow up from childhood through to adolescence with a caring mother, a good motivating school and with weekends and holidays spent with my friends in Saltford, which apart from being (then) a small rural Somerset village, is located along the river Avon: ideal for fishing, swimming and coxing/rowing in the local boat club.

My passion was running – track and cross country. I also enjoyed playing cricket and rugby during the seasons. My school work was OK, I stumbled along somewhere midway in the form exam results, sufficient to keep out of trouble and extra homework and just about to satisfy my mother's supervision. How different it might have been had I been born with some physical or mental disability! As it was, my one problem was my stammer which I have had to cope with all my life – including until today. Fortunately I have managed to live with it to such an extent that in some ways it has turned out to be more of an asset than a liability. More about this later.

All my contacts in those days were male. King Edwards School was for boys only. All my village friends were boys. No girls ever featured in my life during those early years. I never much thought about it. I was a male, so were my school colleagues, so were my village chums. All boys. So what? Except two – my mother and Shelley my elder sister.

I grew up to be an average kid – healthy, accepting everything I learnt and was told. During those early years I never thought about whether I was or was not "normal". Who does at that age? That's just the way it is, or was then, as we grow through the early puberty years.

I never gave a thought about religion. Apparently, my parents had me baptised as Church of England (C of E) and that term was shown on school and later, army documents. But it was just a registration term and meant nothing special to me.

It all changed when, at the age of about twelve, I was approached by one of my classmates at King Edwards school. His parents and he were, I later discovered, Jehovah Witnesses but I never heard that term mentioned at that time. He asked me if I would come to a meeting in Bath on a Sunday afternoon where I would be introduced to his faith. For reasons that now escape me, I agreed and turned up punctually the next Sunday. I found myself in a group of some forty and fifty people of varying age groups in a small somewhat stuffy, overcrowded room. The meetings were led by a gentleman who turned out to be the father of my school classmate. Somehow, I became seduced by the Christian messages proclaimed at the meeting both by my classmate's father and by others who spoke after him. At the end of the first session which lasted over an hour, I was asked if I would like to attend the Sunday meetings on a regular basis. I don't know why but I agreed and from then for the rest of that year I faithfully turned up every Sunday. I was given a little lapel badge and was called a "crusader". I was so regular that I was even given a free bible as a reward for having not missed a single meeting for fifty-two consecutive weeks.

I've often wondered since why I was so faithful to this group at that age. Perhaps I was naively feeling the need to understand what purpose there was to my life and thought the Jehovah Witness message provided some sort of answer. Or perhaps it was just out of loyalty to my class mate, who I realised didn't manage to make many other friends at school. I have no idea except that, after all my months of faithful attendance, I started to question the validity of some of the assertions made by the group. They all seemed so earnest and serious in their conviction that they understood and agreed with both the Christian bible and their interpretation of it. I became restless and began to find the meeting room restricting and claustrophobic. By then, I was growing into a phase where I could no longer blindly accept what I was being told at these meetings. Something inside me didn't actually rebel but I sought more convincing evidence than I was hearing each week from the Jehovah Witness version of faith. I needed to explore other versions of religion.

At about that period of my life, several of my friends attended the evening service in Bath Abbey, a beautiful historic building in the very centre of the city. I decided to leave the Jehovah's to their Sunday meetings and instead to join with my friends in the Abbey. I enjoyed the whole atmosphere – the fabulous architecture of the building, the reassuring ritual of the service and the chance to sing lustily all the stirring hymns. Initially I was content to join in with all that was required of the congregation, accepting the sequence and content of the service that had been developed over the centuries. For some time, I didn't think to question or challenge any part of the service. But then, subconsciously, I started to listen more closely to the words of the weekly sermons. Maybe it was just an evolution of growing up but more and more I started to wonder if the preacher really knew the detail of what he was saying. One particular example was when the rector told us "When Jesus Christ said (Mathew 5:5) "Blessed are the meek for they will inherit the earth, what he really meant was – etc". I remember thinking to myself. "How does he know what Jesus really meant? The event he quoted, even if true as narrated in the Bible, occurred two thousand years ago. It was not written down until many years later and then in a language that has been translated several times over the last two millennium. It's a wonderful story as are the rest of the ten "beatitudes" from the Sermon on the Mount collection. I thought to myself "That's what the rector thinks, and it fits the flow of his sermon, but he can't possibly know. There was another thing. During the Easter service that year, we all sang what I later found was an interpretation of Samuel Medley's music (written in 1775), with words from Job 19.25 beginning "I know my redeemer livith". Again, I inwardly rebelled. How could I or anyone else possibly know? It is beautiful music but there was absolutely no evidence to say these words with such conviction. One might think, believe or have faith but to know! From that time, my feeling of respect, even awe, of the church began to dwindle. I started to question the existence of God, a God, any God. In a totally immature, unstructured way at this stage of my life, I wondered if there really was something else there or did the world we live in just evolve over time?

I also had a problem with praying. As it was part of the church services and usually just preceded or followed hymn singing which I really enjoyed, I always went along with the ritual of praying. I would follow the example of those around me and go through the accepted motions: get down on your knees, position your hands together and adopt a suitably devout look on your face, listen to the words of the prayer intoned by the priest or just hold the prayer position in silence. I had learnt to have respect for those who did feel that their prayers were answered or at the least found comfort and inner strength from praying. I tried hard to be receptive, to admit all my faults, frailties and weaknesses, of which there were many, to put my mind in a place where I was ready, willing and eager to find some response. I would say the words "Amen" as and when required. I didn't know what to expect – some message from a higher place, some feeling of peace, or perhaps just an inner tranquillity? But it didn't work for me! In my case – zero. zilch, nada, rien, nothing at all!

During a later time during my youth, I remember another incident that reinforced my scepticism of the Christian faith. Whenever I had the free time, I would go for a training run. One Sunday on a fine, fresh, bracing spring morning, I took a route which led me up a steep hill. The gradient was sharp and I remember pausing at the summit of the hill. The views were spectacular. The effort of the run had loosened the joints of my body. I felt immersed in the beauty of nature. I felt fresh, alert, in tune with life. Then I looked down into the valley below. There was a village in deep shadow with a church in its midst. It was mid Sunday morning and I could make out the sound of the church organ playing a hymn. Then it was quiet and I knew that, at that part of the service, the congregation would be on their knees in prayer. I thought of the physical state of the congregation, kneeling on the hard wooden church pews and being physically cramped and uncomfortable. I contrasted their situation with my own feeling of being at one with the world around me. I remember throwing my arms aloft and thinking; "Here I am, embracing the joys of nature while all those people down in the dark village church are crouched down, not using the physical assets they were born with and with their eyes closed to the miracles around them. If indeed there is a God, a creator, who does he think honours him more; those worshippers down there in the dark or me up here on this glorious morning?" Of course, there was no answer. There you go!

xxx

Chapter Seventeen

From Timid Teenager to Stroppy Adolescent

King Edwards in the 1950s was a boys only school. I enjoyed acting in our school plays largely because of the verbal freedom it gave me. I discovered that if I put on a different voice accent, or when singing, for some reason I lost my stammer. In the mid-teen years, my body went through a major physical change. At fourteen I was one of the shortest boys in my form but after not much more than a year, I was one of the tallest. When I was still short and my voice had not yet "broken" I was often selected to play girls roles in our school plays such as Katherina in Shakespeare's "Taming of the Shrew". As my height shot up and I developed a baritone voice, I changed acting gender and took roles such as Edmund "the bastard" in our school's stirring version of "King Lear."

My physical body change also led to the realisation that Sunday evenings didn't have to be solely about going to church. After the Bath Abbey evening service, it was the habit of many of my school chums to go to a local coffee bar called the "Salamander". The bar was usually full and lively, and although only coffee was served, it was regarded as a very cool place to frequent. Apart from the chance to unwind after the formal ritual of the abbey service, I found there was another attraction. The "Salamander" didn't only serve boys. There were girls there as well and it was during that phase that my first stirrings of attraction for the opposite sex were aroused. I had not previously met any unattached girls and I liked the experience! How ridiculously innocent it all was as nothing ever happened at the "Salamander" except drinking coffee and chatting to girls but at the time I remember my desire to go to the bar on Sunday evenings outweighed any fulfilment in the service in the abbey.

My first "girlfriend" was a lovely girl called Marjory. I met her in the famous "Salamander" when she was with a group of her school friends from Bath High school, the girl's equivalent to King Edwards. I was mesmerised by her Eurasian looks, later discovering that her mother was Indian and her father was native British. It took me a long time to pluck up the courage, and fear of my stammer, to ask her out. To my delight, she just replied "OK!" We were the same age (I think fifteen) and for a time we saw each other regularly. We would walk together in Lansdown Park, Bath or along the River Avon footpath at Pulteney bridge. We talked a lot about our background and life in general. Eventually I plucked up enough courage to hold her hand and to kiss her. This was a big deal – and very memorable as for me it was my first foray into having a physical relationship with a girl. Neither of us really knew what we should do but I remember the sweet femininity of her, the tingle of emotion at the softness of her body. I realised that, while all my male friends were great personal and sports colleagues, there is a unique, magical and special chemistry in a one-to-one relationship with a pretty girl. May it always be so! Regrettably, I can no longer recall what happened between Marjory and me, but after some months, we stopped seeing each other. No matter, I will always feel grateful to that dear, sweet girl for our mutual initiation into the mysteries and pleasures of being with the opposite sex.

Those late school years were relaxed and pleasurable. My main interest continued to be sport. King Edwards was then a very small school compared to others in the area such as Bath and Bristol Grammar schools. We played against them at cricket and rugby. Those schools had many more pupils to choose from to represent them and we always felt rather intimidated. But we had one major advantage. We knew each other really well and could coordinate our team work closely and instinctively. This gave us good team morale and we often ended up winning our matches. My two best friends at school were Christopher Warburton and Michael Andrew. Christopher was a natural sportsman who excelled in all ball games including cricket, rugby and hockey – the three main sports played at our school. He was our year captain in all these sports – in cricket, a left-handed batsman who dominated the number three spot, a natural number ten fly half at rugby who could always "read the game" and an accomplished hockey inside forward.

Michael was wiry and had very quick reactions. In cricket he was wicket keeper and in rugby he was a natural scrum half. My own sporting ability was far less distinguished than those of Christopher and Michael. In cricket, I usually opened the innings and sometimes managed to give our team a reasonable start before Christopher and Michael came in and piled on the runs. In rugby, I was usually put on the wing to exploit my running ability, which remained my passion. I concentrated on my running, competing in Somerset schools middle distance and cross-country races.

Life in my mid/late teens was quite standard for a boy of my background and age. My school work was low on my priority list. I managed to keep continuing to peg along but in hindsight, I should have worked much harder. Many of my King Edwards class mates achieved places at Cambridge University and I suppose I thought I would be able to do the same. It was not to be. I passed all subjects at "O" level and two years later, my "A" levels but not at grades high enough to qualify for Cambridge. I could have applied to other universities and would have been accepted straightaway at Bristol. But in my naïve snobbish way, for me it was Cambridge or nothing. My arrogant youthful attitude had significant later implications.

Digression – social attitudes

What a fundamental change in social attitudes there has been from the 1950s to the present 2020s! Our 1950s King Edwards students were well led and well taught. Discipline was firm but fair as were the school rules. Any boy who disobeyed the rules or who was cheeky or insolent was punished, usually by being caned on the backside by Mr Porter, the Headmaster. I remember that I had three such canings. After each misdemeanour, the boy was sent to stand outside Mr Porter's study. It was customary to be made to wait there for quite some time, as part of the disciplinary process. At last, from inside his study, Mr Porter's booming voice would summon the offending pupil. With trepidation, the boy would enter and stand before the seated Mr Porter. "Boy, you broke school rules by – (he would then give a short description of the offense)." He would then inform the boy that the degree of gravity of the offence dictated how many whips of his cane would be given. No excuses or mitigations were considered. Mr Porter would then tell the offending boy to bend over the desk and punishment would be administered. Wow, did it sting! But that was it. Nothing further, no continued issue. Done! Back to class and carry on. As far as I know, no boy ever suffered any after effects other than realising it was not a good idea to break the school rules! I never heard anyone, including the parents, suggest that this type of short, sharp discipline was anything other than a simple and effective way of keeping young healthy boys in good order. I remember I once told my mother about getting the cane. She asked what I had done to deserve it. When I explained the reason, all she said was, "Quite right, I hope you learned your lesson." Today such action as caning would never be tolerated. It would be defined as corporal punishment and be legally forbidden. Indeed the master who administered the caning would most likely be charged with criminal assault and face a prison sentence.

Another major social change is the attitude to sex and gender. In the 1950s, your sex was clear and biologically determined. You were either male or female – period! There was no obsession about a youth's sexuality and the word "gay" merely meant pleasant or bright. The term LGBTQ+ etc had not been invented. There was no Stonewall, Pride rainbow marches, Tavistock gender identity Institute, Mermaids, Gendered Intelligence, All about Trans; and no terms such as "gender neutral", "sexual equality", or struggling to find the best term to use to describe a human being, e.g. man, woman, person, individual, it, they, humankind, homo sapiens. There were also no such terms as "diversity", "me too" or "cancel culture". There was no navel gazing about colonial slavery and denigration of past pioneering Brits. For young people in the 1950s, life was far less complicated – for boys, girls, white or coloured. Individuals could get on with their lives without these complexes. Concerns such as personal responsibilities, national and global poverty, employment, health provision and charitable work were more pressing issues than endless self-analysis.

While it can be argued that today's cultural shift has produced a more caring and inclusive society, conversely the emphasis on gender can be excessive. More young girls now have eating disorders and self-harm and many young boys feel lost, insecure and traumatised. It is not surprising that there remain such wide divisions in our society in the 2020s when so much emphasis is placed on sexual inclinations and individual rights. Young white males are assailed in social media by expressions such as "male, pale and stale". Is it any wonder that many feel disenfranchised and search social media for influencers such as Andrew Tate, KSI, Beta Sqad, Mr McBeast and others, as distasteful as their philosophy may be, to restore their confidence as healthy young men? Critics who blindly accuse Tate of "toxic misogyny" only reinforce their attraction as role models for some young men. Have we really progressed to a more open and inclusive society or regressed to obsessing about our gender, personal and civil rights at the expense of wider society priorities and responsibilities?

End of digression!

Back to my own life and my failure to be offered a place at Cambridge. After my only average "A" level results, Mr Porter called me into his office "to talk about my future!" I was then just seventeen. He told me to forget Cambridge but that my grades should be sufficient for acceptance at Bristol and some other provincial universities. Had I already applied? I told him that I had not nor did I intend to as I had decided I wanted Cambridge or nothing. Looking back, I realise how stupidly arrogant that attitude was – but there you go, the brashness of youth! Clearly Mr Porter was not at all impressed but decided to give me one last chance although I didn't deserve his gracious help. "Right," he said: "If that's what you want, I'll accept you back for another school year but you'll have to apply yourself far more conscientiously to your studies. It will be a year with your studies as your top priority and sport and other activities much reduced. With hard work and real application, you might just scrape it to Cambridge next year." I remember thinking how unattractive the idea was of having to endure another year as a schoolboy. All my form friends would have left, I'd have the "indignity" of dropping down to the form below, having to start all over again with a pile of boring text books. I felt ready now for a complete change. And what was really bugging me was that I was perpetually broke. I also thought about my parents' finances and knew they could not afford to support me for another year at school.

With these muddled thoughts I found that my stammer had returned which made me even more frustrated. Rudely I told Mr Porter that I just couldn't bear the idea of staying on at school and I would try to find a job somewhere. I didn't even have the politeness to thank him for his offer or indeed for all the great support he and the other teachers had given me during the years at his excellent school!

Now I was nowhere – left school without further education, no money, no job. It took me a long time to tell my mother what an idiot I had been.

xxx

During my last school holiday, I had got a part time job working at a large department store in Bristol called Jones and Company, part of the then Debenhams Group. I had been given a range of menial tasks – cleaning the outside of the store, acting as a porter, even washing up in the store's restaurant and/or staff canteen. I didn't care much what they had given me to do as the wages allowed me to buy a few rounds of drinks at the pub with my friends at weekends.

Without any other idea of what to do, I went back to Jones and applied for a permanent job there. Fate took a hand. The personnel manager of the store was a rather large single lady called Miss Clutterbuck. During my part time work, she had sometimes been the one who allocated me with my tasks of the day. It was this same Miss Clutterbuck who interviewed me for the permanent job. For whatever reason, she seemed to like me. She told me she had reviewed my background, i.e. a King Edwards schoolboy who just passed his "A" levels and who seemed fit, healthy and presentable (big deal!). She explained that the store was about to start a management trainee package. Two trainees had already been selected. They were about the same age as me, were both sons of managing directors of other Debenhams stores. Would I care to join this package? Sounded good to me. It was a job; it would be paid. I readily accepted. My first job marked the start of a year which allowed me to transition from innocent schoolboy into an independent but somewhat shallow and arrogant young man. I got on really well with my two fellow trainees. The job was interesting but not demanding as we were shunted around the various departments of the store. I even enrolled in a night school to learn about bookkeeping and stock control. I had no idea where this job might take me and had no great interest to find out.

At last I accrued enough money to buy my dream – a second-hand motor scooter – a rather exotic German machine called a Zundapp Bella. It could outpace most other scooters around, then mostly Lambrettas and Vespas It cost me eighty-five pounds plus another fiver for a helmet. It was my first material possession and I treasured it as if it was made of gold. Although I'll never be a good mechanic, I learnt to take it to bits and put it back together again. It was so precious to me because for the first time in my life it gave me a freedom of movement I had not previously experienced. Until my scooter, I had always been restricted to either walking or cycling everywhere or being governed by our local bus service timetable. This was limiting as the last bus to our home in Saltford from both Bath and Bristol left at ten fifteen p.m. With my scooter, I could make my own time-table and come and go as I liked. What was more, and this was a really big deal at the time, I found I could pull the girls – at least those who were brave or foolhardy enough to ride behind me.

I really enjoyed this first feeling of independence and found that I soon forgot my earlier passion about going to Cambridge. I still managed to keep up my running training and was lucky to meet a girl who was equally keen on athletics and was also reckless enough to enjoy riding pillion on my scooter. Her name was Diana – she was tall, willowy, and very fit! I also found her very sexy and I loved to feel the contours of her body as she pressed into my back as we roared along on my motor scooter!

Diana and I often trained together. One day we both entered for races in a local athletics event, me for the men's', Diana for the women's. Boastfully, I remember I won almost every race from hundred yards (this was before we went metric) up to three miles. Diana, also won all her women's races. Our problem was how to carry away all our trophies on the scooter. I remember wedging some between my knees while Diana stashed others in a bag she slung into a backpack. When I refer to Diana as my girlfriend, that is something of an exaggeration. We certainly got on very well while we were out on our training runs and we had a lot of laughs together. I think I would have liked for us to have a more serious relationship but Diana had her sights set somewhere higher than a poor trainee working at a department store. She was a beautiful young woman who later become a TV icon presenting early morning keep fit programmes. Still I had my moments with her. In any case, the late teenage years were far too early to get seriously involved and I was lucky enough to find several other great young ladies willing to ride pillion on my scooter and sometimes more!

I fear that my earlier interest in religion or what my life was about, was put on the back burner during that "freedom" year. Other priorities had taken over. The meaning of life was then to enjoy the moment, have fun, chat up the girls and enjoy a pint and a few laughs in the pub with my chums on a Saturday evening. That was enough.

XXX

Chapter Eighteen

National Military Service: Nigeria, Cameroons, Congo

1959–61

My cosy little world came to an abrupt end when I came home one day and found a letter marked "On Her Majesty's Service" informing me that I was required to serve two years national military service. The next two years changed my life completely as I described in my book: *Adsum: Mission and Passion.* Rather than repeating many of the details of the book, below is the synopsis which I wrote, in the first-person present tense, when presenting that book to my publisher. This summarises the next two years of my life.

"England, 1959. I am a naive eighteen-year-old. I receive a formal summons to serve two years' compulsory national military service. I could have got a deferment by going to university or taking an apprenticeship, as compulsory service was due to be abolished in two years' time. But I decide to obey the summons.

I complete twelve weeks training as an infantryman then, after officer training, am commissioned as a second-lieutenant and posted to join the Nigerian army. This is the period (1959–60) of rapidly changing African politics as many countries gain independence. I am sent to Kaduna where I'm put in charge of a platoon of forty Nigerian soldiers. Initially, I find these soldiers difficult even to tell apart, but after living and intensively training with them every-day, I learn about their culture, to speak the Hausa language and to appreciate the individual qualities of these soldiers. I also learn to respect their strong and sincere devotion to Islam and to question why our spiritual leaders in UK seemed so convinced by our Christian interpretation of faith.

The first operational mission of my platoon is in the British Cameroons. There, I experience my first taste of jungle guerrilla warfare and learn the hard lessons of combat soldiering.

I have to confront my inner conflict of having to kill, then mourning the lives of those I killed. I also meet the tribal Chief of Bafali, whose wisdom and leadership have a profound impact on my life. He is neither Christian, Muslim or any declared "faith" but has a strong moral sense in his benign rule of his people – a microcosm of how humans can live in peace and love with no spiritual input!

In the Congo, as part of the UN Peacekeeping Force, I experience the clash of political manoeuvring by the world's superpowers and the conflict between the official rules of military engagement and the harsh reality of conflicts on the ground. My duties require me and my soldiers to carry out many challenging and often brutal operations in support of the local authorities. One involves the harrowing task of rescuing abused Catholic nuns from a mission hospital where my best colleague is shot, seriously wounded and later dies from his wounds.

After two years' military service, I am demobbed to return to UK to re-join my parents and friends. My naïve youth is gone forever. It's replaced by my experiences of living in the tough world of the military, of surviving the dangers of combat, of facing down a mutiny and of having to kill or be killed. I have learnt about falling in love with a beautiful woman for the first time and the pang of having to let it go. In summary, I learnt the true meaning of comradeship, respect for other cultures and the intelligence and wisdom of people of different nationalities."

Full details are in: *Adsum: Mission and Passion* by Mark Durman. Published 2020. Available on Amazon, Goodreads and all good bookshops!

xxx

I was now no longer the brash young adolescent, content to roar around Bristol on my Zundapp Bella scooter. My experiences on operations when

I was engaged in direct short-range shootings – a kill or be killed situation had a profound mental effect. Not at the immediate moment of contact when our training took over and we used the skills that had been drummed into us. Not then, but afterwards when we had the time to reflect. One was the feeling of relief still to be alive, the other was to mourn for the soldiers we had shot, for their mothers, wives and children who would never see them again. Their young lives had been ended far from their homes and families. These were rebels who had terrorised the local population, killing, raping, destroying the homes of innocent local villagers. Our job had been to protect those villagers and to seek out, capture or if necessary, kill those involved. That had been our mission. We had buried their dead as we did our own. That took care of their physical bodies. It was hygienic but was that it? No afterlife? Nothing more? I didn't know their religion, or even if they had one. But it seemed so bizarre and desperately sad that lives should end so abruptly and when so young. These feelings didn't make me return to the religion I had followed back in Bath. I didn't pray. I was just confused. We never had time to dwell on these thoughts as at that time, there was always the next emergency to respond to.

xxx

Returning (slowly!) home to UK

I didn't find it easy trying to adjust back into civilian life after my two years' military experiences. When writing *Adsum: Mission and Passion*, I shortened the end part. I wrote that I had come back directly from the Congo to UK, reasoning that by immediately contrasting the situation in the Congo to the mundane social life back in Bath would have the impact I wanted to portray in the book. What actually happened to me was this. I was flown back from Leopoldville to Lagos, Nigeria and while there I learnt about a shipping line that sailed between West Africa and UK via a number of stopping off points along the coast. These included ports such as Takoradi in Ghana, Freetown in the just then becoming independent Sierra Leone, Banjul in Gambia, Tenerife in the Canary Islands and finally Lisbon, Portugal before ending up in the port of London. This was intriguing as I had not been to any of these places and a long sea trip back to UK seemed far more appealing than flying directly home. What was more, I received a telegram from the UK War Office informing me that I was now officially demobbed and I had the option of the free flight back to UK or, alternatively, I could be paid one hundred guineas (worth a lot then!) and be free of any other commitments. I was attracted to this second option. I contacted the shipping company (Palm Lines) and was accepted as a passenger. I then replied to the War Office that I would take the hundred guineas. It was the end of April 1961; I was again a free individual.

A few days later, I boarded MV Burutu Palm in Lagos port. I was allocated a small cabin to myself and shared all meals with the ship's officers. I got to know all of them well during our four-week voyage. The Burutu Palm's top speed was only some twelve knots as she meandered along, sticking close to the West African coast. Every few days we would arrive at one of the ports I have described and stay for a day or two while offloading some stores and onloading others. The basic goods were machine parts, picked up in London and Lisbon and offloaded in the various West African ports, and palm oil and other indigenous products taken aboard and brought back to Europe. While in port, the ship's officers took time to socialise on shore. If there was any local attraction or event taking place at that time, mysteriously (!), the ship seemed to develop some minor technical fault which took the duration of the event to repair before we again got underway. Neither the crew nor the company bosses back in London seemed to complain about these manufactured delays: a sensible and pragmatic arrangement for all sides!

While at sea, those not on duty on deck, would meet for supper in the little room, grandly called "the Wardroom". Supper was lavishly washed down with copious quantities of beer and/or whiskey. I enjoyed these evenings both because of the interesting discussions covering a wide range of subjects new to me, and because it was the first time since arriving in Nigeria that I had no responsibilities. I could just relax, learn from the experiences of these merchant naval crew officers and enjoy what for me was a sea cruise holiday.
One evening, the topic of conversation was about the spiritual world with particular links to nautical experiences. The ship's chief engineer, a big

hearty guy named Arthur Robinson, was a mine of information. He was a great storyteller and kept the rest of us entertained with stories about shipwrecks and unexpected horrors of the sea. I think most of the other officers had heard these tales many times before but were happy to listen to Arthur's tales again. Arthur related well known tales such as what happened to the captain, his wife, daughter and crew members of the Marie Celeste in the 1870s, why in the 1940s, all the crew of the Dutch freighter SS Ounang Medan died for no apparent reason. Arthur went on the tell of monsters of the deep but by then I, even as inexperienced as I was about such matters, began to realise that some of Arthur's stories were either exaggerated or just plain fabrications. We had also had a few beers and Arthur had broken out the whiskey. I remember that Arthur wound up his narration by telling me, being a newcomer to being at sea, that the spirit of a former captain of our own ship was regularly seen at night on a particular deck, always at the same spot. Apparently, he had died on the ship from causes that were no longer clear. Had he suffered a heart attack or been murdered or accidentally fallen overboard? No one knew for sure. Somewhat unsteadily, Arthur led me out onto the deck. It was completely dark with only a half-moon for illumination. Jock held my arm with one hand while pointing with the other to a spot on the outer rail of the deck. "Do you see him?" he asked me. I stared at the spot where Arthur was pointing but could see no one. But I did get a vaguely strange sensation that someone and something was there. By then I was seriously sceptical, thinking that Arthur was just making it all up just to tease me. So ended an amusing evening. I decided to take Arthur's tales with a pinch of salt.

But that wasn't the end of it. The next day, I asked a couple of the ship's officers, not Arthur, if they had independently heard the story of the spirit or ghost of the dead captain being seen on the deck at night. I was surprised that both said that they believed it to be true and, yes, they had themselves experienced unusual feelings when on that particular deck at night. Again, I was suspicious that there might be a conspiracy just to wind me up. After the evening meal that day, I excused myself saying I wanted an early night. I purposely kept off the booze. I decided to prove to myself that this was all a joke on me. After all my army experiences, I felt pretty hardened to being affected by such a silly tale. Without, I hoped, being spotted I found my way up to the same area of the deck that Arthur had led me to the previous night. Again, it was lit only by the half-moon. I blithely walked past the area that Arthur had pointed to, expecting to prove that the "dead captain" story was just that; a story. But as I walked past the precise spot, I suddenly felt strangely odd – at one moment instantly cold then I started to sweat. I had never before experienced such a strange unnatural sensation. I looked around but could see nothing unusual there, certainly no ghost of the famous captain. There was just this weird feeling that someone, something was there. At that moment I "lost it". I edged away from that spot on the deck, and made my way as steadily as I could to the sanctuary of my cabin. Once inside, I tried to relax and rationalize the experience. I never really did nor have since. To this day, I still have no idea whether there was indeed a spirit of the dead captain on that deck or whether I had subconsciously been affected by Arthur's storytelling. I also tried to relate this experience to some of the stories I had read in the Bible, particularly the Old Testament. But nothing made sense.

xxx

Digression – the "arrangement"!

I became particularly friendly with the ship's Scottish communications officer, Jock Howard. In the military I had learnt the basics of radio communications. I knew the Morse Code and other comms protocols. I found it interesting to understand how Jock contacted the ports we visited, our London owners and other ships in the area. I spent some of my days on board in Jock's communications domain listening to him chatting away to his maritime contacts. Jock would sometimes let me deputise for him and I enjoyed the easy rapport of chatting with his opposite numbers on the other ships of Palm Lines. Despite Jock's affability, he did have one weakness; he loved his whiskey – too much! On occasions, rather than supervising my amateur attempts to operate his network, Jock would be slumped down in his work desk, having succumbed to the inebriating effects of consuming a bottle of Johnny Walker.

The officers of the Palm Line Company's ships operated an efficient scheme of ensuring there was always a young lady to greet each of them at every port. The scheme worked like this. There were about the same number of ships at sea as there were ports they stopped at and no two ships would normally ever be at the same port at the same time. Each participating officer in the scheme paid to maintain one young lady in one port, ensuring that there was always a lady ready waiting to welcome each officer when a Palm Line ship docked. There was a dedicated captain's lady, first mate's lady, chief engineer's lady, communication's lady etc irrespective of which ship arrived at which port. The ladies did not need to know individual names – they were just hired to greet an appointment not a name. Very neat, tidy, everyone was well looked after. Each officer only paid for one lady but had one available at every port, each lady was well maintained, had regular medical check-ups, and never had to be with more than one gentleman at a time.

On one occasion, when we docked at a port, my chum Jock had passed out and was not able to honour his tryst so, merely out of loyalty not to disrupt the system or disappoint the young lady, I felt honour bound to deputise for Jock. And very charming she was to her acting communications officer. Of this incident, I will say no more!

End of Digression

Slowly, the gallant MV Burutu meandered her way back to Europe. After a final evening when the ships officers gave me an outstanding farewell party, I remember waking up one morning, looking out through the small porthole in my cabin and seeing a drab, grey, rain filled sky. We had docked back in the Port of London.

My African adventures had ended. During the past two years I had learnt much about the strengths and frailties of life – I was still only twenty-one years old.

XXX

Chapter Nineteen

Back in UK. Marshall and Snelgrove, Birmingham

1961–3

It hardly seemed any time since I had left my parents' house in Saltford two years before and made my way to Devizes at the beginning of the extraordinary experience of military service. If I had got a deferment from the conscription, by then I could have a trade or be well under way to getting a degree. But I thought about what I would have missed – all I had done and learnt during these two years. In basic training in Devizes I learnt to handle rough Portsmouth bullies and had my first lesson that nothing is for nothing. In officer training, I learnt about self-sufficiency and that leadership is all about showing not just telling. In Africa, I had learnt to grow up and had survived the dangers of being in combat. I had experienced many different situations and emotions, always with something new ahead. I realised that phase of my life had ended. I had looked forward to seeing my parents again but then what? I had not been to university and had no job to go to. I wasn't sure how I would reconnect with my past life, my friends both from school days in Bath and in Saltford village. I knew I was not the same person who had been conscripted into the military two years before.

As I had feared, the initial pleasure of being reunited with my family and my local friends in Saltford soon wore off as I realised I had to start from scratch to find a job. I was then twenty-one years old. As the summer of 1961 rolled by, I began to have serious regrets about my stubbornness to stick with completing my military national service.

I fired off a few job applications in response to newspaper adverts but either got negative replies or no reply at all. Except one. This was from

Debenhams, the department store group (now sadly gone into part liquidation in 2021) where I had spent the year as a trainee at Jones in Bristol before being called up for national service. Their letter said they had a record of my time at Jones and asked me to come to their Oxford Street, London store for an interview. I was pleasantly surprised when I learnt that, prior to my interview, the chairman of the interview panel had spoken to the War Office in Whitehall and been given details of my army service in the Nigerian Army. Indeed, most of the interview involved questions about my African experiences and ended with the job offer as "executive trainee" at the Debenhams owned store in Birmingham. The chairman asked if I could start immediately. I thought, "At last I've got a job offer. It sounds interesting so why not?" The chairman told me to report myself to the managing director of Marshall and Snelgrove, New Street, Birmingham the following week. That was it. I had a job and a new direction, a new phase of life.

Marshall and Snelgrove group was regarded as the top end of Debenham's retail enterprise. It specialised in the most expensive brand of ladies' fashion and accessories. The Birmingham branch occupied a spacious and prestigious corner of New Street, which was the most elite shopping street in the city. The store comprised several floors, with cosmetics and jewellery dominating the ground floor and various clothes specialities, such as gowns, furs, coats, millinery etc on the higher floors. It had a top-class gourmet restaurant, a ladies' "sitting out" area, a hairdresser, numerous fitting rooms and a tailoring section geared to making clothes alterations/adjustments ready for the customer in record time. It was "the" place for the ladies of the Midlands counties to shop, to socialise with colleagues, to "see and been seen".

There were four hundred and fifty permanent staff, four hundred and twenty of which were female and mostly young and attractive. Of the thirty male employees, there was the Managing Director, his deputy and a senior "buyer" from the fur department. The remaining males were porters, van drivers and security staff. To this employment roll was to be added one more – a twenty-one-year-old, single male – me! I had no idea what to expect or what my duties might entail but with a male/female ratio like that, I didn't much care.

On my first day, I found my way to the managing director's office suite and was invited to wait in his outer office, occupied by two pretty young secretaries. I had no idea what would happen next and I spent some time trying not to stare too hard at either of the two lovely girls. They seemed as unsure about what I was doing there as I was myself. Eventually the phone rang, was answered by one of the secretaries who merely said "Yes, Sir" and put the phone down. She looked at me and (in the style of the renowned TV series *The Apprentice*) told me "Mr Wellington will see you now!"

Mr Wellington was a middle-aged gentleman who was quite short and rotund, which surprised me as I had imagined the MD of this prestigious establishment to be more elegant and suave. I thought he looked more like a farmer than the head of a fashion store. He had a blunt Yorkshire accent and I had the distinct impression that I had been foisted on him by the Debenhams London head office against his wishes. His instructions to me went something like this: "Right lad, you're here to learn the trade. You are to spend time in each of our departments and make sure our customers are well looked after." That was about it. I left Mr Wellington's office without the faintest idea what to do or where to start.

I didn't really care too much that, for most of my time at Marshall and Snelgrove, I was given no direction whatsoever. I was being paid, though not much, I had reasonable accommodation and began to develop an interesting social life. I had bought a new suit and made sure my appearance was always neat and smart – clean shirt, tie with straight knot, trousers pressed, shoes polished and shiny. I remembered to walk with head up, shoulders back, chest out and stomach in – good military training. I would always arrive five minutes before opening time, took no more than thirty minutes for lunch and made sure the store was correctly closed down at the end of each day. But what did I actually do? I would walk around the various departments pretending to look busy. I would meet important customers arriving at the store, escort them as required and make sure their needs were attended to. Many of these good ladies were, in my opinion, fussy and over-cossetted. They would complain about their personal petty problems which I made myself listen to and appear to be sympathetic and understanding. I felt that was part of my role to contribute to the attraction for these ladies of visiting Marshall and Snelgrove. I kept to myself what I really thought about their trivial self-indulgences.

Many of the lady customers would make visiting Marshall and Snelgrove a day long social event. They would arrive at mid-morning, have a fitting for a new dress, meet friends for coffee, have a hairdo, facial or a massage or all three, back to the restaurant for lunch, try on the dress which had by then been adjusted in the tailoring section, visit other departments such as choosing a new hat in the extensive millinery department. They would eventually leave in mid to late afternoon, laden with smart Marshall and Snelgrove carrier bags, having enjoyed being spoiled in the store. Sometimes, well known stars and celebrities would visit. I remembering being genuinely honoured to escort Ella Fitzgerald around the store when she took free time from performing at the local concert theatre to do her shopping. I found her a warm and delightful lady, polite and courteous. On that occasion I actually felt I was performing a useful duty. Many other lady customers were not so gracious!

There were certainly attractions for a young single guy to be working in an almost female only environment. Soon after starting my job there I was attracted to a very "English rose" looking girl who represented one of the leading perfumery companies. She was single and unattached so I asked her out for a date. She was a charming girl and we got on really well in a rather innocent way. Unfortunately, her very protective mother once saw us together, embracing in my little Austin car and took exception to this behaviour. She wrote me a very sharp letter telling me I could not see her daughter again. I decided that I did not need to have an angry mother on my back and had to tell the poor girl that we should stop our light relationship. This merely caused embarrassment for the girl, who of course I would still regularly see as I did my patrolling rounds.

After that episode, I learnt to tread warily among these delightful girls working for Marshall and Snelgrove. However, I was then a healthy single guy in my early twenties and the city of Birmingham had a wide selection of attractive girls to choose from. During my time there I was lucky enough to have "dates" with several but, neither I nor they, wanted to form any serious or permanent relationship.

After some time, I found the heady atmosphere of perfumes and the almost exclusive female staff and customers of my working environment needed to be counter balanced with more male company. I learnt there was a thriving local Territorial Army (TA) unit based in the Erdington district of Birmingham, the TA element of the Royal Warwickshire Fusiliers. I contacted them, met their company commander and his supporting officers. We got on well and after checking out my background, I was offered a TA commission in the initial rank of second lieutenant. We met in a "drill hall" once a week and also had some training weekends scheduled throughout the year.

I was also keen to start playing rugby again. Near to the Erdington TA drill hall was the home of the local rugby club. I approached the club management, was invited to a mid-week training session, then picked to play in their next match. This combination of TA soldiering and rugby suited me well and I now had more balance in my life which made the need to be ever courteous to all the ladies in Marshalls easier to handle.

xxx

There was one department in the store which particularly interested me. This was the fur department, run by the impeccable Mr Brent, the only male Head of Department. Mr Brent was a very smart operator. He knew his lady customers very well and maintained an efficient card index system on them all. To be more specific, his research was primarily about the wealth and income of his customers' husbands and his analysis of the relationship between husband and wife. This intelligence led to his assessment as to how much the husband would be willing to spend of his wife's next fur coat.

My conversations with Mr Brent were not only about fur coats! I had noticed he was never at the store on Saturdays and one day I innocently asked him why. He explained that he was Jewish and that he and his family celebrated the Jewish festival of Shabbat. This was considered by practising Jews to be a day of rest and prayer. Shabbat traditionally begins at sunset on Friday and lasts until nightfall on Saturday. Mr Brent explained his faith to me and during my time at Marshall and Snelgrove, he educated me in its traditions and beliefs. He was a good and patient teacher and I learnt a lot from him. I had always heard stories about how Jews were very adapt in money matters and business and indeed Mr Brent was a good example of this. I once had the cheek to ask him about this. His replied that he thought it was probably because most Jews were very aware that, throughout their history they had been a persecuted people. He gave examples of the 1066 Granada massacre when a Muslim mob killed more than one thousand Jewish families, in 1492 when the newly established Christian authorities in Spain issued a writ that all Jews who refused to convert to Christianity would be expelled. Now of course we are all aware of the Nazi organised Holocaust where some six million Jews were killed. Mr Brent felt that, due to this history of persecution, Jews today were determined to be financially secure as some sort of personal and collective security. After time spent with Mr Brent, I have always had much respect for Jewish people. Later in my life I spent a good deal of time in Israel as I explain in a later chapter.

Digression – business intelligence

Mr Brent taught me about the fascination of mink – the differing types and qualities. In those days, there was no taboo on wearing animal fur. He showed me how to present such coats to his customers by holding them by the top collar and shaking them out to emphasis the glorious sheen they displayed. One evening we stayed in his department after the store had closed and Mr Brent gave me a mission for the following day. I was to take a selection of mink furs to the residence of one of his lady customers and "sell one to her". He then proceeded to give me comprehensive instructions as to how to achieve the sale. He packed ten valuable minks separately in Marshalls cardboard boxes, each coat folded among many layers of tissue in a special way. Mr Brent then taught me exactly how I should conduct myself at the lady's residence, what I was to say in describing the coats to her, the order I was to present them and which one she would buy!

Mr Brent made me rehearse my performance, only concluding when he was satisfied I was proficient in the precise procedure. All was prepared for me to drive a Marshall's van to the lady's residence the following day.

This is how it went. Early the next morning, I checked into our security office, located in the Marshall's underground garaging, signed for one of our vans and for the ten cardboard boxes that Mr Brent had prepared and set off to the good lady's residence. Mr Brent had given me her address and the route I was to follow. The journey took about two hours and at ten thirty sharp, I pulled into the driveway of her residence. I found myself facing a large country house with a set of stately pillars supporting a porch outside the front entrance. I rang the doorbell. It was a palatial property and I was half expecting a butler to respond to the ring. But no, it was the lady of the house herself. She was in her late fifties, slim and well preserved (Mr Brent of course knew her precise measurements, date of birth etc!) She was wearing an elegant dress and already had made up her face. I shall call her Lady Russell to preserve her anonymity though this was not her real name. I could tell she had eagerly been waiting for my arrival, no doubt encouraged by speaking to Mr Brent on the phone. After leading me into a beautifully furnished spacious drawing room, her first words were, "Have you brought my mink?"

I then proceeded faithfully to follow Mr Brent's precise instructions. "Oh Madame," I said, "what a beautiful room this is. And I do like that painting. Could you tell me a little about it?" Lady Russel was well bred and indulged in my question. Whereupon I asked about some other item and its provenance. Again, she replied politely but I could tell she was getting ever more impatient to see the furs. Mr Brent had told me to prolong this diversionary conversational tactic for a while but not to over-do it. When I felt the time had come, I told her, "Ah, yes, of course the minks! Shall I bring them in for your inspection?"
Of course, she eagerly agreed.

I went out to the van, collected the ten boxes and said to Lady Russell, "Madame, may I suggest we go to your dressing room so you can try these minks on, then you can select your favourite?" She of course again eagerly agreed. She led the way up the stairs to a large bedroom, to the side of which was a dressing room with a full-length mirror. Following my brief, I took my time to pile up the boxes on the single bed in the room taking care to arrange them in the exact order that I had been told. I could sense Lady Russell's impatience and anticipation. I opened the first box and made a show of grabbing the coat by its collar and roughly shaking it free from the tissue. The mink gleamed and displayed its sheen. I indicated to Lady Russell that she should stand in front of her mirror and I then proceeded to fit it around her shoulders. Hardly had she had the chance to admire the effect in her mirror when I immediately lifted the coat back from her shoulders and threw it on the bed exclaiming "No, no, Madame, that is just not you!"

So our fitting continued, I introduced each coat with the same flamboyant flourish, and arranged it on Lady Russell's shoulders. With each coat, I had been taught what comments to make, for example, "Yeees, Madame. This fits well and complements Madame's figure but, you see there, the collar line is not quite perfect." Or "This one fits on Madame's shoulders nicely but I feel we could do better with the hem". I would then remove the coat from her and throw it roughly on the bed with the others. Each time, Lady Russell would preen herself in front of the mirror and I could tell she was eager for me to find the 'right' coat. As per my brief, I got to coat number eight of ten. Mr Brent had stressed not to wait until the final coat number ten as that would have been too obvious. I took my time again to highlight its sheen, slipped it over her shoulders, stood back in feigned admiration and said simply, "Madame, need I say more!"

That was it. I left Lady Russell to admire herself in the mirror, piled the remaining coats in the van, and stayed just long enough for her to give me a cheque for six thousand pounds before heading back to Birmingham. Mr Brent had told me I would get one per cent of the sale price as my commission, that meant sixty pounds. A great pay day!

Mr Brent taught me a great deal about how he ran his fur "empire". His comprehensive filing system recorded details of all his key customers. The statistics of the lady, age, address (including value of property), figure measurements, character, style preferences. Then details about her lifestyle, husband/partner (if applicable!), husband's job, income and estimated wealth, relationship with partner (close/loving, cool/distant), record of past purchases with price etc. All this information led to an assessment of what the lady would likely buy next. I suspected his intelligence system was as accurate with all his other ladies as it was about Lady Russell!

xxx

Punch up in the car park!

After my daily working life in the world of ladies' fashion, it was a welcome change to get involved and scruff it with the Erdington rugby club. Apart for the Saturday match fixtures, the club organised mid-week evening training sessions which I attended both as a means to get to know the other team members and also to improve my own level of fitness which had begun to decline after the end of my time in the army. Erdington was quite a poor suburb of Birmingham and had a high crime rate. My fellow team members came from a range of differing backgrounds and we didn't have too much in common except our mutual love of rugby. After one mid-week evening training session, I was invited to join a group of six others to go to a nearby pub for a pint or two before dispersing for the evening. The pub was busy with late evening drinkers. We had been there some time when I noticed a group of seven or eight rough looking guys had come in and pushed their way through to the bar, elbowing another guy out of their way whose turn was ahead of theirs. So what, I thought, this has nothing to do with us. That was until, one of our team named Jim went to the bar to order another round of beers. I couldn't hear what was said but saw that Jim was being surrounded and threatened by guys from the other group. My colleagues also saw this and were quick to react to go over to the bar to support Jim. I did not want to get involved. I was neither a local of the area nor yet a regular in the rugby squad. I knew that my colleagues were all fit guys and reckoned they were well capable of handling the confrontation. But I felt a sense of loyalty to my newly met rugby colleagues and duty bound to support them not least because we were outnumbered by this gang. There was a session of pushing and shoving, then I heard one of the gang shout out, "OK, let's settle this outside!"

We all faced up to each other in the pub's carpark. It was a dank, wet winter's evening, and very dark in the enclosed pub parking area with only faint streetlighting to illuminate the scene. I was confronted by some guy who seemed to have picked me out as his target. In the darkness, I couldn't gauge his age or physical attributes. I only knew that I was now in a fight which had to be resolved. It was too late to back out. We squared up. I hit him with a solid punch and he began to back off. But before I could follow up, he whipped out something from his clothing and, in the half-light, I saw the glint of the steel from a knife. That was not good! Initially I had felt capable of looking after myself in a wrestle or punch up, but knives being used in close contact – that's another dimension. I did not enjoy being in this situation!

This was no time for hesitation – even if I had wanted to be a coward and try to get out of there, I was already hemmed in. In any case, by then I was fired up and pissed off with this group of thugs trying to boss the local community about. I had no choice but to go on the offensive which meant diving straight for the knife. I aimed for the knife's haft hoping that I would get the thug's wrist. I reckoned that even if I got cut on my hand or arm it was better than the blade lunging into my body. He didn't expect this and before he reacted, I had grabbed his wrist with both hands and twisted hard. I was relieved to hear the knife clatter onto the ground. By then, my blood was up. I had lost it and overreacted. I continued to hold hard onto his wrist with my left hand then grabbed him around the neck with my right. I held him in a neck grip and forced his head down while jerking my right knee up to connect with his head. I heard a bone snap – I think it was on the bridge of his nose. He slumped down at my feet. I had an awful feeling he was seriously injured or maybe even worse! I tried to control myself and rationalise the position I had got myself into. It was then I heard the siren of a police car approaching. I had a quick look round and saw, or perhaps hoped I saw, that my rugby friends were holding their own. I knew then that it was time to get out. We were about half a mile from my apartment room and I was glad I had not come to the rugby training by car. As the police siren got louder, I managed to extract myself from this mêlée. I had left my sweaty training kit in a bag in the pub so made a quick return to retrieve it then got straight back out again. I controlled myself enough to walk rather than run away and be clear of the pub as the police car (or cars I will never know) screamed to a halt outside the pub. I forced myself to walk calmly away and was not apprehended or challenged as I returned home.

The next day. I arrived at Marshall's promptly and smartly dressed as usual. Everything seemed normal, I was not summoned to Mr Wellington's office and no police showed up at the store. I waited until mid-morning then slipped out to buy the local Birmingham newspaper. I scoured through the headlines but was relieved that there was no mention of last night's pub fracas. I gradually began to relax. Perhaps pub fights were routine events in Erdington and didn't merit press coverage.

The following Saturday I turned up as usual for the match. I met up with Jim who told me that the fight had come to a stop when the police had arrived. No one had been seriously hurt and the gang had run off not wanting to face police enquiries. The police had asked a few questions but did not seem to want to take further action. Jim said it best to forget about the incident. Much relieved, I agreed.

End of Digression

xxx

Back to the Marshall's story. There was one part of the store's business that I had not learnt about. That was the publicity and advertising department run by Mary Hardy, an elegant, polished lady of about forty; a delightful person; intelligent, professional but also with a great sense of humour. She enjoyed a very high business reputation. Mary taught me about how to get the most out of her business. She had many close contacts in the press and broadcasting world. She produced weekly advertisements of Marshall's products and arranged fashion parades both in the store and at various venues within the Marshall's catchment areas such as Leamington Spa, Stratford upon Avon, Warwick and Worcester.

The outward persona of Mary Hardy was of a lady who was always impeccably groomed, impressively confident, affable, personable and professional. I was flattered that she seemed to befriend me – being some seventeen years younger than her. During that period we often took our lunch breaks together and developed an easy rapport. One day I noticed she seemed to have lost her usual positive manner and asked her if something was troubling her. I then discovered there was another side to Mary when she confessed that despite always putting up a pretence of been happily married, in reality she was deeply troubled due to her husband being both an alcoholic and having a number of sexual affairs. She said that he was also often violent to her, especially when he had been drinking. Once she had taken me into her confidence, she freely opened up about her many inhibitions that outwardly she concealed to those around her in both her personal and professional life. She also told me about a medical condition for which her doctors could find no cure. This led to our many later discussions about life, its meaning and purpose. Mary felt that her life span would be short, that she could not relate to any religion and dreaded the idea of death. Until these discussions with Mary, I had not seriously considered these fundamental issues.

Mary asked me to assist her in organising the travelling fashion shows. The venue, usually a theatre or dance hall. The role Mary allotted to me was to help in setting up the flower bedecked catwalk, welcoming our guests, producing the music, and ensuring the girls came on stage in the correct order and in the correct dress. I really enjoyed myself, what healthy young male could not, surrounded by a squad of gorgeous scantily clad model girls. It was just as well I had a full social life outside of Marshall and Snelgrove!

Mary had an excellent and confident stage voice – she also frequently appeared on radio programs dealing with fashion subjects. She always gained her audience's full attention giving a short formal welcome then introducing each of the fashion exhibits modelled by the girls. My job, from behind the stage, included setting each girl off onto the catwalk in sync with Mary's introduction while ensuring the music matched the mood. I enjoyed working with these beautiful and delightful girls. Mary gave me one further role. She squeezed the Marshall's budget to send me to the local branch of

Moss Bros to buy a made-to-measure wedding suit with all accessories – top hat. dress shirt, waistcoat, bow tie, cuff links, pocket square, patent leather shoes. The shows always ended with modelling a bridal dress. This was my cue, dressed up as "the groom" to link up with the model "bride". She would take my arm and together we would sidle down the catwalk as if it we were returning from the alter! Our procession, fluently presented by Mary, never failed to wow our audience. I have no idea of actual sales figures but I know that Mary's publicity department led to good profits for the store.

Digression – Sexual relations

My role at these fashion parades would probably not be permissible in today's society. Back then, the young models were professional in their work but charming, easy and confident in their relationship with men. Attitudes have changed so much in today's over sensitive world where many young women are hyped up to accuse men of "inappropriate behaviour", "unwarranted touching", "sexual abuse", "down-blousing", "up-skirting", even "attempted rape" or any combination of these. Some accusations may be justified, many others not. Men must have respect for women, as indeed should women for men, but the pendulum of sexual relations has, in my opinion, swung too far. The law has become intrusive, judgemental and pseudo protective in an area of one of the most natural areas of human interaction – the relationship between men and women. Of course there are instances where men in powerful jobs exploit their position to gain sexual gratification. Hence the fully justified charges against, for example, Sidney Weinstein and others. But the so called "me too" movement has too often become an excuse for some young women to gain notoriety and/or an easy pay off. In the first instance, if a woman does not wish to develop a relation with a man, she can just firmly say "NO!"

End of Digression

xxx

My hobby in the Territorial Army became increasingly more important to me. I very much enjoyed our training evenings with our volunteer soldiers.

There were several weekends held in army camps located away from Birmingham and which required travel time during the working week. On each of these occasions, I asked Mr Wellington for time off, explaining that my TA duties were for the benefit of the defence of our country etc. Grudgingly, Mr Wellington gave his permission for "leave of absence." I wondered why he should be "grudging" as he rarely took any interest in my work. The odd edict I would receive via his PA was to meet, greet and escort some rich lady or celebratory during their visits to Marshalls.

My life style in Birmingham was generally light and pleasant. I still mainly followed my own self-motivated programme at Marshall's: arriving early, spending some time walking around the departments, greeting both staff and customers, then repairing to my two favourite departments viz: Mr Brent's furs or Mary Hardy's publicity. But after nearly two years in Birmingham I began to take stock, by then being twenty-three years old. Here I was, poncing around all day in a female heavy environment, with no clear career path ahead. I realised that I should have pushed to spend more time in the accounts department, learning the financial side of the business. A full understanding of expenditure, income, stock control etc would be critical if I were to progress as an executive in the department store business. I realised I probably should also be pushing to attend night school studies in accounting. I should have but I really didn't feel motivated to do so. I kept thinking about my army days and realised I was missing that life-style.

One day, I had a call from my TA company commander asking if I could take a squad of soldiers down to Warminster for a week's live firing practice on the ranges there. Before replying I reported myself to Mr Wellington and asked permission to be absent from the store for that week. In his typical blunt Yorkshire way, his reply was direct. He told me. "Look son, you either work here or in the f***ing army. Which is it to be? Make your mind up!" In that moment, I realised Mr Wellington had summed up the situation perfectly. All I could think of in reply was: "I understand, sir. I prefer to be in the f***ing army". Mr Wellington seemed rather taken aback by my curt reply but, I think for the first time, I saw him smile. He came over and shook my hand and said, "Good luck to you, son!" When I went up to the accounts department to collect the pay, I was owed. I found they had already been contacted by Mr Wellington's office and that, to my surprise, I had been given a good bonus payment. I routed via the departments of Mr Brent and Mary Hardy to say goodbye, then left Marshall and Snelgrove, never to return. One postscript. I continued to keep in regular written contact with Mary until sadly she succumbed to her incurable medical condition and died fourteen years later at the age of fifty-two.

I contacted my TA commander, agreed to the live firing assignment, and told him I would meet up with the TA soldiers directly in Warminster. I then packed my few belongings, left a month's rent at my apartment and drove my little car away from Birmingham back to my parents' home in Saltford. It was January 1963.

xxx

Chapter Twenty

Back Home

It seemed strange to be back once again in the room in our house in Saltford where I had been born. My parents were welcoming but I was aware that my artist father was not well. He was recovering at home from a stroke, the second he had had in the past two years. Although he seemed physically normal, he was very distressed because the stroke had left him partly paralysed on the right side of his body which resulted in his ability to continue painting being seriously impaired. Art and painting had been his life, his profession, his motivation, his whole world. Losing part of that ability left him hollow and depressed. Shortly after I had arrived, my father was taken ill again and admitted to hospital. A few days later, I was woken in the middle of the night by my mother, who was sobbing. Between her tears, she told me there had just been a call from the hospital to tell her that my father had died. He was only fifty-eight years old.

At least I was at home to comfort my mother. She had always been so stable and responsible for my upbringing and development. She had always been there to care for my sister and me. My father had been the character, the extravert, the "penniless artist" often away for weeks with his arty friends. My mother had been caring, loving, pushing our father to make sure we at least had enough money to buy the basics of food and clothing. Now she was distraught. It was my turn to step up and act responsibly. I knew nothing about how to handle the rules following a death and it took some time to arrange for doctor's certificates and notify the relevant authorities. Then to the funeral arrangements. I asked my mother about this – burial or cremation. She didn't know and told me to decide what was best. I knew that our little family had no reserved burial plot and somehow felt repelled the idea of my father's body stuck for ever in a coffin as it slowly decomposed and rotted away. I knew that burial has been the chosen funeral form for many millions and that it was still preferred to cremation by many Christians as it conforms to their beliefs on resurrection and the afterlife. But that didn't mean much to me and I knew my father was not religious except in his own style of respecting and loving nature. After taking some advice, I decided that a cremation seemed more appropriate.

My father's death prompted me to rethink about the meaning of life and what happens to us when we die. Except for my discussions with Mary Hardy, I had rarely had such thoughts before. When I was on active service in Africa and had to deal with the bodies of dead terrorists; except the great feeling of distress and emotion when my best chum was shot and I could see him fading away as we tried desperately to stop his bleeding. (See p 294 of Adsum: Mission and Passion). But my thoughts then had been shallow. At that time, there were always so many other priorities to deal with. But this was my own father. I tried to pray for him, to wonder if a part of him, his soul, his spirit, his conscious might live on, somehow, somewhere. I wondered if one day I might find out, maybe even meet him in some form again. These "spiritual" thoughts led to no conclusions. My main priority then was with the living and doing all I could to help and comfort my poor mother.

xxx

I have, to my cost, always been far too impetuous. I now realised I had responded to Mr Wellington's remark about the army by quitting Marshall's before I had even made any enquiry to the War Office, what vacancies there might be and what procedures/applications were required. Now I was out of a job again and my savings would quickly be exhausted.

As I feared, it was a complicated and long-winded process to re-join the army as a "regular" officer. It was made even more difficult in my case as, although I had been commissioned as a national service officer in the infantry, and later a TA officer, I had never served with my original regiment, The Royal Hampshires, having been seconded to the Nigerian Army for all of my commissioned service. As an individual, I was unknown to any British county regiment and had no one to sponsor me or act as a reference. As a result, I had to start the application process from scratch. This was how it worked. First the applicant had to appear before the Regular Commissions Board (RCB) based in Westbury, Wiltshire. If successful, he/she had to apply to be accepted by a particular county regiment i.e. Royal Hampshires, or a specialist Corps who would consider the application. If they were interested in the applicant and if there was a vacancy, the applicant would then be called for at least one interview. All this took time and there was absolutely no guarantee of being accepted. Meanwhile, I needed to earn a living.

I put job hunting temporally to one side when I received a letter from the War Office inviting me to attend the Regular Commissions Board (RCB) in Westbury, Wiltshire. This three-day process was designed to assess the suitability of young British men (as far as I knew it was male only at that time) for training to be regular officers in the British Army. I did have an advantage here because, back in 1959, as a national serviceman, I had been required to undertake a similar selection process. I had managed to pass that selection which led to my training at Mons Officer Cadet school, Aldershot and eventual commission as a national service officer. Although the War Office still had records of my passing the previous selection tests, apparently this did not count. The regulations were that I would have to do the tests again.

I explained the selection process in some detail in my earlier book *Adsum: Mission and Passion* (Chapters 9 and 10). In summary, over a three-day period, candidates have to carry out a wide variety of tests, some verbal, some mental and some physical. Indoor tests include: discussions about world current affairs, individual presentations, personal interviews, written tests involving short essay writing, arithmetical and psychometric tests. Outdoors were a series of "command tasks" involving working as a group, designed to test candidate's ability both as a leader and as a group "player" within a team. And finally, candidates had individually to complete an obstacle course to assess physical fitness and determination.

At the end of the process, all of us candidates were required to collect an envelope when our names were called. I opened mine and was relieved to see that I had passed! Relieved but not ecstatic because this merely meant that I had passed the first hurdle. I was told that my operational experience in Africa negated the need for further officer cadet training in Sandhurst but now I had to persuade some Regiment or Corps to take me on as a regular officer. That was the next big challenge.

As soon as I got back to Saltford, I wrote to the colonel of the Royal Hampshire Regiment, explaining my background, that I had just passed the RCB, and requesting a regular commission in his Regiment. Now I could only wait and hope.

xxx

Digression – the "Crunchy Bar spreader"

Meanwhile I was getting seriously broke again and needed a job. The only local work available that I could find at that time was a vacancy to work at Fry's chocolate factory, located in the nearby village/small town of Keynsham. I applied and was told I could work on the night shift. Hours were from eight thirty p.m. to six thirty a.m. I was issued with a card to punch into a machine at the entrance to my allocated section of the factory. The card recorded precisely when I clocked in and clocked off.

My allocated task was on the "Crunchy Bar" section. It had an all-pervading sickly sweet aroma. It was repetitive work. In front of my work station were three wooden rectangular slabs. The guy working ahead of me would pass me a large copper bowl full of a steaming liquid. My task was to pour the liquid to fill the first wooden rectangle. I then had to wait until the liquid cooled sufficiently then to pass a large spatula over the liquid to flatten it out. While it was hardening, I had to bring down a hinged partitioned cover (which resembled a suitcase lid) over the drying liquid which cut it into small slices. I then had to pass the sliced product to the next guy in the production chain while presenting a cleaned section back to the first guy ready to be filled again with hot liquid. That was it! The procedure took a while to get used to but became automatic after repeated constantly during my working shift. My job was called, "A honey-comb centre spreader!" A bit of a change from operational soldiering in the Congo, to selling Mr Brent's fur coats to wealthy ladies or to poncing down the catwalk during Mary Hardy's fashion parades!

The procedure in the "Crunchy bar centre" was that a stipulated quota of this "glorious" product had to be produced by each shift. No less, no more. While I was there, this is what happened. Having clocked on at eight thirty p.m., everyone would work feverishly at our tasks. For the first few hours, our production line was roaring along at top speed. Our efforts were rewarded when, usually by two to two thirty a.m., our foreman would announce that we had reached our target quota. We would then spend half an hour, cleaning all our tools and work spaces ready for the day shift to take over later that morning. The noise and bustle of the factory floor would then cease completely and everyone would rest either by finding a comfortable spot to sit on or, in some cases, to stretch out onto the work top and drop off to sleep there for the remaining hours of our shift, being sure to wake up in time to clock off at precisely six thirty a.m.

Still, it was a job. Then, and many times in later life, I learnt never to be too proud to take any legal job when you need money. You have to do what you have to do!

There was a catch to this work at Fry's. To begin with I found both the managers and my fellow workers were friendly and helpful. Slowly, attitudes began to change. After about a week, I was approached by an older gentleman. He told me he was the local union representative and asked to see my membership card. When I told him I wasn't a member, his attitude hardened. He told me that Fry's was a "closed shop" and that only union members could work there. He said that I would have to join or lose my job. This was my first experience of union power and I didn't take it too seriously. The following week, the same guy asked me if I had yet joined the union. I tried politely to tell him that I had no strong political views and had nothing against his union. I said I didn't really care about the subject but preferred at this time not to join. This was not an acceptable answer. The union rep told me that the union would not make any exceptions. I either joined the union or I would lose my job.

I wondered if this guy had the authority to have me fired merely for not joining his union. In my naivety about industrial relations in UK at that time, I found it hard to believe that a successful company like Fry's would allow such power to a union. Surely it was for the management to decide who could be hired or fired?

I again disregarded the gentleman's threat. This was not a good idea. The following days I found the attitude of my former friendly work colleagues had changed. Smiles turned to scowls. I tried to talk to one or two guys, asking if they thought it right and legal that anyone should lose their job merely for not belonging to a union. All I got were shrugs. One guy who replied, "That's the way it is, mate" summed up the general attitude. I thought perhaps as a matter of principle I should report my situation to the management. Then again, I realised that this was indeed "the way it was" and some feeble gesture of mine would have absolutely no effect. In any case, why the hell would I need to get involved with fighting a lost cause about my job as a "crunchy bar" spreader? I knew I had to keep a sense of proportion. So, I accepted the inevitable and quit. I had found it a fascinating vignette into industrial life in UK in the 1960s. Time to move on.

End of digression.

xxx

About the same time as my Fry's job reached its conclusion, I received a reply from the Royal Hampshire Regiment. I was told to report to the barracks in Winchester for an interview the following week. I got out my best ex-Marshall's suit and on the appointed day, drove my trusty Austin to Winchester.

I found myself in front of a panel of four officers. The chairman, wearing a civilian suit with regimental tie, introduced himself as Colonel Forester. The other three were all in uniform each with the rank insignia of lieutenant-colonel. The interview was cordial and all had apparently read up on my background as a national serviceman, commissioned into their regiment. We discussed the operations in the Cameroons and the Congo. I was thinking: “So far, so good”. Then we came to what I came to realise were the key issues. The conversation continued something like this:

“Mr Durman, do you have family connections in Hampshire?”

“Not that I’m aware of, sir, I was born near Bath in Somerset which is still my family home.”

“Was your father connected to the Royal Hampshire Regiment?”

“No, sir, he was only in the army during the war. He was in the Royal Army Service Corps”

“What is his profession?”

“Actually, he has recently died. All his life he was a professional artist”

“I see. Why have you asked particularly to join the Royal Hampshires?”

“Well, sir, I was assigned to the regiment as a national serviceman and was honoured to be commissioned into the regiment.”

“But you did not remain with us on commissioning. Instead, you elected to be seconded to the Nigerian army. Why was that?”

From this point on, I felt my chances were slipping away. I realised that, with no family connections either to the Regiment or to the county of Hampshire, it was unlikely that I would be accepted.

At the end of the interview, which remained cordial, I shook hands with each member of the panel but I left feeling I was on a loser with the Royal Hampshires. And so it was. The following week, I received a letter from the colonel telling me his panel had been impressed with my background (blah, blah etc) but, with regret, they did not wish to proceed with my application.

I felt deflated and depressed as I realised that infantry county regiments, such as the Royal Hampshires, are very parochial organisations. That is the nature of their formation, history and continued culture. Due to this, it would be unlikely I would be accepted into such a regiment. I could keep trying – perhaps the Duke of Edinburgh's Royal regiment (a recent amalgamation of the Wiltshire and Berkshire Regiments) or the Glosters etc. But I realised that probably none of these would accept me as I had no family or county background ties. There was another thing. I reckoned that, even if I were to be accepted by one of these regiments, I might make it up to the rank of major, but to go on to command the regiment as a lieutenant-colonel with no county background, and any subsequent higher rank, would be most unlikely. It was time to rethink my future.

I had set my goal as re-joining the army as a regular officer. Until now I had only been considering infantry regiments because that had been my previous military background. But there are many other elements of the British Army other than the infantry. I drew up a list of alternatives. There was the cavalry – (but that was even more closed to non-family connections than the infantry), the tank regiment, certainly a possibility, the artillery, also possible but perhaps too technical for my background, the engineers and electrical engineers, again, not with my non-technical background, ordnance – certainly a starter but didn't really appeal, military police, likewise, signals, yes, a strong possibility (I put it on my short list).

Lastly, I thought about The Intelligence Corps – I didn't know much about that Corps but I was certainly intrigued. During my time on operations in Africa, I'd learnt to appreciate how valuable it was to have good intelligence about a potential enemy. I remembered that our battalion in Nigeria had a dedicated intelligence officer (IO) and how vital the information he produced was to the planning and execution of our tactics. In my own recent experience in Marshalls, I had great respect for Mr Brent and his invaluable "intelligence system" about his fur buying customers and how that drove his sales campaign. I couldn't find much out about the

Intelligence Corps, only that their headquarters was in Uckfield, Kent. On impulse, I wrote to the address I found, described my background and asked if I could be considered for a commission with their Corps. I had no great hopes that I might get a good response but decided to wait a week and, if there was no answer, to apply to join the Royal Signals.

xxx

Meanwhile, back to trying to earn some money. By now it was mid-April, winter had passed and the weather had turned mild. I heard about a construction project in Keynsham that was building a new shopping and civic centre in the middle of the town. Work was already underway. I checked in to the work's office where I was told they were taking on part time labourers. This was just what I was looking for: outdoor manual work, flexible hours, no union control (yet!). I reckoned that was far better and healthier than the night shift at Fry's. I applied and was told I could start straightaway. For me this was the perfect temporary situation.

Digression – Ray the Baptist

The west country enjoyed an excellent summer that year in 1963. I spent much of it digging construction trenches or climbing up and down scaffolding with a hod over my shoulder, supplying the permanent "brickies" with constant refills of cement and bricks – tough manual labour but excellent for restoring torso muscles that had softened up during my Marshall's period. Most days were hot and sunny so we could strip off to the waist and build up healthy tans. I spent much of the time working alongside a guy of about my age, called Ray Harris, who was waiting to be accepted as a Baptist priest. He was a bright guy and between our manual efforts we regularly discussed religion and current affairs. We didn't agree on much but always enjoyed the good-natured banter. I was mystified why Ray should be so motivated to absorb himself in a religious faith and I pressed him to explain his reasons. Ray was exuberantly enthusiastic about his "calling". He told me that when he was a young teenager, out of curiosity, he had gone to a rally in Harringay Arena where the evangelist Billy Graham was preaching. Ray said he had never really thought about religion before but he found Graham's message to be utterly compelling about our needs in life and God's solution. After the rally, he learnt that Billy Graham was also to preach at Wembley stadium later that summer of 1954. He had pushed his way in among the many thousands who attended and readily joined the throngs who signed up their "decision" that day. Since then he had become certain that his future lay in becoming a Baptist minister with the mission of spreading the Lord's gospel. He had signed up to Oak Hill Theological college, carried out the syllabus of religious studies, passed his finals and was now awaiting confirmation that he would be accepted as a Baptist priest. Ray told me all this while, side by side, we shovelled our way through the trench foundations of the new Keynsham civil centre project. I quizzed Ray about why he had been so seduced by Graham's message. I liked Ray's personality and was impressed by his infectious enthusiasm but we could never reach agreement about the validity of Graham's interpretation of the gospel message. I think Ray found it equally baffling that I wanted to have a full-time career in the British army. We had mutual respect but agreed to disagree about these fundamental issues.

End of Digression

xxx

After about two weeks working on the building site, I received a reply from Headquarters Intelligence Corps informing me that the Corps was indeed recruiting and requested that I attend for an interview the following week in the War Office building, Whitehall.

I had no idea how best to prepare for the interview and could get no advice about this. As I did before the RCB, I bought copies of the serious newspapers and bulled up on current national and world events. Other than ensuring I was up to date on current affairs, I decided just to be myself and hope for the best.

Lying awake on the night before the Intelligence Corps interview, I suddenly had an idea: to contact Lieutenant Colonel (Lt Col) Johnson, the commanding officer of our battalion in Nigeria. He had been the last British CO of the battalion and had handed over his command to a Nigerian officer who had been our CO during our time in the Congo. I had heard Lt Col Johnson had since been promoted to full colonel and assigned to a staff appointment in the War Office Building where my interview was scheduled the next morning. I wondered if he was still working there. I knew he had thought well of me, particularly during our time in the Cameroons. Perhaps he might give me a reference or help in some way.

Next morning, I took the train from Bath Spa to Waterloo station and arrived at the War Office in Whitehall a good hour ahead of the interview time. At the security post, I presented my passport and interview letter and asked if Colonel (Col) Johnson was still working there. To my good fortune, not only was he still in that post but was actually there that morning. He invited me up to his office and I explained about the interview I was to attend. He heard me out then proceeded to press me about the battalion's tour with the UN in the Congo which had begun shortly after he had returned to UK. He had followed the news in the Press with interest but was keen to hear about the details including the full circumstances about the shooting and death of my colleague, Bill Holding. Bill and I had been the last two Brits in the battalion. Col Johnson was in no hurry to end our conversation and I had to excuse myself as the time was approaching for my interview.

I will never know exactly what Col Johnson did or said – only that, after I left his office, he had either gone in person to speak to the Intelligence Corps interview board or had a phone conversation with the board chairman. Either way, when I was called into the interview room, the chairman said he had been contacted by Col Johnson who had given me a glowing testimonial! I can't remember much about the questions I was asked but I felt the interview went well and I left with a good feeling. A few days later, I received a letter from Headquarters, Intelligence Corps informing me I had been provisionally selected for a commission in the Corps, subject to clearance by "positive security vetting". I knew much of this success was due to the intervention of Col Johnson. I was pleased to have thought to contact him, that he happened to be in his office that morning and that he had decided to speak up on my behalf. I shall always be grateful to him.

Digression – Luck

I have often wondered what part "luck" plays in life. In the example above, how lucky I was to have thought, at almost the last moment, to contact Col Johnson, that he was still in the same War Office job, that he would be in his office at that time and day and that he would feel sufficiently well disposed towards me to intervene on my behalf with the Intelligence Corps board. As a result, my professional life was determined for the next thirty years!

Luck, chance, fate. I have two English dictionaries. One defines "luck" as: "Force that brings good fortune or a force that operates against a person or favourable to a person." The other just says: "Fortune good or ill." I'm not sure either definition really applied in my situation. I wondered what others felt about the role that luck has played in their lives. Abraham Lincoln is quoted as saying "The harder I work, the luckier I get" Sounds good but I'm sure many people work and strive really hard but just don't get the breaks.

I like a comment reputedly made by Frank Sinatra: "People often remark that I'm pretty lucky. Luck is only important in so far as getting the chance to sell yourself at the right moment. After that, you've got to have the talent and know-how to use it." That sounds more realistic than Abraham Lincoln's quote in that it implies that luck only grabs the right chance for you. After that, you have to apply yourself to make it work and prove you are worth that luck.

End of Digression

XXX

While I was waiting for the follow up from the Intelligence Corps, I resumed my temporary employment working as a labourer on the building site in Keynsham – a job which lasted through the rest of the sun filled summer of 1963 while the security vetting process was been carried out. I renewed my friendship with Ray Harris. We were both in good spirits. I had been provisionally accepted as a regular officer in the British Army and Ray had heard he had been formally accepted as a trainee Baptist minister. As a result, we were both more relaxed about the direction of our futures. Our labours made us enough cash to support ourselves that summer, restored our physiques and gave us a healthy tan.

Clearly, nothing adverse was found in the vetting process as in early September 1963, I received formal notification that I was to report to the adjutant of the Intelligence Corps at Maresfield Camp, near Uckfield, Sussex on the morning of Monday 23 September. I was offered a commission, on probation for six months, starting with the rank of second lieutenant.

XXX

Chapter Twenty-One

The Intelligence Corps. A New Career

For the next three months, I attended an Intelligence Corps "Young Officers" Course held at the dilapidated military barracks at Maresfield Camp, Uckfield, Sussex. My fellow students were from very diverse backgrounds concerning families, previous experiences and the route we had taken to applying to join the intelligence corps. Underlying our motivation was the serious will to succeed in our new chosen careers in the British Army and to serve our country.

During the day we learnt the principles of sources and management of intelligence at tactical, operational and strategic levels, of photographic interpretation, of signals intelligence and of security principles and planning. In the evenings we would gather in a rambling old Nissan hut which was grandly called the officers' mess where we would drink, tell stories, sing smutty songs and laugh a lot. We had many long and deep discussions about life, its meaning and how we saw the future. As expected, there was no consensus, just enthusiastic anticipation of how our lives would develop in the varying military situations we would face after our intelligence training.

Another major event in my life occurred during that period. I met the woman who was later to become my wife and the mother of our two sons. My life story demands that I devote time exploring marital relationships and the effects they can have on the meaning of life – close, loving, demanding, exasperating, controlling. Emotions of togetherness, understanding, divisiveness, bitterness, temptation, unfaithfulness, guilt. Over the following sixty years, I have experienced and deeply felt many of the above emotions. Better to explore them later rather than at this stage of my story.

xxx

Our Intelligence Corps training course lasted until late December 1963. We were then permitted a few days leave over the Christmas period after which I was told I was to be posted to a security unit in Colchester, Essex where I could consolidate the principles I had been taught. That was the plan but I had only been back at my home in Saltford for one day when early the following morning, a Friday, I had a phone call telling me to report back to Maresfield straight away. As directed, I drove to Maresfield in my trusty Austin A30 wondering what on earth it was about. As soon as I reported in, I was ushered into the office of the imposing Brigadier Bill Vickers, Director Intelligence Corps. The brigadier told me that my Colchester posting was cancelled. Instead, I was to be the officer in charge of an intelligence platoon supporting the headquarters of 51 Gurkha Brigade which that week was being despatched from UK to Brunei, Borneo on operational duties. I was to replace a more senior officer who had just sustained an accident. Brigadier Vickers gave me three instructions. Firstly I was to go immediately to Tidworth military barracks in Wiltshire and report myself to the brigade commander who would give me my specific duties. Secondly, I could expect to be away for at least one year. And thirdly, the move was sensitive and classified: I was to tell no one about this new deployment. No one included my own family and personal friends.

I suppose I should have been annoyed that, with no prior warning, I would have to miss Christmas with my family plus not seeing my new girlfriend and that I would not be able to explain the reason. But inwardly I felt elated. After years of drifting through life – national service, poncing around at Marshall and Snelgrove, then a series of temporary jobs just to keep financially afloat, at last I had been given a real assignment and the chance to prove myself as a regular Intelligence Corps officer. I had only the vaguest idea what the political situation was in Borneo, and I knew nothing about why the British were involved there, or even about the Gurkha Brigade – only that the Gurkha's were Nepalese soldiers who for many years had fought for the British army. I knew they had a fearsome reputation for their bravery. I also had yet to learn what our mission would be, and what might be expected of me.

As instructed, I drove directly from Maresfield, Sussex and eventually found my way to Tidworth, Wiltshire and located the signs for HQ 51

Gurkha Brigade. I pulled up outside the HQ building. It was mid-afternoon. I was still wearing civilian clothes having earlier deposited my army kit at my mother's house in Saltford. I gave my name to the duty officer and produced my military ID. I was then ushered directly into the Brigade Commander's office. It was my first meeting with Brigadier Harry Tuzo, a distinguished officer who, during the next year, I would learn to respect and admire. The brigadier was welcoming and told me he had been expecting me having talked by phone earlier that day to Brigadier Vickers. He told me that he would be flying to Brunei in the next few days. My first mission was to go ahead of him and arrange working and living accommodation prior to his own arrival with his key staff officers. He said that seven seats had been booked on a BOAC flight leaving from Stanstead airport for Singapore that evening. I was to gather any available personnel and together fly to Singapore, then onto Brunei town. He concluded by saying that I was to collect relevant classified documents from his staff and take these with me. These documents explained the background to the political situation and the UK government's involvement. I was to familiarise myself thoroughly with the content of these documents. He looked forward to meeting up with me again in Brunei the next week.

I duly collected and signed for the documents, a briefcase and keys and was given the seven tickets for the flight to Singapore. I was startled to see the flight was due to depart from Stanstead, an airport on the other side of London from Wiltshire, at 2230 hours that same evening. I got directions to my new unit – Intelligence Platoon, 51 Gurkha Infantry Brigade. There were only four personnel on duty in the platoon office, two sergeants and two corporals as, in common with the rest of the British Army, this was the Christmas stand down period. I introduced myself, told them of the mission I had been given and was impressed by their immediate positive response.

During the afternoon, a lot of things happened. I found the Quartermasters' stores and was issued with a basic set of olive-green tropical uniform, arrangements were made for two of the four on-duty Intelligence Corps personnel to accompany me on that evening's flight together with three Gurkha soldiers. A minibus and Gurkha driver were booked to get us to Stanstead. I also reported to another officer, who was to be my immediate staff superior. He was Captain, (soon to be promoted to major) Peter

Morrison. During the next year, Peter was always supportive and mentored me through my inexperience during the early part of our tour in Brunei. I learnt to appreciate his sound judgement and advice. He told me he would accompany our group leaving for Stanstead that evening.

I also phoned my mother, told her I wouldn't be back for Christmas, that I would post her my car keys and details of where the car was parked. I asked her to arrange for the car to be collected and returned back to our home. My mother, calm as always, told me she would fix it.

Our motley little band of hastily assembled personnel drove out of the barracks from Tidworth at 5.30 pm on Friday evening, 20 December 1963 driven by a young Gurkha soldier who had very little experience of driving on UK roads. It was already getting dark and to complicate our journey, it started to rain. As we approached London, the Friday evening traffic built up. We had only a rudimentary road map and none of us had ever been to Stanstead before. Our navigation around the edges of London was challenging and I had every sympathy with our young driver who valiantly struggled on as I tried to give him clear directions. It was already after ten p.m. when eventually we arrived at Stanstead airport and found our way to the departures entrance. Our flight was due to leave in less than half an hour.

As soon as we pulled to a halt, one of our sergeants took the initiative, leapt out and ran through to the BOAC desk. I never knew exactly what he said but he was soon back with a BOAC official in tow who guided us through the runway controls and directly up to the waiting aircraft. With only minutes to spare, we all boarded the plane, leaving our poor young Gurkha driver to find his own way back to Tidworth through the Friday evening rain.

xxx

Istanbul

I felt relieved that we had succeeded in our first mission: to catch the plane. But my relief was premature. Some hours later, the announcement was made that we were descending to land in Istanbul for a routine refuelling stop. By then it was the middle of the night. We stayed in the waiting area until we were told to re-board and were soon underway again. I was hoping to get a few hours' sleep before our next stop. It was not to be. Soon after take-off, the pilot made the announcement that the aircraft had developed a technical fault and would be returning to Istanbul. Soon, we again found ourselves back in the airport waiting area. After over an hour, an announcement was made that the aircraft was unable to continue and a replacement would have to be flown out from the UK. Arrangements had been made for all passengers to be accommodated in local Istanbul hotels at BOAC's expense. My new found military contingent and I were the last names to be called out. Apparently, most hotels were full and the only option was for my team to be accommodated in what we later learned was one of the most expensive hotel in the city. We were allocated to four penthouse suites: one to be occupied by our three Gurkha soldiers, one to be shared by our two Intelligence Corps sergeants and one whole suite each for Peter Morrison and me! We were told that the delay could last up to three days. Having been relieved that we had caught the plane and would fulfil the brigadier's task to be ahead of his arrival, it was now likely that he would arrive in Brunei before us. How our fortunes had changed within the space of a few hours!

Fate can often determine how life can change so quickly! I had to adjust to our new situation. First, that I would not be spending Christmas in UK but instead would be on military operations on the other side of the world. At this point, my new found military colleagues and I had expected to be on route to Brunei via Singapore. Instead fate had landed us in the finest rooms in one of Istanbul's most expensive hotel with all expenses paid – Wow!

When at last we were shown to our rooms, I made a tour, marvelling at the quality of the bedroom, en-suite bathroom and the adjoining sitting room. I had never before seen such a luxurious setup. Still clutching my precious briefcase, I lay on the bed and, through a mix of excitement, bewilderment and exhaustion, crashed out to sleep. When I woke up, the bedside clock said it was four p.m. I found I was still clutching the briefcase. I felt refreshed and decided it was time to open the case, do some serious reading about the political situation in Brunei/Borneo, learn about why the British army was involved there and what our likely mission would be.

In summary, this was what I read. Three months earlier, in September 1963, the Malaysian Federation had been formed. This comprised the Malay Peninsula, Singapore and the states of Sarawak and North Borneo, recently called Sabah, both located in the northern part of the island of Borneo. The larger southern portion of Borneo, called Kalimantan, was part of Indonesia. Brunei, wedged between Sarawak and Sabah, was an independent Sultanate. It retained close links with the UK which, in 1963, still retained responsibility for its defence and foreign affairs. Earlier that year, there had been an uprising in Brunei and the Sultan had called the UK for assistance. This was rapidly provided using British troops stationed in nearby Singapore. The insurrection was put down and the main rebel leaders were either killed or dispersed but there were still pockets of these forces active within Brunei state. The wider issue that most concerned the UK government was that Indonesia's President Soekarno was fiercely opposed to the formation of the Malaysian Federation and was determined to destabilise it. His present tactic termed "confrontation" was an undeclared war waged particularly in the border areas aiming to exploit the ethnic and religious diversity within Sarawak and Sabah. His forces infiltrated from their bases in Kalimantan into the border areas and made attacks on local villages killing many villagers and burning their crops and the "long houses" in which they lived, before withdrawing back across the border. These attacks successfully resulted in intimidating the local indigenous people. After discussion with the Malaysian leaders, the UK had agreed to coordinate the defence of these territories and their peoples against Indonesian aggression. Our headquarters, 51 Gurkha Infantry Brigade was to be deployed to Brunei town and have operational responsibility for Brunei state, 4th and 5th Divisions of Sarawak and the interior (western) residency of Sabah. Our flanking brigades where 99 Gurkha Infantry, based in Kuching, Sarawak and 3rd Malaysian Brigade based in eastern Sabah.

The files in my briefcase also included the latest intelligence about the composition of Indonesian forces. This was very broad brush with little detail below battalion level. Also included were a series of very old maps of the area which I noted had been produced initially by the Dutch. These were detailed along the Borneo coastline but very vague about the interior, much of the map merely shown in green and labelled "jungle"!

Although the information in the files was very general, at least I learnt from them what our mission was all about. I realised I was going to be very busy. But that would be for later.

xxx

Digression – If fate intervenes; enjoy!

I finished my study of the papers by nine p.m., closed the briefcase and wondered what I should do next. I was hungry and decided to try out the hotel restaurant. My immediate problem was what to do with the briefcase and the sensitive papers it contained. I reckoned it would look very odd if I turned up for supper with it permanently tucked under my arm. I decided to take a chance and get the Gurkha soldiers to guard it at least while I got something to eat. I had earlier arranged for them to have separate food prepared and taken to their room and that they would stay there until the replacement plane was ready.

The Gurkhas' room was along the same corridor as mine. I went there and knocked on their door. They were all there, still smartly dressed and alert. I told them that I needed to go out and that they were to look after the locked briefcase. Its security was to be their special responsibility. They told me they would guard it with their lives and I think I believed them. I left the case with them but I still was not sure I was doing the right thing. I waited five minutes then went back and hammered on the Gurkhas' door hiding outside out of sight of the spyhole. Suddenly the door was opened and one of the soldiers appeared brandishing his drawn kukri, the traditional curved knife of the Gurkhas. When he saw it was me, he relaxed and returned the knife into its scabbard. That was my first experience of a Gurkha in action. Now I felt I could relax about the security of the briefcase.

I hoped the hotel restaurant would still be open but I also realised I was in a five plus star hotel and was still dressed in the same casual clothes I had put on the previous morning. Too bad, I was hungry and that was that. I took the lift down to the floor marked "restaurant". I didn't know quite what to expect but it was nothing like the scene I found in front of me. The circular shaped room had large pillars surrounding its perimeter. Tables were arranged around a large centre stage. Lighting was subtle and subdued. Most of the tables were occupied and waiters were moving around them serving their guests. The guests themselves all seemed to be smartly dressed, gentlemen in suits and ties and their ladies in elegant dresses. They all seemed to be middle aged – at least significantly older than me. I felt distantly out of place in my scruffy clothes and decided this was not the place for me. Too late! I was approached by a gentleman wearing an immaculate dinner jacket who introduced himself as the restaurant manager. I didn't blame him when he looked disdainfully at me and asked me what I wanted. I mumbled that I was staying in the hotel and showed him my room key. He looked at the key and his manner abruptly changed. He led me to the front of the centre stage and gestured that I should sit at what was clearly the premier table, situated immediately in front of the stage. The only occupant at the table was Peter Morrison who had beaten me to it and already had started on the complimentary bottle of champagne which was resting in a cooler with glasses which I assumed were made of the best crystal. Peter also put me to shame in that he was smartly dressed in a suit and tie.

I later learnt that Peter and my VIP treatment was solely on account of the rooms we occupied, in our case the most expensive in the hotel. They had been the only available rooms that the BOAC staff could find at the time. I had never tried champagne before and after a couple of glasses I started to relax. I even noticed the guests around me were smiling warmly. Or at least I thought they were. Perhaps they saw me as some sort of eccentric young millionaire. What followed was an evening I shall never forget – excellent food and drinks, prime position for the cabaret which included some exotic dancers all whom had been briefed to pay particularly good attention to the occupants of Table Number One. I vaguely remember staggering up to my room in a daze and feeling ever grateful to the generosity of BOAC!

That day I learnt a good lesson of life. Be flexible and take what fate offers. You never know what might be round the next corner! I learnt that if you find yourself in unforeseen circumstances through events outside your ability to influence, try to be positive and find some way to turn things round to your advantage.

End of Digression

xxx

The next day, the two sergeants, McVeigh and Samways, had arranged for us to be taken on a tour of Istanbul; provided free by the management of our up-market hotel, minibus and guide included. This was my first real contact with Intelligence Corps NCOs who I would be fortunate to work with throughout the next year, and then for many years more. We spent much of the day exploring the magical city of Istanbul, visiting the Blue Mosque, with its thousands of blue hand-crafted tiles and taking coffee at a terrace overlooking the bridge spanning the two sides of the Bosporus which marks the boundary between Europe and Asia. Our tour included visits to the Galata Tower and the architectural wonder of Hagia Sophia. We strolled through the narrow passageways of the Grand Bazaar being pressed by insistent traders to buy their goods. They got no sales from any of our group, I fear, as we were very conscious of the fleeting transitory nature of our bonus time in this amazing city.

The following morning we were told that the replacement plane was due to arrive in Istanbul shortly and we were to reassemble at the airport. After two further days we eventually reached Brunei town, a full day after Brigadier Tuzo and his staff. I had failed my first mission in the Intelligence Corps which was to prepare for his arrival. Fortunately he was gracious enough to forgive me and in fact to laugh it off when I stammered my apology. He had already been informed about the defective aircraft in Istanbul and that we had been stuck there for reasons beyond our control.

xxx

Borneo operations

Shortly after our Brigade HQ arrived in Brunei, we learnt that the Indonesians had stepped up their infiltration attacks against local inhabitants in Sarawak and Sabah, in many cases leaving behind them a trail of death and destruction. Most of the local population lived in communal family "long houses". Several of these in the border areas had been attacked by Indonesian forces, their "long houses" burnt and destroyed, the men killed and their women and girls forced to flee or taken prisoner to be used as captive slaves back over the border. It was assessed that Soekarno's political objective was to use these savage tactics to destabilise the newly formed Malaysian Federation.

Comment. It was only some years later, that I fully appreciated Soekano's many positive qualities as outlined in Part One above. In 1964, the British were allied to Malaysia and therefore was strongly opposed to Indonesia's actions in Borneo.

Our mission was to counter the Indonesian attacks and restore security, stability and confidence to the local people. To fulfil this mission, we first had to have accurate tactical intelligence about the attacking Indonesian forces, their organization, their capabilities, strengths and weaknesses, their tactics and their weapons systems. Once we knew all the above, our own troops could provide protection to the local indigenous people, neutralise the threats against them and enable them to live their lives again in peace and security.

It was a steep learning curve during my first few months in Brunei. The briefing papers from the briefcase that I had been given back in UK, were mostly out of date. We had to start virtually with a blank sheet to gain intelligence about the Indonesian forces opposing us in the border areas. But even before we could commence our information gathering programme, we had to understand more about our operational area: the terrain, the precise geography between Malaysian Sarawak/Sabah and Indonesian side known as Kalimantan.

The only maps we inherited had been drawn up by Dutch cartographers many years before which had absolutely no detail about the interior of vast jungle clad interior of Borneo island. We were fortunate to have Staff Sergeant (SSgt) Philip Brown as part of our Intelligence Platoon. Philip was a trained photographic interpreter and a skilled artist. His initial task was to produce mapping by scaling aerial photos of the area and producing temporary maps to 1:50,000 scale, later reducing to 1:25,000. The early drafts of these maps were relatively light on detail but we issued these to all foot patrols, special forces, the crews of any aircraft flying over the area and to trusted indigenous locals. Each time, Philip tasked them to check the draft maps and give us feedback and comments on their accuracy. Where errors occurred or more confirmed detail could be given, Philip made further drafts and reissued these until there was consensus as to their accuracy. We then produced a final draft which became the accepted mapping "bible" of the whole of our operational area.

Once we established with a good degree of accuracy where the border was and the terrain detail of the main features in our operational area, we could then accelerate the process of gathering intelligence about the composition of Indonesian forces opposing our operational area and where their most likely future attacks would be mounted. This process involved using the strategic intelligence overview we received from HQ Borneo Operations based in Labuan island, which included signals intercept, and adding the results of our own air reconnaissance, our patrols and building up our networks of the local sources we recruited, whose reliability we tested thoroughly before accepting any information they provided; then by integrating all the above, we gradually built up an intelligence picture. Our task was then to produce daily verbal briefings to Brigadier Tuzo and his operations staff and written intelligence summaries (Intsums) sent to all our supporting troops.

It took some months before our intelligence was sufficient to be able to make accurate intelligence-based predictions but Brigadier Tuzo gave us both his personal support and the provision of the resources we needed. The initial collecting, collating and interpreting process was a period of solid graft for my team and I learnt to respect the skills and professionalism of our Intelligence Corps soldiers. I must have done something right because, in early April 1964, Brig Tuzo told me that my probation period had expired, that he had sent back a good report of my work and I had now been accepted for a permanent commission in the Intelligence Corps and promoted to full lieutenant. It was a relief to know that at last I had a fulfilling job with a long-term future! I felt highly motivated by the challenges of our situation in Borneo and realised that I was in the right job at the right time.

xxx

Our major military constraint at that time was that our forces were under strict political orders to restrict our operations to the Malaysian side of the border. By mid/late 1964, our military commanders argued that we could achieve a far greater degree of protection for Malaysians in Sarawak and Sabah if we could attack the Indonesian forces in their own bases over the border particularly now that we had built up good intelligence about the locations and composition of Indonesian forward base camps. In order to mount any cross-border attack we would require specific political authorisation.

The visitors from Whitehall

From my very junior rank at that time, I was not privy to the higher-level discussions that took place in late 1964, when our military commanders requested political authorisation to mount cross border attacks into Indonesian Kalimantan. My first personal involvement was in early December when I was told that there was to be a political delegation visiting in a week's time and that I was to give the intelligence briefing about the composition of major Indonesian forces in northern Kalimantan facing our operational front. I was to give particular reference to the settlement of Lumbis as we had established this was the main Indonesian forces base from which incursions were made across the border into Sarawak.

Of political relevance was that a General Election had been held in the UK in October 1964, which was narrowly won by the Labour Party. Prime

Minister Harold Wilson appointed Denis Healey to be Secretary of State for Defence and Frederick Mulley to be Minister of State for the Army/Deputy Secretary of Defence. It was Mr Mulley and his aides who would visit us in our Brunei brigade headquarters.

In the briefing room of our brigade HQ in Brunei, Sergeant McVeigh produced a model of the Lumbis base camp working from confirmed collateral intelligence. The model included all buildings, and perimeter defences. Alongside the model we made detailed mapping of the area between the base camp, the border, the closest Malaysian villages and our own forward troop positions. These visual aids were the templates for our briefing to our political visitors.

Mr Mulley and his entourage's visit was not without drama. The month of December is in the midst of the rainy season in Brunei and our VIP visitors were delayed due to a heavy monsoon storm on the day of their arrival. The temperature was just over thirty degrees; as hot and humid as it is all year round. Eventually their helicopter from Labuan was able to land in Brunei town and the party was transferred to a convoy of Land Rovers from the airstrip to our brigade HQ. On route, the visitors were bombarded by penetrating torrential rain. Brigadier Tuzo and his staff did their best to make our bedraggled visitors as welcome as was possible under the circumstances. Our political visitors comprised Mr Mulley himself, a bespectacled studious looking gentleman and his team of advisors, a mix of (to me) middle aged ladies and gentlemen. Somehow, they had been kitted out with olive green tropical uniforms and bush hats which were sodden through when eventually they made the sanctuary of our dry HQ building. With their December lily white skins, they had come directly from a cold winter's day in London to the tropical humid heat of Brunei. We all did our best to comfort them with cups of tea and cordials. They declined our offer of a change of clothes and slowly steamed away during our conference as they dried themselves out.

The visitors had been accompanied from Labuan by the overall British military commander of our operations in Borneo, General Walter Walker and several of his staff officers. General Walker had a formidable reputation, not least for his knowledge of the intelligence process and its value. This was the first time I had met him and was duly impressed by his clipped air of authority.

This was the background to the presentation we gave to the UK Secretary of Defence. When all our sodden guests were seated, General Walker gave some short welcoming remarks, then handed over to Brigadier Tuzo. The brigadier set the political and military background and summarised the recent operational contacts resulting from Indonesian incursions. He stressed that although our Gurkha troops had succeeded in ambushing several of these incursions and driving the aggressors back over the border, our troops could only ever react to events. We were constrained by the political order not to cross over the border. In order to stabilise the situation, provide more permanent protection to the local people, to seize the initiative and put Soekarno's Indonesia on the defensive, it would be necessary to carry out limited and targeted attacks on the Indonesians own bases. Hence our request for political authorisation.

Mr Mulley then spoke about wider British aims in the Far East, namely to give political support to the development of the newly formed Malaysian Federation but not to get involved in a major conflict with Soekarno's regime. The UK government would need to be convinced of success before authorising any cross-border actions. Additionally, any such operations would need to be strictly limited in scope and conducted under tight security. Mr Mulley stressed that the UK needed to be seen merely to be in support of Malaysian forces as the UK progressively withdrew from any direct conflict. Above all, the UK would not engage in any messy fighting that could detract from the above strategy.

Brigadier Tuzo resumed by saying that we believed that a direct attack on one base, i.e. Lumbis, could succeed in striking a major blow to Soekarno's troops with minimal risk to our own. He stressed that the area was isolated from outside observation particularly from the world's press. He introduced me as "his" intelligence officer. I was relieved that this briefing came only after we had been in Borneo for several months and we had the time to build up our intelligence picture. By that time I knew my subject thoroughly and had, though temporally, lost my stammer!

My briefing revolved around the detailed model we had made of Lumbis and its defences. The briefing became more of a discussion session as Mr Mulley, and at times General Walker, interrupted with a series of questions. Eventually, the session concluded with Mr Mulley saying to me: "That was a good, clear briefing Lieutenant, but before I can agree to any attack, I have one question – are you absolutely certain of all these details about Lumbis?" I was rather taken aback by this and could only reply, "No, sir, not absolutely certain because I have never personally been to Lumbis. But am I absolutely sure that our intelligence is accurate, then Yes, I am." That was the end of the briefing.

Soon after our VIP visitors had left on route back to Whitehall, General Walker contacted Brigadier Tuzo to tell him that we had authorisation to attack the base at Lumbis. This was to be limited to Lumbis only and to be conducted with full security. Brigadier Tuzo acted without delay. He ordered Sgt McVeigh and me to set up the briefing model at the HQ of the Gurkha company that had been designated as the attack unit. Here, we carried out briefings with the company officers covering both details of the Lumbis basecamp defences and the optimal routes to and across the border. I was at last performing the task I had been trained to do – to provide timely and accurate tactical intelligence for a specific offensive operation.

The Gurkha company carried out the attack with their customary professionalism which achieved total surprise and success. Our intelligence proved to be completely accurate in every detail! The Lumbis attack was the first cross border operation in our brigade area. It was followed later by other such operations, known under the code name Operation Claret, both in our area and those of our two flanking brigades in north Borneo.

In mid-January, I received notification from HQ Intelligence Corps that my tour of duty in Brunei was shortly to end. A replacement, Lieutenant Bob Langstaff, had been nominated to replace me and I was to hand over to him on 1 February 1965. That ended my first operational tour as a now substantive Intelligence Corps officer.

The "meaning of life" to me then was the feeling of satisfaction that, by our actions, the British military had done a superb job of restoring confidence and peace to those villagers living close to the border area with Indonesian Kalimantan. Not only did our operations succeed in reducing and eventually halting cross border attacks by Indonesian forces in our sector but, with the assistance of our engineers, the local people were able to rebuild their village long houses and return to the type of peaceful lives they had previously enjoyed. I was proud to have played a part in this successful mission. That was enough.

xxx

Malaysia: Rest and Recuperation

Although all of us in HQ 51 Gurkha Infantry Brigade worked long hours often with very little sleep over extended periods, life wasn't all about work. Brigadier Tuzo ensured that all his staff got frequent physical exercise and, about every six months, were given a week's break, aptly called "rest and recuperation (R&R)."

Digression: R & R – a ski too far.

Brunei Town is only a short drive away from the sea and the calm waters of Brunei Bay. Peter Morrison and I had written to the Nuffield Trust in UK, giving a sob story about us being hard pressed soldiers on operational duty and without any decent sports facilities. We had asked if the Trust could see its way to providing any water ski equipment. We heard nothing for a while then, to our surprised delight, we received a delivery of: one Gemini boat, one Evenrude 500 engine, water skis and associated equipment. We notified everyone in our Brigade Headquarters of our treasure saying it would be for the use of all ranks but the only ones interested to ski were Peter, me and Andrew Carter a Signals Regiment officer and my, by then, good friend and fellow lieutenant. My platoon was issued with a Land Rover and trailer so, whenever we had any free time, we would hitch up the boat and head for Brunei Bay. The conditions for water skiing there were outstanding. None of the three of us had previous experience but soon we became very proficient – first learning to stay upright on two skis, then to perform ever more complex manoeuvres on the two skis and then just one. Later, we graduated to tricks on a circular board and finally to performing without skis at all, just using the soles of our feet. The morale of this episode was: "Never look a gift horse in the mouth!"

Everyone looked forward to the time when our turn came round for R&R. I managed to get my one week off at the same time as Andrew Carter. We were allocated seats on an RAF flight back to Singapore then were on our own. We decided to explore as much of Malaya as we could pack into our week's freedom. We boarded a train at Johor Bharu which trundled its way through the Malay peninsula, dropping us off at the far north east town of Kota Bharu. After a day's sight-seeing there, we hired a four-by-four van and drove down the length of the east coast.

Somewhere between Kuala Terengganu and Kuantan, we came across a brand-new luxury hotel, so new in fact that it had not then even opened to the public. It was situated right on the beach and we noticed that it advertised water skiing trips. After our developed skills in Brunei bay, Andrew and I took the chance to ski here. We negotiated a price with the manager who provided us with a brand-new boat with full ski equipment together with a three-man crew. As soon as we were away from the shore, Andrew and I jumped in the sea, fitted our skis, signalled to the boat driver to pull away and were soon upright and enjoying the experience. The boat roared along with Andrew and I in tow. The sea was choppy and needed some care but we found it exhilarating. Our free-time in Brunei Bay had made us both competent water-skiers and we enjoyed testing ourselves in the open sea. We practised crossing manoeuvre realising that here with choppy waves, more care is needed to perform such techniques.

After about half an hour, we began to tire and signalled to the crew to slow so that we could dismount, climb aboard and head back to the hotel. There is a universally understood sign to stop – to use one hand in a circular movement above the head – meaning “stop now”. However, our gallant crew clearly had not been taught this protocol. The driver was continuing to head further and further away from the shore. All three of the crew were facing forward: none even glanced back in our direction. We were now a long way out to sea. Skiing became more difficult as the sea turned increasingly rough. Our trip had begun as a fun ride but not anymore. We kept trying to attract the crew’s attention as we continued ever further from the coast. Then, suddenly, the driver turned round, saw our signal and decided to respond. But he overreacted and swung the control wheel too abruptly which tipped the boat sharply on its side throwing all the crew overboard. Andrew and I both had to let go of the ski ropes and start swimming. We looked up to see that the unmanned boat had righted itself with its engine still running on full throttle. The steering had jammed and the boat was leaping around in a continuous circle. Andrew was stuck in the middle of that circle and I noticed he was holding up one of the crew members. I found myself outside the circling boat’s radius, with the other two crew members close by. One of them could swim but was shrieking with fright, the other was lying face down in the water. I managed to swim over to him and hold his head up in “life-saving mode”.

Our fun trip had suddenly become a seriously dangerous situation. We were stuck out in the middle of the ocean. From my wave top position, I could just make out the shoreline. It seemed a very long way away! Even if I tried to swim back to shore with my non swimming Malay and could encourage the second to come with us, there was still the major problem of Andrew plus one who were trapped inside the circle of the bucking boat. There was no way I could leave them there.

I was treading water while holding up the one crewmember and trying to keep the other calm. The waves were steadily getting even rougher. There was another concern. We were stuck in the middle of the ocean and I had no idea whether this was a shark frequented area. I then realised, far too late, that we had no safety equipment such as life jackets and it now seemed that the crew were completely inexperienced and had been given no training. I was beginning to tire as, while still treading water, I had to continue propping up the non-swimming crew member. I knew that if we continued as we were, I would have to let him go or we would both drown. We were, as they say, in the shit!

I considered whether to try to strike out for the shore and then to get back to the hotel, summon help go and rescue Andrew but we had the only boat the hotel owned and the hotel was stuck in the middle of nowhere. A rescue mission could take hours to organise – far too long to save Andrew and the third crewmember. In any case, the light was already beginning to fade and soon we would have the added problem of darkness.

The boat continued to buck and swerve as it completed each circle around Andrew. He was a fit man and an accomplished swimmer but there was a limit to anyone's ability to keep afloat in those conditions. I wondered if perhaps he might try to swim out beyond the radius of the circling boat, a manoeuvre which would require precise timing. If he were to get his timing wrong, he would be crushed by the boat and would have no chance of survival. Also, he would have to relay his intentions to the third crew member. Andrew didn't speak Malay nor did the crewman speak English!

After what seemed an age, a miracle happened. The engine of the bouncing, throbbing boat suddenly cut out and the boat slurred to a stop. It had run out of petrol! With great relief Andrew and his crewmember swam to the side of the boat: Andrew managed to pull himself aboard and was there to help me and our three charges also onto the boat. For a while we just slumped down utterly exhausted. We realised we had come close to dying and couldn't have existed out there in the choppy open sea much longer. Our three crewmen had collapsed on the floor of the boat, the one I had been supporting became violently sick then collapsed in an unconscious heap on the floor of the boat.

We searched the boat, hoping to find reserve jerrycans of petrol. There were none. Nor were any life jackets, reserve water or any other safety items such as oars or emergency flares. The boat was bobbing around freely in the choppy sea as the evening gloom transitioned steadily into night. At least we were out of the sea but still not out of danger. Andrew and I examined the engine. It was a new Johnson model, probably this was its first outing.

It was of similar design to the Evenrude we used in Brunei, which had a small reserve petrol compartment that could be switched on when the main tank was empty. We checked and both gave sighs of relief when we found this engine also had a small fuel reserve. We switched over to this reserve and pulled on the starter cord. Nothing happened. Pulled again, same result. Nothing! We checked the connections and found the main spark plug had become dislodged probably due to the boat's violent movement during its circling manoeuvres. We refitted the plug and tried pulling the starter cord again. To our enormous relief, the engine finally spluttered into life. At last we could get going.

By this time it was fully dark but we could just make out the lights of the hotel in the distance. As we headed back towards the shore, we even managed to retrieve three of the four skis that were floating in the water. During our return trip, the three Malay crewmen still remained slumped out on the floor decking.

It was about eight p.m. when eventually we found our way back to the mooring area from where we had set out some hours before. The three Malays were all just conscious and we encouraged them to help us stow the boat safely and to store the skis and towing equipment away. Andrew and I then returned to the hotel, summoned the manager and related all that had occurred, we ended saying that all his staff were returned safely as were the boat, equipment and three of the four skis. We told him that it was imperative that the crew should be given proper training and that the boat should be fitted with safety equipment before any further clients were invited to ski.

We expected that the manager would at the least show concern and some sort of gratitude that his staff and his boat had been safely returned. We were wrong. All he said was that we had been out longer than we had paid for and he would also have to add the cost of the one missing ski! Not a word about the welfare of his crew whose lives we had saved. Andrew and I had planned to stay the night here. Not any more – we declined paying any extra, warned the manager we would be reporting his remarks to the local police, got back to our van and left. When we were clear of the hotel, we stopped to change our still wet clothes then found a spot on the beach and, with relief that we had survived the day, we both lay down and fell asleep. The next day we drove down the Malayan coast to the hire car agent in Kuantan, took the train to Johor Bahru, on to Singapore and back to Brunei town via a transit in Labuan. Then straight back to work!

That water-skiing incident highlighted for me again "The Meaning of Life" and what might have happened if that boat had continued its circling and Andrew, I and the three Malay crew had perished. But we had all survived – just! Andrew and I briefly discussed this before we crashed out to sleep that evening. We were both, sort of (!) Christians, the three Malays were all Muslim. Would all five of us have just drifted out of life as we drowned and our lives perished or would our respective faiths have taken over and our souls or spirits or consciousness (or whatever) have separately moved on to some other place. Andrew and I briefly contemplated these deep thoughts. Of course we had no answer and our exhaustion soon took over as we drifted off to sleep. Next day we had forgotten all about the incident as we got on with a new adventure.

End of Digression

xxx

Gizèle

A year earlier, before leaving for Borneo, I had met the woman who was later to become my wife. She was French and was teaching in a UK private girls' school as a French Mademoiselle. During the year I was away, we continuously wrote to each other, our letters taking at least one week each way to arrive. One could say our romance was principally conducted by post, enforced by my posting to Borneo. During that year, I realised that I was no longer a young man. My army commission had been confirmed and I now had the prospect of a settled future and income. In one of my letters to Gizèle I suggested that we might get married. By return, she accepted. Back in UK, my sister got involved and in her tidy, efficient and rather bossy style, she made all arrangements for us to be married as soon as I returned to England. Ahead of me I could visualise a more settled period. No more chasing around as a free-spirited bachelor as I would have to learn to live with one person as a married man. Yet I really didn't know much about my future wife as we had spent very little time physically together. In one of her letters Gizèle had told me she was Catholic but I hadn't considered that might have implications for our future. We were both Christian so what did the denomination matter? Or so I thought at that time.

In this book, to spare any embarrassment to those who knew her, I refer to my wife as "Gizèle", though that was not her real name.

I had been told that I could have ten days leave after returning to UK then I was to be posted to a security appointment in British Army of the Rhine (BAOR) in Germany. As soon as my return flight from Borneo arrived back in RAF Brise Norton, I headed directly to London where Gizèle was staying with a friend, having given up her teaching job so that we could at least spend a little time (two days!) getting to know each other again before becoming man and wife. We were both nervous with each other and in hindsight we absolutely should have been bold enough to postpone our wedding until we were really sure we were doing the right thing. But there you go! That would have spoiled all the careful arrangements made by my sister and somehow neither of us felt we should wait and disrupt all my caring sister's arrangements. So, we didn't cancel. On 20 February we walked down the aisle of the little catholic church in Maldon, Essex and made our vows. Gizèle's brother Frank, flew over from France to give his sister away. That was it. We were a married couple.

After a brief reception in Essex, Gizèle and I headed for Heathrow airport and stayed overnight in a hotel there. The next morning, we caught an early flight to Paris, then one train to Lyons and another to Saint Claude in the Jura region, Gizèle's family home. The train arrived in the evening where we were met at the station by Gizèle's father. Being February, and Saint-Claude being in a mountainous region, we found ourselves in a wonderworld of deep snow, quite a contrast to the humid 30 plus degrees of heat the jungle in Brunei that I had just left! This was my first time in France, with a new wife I hardly knew and able to speak only schoolboy

French. Her family spoke no English. Gizèle's mother was a warm and charming lady who made me feel very welcome as her daughter's husband. We got on really well despite our limited conversations! We spent the remainder of my leave in Saint Claude, with Gizèle and I getting to know each other better and to learn more about each other's characters, habits, likes and dislikes. I think we did a good job but, perhaps not wanting so early in our relationship to venture into sensitive issues, we did not then discuss our religious views or any other subject of potential discord. I looked forward to being with her at the start of a new experience for us both. I hoped that she felt the same. After my few rushed days with my new wife, I had to hotfoot it back to UK, then onwards to my new job in Germany. I left Gizèle still in Saint Claude, telling her I would try to arrange accommodation for us once I was settled in the new job. It would be the first time either of us would be in Germany.

xxx

Chapter Twenty-Two

Germany: Fallingbostel, Minden

Fallingbostel

Headquarters Intelligence Corps had sent me a "Posting Order" for my next appointment. It was very brief and merely told me I was to be posted to 5 Security Company, based in Hannover, Germany. I was to report on Wednesday 24 February to Major Keith Stevens, the Officer Commanding. My Posting Order entitled me to book a RAF flight from Brize Norton to Gütersloh, where I found a train went directly to Hannover. From the station there, I took a taxi to the address I was given, arriving, again in deep snow, at six thirty p.m. on 24 February. I reported to my new boss who I learnt had been expecting me earlier and was somewhat put out at my late arrival. Not a good start!

I found Major Stevens difficult to characterise. He was a tall, slim, good-looking man in his forties. He was pleasant enough and welcoming but instead of asking about my background etc, his first question was whether I could speak German. When I replied that I could not, he launched into a lecture on the three definite German articles: der, die and das. He took the examples of: der löffel, die gabel and das messer (spoon, fork, knife). I duly recited these words back to him not sure where this basic German lesson was leading. There was another thing. I noticed that behind his desk, and also elsewhere in his office were miniature statues of Chinese Buddhas. They seemed completely out of place here in Germany but I didn't like then to ask him why he kept them there. Later, I learnt that the major was a Chinese specialist and a leading expert on Buddha statues. Apparently, the sitting posture of Buddha is considered to be that of love and it symbolizes balance between thought and tranquillity. All very interesting but not what I was expecting sitting here in a wintry Hanover. I couldn't help wondering why the British military had sent a Chinese specialist like Major Stevens to a senior security post in Germany. Come to think of it, I was wondering why they had also sent me!

Comment: Major Stevens, together with a Nepalese colleague later initiated me into many of the wonders and mystiques of the Buddhist faith.

Major Stevens told me I was to be based, at least initially, in Fallingbostel, Niedersachen (some hundred kilometres north of Hanover). He said there was a vehicle with driver standing by to take me to accommodation booked for me that evening. He handed me a pile of papers which he said would bring me up to date with the major political and security issues involving British Forces in Germany and told me to study these closely. He also told me that a guy called Jan Zielinski was based in Fallingbostel and had been there for several years. He would meet me the next morning and fill me in on the job that needed to be done there. I was to learn all I could from Zielinski. I could tell that Major Stevens was impatient to end our meeting so I thanked him, picked up the package of briefing papers, told him I would do my best and left to link up with the duty driver. The drive to Fallingbostel was slow as the driver battled his way through a snow storm and it was after midnight when eventually I was installed in my new home – a plain, but warm room in the Officers Mess in Lumsden Barracks, Fallingbostel. As I fell asleep, I wondered what the hell I had got myself into.

The next morning, I had just polished off a very acceptable breakfast, when the steward told me a gentleman was asking for me. He was dressed in typical German civilian winter clothing with a tweed suit covered by a thick winter anorak. He was, I thought, in his late forties/early fifties, was rather plump and had a round face with a ruddy complexion. He greeted me with a warm infectious smile which I found he used frequently. This was my first meeting with Jan Zielinski.

Zielinski led me to a battered old VW Beetle and we roared off through the snow-covered streets pulling up outside a plain building in the middle of the town. This, he explained, was our office. He introduced me to a couple of guys in civilian clothes, who were both Intelligence Corps corporals and to the unit's secretary, a lady named Frau Ilse Becker. Frau Becker was a neat, polished, well-preserved lady in, I guessed, her fifties. She spoke excellent English with a clipped, precise, Teutonic accent. She was employed as our unit's secretary but, Zielinski explained, she had been with the unit for some eight years, had a deep personal knowledge of the Niedersachen area and added much more value than just her secretarial expertise. Zielinski said that he himself was a Polish national by birth but had now been registered with German nationality. As a young man he had been in the Polish Army but his unit been disbanded after the war and he had found himself a refugee. He had made his way to the western allied zone ending up in Hamburg where he met and married a German lady. He had volunteered to work for the British Army as an interpreter as he spoke Russian, German and English in addition to his native Polish. He had been with the British Army ever since and had been accepted as what was termed a Locally Employed Civilian (LEC). I immediately liked Zielinski and felt we would work together well. I would be relying heavily on his experience and knowledge not only about my new job but also about his fascinating life in eastern Europe.

My new world was a total contrast to the previous one. Before, I had had to learn the skills of tactical intelligence in a low intensity war zone in the steamy tropical heat of Borneo. Now I had to adjust to understanding the complexity of the "cold war" in Germany and the security challenges to the British Army of the Rhine (BAOR). I wouldn't have known where to begin without Zielinski and his team.

This is a resumé of the main global political events at that time:

- The relations in 1965 between the western democratic countries, the Soviet Union and its Warsaw Pact Allies remained strained.
- The threat from Communist China was growing particularly its confrontation with the US which led to an increasing participation of US forces in Vietnam.
- The Cuban crisis had occurred in October 1962 and President John F Kennedy had been assassinated in November 1963. Last year, 1964, Leonid Brezhnev had replaced Khrushchev as Soviet leader and Lyndon B Johnson had been confirmed as President of the US.

I needed to study the geography of the demarcation line here in Germany, which stretched from the Baltic to the Adriatic seas. Main points were:

- The forces of the NATO allies were deployed with areas of military responsibility covered by the Dutch and German Corps to the north of our 1st British Corps sector and the Belgian, a second German Corps and two US Corps to the south.
- Within our own Corps area, HQ BAOR was based near the Dutch border in Rheindahlen and HQ 1 British Corps in Bielefeld in the district of nordrhein westfalen.
- Our Divisional HQs were: 1st in Verden, close to our location here in Fallingbostel, 2nd in Lübbecke, and 4th in Herford.

I learnt from the briefing papers and my conversations with Jan Zielinkski that there were two main aspects to my new job.

- The first was to understand all the ground rules of physical security – designation of key areas or zones of particular sensitivity – for example: units holding nuclear assets, units where war plans were held and discussed and signals intelligence units. We needed to ensure control of access procedures were clear and observed, that physical security measures such as alarms, sensors and fences were in place and properly maintained.
- The second was to understand and investigate the main threats to our security posed by hostile intelligence agencies such as the Soviet KGB and NKVD and the East German Stasi organisation. Jan Zielinski was a mine of information. He narrated examples of recent identified spying cases targeted against British assets and he brought me up to date concerning the present cases under investigation.

Jan Zielinski was a truly valuable asset. He had great knowledge and experience. Also he had his limitations. He had hardly written any information down and his filing system was almost non-existent. I would have to instigate more formal report writing procedures and ensure that our work was properly disseminated. Jan seemed only too pleased for me to give his work more organisation. I also wondered if I could trust him completely. His work here in Fallingbostel appeared to have been largely unsupervised and unchallenged by higher British authorities. But in my present state of ignorance, how could I possibly tell if he was hundred per cent loyal to British interests? For now, I would have accept the situation as it was but start to build up contacts of my own.

xxx

There was also the question of Gizèle. I wanted her to join me here as soon as possible but was told it could be some months before a British military house would be available. Frau Becker seemed to have taken up my case when, about three weeks after starting my job here, she told me she had found an alternative solution; a friend of hers, Frau Müller, whose husband was a local policeman with the Bundeskriminalamt, (German Federal Police) had an apartment in the upper floor of their house. It was free at the moment and she and her husband were willing to rent it to me. I immediately accepted and straightaway phoned my new wife and made arrangements for her to join me on the next possible flight. I thought that Gizèle didn't sound too enthusiastic but she agreed to come. I arranged a flight from Geneva (one hour's drive from her home in Saint-Claude) to Hanover.

I was excited waiting at Hanover airport. This was to be the start of our married life living and sharing our fortunes together. After such a limited and interrupted romance, I hoped we could learn to bond well and build a successful and loving marriage.

It didn't start well. It was now mid-March but still deep winter in northern Germany. Her flight was due to land at Hanover Flughaven at eight p.m. It was delayed due to bad weather and eventually touched down at nine thirty p.m. Gizèle had had trouble collecting her cases and didn't appear into the arrivals hall until nearly another hour later. I had borrowed Jan Zielinski's VW Beetle and had difficulty stuffing all Gizèle's bags on the back seat and the small front boot. Jan was not the tidiest of men. This was reflected in the state of his car which, Gizèle observed, smelt of stale garlic and bockwurst sausages! We had to battle against thick swirling snow for most of the drive up to Fallingbostel, I then had a blind-spot as I temporally lost the way to the apartment. When finally we arrived and I had lugged all the bags up the steep stairs, it was well after midnight. During our drive, I had tried to sound positive and light but I could tell Gizèle was underwhelmed by our situation. I couldn't blame her! She told me she was exhausted and only wanted to go to bed and sleep. I realised there would be no passionate reunion or lovemaking that night! At least the apartment was dry and warm!

XXX

Slowly, I began to make sense of my new job. I made contacts with all the existing security agencies that linked to my area of responsibility. Through Jan's introduction, I met the local German security organisations: the BND – BundesNachrichtenDienst – the Federal Intelligence service and the local chief of the BKA – Bundeskriminalamt. From these organisations I learnt about the activities of local Soviet and other Communist Intelligence agencies who had or were targeting British security interests. I always tried to ask similar questions to each of these agencies and to check their answers for consistency – a technique of collateral we regularly used in Borneo. I also started a "teach yourself" German course.

In mid-April, Major Stevens held a meeting for all his sub units. This was the first time I met my opposite numbers based in Minden and Detmold and I learned how they operated and the particular issues they faced in their areas. Captain Forster's unit in Minden seemed particularly interesting. Not only did he have security responsibility for the major military units of HQ 1St British Corps but also he told me he and his wife were lodged in military housing in the pleasant town of Minden.

Winter didn't lose its icy grip in Fallingbostel during the months of March or early April nor I fear did my relationship with Gizèle flourish. She was trying to adjust to our life here in the north of Germany. She didn't find it easy and I completely understood. As a French woman, she didn't speak the German language and our neighbours had no French and even very few spoke rudimentary English. Gizèle's nature and background did not blend easily with the somewhat tight and industrious ways of the Niedersachen people. She found living here reminded her of the sound of the jackboots of marching Nazi soldiers during her childhood in wartime Saint-Claude.

What was more, she had not felt well prior to her leaving to fly to Germany, had consulted her local doctor and was told she was pregnant!

In early May, we had a lucky break. Captain Forster called me to say that he was having to leave Minden at short notice. He was an Arabic linguist and was being transferred to a new assignment in the Middle East requiring his language skills. He told me he was currently handling some very sensitive security cases involving HQ 1st British Corps that needed prompt action to be resolved. He said Major Stevens was very concerned that the post would be left vacant for some time until a replacement for him could be found. He asked if I would be interested to switch jobs from Fallingbostel to Minden. He reckoned also that I could take over not only his job but also his married quarter house. I didn't hesitate. Although I was just getting to grips with the my present job, a move to Minden had many attractions. Not only was the job there more demanding and interesting but also, the big deal was that in Minden I could provide a far better lifestyle for Gizèle. I straightaway called Major Stevens to tell him about my conversation with Captain Forster and that I was interested to switch jobs. The major seemed relieved that an immediate answer could be found. He told me he would formally recommend me for the switch. A few days later this was confirmed. The twists of fate! I couldn't imagine Gizèle ever being able to settle in Fallingbostel. Now, our new move to Minden seemed to have far better potential for our future together. Not only did we have the prospect of living together in a decent house but on the same day that Major Stevens gave me news of the move, the first daffodils of spring began to bloom. Or so it seemed!

XXX

Minden

I had bought my own car in Fallingbostel, another VW Beetle, second hand of course! I loaded up our few belongings, bade farewell to Jan Zielinski and the 11 CI Det team and Gizèle and I then headed for our new home in Minden. We both liked our new house which was a "military married quarter" grouped with about twenty similar properties, the remainder all being occupied by fellow British officers of similar rank and age. Our new neighbours and their wives did their best to make us, and particularly Gizèle, welcome. There were other wives who also were pregnant or recently had been. They assured Gizèle that there was good local medical support and she would be well cared for during her pregnancy and giving birth. I hoped that now Gizèle could be more relaxed and learn to adjust and enjoy her new life.

The unit in Minden was headed up by Sergeant-Major Gosney. Although he was British and in the Intelligence Corps, Gosney's background was in some ways similar to Jan Zielinski. He also had a German wife and had remained in the same job for several years. He was our "Mr continuity" who, like Jan, had long well-established contacts with the local national agencies. There were three Intelligence Corps corporals, all bright motivated guys, who I soon learnt were as professional and easy to get on with as all those I had worked with in Borneo. Our office was in an old German military barracks in the middle of Minden town – within easy reach from my new house.

It had been a good move. What was more, the weather had completely changed with the coming of early summer. The sun shone most of the time and the temperature was balmy. Everyone seemed to have a spring in their steps, me included!

Moral of this story – Keep your head down when the going is hard, take advantage of good luck when it occurs.

xxx

There followed a period of stability in my life – the first since my adolescence. I got to know the intelligence and security personnel on the staffs of the units I was tasked to support, I familiarised myself with all the main towns in my "patch" – Minden, Herford, Bielefeld, Lübbecke, Osnabruck etc. I learnt to understand the security protocols required in BAOR units and ensured that I gave advice when required and followed through with audits to check recommendations had been implemented. My relationship with Gizèle improved as she settled into her life of being the wife of a British army officer. We arranged our new army quarter to our taste, routinely I would leave and return to our home following near normal "office hours". Gizèle had a standard pregnancy with regular medical check-ups and in November 1965, our first son, Anthony, was born in the British military hospital Rinteln, one hour's drive from Minden. Our son was healthy and we devoted much of our time ensuring that we brought him up as caring parents in a loving environment. I began to feel quite domesticated.

Our unit's role required us to make regular checks/inspections of the headquarters elements of our forces but there were several individual units requiring special security measures. These included three artillery regiments which were equipped with US "Honest John" missiles W31 warheads and nuclear-capable eight-inch M115 howitzers (later replaced by M110 howitzers with W33 nuclear warheads.) There were also signals units which formed part of our intelligence gathering capability in BAOR. These were naturally of considerable interest to the Soviets.

Much of our unit's work at that time was investigating potential or real Soviet financed espionage cases. Many of these involved some of the eastern European civilians employed by the British since the end of WWII. These employees were grouped into a quasi-military force called Mixed Service Organisation (MSO) and comprised former displaced persons from, for example, Latvia, Lithuania, Estonia, Poland and Czechoslovakia. They were employed as drivers, clerks, mechanics and guards. Many, like Jan Zielinski, were now in their forties or fifties. They played a valuable part in the smooth running of the British units. They also were a useful source of intelligence gathering due to their ethnic and cultural ties and the many contacts they retained in eastern Europe. But equally they were exposed to being penetrated by Russian and other communist spying organisations.

Elements of these MSO units were stationed in most of the garrison towns our unit worked in. Via introductions from Sergeant Gosney and my new contacts in the German BND and BKA, I learnt that there were individuals in the MSO who were working with the Soviets to recruit and exploit British personnel to act in spying activities. These cases were sensitive to uncover and involved long hours of counter–surveillance work.

Digression – One espionage case

One particular report that I wrote about an espionage case caused a major reaction back in London. I only learnt of this when I received a call from the senior Intelligence Corps officer in Germany telling me I had to take a flight immediately to UK and report to the Security Headquarters in Whitehall. The report concerned the case of a British Army sergeant, a senior clerk who had been recruited, through blackmail, by a Soviet contact via the MSO organisation. Apparently, this connected with other British espionage reports which had been of major concern to our security authorities. I was told that the Ministry of Defence (which had been established in 1964 by unifying the War Office, Admiralty and Air Ministry) required to get a first-hand briefing from the case officer – me! My summons was on a Friday morning and I was ordered to go directly to the nearest RAF airfield (Gütersloh) where a reservation had been booked on a flight that morning to RAF Brize Norton in Oxfordshire. A car had been laid on to whisk me to London. All very VIP for such a junior officer as me! These arrangements worked like clockwork and by early afternoon I reported to the Security Department in the Main Building of the Ministry of Defence, Whitehall. I was required to give details of this one particular case investigation to a gentleman in civilian clothes who identified himself as a full colonel: then soon after I was also grilled by an unnamed major-general. I had to struggle to recall all the precise details as concurrently there had been several other similar espionage cases. I was then told to wait for further instructions. After about another hour, I was escorted to a different part of the building and into the office of another gentleman who I recognised from press photos. His name was Mr George Wigg. This gentleman seemed to have a thorough knowledge of the case I was investigating in Germany. He asked several pertinent questions about the case, how it had been uncovered, who and which agencies were involved, the degree of access to information the sergeant had about the nuclear weapons deployed in both the British and US zones in Germany and many other details. I found the cross examination rather daunting but, in a way, I felt chuffed that our work in Germany was being studied at this level. After about one and a half hours, Mr Wigg wound up our meeting saying something like: "I'll go and tell Harold. Wait here in case he wants to talk to you himself." By this time, it was about eight thirty p.m. on the Friday evening. I duly waited as I had been instructed but nothing happened until ten p.m. when the officer I had first met came in and told me: "It's OK, the PM won't need you to brief him, you can go back to your unit." I remember having mixed emotions. One was when I realised who Mr Wigg had meant by Harold. It was Mr Harold Wilson – the Prime Minister no less! I wondered what the heck I had got myself into. My second emotion was rather more mundane. I realised it was late on a Friday evening. I was still in London. I had been supposed to be going out with Gizèle that evening and hadn't even told her I wouldn't be there. A weekend ruined. As it was, the army paid for me to stay in a London Hotel that night and fixed a flight back to Gütersloh the next morning.

Later, I learned that Mr George Wigg had at that time been the Paymaster General in Harold Wilson's government but also was a close confident of the PM. He took a special interest in espionage cases including the recent exposure of John Profumo, then UK Minister of Defence which involved Stephen Ward, Christine Keeler, Mandy Rice-Davies and the Soviet diplomat Captain Eugene Ivanov. My humble investigation in Germany had by chance connected with this major spy case in UK that Mr Wigg was following.

End of Digression

Comment: I ask myself what this experience in Germany had to do with the "development of a man's life"? Perhaps it firmed up my view to "Go with the flow, do your work and don't ask too many questions!" The reality was that I was getting complacent in my developing role of being a husband and a father and this incident shook me up and made me realise the conflict I had between work and home, an issue which was to intensify later in my life.

XXX

Chapter Twenty-Three

The Gulf: Bahrain, Sharjah

Soon after the George Wigg incident in early 1967, I received a new "Posting Order" from HQ Intelligence Corps. I was to hand over my job in Germany and become the "Officer Commanding Security Unit, (Persian) Gulf". I discovered the unit was based on the island of Bahrain and had a sub unit in the Gulf state of Sharjah. Fortunately, unlike my two previous postings, on this occasion I was at least given one month's notice before I had to move. This gave me time to research, at least at a superficial level, some of the political and cultural background to the region. The main political issues at that time were:

- The Vietnam War. The US had been involved in Vietnam since the mid-1950s and by the mid/late 1960s, their forces were heavily engaged. The US press was beginning to become less supportive of US involvement in the Vietnam war and more sceptical about the outcome. Some journalists were even writing that the US were unlikely to win the conflict which was becoming a major drain on US resources and the lives of American service personnel.
- The "six-day war" between Israel and Arab states took place in June 1967, just as I was preparing to leave for Bahrain.
- The Harold Wilson government announcement that Britain's base in Aden, the Yemen, would not be retained after South Yemen's independence in 1967. This premature announcement escalated the push by indigenous groups, backed by the Soviet Union and communist Chinese, to fill the political vacuum in that region.
- In the mid-1960s, the UK decided to transfer UK assets from Aden to the Gulf region which at that time still comprised a number of individual states controlled by traditional families such as Al Khalifa in Bahrain, Al

Maktoum in Dubai and Al Qasimi in Sharjah. Production and processing of Gulf oil was fast becoming a major resource.

It was a shock to the system to arrive in Manana, Bahrain in late June 1967. I had to leave Gizèle and my now two-year-old son back with her mother in Saint-Claude again while, as in Germany, I went ahead, started my new job and looked for accommodation for our family. The plane landed at ten p.m. well after it was dark but, despite the hour, I was hit by a wall of heat as we descended from the aircraft. Then there was none of the massive air-conditioning that is omnipresent in the Gulf states today.

I spent the first week in a hand over/take over with my predecessor, Major Clare. Doing the rounds of the contacts that I would be working with during the next two years was very new and different than any previous experience. I learnt that the UK was trying to find its way politically after the dirty and painful withdrawal from Aden. Several of the troops being withdrawn either routed via Bahrain island or were being redeployed there or in Sharjah on the Gulf coast.

My new job involved working with many local Arab citizens. As I was not an Arab linguist, I always had to work/travel with local Arabs who had been attached to our Security Unit. As, for example, in Borneo, we "multiple tested" all these employees for loyalty and trustworthiness. These excellent individuals had all been recruited and vetted by my predecessor and it was my good fortune to continue working with them throughout my time in the Gulf. The work itself involved developing a thorough understanding of the many and varying security threats against British interests in the region (both local and strategic) in compliance with the priorities of both the British High Commissioner and the military commander of British Forces Gulf. As a cover for our security work, my inherited unit was called British Forces Employment unit, Gulf, a task of recruiting local employees to work for the British forces which we genuinely fulfilled. This overt work enabled us to have an office in the middle of the capital, Manama, to work in civilian clothes and move freely in Arab circles.

Digression – work versus married life!

Accommodation for all unaccompanied British military was initially within the perimeter of our main base at Jufair, a few miles north of Manama town. I was told that although some houses were being built for our families, these would not be completed for several months. Meanwhile, we had to find our own accommodation if our families were to join us. I was keen to have Gizèle and our young son Anthony with me again as soon as possible so I set out to explore the local property market. In 1967, there were few British and other non-Arab expats living on the island so finding somewhere suitable for my French wife and my son was not easy. However, a block of quite stylish apartments had recently been completed and I rushed to rent one of these. As soon I had the keys, I contacted Gizèle and made arrangements for her and our son to fly out as soon as possible. I had felt that, after a naturally difficult adjustment period in Germany, Gizèle had begun to settle into her life of being married to a Brit Army guy. I hoped our mutual love of our son would help us to bond together as a family unit. I was excited by the idea of starting out again in a different part of the world and gaining the (I hoped!) enriching experience of living and working among people with a different language, culture and religion to our own.

I was probably being too idealistic. Gizèle and I did not get off to a good start in Bahrain. Her journey from her parents' home in Saint-Claude to Bahrain had been tortuous for her, particularly as our son had not been well. She was exhausted when I eventually got her to our new apartment. To add to the situation, the climate was still debilitatingly hot, and the one and only air conditioning unit in the apartment had packed up on the very day she arrived. Poor Gizèle – I tried my best to console her but I realised it would be an uphill struggle. There was more. I needed to get medical support for our young son but the nearest medical centre was in Jufair, some three miles away from our apartment. We only had the one car I had just bought and, in any case, Gizèle couldn't then drive. My name was on the list to be wired up for a phone but I was still waiting. As a short-term interim arrangement, I enlisted the help of the wife of one of our office personnel to visit Gizèle every day and to escort her for shopping etc. I also recruited a local taxi driver to be on call to provide her with any transport needs – for example to visit the nearest British hospital which was run by the RAF at their Muharroq air base, a half hour's drive away – but then she would have to get to a phone to call him! Just after Gizèle was installed in our rented apartment, I received an urgent message from my sub unit in Sharjah about a security issue which I was required to resolve. I had no option but to respond and temporally leave my poor wife to cope on her own. My idea of an idyllic and harmonious married life in this exotic part of the middle-east was quickly dispelled!

End of Digression

I soon realised how fundamentally important the Muslim faith was to the local people. Our Arab employees educated me about some of the major differences between the Sunni and Shi'a factions. One peculiarity about Bahrain was that the majority of Bahrainis were Shia but the ruling family and most of the business fraternity were Sunni. My advisors stressed that Sunni and Shi'a communities have a lot more in common in their beliefs and practices than they have differences. I learnt that the main Islamic beliefs and practices shared by both factions are the centrality of the Qur'an, the basic sayings of the Hadith and the five Pillars of Islam – Shahada, "There is no God but Allah and Muhammad is His messenger", Salah, prayer, Zakat, charitable giving, Sawm, fasting in the month of Ramadan and Hajj, the pilgrimage to Mecca. As described in Part One above, the main differences between Sunni and Sh'ia concern the question of religious authority and the leadership of Muslims following the death of the Prophet.

I was told that some Shi'a practices include a session of self-flagellation which in Bahrain was practiced as part of an initiation ceremony for young believers. I had never heard about this before and pushed two of our Muslim employees to explain. This led to quite an animated discussion between them as they switched to Arabic and got quite heated with each other. When translated I learnt that one had explained that self-flagellation was used by some Shi'as for young men (only men I noted!) to demonstrate their allegiance to the faith – a sort of devotion symbol. The other argued that the more recent teachings by the Mullahs had said that this tradition was now considered unacceptable in the modern Shi'a world. This discussion ended in an impasse. Another of our employees had witnessed the dispute but had not expressed an opinion. His name was Rasool, a remarkable individual who I later learnt to respect for his sound judgement and excellent work. Rasool was Persian by birth but had been working in Bahrain for several years mostly for my predecessors in the Security Unit. After this discussion, Rasool told me that a self-flagellation ceremony was due to take place the following week and that his own flat overlooked the square where it would be held. He told me that "non-believers" were absolutely NOT invited to spectate but that we could discreetly watch from his balcony. I had been intrigued by the earlier discussion and readily agreed.

Rasool collected me from our office in downtown Manama and we walked together to his apartment. On his advice, I had dressed in Arab robes. We were installed on the balcony by eleven p.m. and watched as the organisers did their preparations but it was close to midnight before the ceremony got underway. This is how it was. There were about fifty participants who, as far as I could tell, were all were young men in their late teens. Each carried a long metal chain which had knife blades attached to the end. At the instruction of a robed older man, I presumed he was a senior Islamic cleric, the youths began to shuffle in a clockwork direction around the small square. Each would chant the same repetitive prayer and, in time to the chant, they would beat their chest on the right side while holding the chain and throwing it over their left shoulder so that the knife blades hit their backs. For some time, the youths seemed to withstand the effects of the knives then gradually, blood began to flow as the knife cuts bit into their skin. The ritual continued with the same prayer chant, the same shuffling round the square, repeating the waving of the knife-attached chains over their shoulder striking into their backs. This same ritual was repeated over and over again. As the youths' injuries got progressively worse, older men would appear with what appeared to be simple cloths and begin to mop the blood from the young men's chests and backs. The men would move from youth to youth. I saw no sign of any antiseptic or other sanitary medical supplies. As time passed and the condition of the youths continued to worsen, some youths eventually succumbed to the situation and either began to stagger around the square or to collapse through loss of blood. But still the ritual continued – those youths who were still on their feet continued their ritualistic chanting and shuffling round the square sometimes slipping in the blood that had seeped onto the ground.

I continued watching this macabre scene for some long time wondering how it would end. I noticed that the youths participated with an unquestioning obedience and I saw none who showed any dissent or resistance. The seniors continued to administer a crude form of staunching the blood from the skin of the bleeding youths but none intervened in the continuance of the ritual. I also noticed that all participants, both the youths and their elders were male – I saw no women present anywhere at any time. Rasool had told his wife that she and their two children were to stay well away from the balcony that night.

I never got to see the end of the ceremony. By four a.m. I had frankly had enough of witnessing the scene of ever more bloodshed and the desperate state of these young men. I signalled to Rasool and together we slipped out of his apartment and away from the scene. Rasool told me later that routinely the ritual would continue until dawn (due about six thirty a.m.) then the elders would halt the proceedings and tend to the wounded youths. I left wondering what to make of this event. In some ways it seemed barbaric, like something out of the middle ages. But I had been impressed that the youths seemed to participate without questioning its validity as if they viewed it as an essential way of proving their devotion to their faith.

Living in Bahrain at that time, I learnt that although the strict interpretation of faith in Islam and its male dominated customs seemed very alien to my Christian upbringing, there are in fact many similarities between the two faiths; principally that both worship a prophet and believe that God is the creator of all things. Christians believe that Jesus Christ was the son of God whereas Muslims believe that Muhammad was the chosen recipient and messenger of the word of God through divine revelations. Muslims see the Prophet Muhammad to be the last in a long line of prophets that included Moses and Jesus. Although the interpretation by the two religions of the "meaning of life" may seem to be incompatible, in reality they both see the "meaning" as following the dictums of "God's Prophet", whether Jesus or Muhammad.

Digression – Arab hypocrisy

Of all the different races and cultures that I have lived and worked with, I found the Bahraini Arab the most distant from my Anglo-Saxon background. There were positives and negatives. I found our Arabic team in Security Unit Gulf to be straight forward, co-operative, intelligent and a pleasure to work with. Not so, several of the higher-level locals I got to know. Here are two examples. My job required me to liaise closely with a certain gentleman, a successful local businessman, who was close to the Al Khalifa ruling family. Fine, all part of the job! This gentleman enjoyed playing tennis and asked me to be his doubles partner. I don't know why as I was never more than an average player. When we played a match against another pair, I found my gentleman colleague was a terrible cheat. He had a driving will to win at any cost. Often when our opponents sent down a return which was clearly "in" he would immediately loudly declare "out" and claim the point. For diplomacy's sake, I found I had to go along with this cheating but I never could understand why he felt so compelled to lie about what after all was just a game. I suspected that he and others also cheated in their business dealings.

Another example was the double standards I experienced by some of the Arab ladies. When out in the street and public places they would wear the full Arab Burqa with the face covered by a mesh screen. Their actions were demur and their demeanour was modest. When accompanying a male, they would meekly walk behind him. On occasions, I was invited to social events in the homes of these same ladies. However, once inside their houses, there was no sign of Burquas or any other outer covering. Quite the reverse. The ladies delighted in wearing the latest western fashion with full make up and would freely mix with the men. In addition, both the men and the women also enjoyed alcohol and would drink copiously. I thought how hypocritical it was of some Arabs to pretend to be honest, modest and abstemious in public while acting in completely the opposite way when away from the social gaze. However, part of my job was to integrate with these good people so I kept my opinion to myself.

End of Digression

As the months of my tour in Bahrain went by, I felt more confident in handling the work aspects. It was a very volatile period as the Gulf states moved towards forming a grand alliance which came to be termed the United Arab Emirates. At that time the UK was reassessing its strategic role which was soon to become a policy of withdrawal from "east of Suez". The US became ever more bogged down in Vietnam, the Shah's power in Persia was being threatened by internal Islam dissent and the strategic vacuum from the Yemen to the Gulf was being challenged by indigenous groups backed by the Soviets and China. My job often required me frequently to visit not only our sub unit in Sharjah but also to Dubai and other Gulf states and to the then primary oil rich state of Kuwait.

While involved with this work, my poor Gizèle was having to cope in our isolated apartment with our son who was now learning to form his own character. Then one day I returned home and Gizèle had some important news for me. She was pregnant again! My immediate reactions were mixed. I was so pleased that we were expanding our family and that our son would not be an only child. But then, Gizéle's news reinforced my concerns that I must do all I could to improve our accommodation. Gizèle needed more support, more social contacts and, now, more medical cover to help her through her pregnancy.

Then came another jolt to the system. I arrived back at our apartment in Bahrain late one evening on returning from working in Sharjah, in an area of the state where communications was difficult. An army major from our administrative department was there waiting for me. He told me he had been trying unsuccessfully to contact me for the past two days. He had bad news. He had been notified by my sister Shelley that my mother had died of cancer. I was shocked as I had no idea she had even been ill, let alone had cancer. We still had no phone in our apartment so I immediately drove to my office and called my sister. She told me that my mother had not wanted me to know about her condition and that her funeral was to take place the next day. I did a quick calculation. I reckoned that if went immediately to Bahrain airport I just might be able to hitch a flight back to UK that night or early the next morning. Then with luck I might get to my sister's village in Essex in time to attend my mother's funeral. Then I reflected that the time to be with my mother would have been while she was still alive and I could have comforted her and told her how much I loved her and appreciated all she had done for me while I was growing up. But it was too late. I would now never have that chance. So, I decided not to try to get to her funeral – in hindsight, something I have always bitterly regretted. My mother was a caring, wonderful person. I absolutely should have been there to mourn her at her funeral. I suppose I was then too selfishly wrapped up in my own life and situation in Bahrain.

Digression – news: good and bad

Life went on. A short time later I had some good news and some bad news. The good news; the ship that had carried our one crate of baggage had just docked at the Jufair jetty. Being early in married life, Gizéle and I hadn't accumulated many personal belongings that we could not bring in our hand luggage on the plane – just one crate which we had packed in Germany before we left. It contained spare, mostly winter, clothes, some ornaments that we had bought to personalise our military house there, toys we had bought for our son and a set of framed photos, some from our wedding, others that Gizéle had kept and were precious to her as reminders of her past life. The crate had been loaded with those of other service personnel onto a ship which became a casualty of the 1967 six-day war between Israel and its Arab neighbours. The last we had previously heard about its whereabouts was that it was stuck "somewhere in the Suez Canal". I was relieved to learn that it had at last been freed and had found its way to Bahrain.

The bad news: I was informed that while it had been anchored in the Suez Canal, the ship's hold had been broken into by thieves searching for valuables among our belongings. The crates belonging to several service personnel including me had been offloaded at Jufair, Bahrain but their contents had been mixed up. I was asked to go to the jetty straightaway with the other owners and try to identify our own possessions. I hurried to the jetty to find that my crate and those of others had been offloaded and the contents had been strewn around the edge of the harbour wall. Several of the other owners had also arrived there and we spent the next hour in the mid-day Bahraini heat, rummaging around the scattered belongings, trying to establish and agree who owned what. I identified Anthony's toys and a couple of our lamps but had to haggle over whether or not some of the lady's lingerie belonged to Gizéle or someone else's wife. Worse: I could find no sign of any of the photos we had packed – these had no financial value but were irreplaceable souvenirs for Gizèle. My poor wife!

At last, after nearly one year in the job in Bahrain, we had a lucky break, which had similarities to our time in Germany. Although my substantive army rank was then Captain, my job was formally graded as a Major's appointment. I learnt that not only was I to be promoted to "acting Major" but that the local housing project had just been completed, these houses were being allocated to those of Major rank and above and one had been reserved for me! With much relief, I hastily installed Gizèle, Anthony and our few remaining belongings in our new little house in Jufair. All our neighbours were British nationals, and soon after our move, Gizèle was befriended by the charming wives of my service colleagues some of whom had cars and willingly included Gizèle in their shopping trips, other social visits and, as mothers themselves, could counsel Gizèle through her pregnancy. I realised that my wife still found it difficult to adjust to our life together in this somewhat unsettled world of the Persian Gulf, but at least she now had better support. We also had our mutual love for our young son who, during this period in Bahrain, continued to develop into a lively young boy.

End of Digression

Having at last settled Gizèle into a more stable home situation, I was able to concentrate more fully on my job. As in Borneo and Germany, I was fortunate to have the support of our outstanding Intelligence Corps personnel, backed up by the professionalism and loyalty of our locally employed civilians. It was a job like no other I experienced before or after my years in the military, involving a mix of political, military and security issues, research and investigations. Few days were ever alike, some mundane, some extremely challenging and some verging on the edge of legality: but always highly motivating.

In November 1968, Gizèle gave birth to our second son in the RAF hospital at Muharroq. We called him William. Gizèle seemed to be more settled as a mother with one son who was growing up well and a new baby who was also healthy. Our medical support was now well established for Gizèle at RAF Muharroq hospital and we always had our local taxi service on hand when required.

In mid-1969, I received my next "posting order". I was to spend a few months at our UK Headquarters, which had now moved from Maresfield, Sussex to our new purpose-built barracks at Ashford, Kent. I was to attend upgrading training courses there, reverting back to my substantive rank of Captain, then I was to be sent to a staff appointment in Cyprus.

xxx

Chapter Twenty-Four

Cyprus

Cyprus: what a wonderful change! Although I had enjoyed Bahrain professionally, I realised it had been very difficult for Gizèle. I hoped that our next couple of years together based in such a lovely location would be easier and more relaxing for her and that we could find good accommodation where we could allow our marriage relationship to deepen while we brought up our two young sons in the early years of their lives. I celebrated this news by ordering my first ever new car to be delivered to RAF Brize Norton for our return to UK.

We were in the UK for three months and were allocated a small house within the barracks at Ashford while I attended training courses. This short period gave me the chance to reconnect with the UK, the country of my birth, though my roots back in Saltford, Somerset were no more as now both of my parents had died.

The UK seemed different – smaller, more parochial. But it was green and comforting after the barren harshness of the Middle East. Gizèle and I enjoyed bringing up our two young sons and taking rides along the little winding country lanes of Kent, a county and part of the world which then was new to both of us.

I also read up on the history of Cyprus as at least a basic knowledge was fundamental for my next job. Main historical points about this island which is often described as being; "blessed by nature but cursed by history" were:

- Many middle-eastern civilizations in pre-Roman times had at some stage controlled the island – Phoenicians, Assyrians, Egyptians.

- Cyprus became a Roman province in 58BC and remained in Roman hands for several hundred years.
- Later, control passed through many different powers – Justinian, Byzantine, the Knight Templar Crusaders, French (Lusignan), Genoese merchants.
- From 1571, it was controlled by the Ottoman empire.
- In 1914, it was annexed by the UK.
- Armed conflict erupted on the island between 1955 and 1957. This stemmed from an underground Greek Cypriot movement, dedicated to ending British colonial rule in Cyprus and to achieving eventual enosis (union) with Greece. The military element, EOKA, was primarily organised and led by Georgios Grivas, a former Greek army officer with the support of the Machiavellian Archbishop Makarios. During this period, the Greek orthodox church under Makarios colluded with General Grivas's Eoka movement in the armed campaign. This was one of many examples when religious faith became blurred and hijacked by political or racial interests. When Makarios became primate of the Greek Orthodox Church, he took a leading political role, proclaiming "Cyprus is Greek and has been since the dawn of history and it will always remain Greek." His assertion was completely incorrect as it had been ruled by many differing outside powers – details above. Makarios's close involvement with Eoka also ignored the legitimate interests of the Turkish-Cypriot inhabitants, who accounted for more than one third of the Cypriot population. (Details of this conflict is well described in David French's book, *The British counter-insurgency campaign of Cyprus 1955–59.*)
- In 1960 a treaty of establishment had agreed that Cyprus was to become an independent Republic, free from British control. The country was to be led by a coalition with a Greek-Cypriot President and a Turkish-Cypriot vice-president. Within the agreement, two Sovereign Base Areas (SBAs) at Akrotiri and Dhekelia were identified as real estate that would remain as British sovereign territory and therefore remain under British jurisdiction. The Cypriot capital, Nicosia, also a divided city, had been the flashpoint of past intercommunal violence. This had resulted in the deployment in 1964 of UN forces (known as UNFICYP) to Nicosia with the aim of preventing fighting between the two communities. UNFICYP

established a physical partition of the city, colloquially known as the "green line".
When I was posted there in 1970, the island was populated by approximately two third Greek-Cypriots and one third Turkish-Cypriots. The majority of Greek-Cypriots lived in the south of the island, the majority of the Turkish in the north. However, most towns and even many small villages were then divided between ethnic Greeks and Turks.

xxx

My job was an intelligence staff officer working in HQ Near East Land Forces (NEARELF), located in Episkopi in the Akrotiri SBA. There was no family housing in Episkopi and all accompanied married personnel lived in rented accommodation in Limassol, about a half an hour's drive away. Although the army would provide a service flight to Cyprus, if I preferred, I was told I would be free at my own expense, to organise my own travel arrangements. This was a whole new situation as it meant that not only could our family stay together but I could arrange our own programme and even bring our precious new car with us.

My work in Cyprus involved analysis of political aspirations and military capabilities of both Greek and Turkish Cypriot communities and how these might impact on British interests on the island. The intercommunal disparities and constant friction between the Greek and Turkish Cypriots highlighted their differences in their fervently held religious beliefs. There were regular incidents of intercommunal disputes, violence and occasional shootings: but none of these escalated into a major conflagration during our time on the island.

Socially, Gizèle and I made friends with both Greek and Turkish-Cypriots who often invited us to their homes. The format regularly went like this. Initially, the conversation with our charming hosts would be about general subjects – life in Cyprus, its climate, its geography, cultural sites, local events. After a short while, our host's conversation would turn to intercommunal issues – our Greek hosts accusing the Turks of some recent misdemeanour and how much better it would be if there were no Turkish people living in Limassol. It was exactly the same in reverse with our Turkish hosts who would berate the Greek community. Gizéle and I would nod our understanding of our hosts concerns but we learnt to be very discreet and never openly side with either community.

My tour in Cyprus came at a great time in my life. I was 30 years old when we arrived there in 1970 and we stayed until the summer of 1972. My job enabled me to be at home regularly and spend good quality time enjoying the growing phase of our two sons. We found a small two bedroomed house in a quiet and peaceful area of Limassol and at last I felt we could reach a balance of life between job and family.

This was a time before package air tours and mass tourism in Cyprus. There were very few tourist hotels, indeed very few tourists. The beaches were still unspoilt by development. Shortly after we left, there were two invasions – the first was the Turkish military invasion in July 1974, the second was the invasion of mass tourist packages. These totally transformed the image and culture of the island as hotels and associated tourist facilities: bars, restaurants, night clubs sprung up to cater for these tourists.

Digression. The Staff College exam/family life

There was one big professional niggle. Back in 1963, I had leapt at the chance to become a regular army officer and so far had really enjoyed my very different postings around the world. I hadn't given much thought to the long-term future. But now I was faced with the reality that this year was the last chance I would have to take the exam for both promotion to the rank of substantive major and selection to the Army Staff College. The rules were that an officer had to take the exam, between the ages of 29 and 31 – and I would be 31 this year! During the two previous years when I was in Bahrain, it didn't really register with me that I should have studied for and taken the exam then. Perhaps it was because I was in a "civilian clothes" job and seemed detached from the regular army or more likely, because I was too idle to involve myself in the studying needed to prepare for the exam. Without passing the exam, I might be required to leave the army when still in my thirties. I now realised that, as a husband and father of two boys, I had the responsibility for their future as well as my own. I had no degree and no other employable trade to fall back on if I were to get kicked out of the army. There was another thing. So far, I had done well in my army career. I had been given good grades in all the annual "confidential" reports that are written on every officer. I now felt confident that I could hold my own professionally and intellectually with my fellow officers. But if I wanted to have any future chance gaining a senior rank, say colonel or brigadier, the only way was to be selected to attend the Staff College and perform well there.

I decided I would have to defer full exploitation of all the social pleasures of living and working in this beautiful island until I had knuckled down to study for the next exam which was to be held in November/December that year. The Staff College exam at the time consisted of eight separate subject papers. Three hours were allowed for each. All were taken in the same week, commencing on Monday morning and concluding on Friday morning.

In mid-November, the week before the exam, I was suddenly ill. I had a fever, was physically sick, had no energy and felt like death. I staggered to our local military doctor who diagnosed jaundice, (hepatitis) and insisted I be admitted to our hospital in RAF Akrotiri. That was the bad news. The good news was that my senior officer at that time, Major Nigel Flower, was well aware that if I missed the exam, the following year I would be above the eligible age limit and would be ineligible to re-sit the exam then. It was now or forget it! Nigel took it on himself to contact the exam coordinator and press for a special examination centre to be set up in my hospital room, with independent personal invigilators appointed. Through Nigel's drive and persistence, this was agreed and I will be always grateful to him. The result; each day of the week 30 November to 3 December 1971, a different invigilating officer, always with the rank of Major, turned up in my hospital room, gave out my exam paper, sat in the room patiently for the stipulated three hours, then collected the papers and submitted them for central marking. It was the same for all eight exams.

After a further two weeks, I was discharged from the hospital. The doctor told me I could resume my normal work duties but gave strict instructions that on no account was I to drink alcohol for six full months. Surprisingly I found this restriction easier to follow than I had thought and it gave me the incentive to regain fitness and restart running training.

I had no idea how well or badly I had done in the Staff College exam. It was not until the end of February 1972 that I was notified that I had passed. That was not the end of the process. There were a fixed number of places on the course and it was normal for more candidates to pass the exam than there were places available. There then followed a selection procedure from those who had passed. Finally in early April 1972 I learnt that I had been selected. I was to attend the Royal Military School of Science (RMCS) in Shrivenham, Wiltshire from October to December 1972, then the full Army Staff College course at Camberley, Surrey from January to December 1973.

End of Digression

With this great weight off my mind, I still had a few months to be able to enjoy the delights of Cyprus. I particularly wanted to give maximum free time to spend with our two sons. We spent good quality time at the beach and our sons both became strong swimmers. On several weekends we camped out on an unspoiled stretch of sandy beach called Pantachou near the tiny settlement of Ayia Napa, and spent our whole time there without meeting another human being. Ayia Napa then consisted of a Venetian style monastery and a small collection of fishermen's houses. Today, this formally idyllic area has been transformed into a tourist destination, particularly favoured by young clubbers wishing to party through the night!

We explored inland parts of the island. We came across a beautiful isolated area in a grove of olive, eucalyptus and cedar trees that we came to call "our place" and would often spend week-ends there. We would build a barbecue structure out of local stones, collect sticks as fuel and cook our lunch, then, ensuring our fire was fully extinguished, our boys and I would explore the area while Gizèle enjoyed a siesta in the shade of the trees.

We matured together as a family and this was the best time of Gizèle's and my relationship together. There were though a few issues. Gizèle did not swim and, although she came with us on our beach camping sessions, I could tell that she came out of loyalty/duty rather than pleasure. This detracted from the enjoyment for both of us. We also had disagreements about language. Gizèle was French and I was keen for our sons to grow up as bilingual. I planned always to speak directly to them in English and I pressed Gizèle to speak to them in French. Gizèle refused: I never knew why!

I wrote earlier that I had had the opportunity when in Borneo to learn to water ski to a high level. This capability really payed off in Cyprus. The beach at Limassol then was quiet and occupied along its length by a series of simple Greek-Cypriot beach bars. A fellow officer working in Episcopi at the same time had the same interests as me. Together we approached the elderly (to us) owner of one of these beach bars, his name was Stefanos, and made him a proposition: to let us use his beach site as a base for a water ski club and we would bring him regular business from our members who would always buy their drinks from him. To our delight, he agreed. Nothing was put in writing; just a handshake and a few beers together to cement the deal. During the summer months, Bill and I formed a water ski club which soon had a healthy membership. The army welfare fund loaned us the initial boat and engine, the rest of the equipment was financed by our members. So it was that we were able to water ski every day for free. Bill and I would share our instructing duties.

Nature: the true meaning of life.

When it was my turn to be the water skiing instructor, my habit was to get up at about five a.m., drive my Lambretta to the beach, park up, swim out to our boat which for its protection, was moored each night some fifty metres from the shore, climb aboard, dry out the engine's starter motor from the previous night's dew, start the motor, steer away from the shore for about a kilometre, I would stop the engine and wait; **then marvel as the sun rose majestically from beyond the horizon. Just to be there alone in nature! I remember finding that to be a stronger spiritual experience**

than I ever had in a church! The chill of the early morning and the swim out to the boat soon evaporated with the warming rays of the sun. I had the feeling then that I was as close to being in paradise as it is possible to be! At that time, this was for me "the true meaning of life"! After some time of this period of wonder and reflection, I would steer the boat back to the shore in time to welcome the first arrivals for water ski lessons. These would finish by seven fifteen a.m., in time to change into army uniform, hop back on the scooter and get to the office in Episcopi in time for our start of work at eight a.m.

XXX

Digression: Ankara – the Atatürk Legacy

Due to my job on the intelligence staff, on occasions I was required to visit Ankara and other parts of Turkey. Here, I was sponsored by the UK Defence Attaché to Turkey, at that time Brigadier Dennis Sole. On one occasion, I was invited to a cocktail reception hosted by the deputy head of the Turkish Defence forces. It was a rather formal and grand occasion held in a historic building in the Ulus district of central Ankara known as "The Museum of the War of Independence". I wasn't sure why I had been invited but I jumped at the chance to absorb some Turkish culture at this high level. The event occurred shortly after my alcohol prohibition had expired and I took advantage to accept a couple of glasses of the excellent champagne that was being offered. There followed one of the most memorable evenings of my life but not, I'd like to believe, due to the champagne! This is what happened. At one point during the reception, silence was called and short speeches were made by a senior Turkish general, followed by a civilian gentleman who I had been told was the defence minister. The speeches were in Turkish, which I did not understand, but to my surprise, the words were being translated into English and whispered to me. I half glanced round and noticed the interpreter was a young lady. I hadn't even been aware of her quiet and discreet approach. When the speeches ended, there was applause all round then general conversation continued. I could then overtly turn and face my volunteer interpreter. I noticed three things about her – she was young, probably still in her late teens, she was immaculately dressed, and she was exquisitely beautiful. As I turned to look directly at her, she smiled and said:

"My mother had noticed you here earlier. She knew there would be speeches in our Turkish language and thought you might like a little help to follow them. She sent me over to you. My name is Aysun."

I was somewhat startled by her presence. I felt I should play my British role so I politely held out my hand and, as I took her own, I noticed how slender and soft her small fingers were. I rather stiffly said:

"I should introduce myself, my name is Mark Durman. I'm a captain in the British Army. Thank you for your assistance and please also thank your mother."

Aysun smiled and softly replied:

"I know your name, Mark! And why don't you come over and thank my mother yourself?"

She led the way to another part of the room where a Turkish officer, with General's rank insignia, and a lady were standing together. They both looked up as we approached and the General stretched out his hand in welcome. He was a tall, good looking man whose dark hair was flecked with just a hint of grey. He smiled and said:

"Ah – I see our daughter has trapped you. It's Captain Durman, isn't it, may I call you Mark? I'm General Burak Gulden. I'm a long-term friend of your Brigadier Dennis Sole. We discussed your visit to us here in Ankara and both thought this evening would be of interest to you. I hope our daughter looked after you all right!"

I stammered out my reply, "Very much so, sir, I really appreciate it."

"Good, and I must also extend our introduction to my wife, Yildiz. We've all been keen to meet you."

I duly shook her hand. I couldn't help but notice that his wife too was a deeply attractive looking lady – immaculately coiffured hair, stylishly dressed and as beautiful as her daughter. She was perhaps in her early fifties but had still retained the slender figure of her youth. I was frankly stunned by the General's effusiveness but he quickly put me at my ease. He told me that Brigadier Sole had informed him that I worked on the British staff in Cyprus and that his own job required him to have an up-to-date knowledge of Cypriot affairs. He asked me how I assessed present relations between the two Cypriot communities. At first, I felt defensive and concerned that he might have been trying to compromise me by requesting classified information but, as our conversation developed, he seemed, or at least I hoped, merely interested in developments of Greek and Turkish Cypriot political affairs. None of his questions in any way related to British sensitive issues. To be sure, I decided I would report this conversation back to Brigadier Sole the next day. We talked for some while, as his two ladies stayed with us seemingly also interested in our conversation. Then the General said:

"Look, Mark, I really enjoyed our chat and by all means come to my office in our defence headquarters if I can provide you with any information to assist your job. I ask you to excuse me now as I have to attend a meeting with some of my staff. Meanwhile, may I leave you in the company of my ladies who I know are anxious to talk to you about non-military matters."

With that, he shook my hand and walked away, joined by another Turkish officer. I wasn't quite sure what I should now do but the general's wife was quick to step in.

"Captain Durman, may I call you Mark, look – the reception is now about to end and already guests are forming up to say goodbye to the presiding general. I suggest we do the same – but I do have a suggestion that may interest you. What do you know about our famous Mustafa Kemal Atatürk?"

I fought to find an answer, weakly saying:

"Well, I know he is much revered and known as the father of modern Turkey."

"Would you like to know more?"

"Certainly, what do you suggest Mrs Gulden–er?"

"Please, it's Yildiz! Just follow on and we'll show you."

Follow on? Show me? I wondered what this fascinating lady had in mind. But already I found she and her daughter, Aysun, had me filled with curiosity. I meekly followed the ladies and stood to one side as Yildiz said an effusive goodbye to our host. She gave me a wink and winkled her little finger in a conspiratorial "follow me" sign. Of course I duly followed.

Yildiz Gulden led us out of the main reception room and along an attached corridor. At the end was a large locked door, Yildiz produced a key from her bag and opened the door leading into the darkened room. She expertly found the light control panel and switched on a few lights which revealed a circular chamber with seating around the whole of its perimeter. She led us along one of the rows and had illuminated just enough of the building to enable us to have a full view of all the seating but the lighting was still low and atmospheric.

I looked around to try to familiarise myself with our surroundings, still wondering what on earth was happening. Yildiz sat down on one of the small seats and gestured for me to sit next to her with daughter Aysun close up on my other side. I didn't care anymore. I was totally seduced and I didn't think the two glasses of champagne had much to do with it! Yildiz let me adjust to our situation and to take in the atmosphere. Then she began her lecture in a strong but melodic voice, speaking in perfect English.

"Mark, firstly I want to tell that all I and my daughter have – our western culture, our education and freedom to study, to live our own lives as we wish; all this is totally due to one man – Mustafa Kemal Atatürk. If it had not been for him and all he achieved for our country, it is likely I would still be speaking only Arabic, wearing the burqa and following my husband's every command. As it is, I was educated first here at Ankara university then took my doctorate in PPE (that's Philosophy, Politics and Economics) at your London school of Economics. I also later studied at Harvard. Now my daughter is at an early stage of following a similar path. This evening, I have brought you here for a particular reason. We are now in the former Turkish Assembly building where Atatürk spoke for many sessions after his arrival in Ankara in December 1919. On his instructions a newer building was constructed just hundred metres from here which housed the parliament for some thirty-six years until the present parliament building, which, after delays caused by the WWII, was finally opened in 1961."

Yildiz paused to see my reaction which she could see was one of rapt attention before she continued.

"It was in the second building, just across the way from here that Atatürk made the speech we call the "Nutuk". This is a Turkish word which translates in English to "speech" but we always call it "the speech" rather than "a speech" as it concluded and defined our country as it is constituted today. He delivered it over six full days from 15 to 20 October 1927 to the second Congress of the Republican People's Party, who were then the governing party of our country. If you are still with me, Mark, I will give you a summary of this amazing speech."

Yildiz didn't need to worry about that. She could tell I was spellbound not merely by the story itself but also by the atmosphere of the chamber and our exclusive use of it and by Yildiz's fluent delivery. I was mesmerised by her lecture but perhaps even more by sitting so close between these two beguiling ladies. Yildiz continued:

"Atatürk began his speech with the words; 'Gentlemen, I landed in Samsum on 19 May 1919.' He then went on in painstaking detail to narrate the history of our country as it was at that time, decimated after the defeats sustained by the Ottoman Empire, the parlous state of the army, parts of the country occupied by the French, English (he used that term rather than British), Italians and Greeks. Atatürk then went on in great detail, quoting from many telegrams transmitted at the time, to tell the Congress of the gradual path to the evolution of his strategic vision to form an independent Turkish state. He narrated the terms of the Erzurum Congress held in July 1919 and the Sivas Congress the following September. Eventually, in 1920, the way was laid to form a new capital in Ankara, some 480 kms from Istanbul and to establish a Grand National Assembly. Atatürk explained that between 1920 and 1926, following the Treaties of Alexandropol (December 1920), Moscow (March 1921), Lausanne (July 1923) the following was adopted:

-Ankara was formally named the Capital of the Turkish Republic.

-The Caliphate was abolished.

- Religious courts and schools were abolished

- The emancipation of women.

-Western style clothing was adopted

- The Swiss civil code, Italian penal code and German commercial code were adopted.

- Plans were under way in 1928 to replace the Arabic language with the Latin alphabet."

Yildiz didn't herself talk for six days; I wish she had! But she certainly held my full attention for about an hour. I can't remember all the details of her talk but the above is the best summary that I can recall. She concluded by saying;

"Mark, you understand now why Atatürk is still omnipresent in Turkey today. Statues of him are everywhere. Since his time, many politicians have claimed to be the inheritors of Atatürk's legacy but none have matched his vision, selflessness and dedication. Ayoun, I and so many other Turkish women like us owe our existence to this remarkable man. I must tell you, Mark, there are three men in my life – Atatürk, Allah and my husband – in that order!"

I didn't know what to make of this last comment!

It was time for us to leave. All I could do was mutter my profound thanks to Yildiz Gulden for giving me a magical and unforgettable evening. She led us out to the exit of the chamber, turned off the lights, relocked the door and we made our way together out of the building. I didn`t know how to bring our meeting to a close. Somehow, I wanted to draw both mother and daughter close, to hold them, to breathe the same air, not to let them go. But I didn't do that. Instead I politely and inadequately thanked them again. We walked together to the nearby taxi stand, I opened the door of the first taxi for them and waved them goodbye. I then took a second taxi to the hotel where I was staying the night.

It took me a long time that night to get to sleep. I was still fantasising about these two gorgeous Turkish ladies. My age then (thirty-two) was mid-way between theirs. Yildiz was some twenty years older, Aysun was at least twelve years younger. I had to get a grip. Yildiz was married, so was I and Aysun was just starting out with her further education. Of course, both were unobtainable but that didn't stop my yearning for them that night. As I eventually felt myself dropping off to sleep, I realised this was the first time since I had married Gizèle that I had thought that way about other women!

End of Digression

XXX

My tour in the paradise island of Cyprus began to draw to a close and I had to start planning our next move. That autumn (1972) I was to spend three months in Shrivenham, Wiltshire followed by the next year in Camberley, Surrey. Gizèle and I discussed possible future housing options. I had been aware that the price of housing in UK was beginning to rise quite rapidly and I knew some fellow officers who had decided to invest in private housing so that they and their families would have a foot in the property market if there were to be further price increases. I was attracted to this idea if we could manage to scrape together enough money for a deposit and mortgage. I knew that Gizéle had never found it easy to adapt to the military life and I thought that she might be more relaxed if we had our own permanent home. Gizéle agreed.

During our short summer break, we spent nearly every day researching and checking out different areas, eventually finding a neat little house in

Winchester, a location midway between Shrivenham and Camberley. It was a small Victorian semi, located in a quiet road within an easy walk to Winchester centre and opposite a large park, which I earmarked as our sons' playing area. It was a stretch to find the financing but we just managed to scrape together enough funds and there we were – home owners to be! We were back in UK; our house could provide Gizèle and our sons more stability and I hoped my attendance at the Staff College would give me the opportunity for further progress in my army career.

xxx

Chapter Twenty-Five

1972/3: The Army Staff College

The first three months of the Staff College course were spent at the Royal College of Military Science in Shrivenham, Wiltshire. Those officers with science or technical backgrounds stayed a full year but the majority of us were let off with a three-month bash – in my case just as well as I had struggled to pass physics and maths at GCE "O" level. We ploughed our way through our course studying, for example, ballistics, explosives; it literally was rocket science, bridge design and radio technology. The course was interesting and informative but I was aware of my technical limitations and that I was never going to achieve more than a basic understanding of all these subjects.

This module ended in late December 1972 and Gizèle, our two sons and I were able to spend our first Christmas in our new home which Gizèle had decorated beautifully in true festive style. During the course, I was able to spend good quality time with our sons. When we moved into the Winchester house, Anthony was six years old and William was three – both active healthy boys. I loved coming home and being with them, teaching William to ride a bike, then the three of us cycling round our local park. With Gizèle, we made weekend trips into the Hampshire countryside to walk and explore, often taking a picnic and being away all day together, often in the nearby New Forest. I hoped our future could continue like this but, in the back of my mind, I wondered how long this lifestyle would last.

The Shrivenham module was just the entrée to the main "Command and Staff Course". In January, all students and directing staff assembled at the college, which was co-located in the same grounds as the Sandhurst officer cadet college. In my year, 1973, our full complement was one hundred and eighty students, comprising one hundred and thirty British – mostly army but also a smattering of RAF, Navy, Marines and civilians – and fifty overseas students from thirty-two different countries. We were directed by fifty-eight instructors – mostly British army senior officers and civilians but also instructors from the US, Germany and France. Quite a turn-out!

Accommodation was arranged so that many married officers, including all the non-Brits were offered housing with their families, while single officers were allocated rooms within the main Staff College buildings. I was able to get one of these rooms but, whenever possible, commuted back to our little house in Winchester.

My first reactions to the Staff College: very impressive organisation, oozing with authority – the handling of our arrival induction, the allocation of syndicates, direct and clipped instructions to students: "how we, the British traditional hierarchy do things!" Another first impression – a total of two hundred and thirty-eight individuals (students and directing staff) all of whom were male – not one female! How our culture has evolved since then! I was impressed by the way the overseas students were integrated with the British. We were initially divided into syndicates of ten students under the direction of one instructor, referred to as the "Directing Staff (DS)" – each syndicate being a well-balanced mix of officers from different branches (regiments) with two or three overseas students in each syndicate. The composition changed four times during the year, ensuring that there was a close integration of all students during the course.

Also impressive was the flow of the course and the high degree of professional preparation and planning. At all times of the day, and sometimes the night, our programme and full itinerary was itemised in detail. There was no doubt about it, we all knew what was expected of us!

The not so positive. I felt somewhat frustrated at what the college considered to be the "right way to do everything". One example was the formal appreciation and plan of a military operation when considering how best to attack an enemy force or to defend against a threatening attack against our own forces. This was a much-used exercise during the course as a means of ensuring we considered every aspect of a situation before deciding what was the best way to proceed. I fully agreed, appreciated and understood that this was a sensible form of "the application of logic" but felt the Staff College teaching of this process could be too laboured and stereotyped.

Often, we would be taken out to an area of the Hampshire countryside, spend time reviewing the whole theoretical "battle situation" scene and consider the above options. We would then return to the college and, as our homework, would be required to write out our appreciation and plan for the hypothetical operation we had been considering. The following morning we would submit our written work to our directing staff for their correction. I considered this procedure to be very valuable as a planning tool but it did have its limitations. Firstly, writing out all the details involved was a time-consuming business, and often, in reality time would not have been on our side. Secondly, our staff had a "right or wrong" approach to the solutions they expected, which included the quality of staff writing and accepted abbreviations and symbols. I accepted that was necessary training but my main criticism of this protocol was that the "enemy forces" were expected to operate in a certain manner according to our staffs' appreciation of their doctrine and tactics. Fine, but what if the enemy did not conform to doctrine and decided to use different tactics? Therefore, I argued, our own plans should be sufficiently flexible to be able to adjust to the unexpected. My first directing staff (DS) leader was a typically rigid infantryman – not from one of the "top" regiments, e.g., Coldstream Guards but with great ambition to reach the top himself. (In the end he did, but more of this later). For some reason I was appointed syndicate leader for that first term module. I suppose our DS wanted to show that "his" syndicate was the best due to his impeccable training, and I fear he found me to be a big disappointment – not a Sandhurst graduate, not from a top regiment, and inclined to be too unconventional in my problem solving and general non-conforming manner. I think he would have failed me at the end of our time together but somehow, I escaped with a warning to try to conform more to the spirit of the college.

That warning was probably the jolt I needed. I did some hard thinking. OK, I reckoned my first DS officer (his rank then was lieutenant-colonel) was far too "old school" and needed to be challenged. But, hey, why was I there? It certainly wasn't to get thrown out of the college. That could have spelt the end of my military career. I didn't always agree with the college solutions. So what? I had worked hard to get to this level of selection for higher military ranks, as we all had, so why throw it away now on a point of silly principle? I told myself to get over my reservations, bite my lip and get safely through the rest of the year. My objective was clear. Get a clean ticket through the course, graduate as "passed Staff College" and then have far greater opportunities for the future. A good lesson learned! The "meaning of life" for me then was simply to graduate and move on!

The grounds of the Camberley real estate were extensive. Behind the college building was, and as far as I know it still is, a large expanse of woodland criss-crossed by long tree-lined trails called Barossa Common – perfect for training runs. Already my fitness level was good but I was able to improve it further during my year at the college. If I felt frustrated by the too structured level of tuition, I put up with it until the end of the day's work, then stripped off into running kit and ran hard along the trails. Not only did this exercise keep me in good physical shape but also it did wonders for my mental condition. I often ended the classes feeling really pent up with frustration and concerns about the particular issue of the moment. After one hour's hard running, I returned feeling both physically and mentally back in balance.

Our course syllabus worked its way through the year with impeccable organisation and planning. In early June, as in many previous years, the course decamped and moved to northern France for what was called "the battlefield tour". Some wags renamed this the "bottlefield tour!" Here, we recaptured the opening days of the Normandy landings in June 1944, with guest speakers who had actually been there – Brit and American naval veterans who had brought the early boatloads of troops onto the beaches, ex-soldiers who had served with the initial invading forces as the initial bridgeheads were seized, German ex Wehrmacht soldiers who were defending against the invasion, British ex glider pilots involved in the operation to secure the "Pegasus" bridge, veterans of the Free French Army who had been members of the French resistance. Each of the above were positioned in the "battle zones" they had occupied in 1944 and gave vivid descriptions of their personal experiences. At the year of our 1973 course these gallant gentlemen were by this time senior citizens and we later heard that ours was one of the last courses to have had the honour of learning from their personal stories. In the evenings, the previous antagonists, Brit, American, French and German all gathered for their own reunion, their original national enmity long forgotten. A truly meaningful experience and one that reminded us of the deaths of so many young men during the war years. The number of deaths was given as statistics but each was an individual life often cut off in its prime. Did any or all have some sort of life after death? That is the big unanswered question!

xxx

Digression – the taxi driver.

In August, the course adjourned for a summer break, an event which highlighted that although we students were all seen as equal during the working sessions, this interim reflected our different backgrounds. Most of the Europeans returned to their home countries with their families as did many of the other nationalities. Some others though, principally those from African countries, could not afford to go home so they either stayed with their wives in the military married accommodation or just carried on living in the single rooms at the college. Amongst us Brits there was also a large disparity. Some of the wealthier officers decamped to various Mediterranean resorts e.g. sailing in the Greek islands or to rented holiday villas in France, Italy or Spain. My own summer break was spent differently. Since I had taken out the mortgage on our little house in Winchester, our family finances had become stretched to the point where I was getting seriously concerned about how to pay our routine household bills.

My solution was to drive for a local Winchester taxi firm, mostly on the night shift. The firm didn't pay high wages but, with a little charm and ingenuity, the tips from passengers were quite generous. Of course, such "black" employment would have been heavily frowned upon by my military bosses but fortunately they never found out. My motivation was simply to improve my family finances. When you're broke, "you have to do what you have to do." I found that my taxi was in particularly high demand on Friday and Saturday evenings. Routinely I would be called to pick up couples who were going out for a social evening. They would be smartly dressed, neat and polite as I dropped them off at their evening venue. Later, when I collected them to take them home, they were often a very changed state – scruffy, garrulous, over familiar – what an evening's drinking will do! – but this was not my concern particularly if they gave me a generous tip! I drove all types of humanity – some courteous, some continuously complaining.

I enjoyed picking up families, typically father, mother and two or three children, needing to be taken to an airport at the start of their holiday. These events were often a wonderful reflexion of human nature and, to me the most important aspect at that time, a source of good tips! An example: I would get a call from the taxi firm that family X needed to be collected to take them to the airport – usually at Eastleigh, Southampton, the closest to Winchester. I would arrive outside their house in good time, usually having to wait while one or other of the family was late with their packing. Often, they would have copious luggage which took time to load. At last all would be squeezed into the taxi and we would proceed for a time then suddenly one of the passengers would fretfully realise that he or she had forgotten their passport so we would hurriedly return to the house. At last, the missing passport would be located and we would get going again. By now, the time was getting on and the father would be getting stressed that the family might not get to the airport on time. I, ever the "patient co-operative driver", would be urged to get to the airport as fast as possible. Usually I made it my business to know the check-in deadline for the flight and would have calculated how long it would take to reach the airport drop off point. Often, there would still be good time but I found it better not to tell this to the family but rather to respond by appearing to be trying my very best to get them there on time. Sometimes, I found a good ploy to increase my passengers' stress level would be to ensure that we approached traffic lights just as they were turning to red. I would be drumming on the steering wheel as we waited then, as the lights turned to green, would rev up and shoot off with the impression of trying to catch up on time. If I could gauge it well, we would finally arrive at our destination with a flourish as we screamed to a halt. I would then help my by now grateful passengers out of the car and, with luck, this ploy would result in a healthy tip. Then on to the next fare!

End of Digression

xxx

My taxi driving job gave me the chance to rethink where I was going in my military career and in my life in general. I had now firmly resolved to do my best to complete the final three months of the Staff College course so as to have a chance of a full military career and therefore continuity finance to support my family and pay off my mortgage. For some time I had felt there was something lacking in my life and it was while waiting to pick up some taxi fare that it fully dawned on me what it was. After I had left school with moderate "A" level results, I could have taken up the offer of a university place, for example at Bristol, but, as I explained earlier, my grades were not good enough to get a place at Cambridge. As it turned out, the two years of national military service had enriched my life and after that experience the idea of then applying to go to university seemed passé and irrelevant. I wanted to get on with the rest of my life. Now I was questioning my youthful decisions. At the Staff College, I appreciated the training we were being given but resented the lack of originality and opportunity for free thinking. Here I was, a thirty-four-year-old major in the Intelligence Corps yet I didn't have a degree, while so many of our smart young soldiers, male and female, were joining us as university graduates. If only for my own self-esteem, I felt I needed to get some sort of university education at least to be on the same academic level as our soldiers. I realised that it would not be feasible to ask the army to give me a three-year sabbatical to attend a university even if any would accept me! But there was another way – the Open University. I realised that if I enrolled on an OU course I could study for a degree in my own time and still continue with my army career. During this summer break, I sent off my application to the OU, was accepted and enrolled in a degree course starting that same autumn. The first year involved completing a foundation course comprising a series of units to be studied then answered by correspondence. I asked to be enrolled as an overseas student as I was expecting to be posted abroad for most of the time during my studies. All the OU work would have to be in addition to my military duties but if I could complete the course, this would give me a BA degree in a few years. I just had to make sure I could allocate enough time to keep up with the course no matter what, where and how the rest my military career would develop.

xxx

When the three-week break from the Staff College was over, the taxi firm and I parted on good terms, my anonymity had been retained and my mission of topping up our family funds was quite successful. I dressed again back into my military major's uniform and returned to the college. It was rather galling to have to endure stories of the wonderful hols that some of my wealthy colleagues had enjoyed at their various exotic venues – all part of life's rich pattern!

The last four months of the Staff College course were for me more enjoyable and relaxed than the first part. I found I could conform to all the requirements of the college, yet in my spare moments could also explore wider insights presented by the excellent OU course material that started in September.

At the end of the Staff College course, students were not given achievement marks, instead they were assigned their next military appointment. These varied in the level of appointment which by its role indicated how well (or badly!) each student had been rated. For example, officers posted to be aides to the military's top generals in operational assignments or senior staff appointments indicated that that officer was highly rated. At the end of the course, I felt I was performing well and I half hoped I might be rewarded with one of these star jobs. However, The Intelligence Corps was required to fill a post, reserved for "passed Staff College students" in a recently formed organisation called the Surveillance, Target Acquisition and Night Observation centre or STANOC for short. As there were only two Intelligence Corps members on the course, it was a 50/50 chance I would be given that job. Despite my vague hope, my posting was as expected. I was to be a staff officer, second grade (i.e. a major's appointment) at the STANOC centre. I was informed that I would have two offices – one in Larkhill, Wiltshire, the home of the Royal Artillery and one in the Old War Office building, Ministry of Defence, Whitehall, London. I was also informed that I could expect to spend extended periods abroad – details to follow!

XXX

Chapter Twenty-Six

STANOC

(Surveillance, Target Acquisition, Night Observation Centre)

I use this chapter to underline the fragility of life in some parts of the world. I took the example of Oman in the 1970s but could equally have chosen other regions of the world which face similar issues. How fortunate are those of us who have been brought up in countries which enjoy peace and stability! All "armchair" clerics, spiritualists and philosophers; please note!

I describe one military operation in considerable detail as it highlights lives under stress socially, personally, domestically and emotionally – our own soldiers, those of our enemies and potential enemies, and those caught up in war zones: lives saved, lost, threatened; the fragility of life and personal relationships. I give examples of the reality of "hands-on", down to earth, life whose "meaning" involves so much more than spiritual theorising. Life can be wonderful and full of love. It can also be harsh, dangerous and inexplicably cruel. It questions if there is a "loving" God, how could he oversee the loss of innocent lives in disasters: some provoked by humans, such as the killing of innocents in war, e.g. Ukraine from 2022, or resulting from disease and/or starvation (Oman, Burundi, Eritrea) or from such events as floods (Mississippi – St Louis 1993), tsunamis (Palu and Sumatra, Indonesia 2018) and earthquakes (Turkey/Syria 2023)?

xxx

I had imagined that, working for an organisation called STANOC, would principally be an office bound job involved in research and development and possibly soldier training in new equipment. In reality, I found the job did indeed involve R and D and training – but office bound – absolutely not! There followed one of the most interesting, varied and dangerous jobs I had during my time in the army.

Dhofar, Oman

My first assignment, resulting from a ministry of defence emergency edict. was to familiarise myself with US produced unattended ground sensors and, if US authorisation could be obtained, to deploy them on operational trials in the Oman. It sounded a reasonably straightforward job until I went into the detail. To complete this mission, understanding the following was vital:

- the political and operational situation in the Oman,
- force structures of the local/supporting forces,
- insurgent forces and their tactics,
- the technology of unattended ground sensors and how the US army had used them in Vietnam.
- how these sensors might best be deployed in support of operations in Oman,
- the political constraints of using US equipment in the Oman,
- how to form a specialist team to support this assignment.

The operational region involved was in the Dhofar, a province in the south and west of Oman, covering about half of the country. For centuries, the Oman has been of global strategic significance as it dominates the traditional trade routes between Europe, India and the Far East and access to the Straits of Hormuz, through which, from the 1960s, a major proportion of the world's oil has been shipped.

For centuries, there had been feuding between local tribes over the key elements of life in the region: land, water and cattle. Life here is harsh, the native Omanis are desperately poor and ill nourished. Life expectancy (1974) was a maximum of fifty years. There were no formal boundaries between these tribes in Dhofar's mountainous regions known as the "djebel". Politically, the country was divided between the Sultan, traditionally residing in the capital, Muscat and the Imam, who controlled the "djebel". Britain had been involved in the region since signing a defence treaty with the Sultan way back in1798, which in essence allowed the Oman to remain an independent country under the Sultan while the British provided external security, advice and support in internal defence matters. Internally, life in the Oman remained of little significance to the rest of the world for many years until events in the 1960s and early 70s brought the region into international focus. The main events were:

- The huge increase in global demand for oil. Oman did not have large oil reserves, unlike Saudi Arabia, Iraq and the Gulf states but the national borders between Oman, Saudi Arabia and Yemen assumed far greater political strategic importance. Saudi Arabia backed the Imam against the Sultan and then declared the interior of Oman to be an independent state. Tensions increased between Sultan bin Taimur, and the Imam, particularly after a new Imam, Ghalib bin Ali, was appointed. Concerned about losing power, the Sultan closed the borders of Oman to the outside world. No journalists were permitted to enter the country resulting in little being known about events there by the world's press.

- Nationalist movements in Yemen and Oman were supported by Egypt and more significantly by the Soviet Union and China, who were both pressing to extend their influence in the region. At that time both communist regimes supported different insurgent groups, the Soviets mainly with weapons and training, the Chinese with financial interest free loans. Both offered sponsorship and invited insurgent leaders to Moscow and Beijing for training. The Soviets and Chinese also saw the potential in Oman for fostering revolution which could spread across the oil rich states of the Arabian peninsula.

- After being defeated during the Arab-Israeli war in 1967, Egypt pulled back from supporting the Yemeni and Omani insurgents leaving the field clear for the communist powers to increase their supply of weapons and money and to wage an indoctrination programme promoting the ideas of Marx, Lenin, Mao Zedong and Che Guevara. The Dhofari groups united under one organisation known as the Popular Front for the Liberation of the Occupied Arabian Gulf, abbreviated as PFLOAG.

- In South Yemen, after an intense terrorist campaign, Britain finally withdraw from Aden and the rest of that country in November 1967. Following this event, the British government was reluctant to get drawn into another major conflict in Oman. Although they still retained their treaty with the Sultan, they opposed his repressive measures and were only prepared to continue support with a small, deniable but highly effective force of SAS special forces and a contract air force. The UK was also instrumental in bringing about a coup d'état in July 1970 which overthrew Sultan bin Taimur and replaced him with his son, the Sandhurst trained Qaboos bin Said. Qaboos immediately initiated a policy of modernization, improvement in living standards and support for the small British led force.

-By early1974 the pro-Sultan forces in the Dhofar region had succeeded in pushing back many of the insurgent forces onto the "Djebel" mountainous region north west of Salalah. These fighters were still very active and continued attempting to reinforce elements of their forces remaining further to the east of the region.

xxx

The Mission

This was "to assess whether unattended ground sensors could successfully detect the movement and composition of insurgent forces through the wadi valleys." The US unattended ground sensors involved were of the design deployed successfully in Vietnam to detect and monitor movement along the Ho Chi Minh trail. They consisted of a mix of sensors which, as an integrated system, could detect movement of armed humans, count numbers and speed of movement. From this information, mortar strikes could accurately be launched.

The US agreed, with some reluctance, to release a supply of these sensors for our deployment in the Dhofar. There were tight caveats. By 1974, the US had already been involved in the combat war in Viet Nam since 1955 (the fall of Saigon was the following year – April 1975). Their government was very sensitive about any further involvement or deployment of their forces or military assets and only agreed to the use of their ground sensors in the Dhofar provided they were controlled by one named British officer who was required to sign for each item and return all after their use. I was to be the named officer! Any operational use had to be covert and deniable.

The US defence department authorized me to travel to the US in order to familiarize myself with the sensors and to learn about their capabilities and limitations. This involved briefings at the Pentagon in Washington, then to a US sensor trials facility in Arizona. I had stressed to my UK MOD sponsors that my background was not in technology and I would need a qualified guy with appropriate technical skills to join my trials team. He should be ready to accompany me to the US, during our visit to the Arizona sensor facility. I was in luck as, the following week, Staff Sergeant (SSgt) Tom Randall reported to me at Larkhill. His Corps was the Royal Electrical and Mechanical Engineers (REME). He told me he had orders to be attached to my team for this Oman mission. I was impressed by Tom's knowledge and enthusiasm. I would need to lean heavily on his technical expertise.

During our visit to the US we learnt that the sensor systems are most effective when deployed in strings as follows: first are seismic sensors which detect any movement within range (these can be calibrated to local conditions), next are magnetic sensors which detect ferrous metal – e.g. identifying a human being armed with a weapon; third are passive infrared, which can record the numbers of persons moving, lastly is a microphone which records sounds such as the human voice. By integrating all these capabilities, the controller can detect and count the number of persons passing through the sensor string and can estimate the time taken to reach a certain waypoint where accurate targeting can be calculated. We had discussions with US personnel who had had first-hand experience of operating these sensors in Vietnam and had used the information provided to mount effective strikes against those who had been detected.

Before leaving the US, I was required to sign for our allocation of sensors giving my full personal details and the threat of terrifying consequences if I failed to return them all intact! I asked how best we could retrieve them once they were hidden along suspected enemy trail routes but only received vague replies. I learnt that was my problem not that of the US military!

Note: Writing this book some fifty years after the event, I can't help thinking it would have been great to have used drones to tackle this mission. However, this action took place in 1974, well before drones were invented. In any case, drones are both noisy beasts and, except when fitted with infrared sensors, can't see in the dark – the very time when we expected the adoo enemy to be moving on the trails! So – unattended ground sensors it was!

xxx

Preparation

Back in the UK, we needed to find some expert to devise a gadget to help us to retrieve the sensors after they had been carefully hidden to prevent their detection by the insurgent forces – seemed like a total contradiction! I wasn't the only one to think that. As I trudged round the various UK defence research and development establishments – in Fort Halstead, Kent, in Christchurch, Dorset, and Malvern, Worcestershire, all the brilliant boffins asked the same question – why on earth would you need to retrieve a sensor which is designed to be hidden – particularly when it's in a dangerous operational location? I couldn't give a sensible answer. Only, those were strict US conditions and delicate relations between the UK and the US were at stake. Probably more out of technical curiosity than confidence, an outstanding young scientist from the Christchurch establishment took pity on me and put his team to work to try to solve the problem. In just a couple of weeks he produced a cunning device which, when activated, gave out a bleep whenever it was within a few metres of the hidden sensor. A major limitation was that the searcher had to wear a headset to hear the bleep – not a good idea in an operational setting!

Before leaving for the US, we assembled a trials team consisting, in addition to SSgt Tom Randall, of a communications specialist, Sergeant (Sgt) John Fuller, Bombardier (Bdr) Jeff Archer, an accomplished free style draftsman and photographer and two young infantrymen Privates (Ptes) Kevin White and Paul Turner from the Royal Hampshire Regiment to act as our protection team.

Our team was complete at Larkhill by 26 January. We had just over a week to get to know each other, and to carry out ground trails of the sensors on the edge of the artillery range on the Salisbury plain. We would arrive in Oman in the midst of the hot season there so we would need to confirm that our findings of the effectiveness of the sensors on the frozen ground of a British winter would also apply in hot, sandy Omani djebel. For weapons we took US ArmaLite AR-15 submachine guns and we also took short range radios to enable us to communicate effectively between us during operational deployment.

xxx

Deployment to Dhofar

The first part of our journey was routine – Brize Norton to the RAF staging post of Mazirah, a small barren island stuck off the coast of Oman, a night stop there then straight on to Salalah. the capital of the Dhofar region. I checked in with HQ Sultan's Own Force (SAF) where I met the force commander who by chance was with Brigadier John Akehurst himself in the process of taking over command of the Force. Our briefing covered a resumé of the events since the coup in 1970 when Qaboos bin Said deposed his father as Sultan of Oman, the gradual improvements to the living standards of local people, the slow turning of many of the insurgent forces (known as adoo) away from their Chinese and Russian paymasters to join the government side, the positive results achieved by the SAS special forces particularly after their dramatic and heroic defence of the town of Mirbat in July 1972 (This amazing episode of SAS courage and resilience is recorded in the book "*SAS Operation Storm*" by Roger Cole and Richard Belfield.) and the efforts to retake inland areas from adoo control.

There was still much to do to achieve a lasting peace in the Dhofar region. In recent months, SAF had been constructing a defence line, known as the

"Hornbeam Line" running north from the coastal town of Mugsayl. A series of outposts located on commanding peaks had been established, linked with barbed wire. These outposts possessed mortars and some artillery to provide cover for patrols and to harass adoo positions and tracks used by them. The principal aim of the Hornbeam Line was to cut the adoo main supply routes from the Yemen into east Dhofar and further into the rest of Oman. The topography of the terrain in the mountainous region north of Mugsayl comprises many high jebel peaks interspersed with deep sided hills dropping sharply down to the wadi valleys. This terrain posed major problems to SAF forces as direct observation from the outposts was not possible. Fire missions into the wadis was not practical by air or artillery, but mortars can be very effective provided they have an identified target. This had been a known problem for some time but, until now, no effective solution had been found. Hence our mission.

The same day that we arrived in Salalah, we were reloaded into a stubby plane known as a Skyvan and flown the short distance down the coast to land at a rough airstrip in the small settlement of Mugsayl, then by Land Rover to a secured holding area to the north. We negotiated a short stay period there before our operational deployment to establish if the sensors would respond satisfactorily in the arid soil of the Dhofar, to test fire all our weapons and to acclimatise ourselves to the harsh hot season in the Dhofar.

After this mini acclimatization period, we were flown by helicopter to our first outpost. The aircrew members wore smart new American uniforms but they were not US personnel. They were all Persian nationals; recently the Shah of Iran had decided to support Sultan Qaboos by loaning a number of helicopters with their crews. As we flew north, the terrain became mountainous, lacking in vegetation and looking like somewhere on the surface of the moon. This is harsh inhospitable country where for centuries the local peoples have survived on sparse resources. The jebel tops were cut by the deep wadis. The pilot was in radio contact with the local forces and brought us in to land on the "H" of the hand-made landing point on the top of a jebel outpost. Our small team disembarked and we were welcomed by a British captain, Mike Shellard, a seconded officer serving with the Northern Frontier Regiment (NFR) of SAF. All his twenty soldiers were local NFR Omanis. Mike's deputy was an Omani national who spoke quite good English. Although Mike spoke some Arabic, it was very basic and he had to rely heavily on his deputy to communicate with the rest of his soldiers. Not ideal! Mike had constructed four sangers built of piled stones in igloolike shapes. He allocated one for our team as our base; necessary as we regularly came under artillery fire from the adoo. Near the sangers was the operations and command post for his unit. Mike explained that his mission was to monitor the wadi trails in his designated area of operations with the aim of attacking the adoo supply movements along the wadi. He liaised with the sub units on other outposts each side of his position. Mike had laid some anti-personal mines and flairs along trails that he assessed were most frequently used. He said that he had had several contacts with the adoo and fired mortar strikes at suspected adoo movements but that he had no clear intelligence regarding their exact locations and little evidence that his actions had hit his intended targets or disrupted adoo convoys. He looked to our team to help him to locate the adoo movements accurately.

From our jebel top location, the ground fell sharply for at least five hundred metres down to the wadi below. At places the slope was almost concave, which completely obscured direct vision. Our team would have to scale down this slope to get to the wadi in order to set out our sensor trails. A complication was that the soil on the hill comprised loose shale making it impossible to descend without dislodging them and revealing our own movement to any adoo in the wadi. Mike said he had found one route down which was the less steep than other options.

We decided to scale down the jebel at first light the next day. I would take four of our six-men team with me but leave John Fuller, our communications expert, behind in Mike's HQ building to keep radio contact with us and test that the sensors could be monitored satisfactorily from the command post. Mike would act as our guide on this first sortie and provide one of his sections as a protection party. A mortar mission would blast off both as we descended and again on our return to cover the noise we would make as we clambered and slithered up and down the jebel.

Our logistics were basic. We would eat when Mike's soldiers prepared their meals. Water was strictly rationed.

The night was noisy and disruptive, typical for life on the Hornbeam Line. The adoo periodically fired off mortars (or some type of artillery) which would explode somewhere nearby. It was spasmodic and interspersed by periods of silence. It seemed to be random and not precisely targeted. Our stone sanger provided protection and during the night nothing exploded directly where we were located or on any of the other sangers.

Deployment

We set out at dawn the next day. Both our own team and Mike's soldiers had our own communications to the HQ building, Mike to his deputy, I to Sgt John Fuller. Mike led with four of his soldiers, then our team followed on with the assortment of sensors we had decided to take on this first trial. The remaining four Omanis brought up the rear. Mike's mortar crew fire mission covered the racket we made when we started the decent and dislodged piles of small stones which eddied down the side of the jebel. Not even the most light-footed soldier could have climbed down quietly.

After about an hour of our slip/sliding descent we reached the wadi, it's base varying between twenty and a fifty hundred metres wide with a flat mostly sandy surface interspersed with rocky outcrops. There was the clear trace of a riverbed which may have had water flowing through it in the rainy season but then in February was completely dry.

We soon identified tracks left by the adoo as they had passed along the wadi – signs of human footprints and much larger prints made by horses, donkeys or camels. To confirm this, we found traces of camel droppings, which our Omani soldiers said had been left within the past few days. We centred our first sensor deployment trail in one area where the track narrowed as it passed between a series of rocks. We laid out the seismic, magnetic and infrared sensors in the configuration explained above. Finally, we found a small area where we felt the group might well bunch up. Here we positioned the HEC microphone sensor which records all sounds including voices.

Jeff Archer, our sketcher, draw a plot, with precise measurements of the layout and took a series of photos to recode each deployment. Then Tom Randall checked that each sensor was correctly armed and its battery tested, then used our precious "sensor-locator" to check that it could detect each sensor when we later would need to recover them. Finally, we established radio contact with John Fuller back in the Control HQ on the Jebel to ensure that when each sensor was activated, John could clearly detect these activations on his monitor. We then hid the sensors so that they were invisible to the naked eye. Our first deployment was complete!

Mike again called his mortar team to initiate a further programme to cover our noisy and laboured slog back up the jebel. Jeff Archer, who was not in good shape, was gasping for breath towards the top.

xxx

Waiting!

Back up on the jebel, we now had to wait for our sensor trail to be triggered. Late that afternoon a helicopter landed on our "H" helipad. It brought much appreciated supplies of rations, water, ammunition and some other items that Mike had requested. Again, the heli crew were all Persian. They seemed to have integrated well into the command structure of SAF (Sultan's Own Forces).

We were now permanently manning our sensor monitoring station with either Tom Randall, John Fuller, Jeff Archer or me taking duty turns. John Fuller patiently took Kevin White and Paul Turner through the procedures and pronounced them both competent enough to take their turn. These two young infantrymen were fitting into the rhythm of our team very well. Both were fit guys, willingly carrying out all that was asked of them, dependable and keen to learn. They were becoming real assets.

It was thought unlikely that the adoo would be on the trail during daylight hours but we manned our monitor set anyway. But during the night – we were hopeful but had no prior intelligence about which day/night they might choose. There were occasional activations of the seismic sensors. Each time we monitored these but neither the magnetic nor the passive infrared were also triggered. We assessed these movements were caused by animals straying in range of the seismic sensors and that no humans were involved. With practice we all learnt to differentiate between animal and human movements.

Throughout that night, we again received the occasional bombardment from the adoo but again no direct hits. Disappointingly, there were no sensor activations of human movement.

During the next days, we kept ourselves as involved as possible – ensuring all our sensors were still operational. We checked our deployed sensors by getting the mortar team to fire close to the end of our sensor trail, switching on the microphone sensor and listening to the blast as the mortar round exploded. This worked well producing dramatic results as we could hear the mortar rounds exploding close to the sensor. We also did some physical training within the tight confines of our outpost perimeter. Jeff Archer, our chubby artilleryman, took these sessions very seriously!

Digression – Open University assignment

There were no sensor activations indicating human movement for the next few days as we continued the same procedure with always one of us on duty manning the monitoring station. The rest were either sleeping inside the sanger or trying to exercise in the defence limited area. The spasmodic shelling had by now become almost routine. For the first time since we had arrived in the Oman, I decided to unzip a small valise that I had stored inside my kitbag. This contained my Open University material. The last unit we had to study was entitled “An Introduction to Sociology”. The OU produced written units containing all the main points of the module then referred to a number of books which amplify and relate to it. We students were required to study all the written units and recommended text books then write an assignment essay to be marked by our tutor (TMA), in my case a lady living in Milton Keynes. I had read the course material just before we left the UK and more while waiting for our flight. Since then, my world had been preoccupied with this mission in the Dhofar. I saw that the relevant TMA had to be received by my tutor by no later than 12 March, that was in less than one week. I was still new to the OU and I must try not to fall behind so early in the course. Mike had told me there was a heli resupply due shortly so if I could finish the TMA essay, I would try to persuade the pilot to take my essay with him and somehow get it to Masirah. From there it could be transferred to the British Forces Post Office (BFPO) system and hopefully find its way to my tutor in Milton Keynes before the cut-off deadline. Partly under torchlight, I reread the course material and skimmed through the two associated text books I had brought along. One was called *Sociological Perspectives*, a series of extracts from such eminence characters as Karl Marx and Max Weber. The other was entitled *Decisions, Organizations and Society*, which again comprised a series of writings by academics, mostly, with a decidedly left-wing flavour! I wondered what these sociologists would make of our life on the Hornbeam Line! As I was writing the TMA essay, there was further frequent shelling overhead, one round exploding close enough to our sanger for loose stones to be blown off over our heads. No one had been hit. I knew I was giving the required text book reading very superficial attention but found what I thought were some relevant quotes and stuck them into my essay. When I had finished writing, I did a quick read through, made a few manuscript corrections, stuck the pages into an envelope and wrote on it my tutors name and address. I realised my work was shallow and lightweight but hoped it might scrape a pass. I also hoped that I would have more time to devote to the next module. For now, I needed to drag my attention back to our military mission.

As much as I hoped we would have an activation during this period, I was relieved that none had occurred while I was in essay writing mode. The next morning the replenishment heli arrived and the Persian pilot agreed to take my package back to Salalah for onwards transmission to the BFPO in Masirah. I hoped it would reach my tutor, be on time and that she wouldn't be too hard on me!

End of Digression

xxx

Contact!

Back to our mission. Our team were still routinely monitoring our sensor trail but until now there had still not been any human activations. We started to have doubts. Were we monitoring the right trail? Had the adoo somehow slipped by without activating the sensors? Had they got intelligence about our trial and taken evasive actions? We had been required by HQ SAF and the MOD to send frequent updates. So far, we had nothing to report. The monitoring procedure required full concentration and I wondered how long our team would keep motivated before their concentration level might decline as there was no human movement to record. Perhaps we should request moving to another outpost and lay another set of sensors.

On our sixth night, we continued the procedure of one always on monitoring duty, the rest of us retiring to our sanger. Just after midnight, Paul Turner shook me awake whispering:

"Can you come quickly? I think we have human movement."

I shot out of my sleeping bag and followed Paul to the control building. We both checked the monitor as Paul explained:

"We started getting seismic activations, several of them, about ten minutes ago. At first, I thought they might be caused by animals passing within range of the sensor as we've noticed before. Then one of the magnetics activated. Then another. Then a third. That's when I decided to call you."

I told Paul he did the right thing and to wake up Mike, his Omani deputy and the rest of our team immediately and for them to join me while I took over the monitoring. While waiting, one of the passive infrareds started to activate. I counted each activation. There were twenty. Mike and the rest soon arrived. I told them I thought we were looking at a party of at least twenty individuals and, judging by the frequent seismic bleeps, it was likely they had a convoy of animals with them. This was our target. Mike stood up the mortar crew ready to fire a sortie on the coordinates of the HEC (microphone) sensor we had previously registered. The pattern and timing of activations enabled us to estimate when the leading group would reach the location of the HEC. We had also registered the time taken for a mortar round from firing to exploding on its target. John Fuller made the key calculation of when the majority of the group would reach the area of the HEC. It was critical to get the correct timing of the mortar explosions/group at the HEC synchronised.

We continued to listen and monitor the movement. In an almost uncanny way, we could visualise who and what was moving in the wadi far below. When we were sure the lead group were about to reach the position of our HEC microphone sensor, Mike gave the mortar fire order. We heard the clump as the firing commenced. Then there was silence until the rounds passed us on their downwards spiral and finally the blast of the explosion in the wadi below. We heard this from our position on the jebel but far more distinctly through the HEC microphone on the wadi floor. We heard screams and shouting and knew we had made an accurate hit. Mike's Omani deputy had a spare headset and monitored the Arab language then translated it to English. He said it was incoherent but he could hear voices in panic and confusion. We then knew we had correctly identified an adoo convoy and had either destroyed it or at the least caused major disruption. When it was light, we would send a patrol to carry out post-strike analysis to determine the full results of the mortar strike. For now, we knew our mission here had been successfully achieved.

It was tempting to stand down our monitoring for the night but we reckoned that, though unlikely, the adoo might send reinforcements to their beleaguered comrades in the wadi. So we continued to monitor the sensors during the rest of the night but there were no further human activations. Using Mike's comms. I sent off a short sitrep to HQ SAF to inform them of our adoo contact, reporting that we would send further details when the post-strike analysis had been carried out and asking for a heli to be on standby to evacuate any wounded we might find tomorrow. I got an acknowledgement from the SAF duty officer.

Early the next day our team accompanied Mike's patrol back down the wadi. The scene was a mess. We counted six dead adoo, and three others who were wounded but too badly immobilized to be able to move. We attended to them with the first aid kit we carried as standard equipment but knew they would need proper medical attention as soon as it could be brought to them. There was no sign of the remainder of the adoo who were in the original group. They must have fled off. There were two dead camels and four donkeys alive and still laden with supplies. They had not strayed far from the scene. The most significant find was a large supply of weapons and ammunition – a mix of Russian AK 47s, Katyusha rockets, three Shpagin heavy machine guns and a mass of associated ammunition. Quite a haul! Mike reckoned we could just squeeze in a helicopter onto one of the wider parts of the wadi and called up for one, asking for medical support. About an hour later we heard the clump of rotor blades and we successfully guided the heli safely down into the wadi. Mike set up a defence perimeter ring to guard against an adoo counter attack. There was none. The heli brought two medics who took charge of the wounded adoos, ferried them to transit at our jebel outpost, then returned first to collect the dead adoo bodies, again to collect the weapons and finally to ferry our own people back to our base. John Fuller tested that the sensors were all still in place and functioning efficiently. He reported that they were all OK except the HEC which had taken a hit from the Mortar strike. We replaced it with the spare we had brought. We also took the opportunity to test out our magic detector. It worked well. This recovery phase was completed by late morning.

I sent a report to SAF HQ itemising the dead, casualties, retrieved weapons, ammunition and other supplies. I wondered what we should do next: should we continue monitoring from this location, or recover our sensors and move to another outpost. While we waited for further instructions from HQ SAF, we were told via Mike radio to remain at our present location and to await a visit from unspecified SAF personnel.

Shortly after being alerted, another heli arrived, out of which alighted a group comprising Brigadier Akehurst and a four-star general whose name I didn't catch. They were accompanied by two staff officers and the general's aide de camp. It seemed we were the flavour of the moment. Mike and I met these worthy gentlemen and I gave a briefing of our mission and the outcome of last night's operation. I explained how our sensors worked and how we were able accurately to assess the composition of the adoo and their precise location. The VIP officers seemed very satisfied. Mike then took them on a tour of his control building.

Mini digression! I stayed to talk to the General's aide who, to my delight, produced a picnic hamper and offered me one of the fresh sandwiches it contained. What a treat! I woofed down the heavenly offering and selfishly snatched a second before the aide could close the box. I know I should have been more dignified and alert to the general's visit but after our time on dry rations, the sandwiches momentarily blotted out all other thoughts! **End!**

When the generals returned to the helicopter, they told us they would be contacting the MOD and we would be informed. Meanwhile Brigadier Akehurst confirmed that our forces with such sensors could now dominate the ground and that the Hornbeam Line could act as an efficient means of ensuring that the adoo could no longer depend on using the wadi valleys to reinforce their assets to the east of the country. With those parting words, the visitors returned to the heli which wheeled away. We had had a good day.

XXX

Trapped in the Wadi!

We continued our monitoring throughout that night but had no further contact. The next morning we received a signal from HQ SAF telling us that our trial had been registered as a success and that we were to prepare to withdraw back to Salalah. I can't say I was disappointed as life on the jebel was basic and we had achieved all we had come to do. Now we needed to perform the final duty: to comply with the rigid US directive to retrieve all the sensors. This would be a great test for John Fuller and our magic detector. We requested a helicopter to get us back down to the wadi but was told none was available except in an emergency which this was not. Mike again produced a section of his soldiers as a protection party plus a radio operator. Again, our gallant team slithered down the face of the jebel with our noisy descent covered by another mortar fire mission. Down in the wadi, I sent the Omani soldiers ahead to cover us while we painstakingly commenced to retrieve the sensors. We used Jeff Archer's excellent sketches and photos to get us to each local area then used the detector to home in on the precise location of each sensor. The system worked but it took time and patience to find each one. We accounted for every seismic sensor except two and after several unsuccessful attempts I decided to abort the search for now and to concentrate on the rest of the sensor types. We found all the magnetics and then the passive infrareds which were positioned at human mid body height and were easier to spot. We then picked up the HEC which we had replaced the previous day. That left the two seismic sensors. We returned back along the trail to renew our search. It was while we were in the search area that we were attacked. The first alarm was a burst of rapid fire ahead of us where our Omani protection section had deployed. The ground around us was filled with sharp rocky outcrops and our team dropped in behind these to use as some sort of cover as we readied are own weapons hoping that the Mike's soldiers up ahead would see off the attack. Mike's radio operator was with our group. I crawled along to his position, got to his radio and signalled through to inform Mike of the situation. I got an acknowledgement. We were hampered by having to protect not only ourselves but the sensors we had recovered. Meanwhile, all we could do was stay tight, cover each other and wait. The firing ahead continued constantly for a time then we saw two of Mike's men appear running back towards us. They dived for cover alongside us. Moments later a further four of Mike's men also ran towards us and, like the other two, dived down near our own positions. One was limping and had clearly been wounded. I knew there were eight in the original section so it seemed probable that the other two were wounded or worse. This new configuration meant our protection party was no longer ahead of us and my group was now directly facing the adoo. I called out to my guys to be prepared to open fire but to wait for my order to do so. I had to do a quick assessment. All my group were soldiers but Tom, John and Jeff were specialist tradesmen and only our two infantrymen were trained to face this type of situation and both of them were young soldiers who had yet to experience this type of close combat. Another issue was that we had each carried a weapon and a full magazine, but no spares and no other extras such as grenades. We would have to conserve our ammunition if we were engaged in a drawn-out fire fight. Not good.

For a time there was a period of quiet then I saw four “adoos” slowly moving up the wadi towards us. We continued to take aim but still held our fire until they were about fifty metres from us, well within the range of our ArmaLites. I aimed at the lead adoo and squeezed the trigger while shouting to the others to fire but only single shots. We clearly hit three of them, but then there were more. Another five or six adoo appeared firing as they advanced towards us. We heard a scream and realised that at least another of Mike’s men had been hit. It got worse. Suddenly we heard bursts of rapid fire from a machine gun. From the deep signature it seemed it was of medium to heavy calibre. It continued on continuous rapid fire for some time and again I heard cries from Mike’s soldiers. Then for a time there was silence. I knew that Mike’s men had a light machine gun, a Bren I think. Why was it not being used? Their own return fire had ceased and for all we could tell they were out of action. We were now on our own. We were pinned down, had limited ammunition and our only withdrawal route was back up the jebel. We were stuck.

I kept in voice contact with our team. So far everyone was still uninjured. I prayed it would stay that way. I was staring out towards the adoo positions and I saw movement which as far as I could tell was from two guys lugging something heavy with them. I realised it was the team carrying the heavy machine gun. They were probably trying to manoeuvre into a position so that they could get a clear line of fire of our group. We had to do something to prevent this. I thought to risk moving ahead myself to see if I could get a direct hit on the gun crew when there was firing from near me. It was accurate shooting and I saw the two adoo fall and lie still. Their machine gun was now unmanned. Our firer was Paul Turner, our infantry private soldier. He had also seen the threat and taken the initiative to take on the machine gun team.

There followed another long standoff and my next concern was that it would soon be dark. I had no idea how that might change the odds against us. Throughout, the adoo continued firing random shots, our side reserving our fire only for clear targets. Then it all changed again. First there was a salvo of mortar fire landing over our heads and behind the adoo positions. Then there was rapid fire from behind us. This increased in intensity until a group of soldiers appeared from behind us, ran through our positions, using fire and movement tactics as they advanced towards the adoo. The arrival of Mike's reinforcement broke our stand-off stalemate. The adoo had had enough and retreated. I told our group to hold their positions until it was clear the adoo had been cleared. I then called out the names of all our group. Everyone answered. By some miracle, we had taken no casualties.

Then Mike himself appeared. He told me he had got my message that we were under attack but in any case had heard the firing and had realised the adoo had tried to take us out. He wanted to send down an immediate mortar strike but couldn't be sure of our exact locations and the risk of hitting us or his own protection section. He followed the action as well as he could but nothing was clear from his position up on the jebel. As the firing continued, he became sure that his own men had been overrun. He knew the only option was to mount a counter attack by sliding down the jebel in the gathering gloom of the evening. It had worked and here he was!

My driving motivation was to get the hell out of the wadi. Our group had already achieved our mission of proving the effectiveness of the sensors. But there was still one nagging problem. There were still two sensors to be recovered if I was to conform to the US stipulation of retrieving them all. I resignedly decided to give it one last shot although I had to think that if we couldn't find the sensor, considering that we had hidden it, how on earth would the adoo?

After half an hour's searching, John Fuller (?) signalled that the bleeps from his detector were increasing and with a sign of triumph he unearthed a sensor from its hiding place. One down, still one to go. Another half hour went by without finding the final sensor. By this time it was half dark as night approached. I made the decision. Enough was enough. We had done our best and nearly got the whole team killed to conform to the US directive. We had recovered all but one sensor. Fuck it, that would have to do!

Mike left a section to attend to and protect his wounded soldiers then called his mortar team to bring down another strike while the rest of us scrambled back up the jebel lugging all the retrieved sensors. The last part was rather a shambles as by now it was fully dark and we had to struggle to keep together and follow Mike's guys up to his platoon outpost. I managed to get off a quick situation report to SAF HQ and requested we be airlifted back to Salalah as soon as a heli could be freed up. Exhausted, we then retired to our sanger and slept through another night of adoo bombardment.

xxx

Withdrawal from the Hornbeam Line

Early the following morning, a heli arrived and ferried us and our equipment back to the SAF base. I had already drafted out a trial report so all that remained was to finalise the report, formalize this with a verbal briefing to Brigadier Akehurst, who sent the report together with his own endorsement back to our MOD. The brigadier was enthusiastic about the effectiveness of the US sensors and pressed the MOD to purchase supplies from the US.

On the flight back to UK, I reflected on all we had achieved during the past few weeks. Our mission had been successful as a military operation. It had resulted in killing about ten adoo enemy and wounding several others. As a professional soldier, I accepted we were doing the right thing to assist in preventing the enemy from moving their personnel and weapons into locations where they could continue attacking our forces. But as a human being I mourned the lives of the poor guys who were killed and I inwardly questioned the morality of our actions wondering, yet again, whether those killed, all devout Muslims, would find that Allah rewarded them in afterlife. A question to which there is no answer!

I had one further key job to do in completing my first STANOC assignment. When we got back to UK, I was directly despatched back to the US to report to our sponsor in the Pentagon, give him a copy of our report and return the sensors that I had signed for – bar one. The staff officer responsible had changed and when, with trepidation, I admitted that we were one sensor short, he said he couldn't believe his predecessor had made such a stupid stipulation and he was amazed that we had managed to recover so many. Such are the vagaries of military life!

xxx

Back in UK

Digression

Back home in UK, I was immediately faced with new priorities. The first was domestic. My sister Shelley had been leaving messages asking me to call her urgently. She had been contacted by the Kent Social services about our grandmother (then aged 98) and our aunt Eileen (mid 70s) who lived together in a rented apartment in Folkestone. The problem was that my aunt was seriously ill but was still being required to look after her mother – a formidable lady raised during the Victorian era. The social services had found a place in a retirement home for our grandmother but she was refusing to go. Social services assessment was that our aunt would only get progressively worse while our grandmother remained in the same apartment. My sister asked for me to join with her to visit our grandmother to try to persuade her to leave. That week I met my sister at Waterloo station and together we took the train down to Folkestone – arriving fortified by a couple of stiff gin and tonics. We had coordinated our trip with the social services who arranged for an ambulance to be standing by. I knew that I needed to be firm with my grandmother as gentle persuasion would not prise the old lady away. I told her that she was being unfair to her daughter and that the time had come for her to leave – and now. My sister packed her main belongings while I called up the ambulance and together with a protesting grandmother, we left directly for the retirement home. All had been set up for her reception. I had to leave my grandmother there still complaining. I felt really bad about having to act so brusquely but our aunt's health was the main priority. The following day, I drove from Winchester back to Folkestone, collected our aunt and carefully brought her back to stay with us where she could recuperate. I was grateful to Gizèle for the care she gave our aunt during the several months she stayed with us in Winchester.

Waiting for me in UK was a package from Milton Keynes with my marked Tutor Marked Assignment from my OU tutor. It had found its way back to her address and apparently within the time deadline. My tutor wrote that she thought my coverage of the child psychology question was rather shallow (as I well knew!) and that I should have given more attention to, for example, the piece by Sigmund Freud entitled *Aggression and Civilization* quoted in our reader *Introduction to Sociology*. She wrote that she could only give me a B grading. I never did get to meet this good lady and perhaps my mental picture of her was not correct. In any case, I thought, if only she knew the circumstances when the TMA was written. But that's the beauty of the anonymity of being an "overseas" student with the Open University!

End of Digression

xxx

There was one further concluding duty to fulfil. My gallant team had to return to their units. I couldn't let them go without ensuring their expertise and loyalty was duly recognised. I wrote to each of their commanding officers commending their achievements: SSgt Tom Randall who returned to REME HQ in Arborfield and Sgt John Fuller back to his research establishment in Christchurch, with the caveat that I hoped he could be made available for future missions. The now slimmed down Bdr Jeff Archer stayed put as he was already on attachment to the STANOC Centre. Then there were Ptes Kevin White and Paul Turner. I made an appointment with the CO, Royal Hampshire Regiment and drove over to Colchester with Kevin and Paul as I was keen to commend both of these guys personally for their outstanding support. Indeed, without Paul Turner's bravery, coolness under fire and excellent marksmanship, our team could well have been overrun and killed!

Back at the STANOC Centre, I was given my next missions. These were in Hong Kong, Germany and Northern Ireland. Each had their unique challenges e.g.: tensions on the border with China during the build-up period prior to the handover by the British of Hong Kong to China in 1997 and the continuing "Cold War" with the Soviet Union. In Northern Island, an additional concern was that it was politically unacceptable to the US for the British to deploy US sensors there; as a result, we formed a mixed team of technical specialists from the UK R&D establishments and private industry to design, test and manufacture a bespoke sensor system which we then deployed in sensitive areas of the province, particularly in South Armagh. Later the MOD sold the design patent to the armed forces of other countries.

My tour at the STANOC Centre lasted for two and a half years. It was a posting that initially I had resisted. In the event it taught me much about the high level of technical expertise that existed in both the R&D establishments and private industry in the UK, how to harness this expertise to solve particular operation requirements, how to improvise in finding solutions to urgent and uniquely challenging situations and how to form cohesive teams from individuals with disparate skills. This experience was to serve me well not only in the military but also in the further jobs during the rest of my working life.

XXX

Chapter Twenty-Seven

Personal Upheaval

By now I was in my mid-thirties and probably for the first time, except for getting a grip to pass the Staff College exam, I began to wonder seriously where my life was going. Events had seemed to happen without a clear idea about what my aims were for the future. In a vague, unstructured way, I found that the army suited me well and I had decided to make the most of it and try to optimise my chances of turning it into a full successful career. My work was absorbing, my two sons were healthy and I enjoyed being their father, being with them and watching them grow up. Personally, I was as physically fit as at any time in my life, training regularly and competing in cross-country running events. I found my new academic interest in the Open University provided a good counter balance to the sometimes over structured life of the military.

But there was one major issue that kept nagging away but that I had consistently resisted to confront: a fundamental aspect that just didn't gel. That was the relationship between Gizéle and me. We had now been married for eleven years. I acknowledged that, if there was fault, it was mainly on my side. We had met by chance at a party in Sussex in October 1963. We had been out together only a few times when suddenly I was posted at minimal notice to Borneo. From then on, our "courtship" had been conducted exclusively by letter. Before we were married, there had been no chance for us to get know each other well, our likes and dislikes, our habits and style of living. I now realised I had been far too immature and impetuous to have asked her to marry me. Instead we should have taken time after my tour in Borneo to get to know each other much better and then later to decide if we were both sure we wanted to get married. In theory! But the reality was that I had been told that my next job after Borneo was to be in Germany and there would have been no viable possibility of Gizèle being there with me unless we were married. I suppose we could have carried on with our long-distance letters for the minimum of another two years, with possible short holidays together, but I had no idea if I would then get a posting back to UK, or even if I had wanted one. (As it happened my posting after Germany had been to Bahrain.) So I was in some ways trapped by the army system. Or was I just using this as an excuse? Gizèle had found it really difficult to adjust to our life in Germany, particularly during the winter in Fallingbostel, our first time together as man and wife. It was better for her in Minden but still I always felt she was not really settled or content. In Bahrain, life was very basic and I absolutely sympathised with her when I often had to leave her alone while I was away in Sharjah, Kuwait etc. I had hoped we at last could settle down to a happy married life with our two healthy, growing boys during our two years in Cyprus – and in a way we did but even there I always thought that Gizèle wanted (perhaps needed) more in life than I was giving her. In hindsight, I realise I should have been more caring and to have appreciated the difficulty Gizèle had in adjusting to the changing situations I exposed her to. I was probably too focussed on my career at the expense of Gizèle's needs and concerns. I know we should have had proper earlier discussions about how we might better reconcile our differences; but we never did.

There were two other major and connected issues that divided us – the education of our sons and the Catholic faith. The military authorities recognised that, as it is likely that service personnel will be routinely posted around the world, an allowance was granted for their children to be educated in a private boarding school in UK. During holidays, depending on operational circumstances, the children could then join their parents wherever they were based. I had always felt uneasy about the idea of sending our sons off to a boarding school from the ages of eight to eighteen then not being able to be with them as they grew up and developed day by day. In most postings overseas where wives accompanied their husbands, the military provided schools, for example the British service schools in Germany had a very good academic reputation. I would have much preferred for our sons to attend military schools near wherever we would be based and to ensure that anything lacking in their education could and should be rectified by Gizèle and me, particularly as our sons could also grow up being bilingual thanks to Gizèle's French nationality. Gizèle did not agree. She had had her own experience as a teacher in a UK boarding school and was adamant that was what she wanted for our sons. We had several strong arguments about this. My fellow officers, with whom I discussed this subject, all seemed to agree with Gizèle and eventually I gave way. Gizèle also insisted they went to Catholic schools in line with her own religion. I was always uneasy about that idea and particularly about our sons being in a school staffed by Catholic priests. But I couldn't justify my uninformed misgivings as these schools had good reputations for educational excellence. Reluctantly I agreed and both of our sons were enrolled in a Catholic boarding school to start when they were eight years old. Being so often overseas, I later learnt to regret bitterly this educational arrangement as I rarely got to support our sons' school activities and was never "on the touchline cheering them on!" as, in my opinion, all fathers should be.

Our relationship, now in 1975–6, continued to decline. I loved change and adventure. Gizèle needed secure surroundings and consistency. We both loved our sons but this seemed not to be enough to bind us together as a couple. We argued a lot, far too much and I was conscious that our sons sometimes heard us and that was affecting their young lives as it was Gizèle`s and mine. The previous year, we had sold our first Winchester house and bought another in a better part of the city. Then, in the summer of 1976, I got my next posting order. I was to return again to Germany. We thought it best for Gizèle to continue living in our Winchester house while I went on alone to Germany.

Then another event occurred which had a major impact on my relationship with Gizèle. While we were living in Winchester, we – mostly Gizèle – made good social contacts. Perhaps we were seen as quite an attractive couple – a good-looking woman with a delightful French accent and her army officer husband. I was then a major. When I came home at weekends, we were regularly invited to dinner parties and other social events. I found these evenings quite enjoyable, relaxing and the chance to meet interesting people away from the military world.

Gizèle became friendly with one particular couple and we regularly socialised with them. They were wealthy and owned a large house on the edge of the city. The husband was a generous host and I appreciated his hospitality – which I later abused! But I found him to be a boorish, pompous and arrogant man – brought up in a rich family, sent to a top English boarding school, then through his father's contacts, fell into a well-paid job in London. An easy plummy life, but, in my opinion, with little personal ability. To me, in my bigoted way, he epitomised all that I disliked about inherited money and its consequences. However, I liked his wife and after several social evenings spent with this couple, I realised that I was becoming attracted to her and she to me. I found her animated, amusing, coquettish and downright sexy. I was excited by this novelty and we began a secret affair. At that time, Gizèle and I had been married for eleven years and I had never even thought of being unfaithful to her. Thinking back, I realise I was never in love with this lady nor was she with me. Our relationship included sex and passion but there was an even stronger element that drew us together. We both had a driving emotional need to fill the gaping void we were both experiencing in our lives. We could let go completely when we were together, with an outpouring of our mutual pent-up emotions. My lover was fully aware of her husband's boorish character. But he was rich and amply provided for her material needs and for those of their three children. For me, there was the additional stupid thrill that when her husband started his long bragging speeches about his "great" achievements, I could put on an admiring outwards expression but secretly was thinking "you silly rich fool, if only you knew what I'm doing with your wife". I would catch my lover's eye; she would understand and keep our little secret. We would see each other whenever we could, finding temporary peace and emotional relief in our illicit relationship together. Of course, it was wrong, totally wrong, both to her husband and to Gizèle, but that was how it was.

That situation couldn't last. It was too explosive. It all came to a dramatic conclusion on the evening we were invited to a ball at my lover's house. She started drinking heavily, and became jealous when she saw me dancing with her sister. She accused me of flirting with her sister and threatened to tell her husband and Gizèle about our affair. I urged her not to but she was a headstrong, rather reckless lady. After the rest of the guests had left and Gizèle and I were also about to leave she blurted out, "I need to tell you that Mark and I are lovers". Both her husband and Gizèle were stunned. Her husband threatened to go to his gunroom, get a shotgun and shoot me. I remember that Gizèle sunk sobbing to the floor. This was a critical moment which, after much swearing by the husband, I left, never to see my lover again.

Gizèle and I then had to face up to the future. We agreed to consult a marriage guidance counsellor to see if we could find a way to rebuild our marriage. It was not successful. I remember the counsellor once asked me, "Mark, tell me what in your lives together makes your wife happy." I struggled to respond but could not find an example. I think then I realised that we were irreconcilable. Soon after that, we began divorce proceedings. I will always feel guilty that I let her down massively. Of course, I should not have had that affair. It was deceitful, selfish and mean but driven by both my natural impulses and those of my lover. We had broken no temporal law but had transgressed the Christian code of "thou shall not commit adultery". To me then, the religious aspect mattered not one jot. Far more important was the hurt it caused Gizèle which also impacted seriously on our two sons during the early years of their lives.

During that period, I also had another doubt. One day I returned earlier than originally planned from somewhere abroad, I can't remember where. I was as always looking forward to being home, to being with my family in Winchester. I had not previously told Gizéle I would come home then as my flight had been changed. I arrived in late-afternoon. I reached my house, was tired but just pleased to be home. I turned the key to our front door and went in. Gizèle was there but not alone. She had a visitor, a tall good-looking guy I had never seen before. Or had I? I remembered seeing photos that Gizèle had kept which included pictures of this guy. I had asked her then who he was and she told me he had been a past lover, the only man she had ever loved until me! And here he was in real life!

I won't give his name but just refer to him as JB. After their initial surprise at my unexpected arrival, Gizèle and JB explained that they had been friends for some years before I had come on the scene, that JB was now working for his company in Brazil. JB said that this was his first time back in UK for some years and he had decided, on a whim, to visit Gizèle. He had booked a table in a Winchester restaurant and had planned to take Gizèle there and they were about to leave. Graciously, he rallied and invited me to join them. I had to admit he was a charming man. Hoping I stayed cool, I declined and said that it would be a good chance for them to catch up with each other's lives. I shook JB's hand and wished them both a pleasant evening. After they left, I reflected that I had never seen Gizéle looking so radiant. Her hair was freshly groomed and she had dressed impeccably. For the first time in my life, I felt a pang of jealousy. But I had to confess it was payback time for my own affair! And perhaps I was at last experiencing the famous Karma law: "actions have consequences, you reap what you sow!"

XXX

Chapter Twenty-Eight

Germany: Bielefeld

As the long hot summer of 1976 turned to autumn, I left Winchester to return to Germany and my next military posting. I knew I was leaving the city and the house I had recently bought and enjoyed but may never see again. Both Gizèle and I knew our marriage was now over and in the hands of solicitors. I realised it would take time to reconnect with my dear sons as we were before – it was only right that Gizèle should keep the house which would be their primary home. I was determined to see them whenever I could but, for now, I was letting them down massively. I yearned for the day I might again be fully reconciled with them. I feared it would not be soon. Meanwhile all I could do was try to make a success of my next job and see how life would develop from this very low point.

My next job was based in Bielefeld at the headquarters of our First British Corps, (HQ 1 BR Corps). It was principally involved with the training of our soldiers based in Germany about the threat posed by the then Soviet Forces.

My predecessor, bar one, in this job was a very formal officer who had produced a well-structured set of lectures which he would deliver from behind a lectern in a strict military manner. I thought this style of presentation was too regimented and that it did not sufficiently motivate his target audience; young British soldiers. This was a period when the nuclear armed Soviet Union posed a major threat to the west. Leonid Ilyich Brezhnev had been General Secretary of the Presidium of the Supreme Soviet since 1964. His speech at the Parade in Moscow's Red Square to mark the 59th Anniversary of the "Great October Socialist Revolution" in November 1976 had been particularly belligerent. It was vitally important that our soldiers learnt and understood the strengths and weaknesses of our potential adversary and were fully motivated to carry out their mission to counter the Soviet threat. It was now my role to perform this training.

The "Threat" magazine and presentation

I had an immediate problem. My predecessor, who had left the job a year before, had been promoted lieutenant-colonel, and would now be my new commanding officer. During the interim period, a younger very talented officer had temporarily filled the post. He had introduced the first edition of a magazine he entitled *The Threat*. This was accurate in detail but presented in a format, partly in comic strip, that was appealing to British squaddies. When I took over the job from this latter officer, I fully embraced his ideas and motivational training style. There also was a, to me fundamental, reason that I rejected the formal lecture style of training. My stammer! After years of being able to cover it up, I knew there would be no way I could stand behind a lectern in formal military uniform and hope to deliver an hour-long presentation using a prewritten script in front of an audience of several hundred bored soldiers. I just could not do it – I worried that at last my speech impediment would leave me tongue tied and useless. Nowhere to hide!

Fortunately the success of *Threat* magazine came to my short-term rescue as already the feedback from the single edition of the magazine was very favourable. Soldiers, who were bored by having to attend the previous formal lectures, were keen to read *Threat* magazine, partly due to its comic strip style, and there were requests for further editions to be produced. My new unit comprised a small headquarter element at Bielefeld with detachments based at all the formation HQs scattered around the British zone area – from Verdun and Soltau in the north to Soest and Padderborn in the west. The Bielefeld team that I "inherited" included some very bright guys. My "second in command" (2 i/c) was a young captain who spoke good Russian and German, as did one of the Corporals. Another was a talented artist. With the aid of these supportive guys, we had the nucleus to make a training team which could be innovative, dynamic and really appeal to our soldiers, motivate them and inspire confidence and enthusiasm.

First, we built on *Threat* magazine, turning out editions once per month and through simple images and cartoons to improve our soldiers understanding of how Soviet Forces were structured, the composition and capabilities of their weapons, a basic understanding of tactics – always acknowledging the strengths while also highlighting weaknesses. The magazine included quizzes about the Soviet Forces that many soldiers competed to answer and showed genuine enthusiasm to learn.

Threat magazine continued to grow in popularity and acceptance within the military in Germany that it was a useful training tool. But how to tackle the verbal presentations which I had been told were an essential part of our soldier training package? My big challenge was how to perform these presentations in an innovative way (and without stammering!) By some quirk of nature, as I had found out during my schooldays, when I act or sing, I lose my stammer, so I hoped that if I could build on that characteristic, I might be able to accomplish the presentations fluently – to use the success of the magazine to promote the presentations and vice versa thus producing a lively motivating overall training package for our soldiers.

This idea led to the birth of a one-hour non-stop show which included strong motivational material for our soldiers to improve their understanding and knowledge of the Soviet forces and build on the written material of *Threat* magazine. I designed the show to include the latest pop music of the day, played very loud, video footage of Soviet forces showing their mobile capability, associated spots, multiple vu-graph screens and other enlarged visual aids, strobe lighting and smoke. All were integrated into a tightly scripted and controlled second by second programme. I knew that for it to be accepted by the military hierarchy, the presentation had to be faultlessly performed with impeccable timing and precision. For the hour's show, I proposed to discard my uniform and wear a trendy bell-bottomed trouser outfit, the fashion at that time. My 2i/c captain took the major narrative lead and one of our Russian speakers played the role of a soviet major, speaking only the Russian language throughout. It took many hours of painstaking work to compile the piece, then many more sessions of repetitive rehearsing to ensure the hour flowed with perfectly timed synchronisation throughout.

As our "Threat Presentation" show was developed and refined, I felt confident we were creating something really special. The next problem was how to sell the concept of performing this live ultra-modern show to our senior officers, most of whom came from highly traditional backgrounds and regiments. My now commander officer (CO) had himself given lectures in the old formal style and expected the same from me. There would be no way he would even consider allowing this show to be performed fearing it might bring discredit to the image of our Intelligence Corps. I knew that if I were to arrange a performance without my COs consent, I would be fired instantly – the end of my career.

xxx

For some months, our "Threat Presentation" remained unperformed. Once a week I continued to rehearse the detailed integrated sequence to be sure that we could give the performance at short notice should the opportunity arise. Then early in 1977, our chance came. I heard that one of our brigade commanders was planning to hold a study day for all the officers under his command. I was told that he felt that the soldiers in his brigade needed an innovative update about the Soviet Forces facing his operational area. He particularly wanted an imaginative format for his study day. Separately I was told that the brigadier had enjoyed our Threat magazine and had ordered extra copies to be distributed to his soldiers. That news was precisely what I needed. I made an appointment to visit the brigadier and explained to him the content of our rehearsed but yet to be performed "Threat Presentation" stressing that the main objective was to motivate as well as train our soldiers. I asked the brigadier if I could give him and his key staff officers a private performance so he could make his own judgement. He agreed and one evening we put on our show exclusively for him in his brigade lecture theatre. The brigadier was enthusiastic and told his staff planners that he wanted the show to be the key centre piece of his officers' study day. I took the opportunity to warn him that the show could be criticised as being too avant-guard for some of our more traditional officers but he said that he would be the sponsor for the show and that I would be performing it strictly under his direction.

This incident taught me the value of "having a patron". By sponsoring my "show", any objection from lower echelon ranking officers, particularly by my own CO, a "mere lieutenant-colonel", would be overridden as the higher ranked brigadier introduced it. It was performed in his name and under his responsibility. This "patron" sponsorship was to serve me well in many other situations throughout the rest of my career.

There had been much prior publicity about the presentation and, on the day of the study, the brigadier's lecture theatre was crammed full not merely by his own officers but also by as many senior officers from other units who could find a seat. They had heard that something original and special was to take place. Needless to say, when my own CO learnt about it, he ensured he personally attended. Our presentation was faultless as I was fully confident it would be after all the rehearsing we had done. As planned, the performance lasted precisely one hour, not one minute more or less. To many it appeared that much of the performance was spontaneous particularly the seemingly "accidental" pyrotechnics. But of cause it was not, every moment was strictly choreographed. And as my own role was more that of an actor than a lecturer, my stammer disappeared completely! The applause at the end of the show told us we had a winner. But of course it was the brigadier who took the credit. It was HIS show. I couldn't resist watching the reaction of my own CO. I could tell he felt my bell-bottomed attire was, to him, totally unacceptable. But there was nothing he could do as the brigadier had shown he was so much in favour of this innovative training style and directed that the show be performed to all the soldiers under his command.

So the "Threat Presentation" which became nick-named "The Rocky Horror Show" was launched. During the rest of that year, 1977, and much of the following year, we performed in all of the local services cinemas throughout the British military area in Germany – each time packing in some two thousand soldiers per performance. We were also asked to advise our US, German, Belgian and Dutch military counterparts, put on separate performances for them and helped them to tailor-make their own shows to suit their unique national styles. I did not admit to anyone that, deep down, the main motivation for designing this unconventional, wacky show was in order to mask to own limiting stammer!

The presentation helped to establish a good reputation for my unit in Germany. I was then able to reinforce this by bringing the disparate groups of the company together with study periods, sports events and group activities such a ski training in the Harz mountains. These all helped to maintain the good morale of our excellent Intelligence Corps soldiers

XXX

Training for the "cold war"

That was a positive element of my tour in Germany at that time: but there was also a negative – when I was temporally sacked by the senior commander in Germany, the three star General whose appointment was the commander of First British Corps, the highest operational command in Germany.

As part of our combat readiness, the British Army in Germany, as the other NATO nations deployed there, took part in training exercises each year when we deployed to locations similar to those we would occupy if a war between NATO and the Warsaw pact forces were to occur. Although these were only exercises, the training was highly realistic. A team of NATO examiners wrote a fully scripted exercise scenario with an imaginary invading Soviet force against which our Corps had to manoeuvre and attempt to disrupt and defeat. The exercise included a phase when we were considered to be under threat of nuclear attack and had to operate wearing full nuclear, biological and chemical (NBC) suits and respirators, thus ensuring we could operate efficiently in this gear should the need arise.

During these exercises, we would deploy from our peacetime barracks to our operational locations usually in wooded areas near the inner-German border (IGB) in the district of Niedersachsen. We would move location at least once each day with the aim of alluding Soviet electronic detection.

Our Corps HQ comprised several armoured vehicles, all designed to be NBC proof when hatches were closed down. The vehicles comprised the main operational elements – around the commander's HQ vehicle were clustered teams dedicated to Operations, Intelligence, Artillery, engineers etc. Communication was by an encrypted intercom system organised by the team from our signals specialists. During the NBC phases, we operated with our vehicles' hatches closed down.

My "war role" was to be in charge of the night shift of the Intelligence vehicle. My team and I would commence our shift at six p.m. each evening, listen to the briefings given by the day shift team, then work through the night and deliver the early morning briefing at seven a.m. the following morning. Our night team consisted of some experienced, well trained Intelligence Corps soldiers. The NATO organisers were very thorough and each night we found we were pitting our wits against a well-researched "enemy" provided by the exercise controllers. All communications were by encrypted radio. Although our living conditions were very basic, I enjoyed these exercises. As ever, I had to hype myself up trying hide my stammer when delivering the morning briefing over our communications system but a mixture of self-belief and a thorough knowledge of the subject seemed to help.

One morning, our confidence turned to personal near disaster. We had been on exercise for over one week. Our British Corps was being tested on our defensive capability to hold out against a concentrated advance by the "Soviet" force facing us across the Inner German Border (IGB). During our night shift, my team and I studied the detail of the "Soviet" forces composition, it's possibility of reinforcement, the relevant terrain and weather features, armoured, artillery, missile and air assets – all these capabilities ranged against our own forces deployed in interlocking "defensive-in-depth" positions. That night was a crucial phase of the "battle". My team was confident that our own forces were deployed in sufficient strength to be capable of holding our current locations, even to be able to counter attack the following day. As per our military protocol, the signals communications team prepared our Corps HQ for the morning briefing. Over the intercom, they would announce: "The commander's briefing will commence in twenty minutes". This was our first warning and we rushed to complete our briefing notes in time. The sequence of briefing was always in the same order: first, intelligence, next operations, then the various arms of service – artillery, armour, logistics etc. The by then "famous" morning and evening intercom briefings had become the centrepiece of the whole exercise, avidly awaited by all those who were entitled to listen in. They were also the means by which our "enemy" exercise controllers could gauge how well, or poorly, we were performing our war role.

The communications count down continued. We were informed "The commander's briefing will commence in ten minutes. Then "in five minutes". Then the last minute by minute notifications until, finally: "The commander's briefing will begin now, over to intelligence, over!" This was the big moment when I had to push down my radio presell switch and begin with the words "Good morning, commander, this is the intelligence briefing". Then I was required to give a summary of the "enemy" activities during the night, an assessment of their present disposition, capabilities and level of threat to our own forces. On that particular briefing I felt buoyant. Our team had done an outstanding job of studying the balance of forces during that night and we were confident in our final assessment that our forces were strong and capable enough to hold our present deployed positions. We even recommended that our forces had the capability to launch a counter attack to drive the "Soviet" force back across the IGB. I remember being in confident mood, ending as per protocol with the wording, "That completes the intelligence briefing, over to operations, over". I then pushed my presell switch to "off", sat back and gave a thumbs up sign to my team as we celebrated what we thought had been a successful night's work.

It was not to be! I was only vaguely listening to the rest of the commanders briefing as we prepared to tidy up our vehicle ready to hand over to the day shift. Then it would be breakfast and time to try to get some sleep before our next night's duty. Our routine was abruptly shattered when the interlock door of our vehicle was opened by a brigadier, the chief of staff to our commanding general. He said, "Durman, the commander needs you to brief him personally on the assessment you just gave." I was rather chuffed, thinking perhaps the commander wished to understand the detail I had given which I could explain more fully using his command vehicle map. I walked over the short distance to the command vehicle and opened the hatch. Inside I found it was crammed with senior officers and support staff. We were all wearing our NBC kit, known colloquially as "noddy suits" which include wearing our respirators making and it difficult to recognise individuals. In the centre was an NBC suited individual whose voice was immediately recognisable. It was the commander. He was furious. He shouted at me and gesticulated. Even through the mask of his visor I could see his face was red with rage. He told me my briefing had been rubbish, I had let him down badly and I was to be instantly dismissed from his HQ. His final words were short and succinct. They were. "You're fired. Now get out of my headquarters!" I slunk back to my intelligence vehicle, re-entered through the hatch hanging my head in despair. I tried to work out what we had done wrong. I went over the detail of the briefing I had just given. I was sure our assessment had been accurate. I had no idea what was going on. I now felt that I had let down my team who had all worked so hard during our shift to produce a clear, succinct and accurate intelligence assessment. I realised that my career was now probably over. I vaguely remembered that an officer has to have served for sixteen years to be entitled to a minimum pension and I even counted up my own years of reckonable service. I hoped I might just qualify. My mood had turned from almost euphoric confidence at a job well done, to one of despair and failure.

Then our hatch door opened again. It was same brigadier, the commander's chief of staff, who had earlier summoned me to the commander. He came in and sat down opposite to me. He said, "I apologise for having put you on the spot before. There are things you didn't know and couldn't have predicted when you gave this morning's intelligence briefing. Firstly, the commander is not in good shape. He doesn't "weather" well on exercises, can't sleep and arrived this morning in a thoroughly bad mood. Last evening he had made the decision to withdraw our troops to a more defensive posture – a decision that had been heavily criticised by other NATO commanders and the exercise controllers. His decision should have been communicated to all his staff but it was not. Your briefing this morning confirmed what other NATO commanders believed, that our defensive posture is strong and there was no need for us to withdraw. In fact, quite the opposite. Unknowingly, you had told him what a grave mistake his decision had been. Don't worry too much about what he told you just now. Complete your handover to your day shift, tell them not to change the assessment, get some rest and report back this evening as usual. Meanwhile I and my fellow staff officers will work on the commander and get him to understand you were only doing your job and that we all agree with the assessment you gave.

That day was a roller coaster. I had gone from confidence of a job well done to one of despair that I would be sacked in disgrace. Then only to be reassured, well sort of. I tried to keep calm during the morning shift change and struggled off to breakfast. Normally this is a chance to meet up with others from the night shift and to relax together before getting our heads down to rest. That morning was different. News of my "bollocking" from the commander had quickly spread and when I came into the Mess area, I found that my usual breakfast colleagues all decided they would find somewhere else to sit. No one wanted to be contaminated by a guy who had just been sacked. I couldn't blame them. Of course they didn't know what the chief of staff had later told me. In a totally confused state of mind, I ate my breakfast alone and slunk off to my sleeping bed-space.

The following night shift was something of a revelation. When I came on duty, I learnt that the commander had reversed his decision to withdraw and preparations were well advanced for our troops to mount a counter offensive. Mid way through the night, I was again summoned to the command vehicle. I found the commander to be in a completely different mood. He asked me to update my intelligence assessment which I did, sticking to our previous positive position. He said he accepted this. He did not actually apologise for his earlier temper but he did go so far as to smile, at least I think it was a smile but it was difficult to tell through his face visor. I hoped I could take that as being implicitly given a reprieve. The following morning I again gave the Intelligence briefing which was accepted without further comment. At breakfast, my former colleagues re-joined my table and I felt I had at last been rehabilitated.

xxx

I recollect that I was frenetically energetic during the two years, 1976–8. In addition to regularly performing the Threat presentations, editing the monthly Threat magazine and exercising my "war role" on manoeuvres, our company took part in a major military parade on 7/7/77 (seventh day of the seventh month of nineteen seventy-seven) in honour of the HM The Queen's silver jubilee. This took place in the Sennelager training area, included an impressive "advance to contact" in our armoured vehicles and later an exhibition stand portraying our role in Germany during which I was honoured to give a short presentation to HM Queen Elizabeth and The Duke of Edinburgh. In my free time, I continued my Open University studies and regularly competed in cross country races as a team member of Güterslohpolizieverain, a local German police sports club.

Why so much energy? Perhaps it was due to the inner turmoil I was experiencing. At that time, I slept very little and would often lay awake at night wondering about life and how fine is the line between happiness and depression. Between success and failure. What did it all mean? Where was I going? I even had another shallow attempt at prayer. But who to? It was no help.

Gizèle and I had agreed to our divorce but in reality, I was the one who had initiated the agreement. Although I continued to believe that it was best for our marriage to end, I was now facing the consequences. In Germany, I was back to living in "single officers" accommodation while Gizèle, rightly, stayed in our house in Winchester. My constant anguish was that I was now cut off from our sons. They were both in the Catholic boarding school in UK of Gizèle's choice then spent their holidays with Gizèle in Winchester. During my first year in Germany, I managed occasionally at weekends to get back to UK to visit our sons. These visits were artificial and painful. I had to take the two boys out to restaurants or walk with them in the local park as I no longer had a UK base. I once managed for them to join me in Germany and together we drove down to northern Italy for a short seaside holiday. All that time, I knew that my sons were resentful and blamed me for leaving their mother and deserting them. I knew they were correct which intensified my feelings of guilt for letting them down. I also was uneasy about their school. I couldn't substantiate what was wrong and my sons made no accusations. The school reports of our elder son Anthony were quite good but William, our younger son, was getting very poor grades. I booked an appointment with the headmaster, a Catholic priest and took a trip back to UK to meet him. He was very charming and professional and sought to allay any criticism of his school or his staff. I had no evidence of any wrong doing in the school and nothing concrete to justify my concerns. But I still felt dissatisfied about having to leave our sons for several months each year in the care of male catholic teachers. I felt cut off from their development caused by the separation of our divorce and the Army's requirement for me to be based in Germany. These emotions all added to my continuing pangs of guilt. Inwardly I longed to see our sons more frequently, to support them at home and at their school. The reality was that a major consequence of our divorce was that I was not being a true father. I suppose my constant work and physical energy was a psychological counterbalance to veil my inner grief and self-guilt.

xxx

There was another thing. I was then in my mid-thirties. Our divorce proceedings were being handled by solicitors in UK and I knew that I could not expect them to be concluded for at least two years, such was the slow speed of the UK legal system. My personal life consisted of socialising with my fellow officers and of training with the police officers of the German athletics club.

In this all-male existence, I felt the need for some female company. In mid-1977, I was invited to give a performance of our Threat presentation in the Brigade troop cinema based in Körbeke, a small town in North Rhine, Westphalia, about one hundred kilometres from my base in Bielefeld. As the performance was to be held at ten a.m., I decided that my team and I would arrive in Körbeke the evening before in order to set up our equipment and rehearse ready for the following day. I had arranged to spend the night in the garrison officers' mess. I had dinner there with some of the officers, one of whom invited me to a small soiree he had organised. I was pleased to accept and was introduced to several ladies who were teachers in the garrison forces school.

That was how and where I met Carol. Immediately, we connected very well. We were the same age, both of us were divorced (or in my case divorcing), both of us were now unattached, both of us were susceptible. At that time, the rules of social behaviour in the British Army were very strict. My divorce was still not completed and it was not considered acceptable in that situation to have a separate relationship – particularly by officers in the Intelligence Corps with its rigid security vetting requirements. Despite being well aware of the rules, I suggested to Carol that we might meet again and get to know each other better. She agreed and the following weekend we met discreetly well away from any British establishment. Thus began a mutually compatible friendship between us. I found Carol to be just the right person I wanted to be with at that time. She was intelligent, well organised and understanding. We became confidents. I told her about my life, the status of my divorce, my deep feelings of guilt about letting down my sons. Carol told me about her former husband and how their marriage had failed due to his drinking and gambling habits. Our first date led to others and after some time we both knew we needed each other and so began a long-term relationship between us.

For a time, my personal life was improved – a great job, a good hobby and at last a close relationship with an understanding woman. Somehow, I hoped that as the years passed and the harshness of my divorce to Gizéle might recede and that I could again regain the trust and love of my two sons. But from day to day, I was living in a shell of a split personality – professionally I was successful but personally my divorce proceedings were grinding along frustratingly slowly, I had no home of my own and was involved in what the army would refer to as an illicit relationship with Carol. Although we were close and supportive to each other, I was not sure if either of us wanted our relationship ever to become permanent. We were both content to keep things as they were.

xxx

Chapter Twenty-Nine

Ashford, Kent

In late 1977, after two years in Bielefeld, I was told that I was to be promoted to the rank of lieutenant-colonel and my next posting was to be the commanding officer of our Intelligence Corps Headquarters and Depot based in Ashford, Kent. In Germany, I was immersed both in my job and the turmoil of my personal life. I knew that my situation of being in the midst of a divorce and living a "secret life" with Carol was fragile and couldn't be sustained for long. I realised this new appointment triggered the need to sort out my personal life and that Carol and I would have to face up to some hard decisions.

The Corps Depot was the home of our main Intelligence Corps headquarters, our School of Service intelligence, and the training facility of all our new recruits. There was a large complement of female soldiers and the wives of our married soldiers, many of whom had personal problems requiring local support. Traditionally that support was provided by the wife of the commanding officer. Yet I was now a supposedly unattached and a just divorced man as shortly before I was due to move back to UK, my divorce was finally legalised and I was again free to marry. Unlike Gizèle, Carol fitted easily into the military world. She had been a teacher in a military school in Germany for some years, she understood the military way of life, and was flexible about where to live. In summary, I knew she would fit in well with the style and requirements of my continued life in the military. But we were both satisfied with our lives together and had no pressing wish to change the nature of our relationship.

This new appointment brought matters to a head. Initially, Carol and I made the decision that I would return to UK and take up my new appointment in Ashford then later Carol would leave her school in Germany some two months later at the end of the term. We never really discussed seriously how we would live our lives, together or separately, when we were back in UK. Early in my new job in Ashford, I was faced with several problems concerning the families of our soldiers, which routinely would have been dealt with by the commanding officer's wife. I was frequently asked by my fellow officers if I was going to remarry as, such was the tradition of the military at that time, it was unusual for officers of my rank to be single. So when Carol left Germany at the end of the year, it seemed only logical that we should be married. Later I realised that this thought process was skewed and should never have been the basis for such a major decision. In the back of my mind even then I wished I had resisted the temptation of reaching an "easy" solution to my life at that time and that Carol and I had taken more time to be certain of our true deep feelings. This was reminiscent of the background circumstance of my marriage to Gizèle! Carol and I both had doubts and knew we should try to resist being pressured by the circumstances. But there we were. That was the reality. Carol and I were both in our late 30s and we needed to have more settled lives. That was the background to our making up our minds. In January, 1978, Carol joined me in Ashford, we got married in the local registry office and started a new life together as man and wife.

I found my new life in Ashford fulfilling and after many years of disruption, I felt personally more relaxed. Carol fitted easily into her new life as the wife of an army officer, supported me by assuming the role of president of the "wives club" and by being at my side at the many social events it was my duty to attend. We were allocated a house within Templar Barracks and settled into the rhythm of our new married life together. Another bonus was that now I had a proper home for my sons to stay when they came to visit. Carol took a job teaching at a local Ashford school and also arranged the music for her new and other schools. Until then I had not realised how talented she was both as a singer and pianist. For the first time in several years I felt my personal life was stable.

In addition to the main role of ensuring HQ Intelligence Centre ran efficiently, it was important to form a close link with the civil authorities in this part of Kent and particularly those based in Ashford. With the permission of the local vicar, we moved our Book of Remembrance (which listed those Intelligence personnel who had been killed in action) from Maresfield to the main church in Ashford and commissioned a stained-glass window to be installed there. It was my job to establish and maintain the main link with the vicar, to liaise with him regarding church services for the annual Service of Remembrance each November and other services such as the funerals of our personal, past and present, who died during that period. It was particularly poignant when, in early 1978, we held a memorial service for one of our soldiers killed in Northern Ireland. The vicar was a charming, broad-minded gentleman and we had many lively personal discussions about the church, the military, the afterlife (or none) and other philosophical issues! If I had thought to believe in Christianity again, it would have been during that time. But by then I think I had seen and experienced too much death and destruction caused in the name of faith in a God.

xxx

One of the most rewarding jobs at the Intelligence Centre was the recruiting and training of our young recruits. My team and I toured and worked with the many army recruiting centres throughout UK to find our required calibre of young men and women who met the criteria we laid down. Our training regime was firm but fair and our standards were high. During my own training I had learnt to appreciate the value of showing rather than telling, of leading by example. It was important for our soldiers to be physically fit as we had commitments around the world often in physically demanding environments. Throughout their twelve-week training cycle, most mornings would begin with a three-mile run commencing at seven a.m. The whole of the training team of instructors, including me and our regimental sergeant major would be on parade. We would run as a formed squad for the first two miles then free run for the remaining mile. All of my instructors would be in the first group home. It was the same with other physical training such as completing our obstacle course and abseiling – and all our classroom work. Our instructors taught by leading by example. Our young recruits arrived as a disparate assortment of young people, often unfit and lacking in social skills. During training, some fell behind but responded well to individual extra coaching, but a few just did not have the aptitude and we had to discharge them. At the end of each course, we held a "passing out" parade with the successful recruits. Their parents were invited for this significant event in the young men and women's careers. A senior dignitary was asked to be the "inspecting officer" and the recruits performed a set of well-rehearsed drills. The climax of the ceremony was the presentation to each successful recruit of the Intelligence Corps Cyprus green beret and "rose and laurel" cap badge. After the parade these soldiers were no longer recruits but would be promoted to the rank of lance corporal and would be given details of their first posting to an Intelligence unit. They were then briefly united for light refreshments with those parents who had attended. It was stimulating when so many of the parents enthused about how the training had changed their son/daughter from being an unfit, unmotivated adolescent when they started their training to becoming a strong, mature and confident young person.

Digression – the Hospital Fête

It was important that we, the military, had good relations with the citizens of the town of Ashford and other nearby areas of Kent and I recognised that our soldiers should contribute to charitable events. However I was regularly being called by local worthy dignitaries asking for our assistance with summer village fêtes and other charitable causes. I was keen to assist, but it soon became apparent that if I were to agree to all such requests, our poor soldiers, who were fully engaged in their training, would lose all the free time at weekends when they needed to be sufficiently refreshed for the following week's training. I decided that the best response was to settle on one major charity event only which would incorporate the interests of many of the areas around the Ashford district. We could then give such an event our full support and decline all others. My chance came in the spring when I was asked by the chairman of the William Harvey Hospital League of friends in Ashford to assist in organising the annual fund-raising fête to be held in the grounds of the hospital in early September. I accepted in principle and suggested that we hold a meeting at the hospital the following week with all the main organising participants attending. I asked for the representatives from a local bank, newspaper and anyone else to attend whose expertise could contribute to the success of the event. The president agreed and said he would invite such people. I told him we could then establish how our military establishment might best assist.

The following Wednesday evening, I arrived at the designating meeting room at the hospital together with my adjutant, a charming young captain named John Tobias, who I co-opted to be our event secretary. We both wore our uniforms. The meeting was scheduled to start at seven thirty p.m. John and I arrived at 7.25 p.m. At seven thirty p.m. no one else was there nor at 7.40 p.m. At a quarter to eight, the first arrival turned up, followed in dribs and drabs by other individuals so that by 8.05 p.m. we were a total of ten people assembled together. Everyone seemed to know each other and seemed content to chat and reminisce about events unrelated to the hospital fête. I began to wonder why I had been invited so decided to "play the soldier". I asked everyone to please be seated, then turned to the chairman and asked why he had invited me to the meeting. "Well," he explained, "Last year our fête was not very successful and we made far less money for the charity than we had hoped. To be truthful it was all rather a shambles. That's why we decided the military might help us to organise ourselves better!" I had suspected that was the case so decided now was the time to impose a little military discipline on these charming and probably talented but somewhat disorganised group of people. I said something like, "Thank you for your honesty, Mr President, and my soldiers and I would be pleased to assist. But if we are to have a successful fête and make a lot of money for the hospital, I must insist that we run our meetings in a military-like manner. I will be honoured to organise the event with your excellent assistance but only if our meetings are held on time, that we record the actions that each of us are to attend to, that full minutes of each meeting are recorded and that progress on all actions will be reviewed at each meeting before moving to the next set of actions. If you agree these basic principles, we can now proceed but if you have difficulty with them please now let me know and Captain Tobias and I will withdraw and leave you to it." I waited for their responses. The assembled group seemed somewhat shocked by my short speech and for a while there was silence. I noted they were looking around to see other's reactions then slowly turned to the president and nodded their agreement. Eventually, the president said. "Yes, Colonel, we would like you to take charge of our organizing committee. What would you like us to do?" I then asked each to identify themselves and allocated jobs to match their areas of expertise. I asked each to give specific progress reports at the next meeting. I concluded, "Thank you for putting your trust in the military. We in turn will do our utmost to contribute to making the next fête a resounding success. I propose we meet again here in one week's time when we can review the progress that together we are making. The meeting will commence at seven thirty p.m. sharp and I expect everyone to be on time. Any questions." As expected, there were none. I realised I had overdone the brusqueness and that I was dealing with a group of disparate civilians who were not used to being pushed along in this way. But I felt that this was the best format to get results and was intrigued to know how they would all respond.

The next week, John and I again arrived at 7.25 p.m. Already half the group were already there and the remainder had all turned up promptly by seven thirty p.m. An encouraging start! As we went round the table, each of our committee members was keen to demonstrate he or she had done the work that had been asked of them. This became the pattern of the meetings that continued throughout that summer. Gradually we began to work together as a team with the pieces of each contribution fitting together in a coherent manner. Finance built up so that we knew what funds we had for the infrastructure of the event, publicity and marketing was well promoted in the local press, the ground plan of the event was drawn up and stalls allocated to the contributing attractions, a showground was earmarked for the various sequenced events to take place throughout the day, car parking spaces were reserved with a field loaned by a local farmer for over-spill parking. Ashford police constabulary provided security cover. The local scouts and sea scouts were designated to act as parking stewards and circulating with collection boxes. As these boxes were filled with contributions, they were to be taken to our finance stall where a temporary bank was established for the day. Our local waste collectors organised rubbish collection during and after the event. Our own military contribution included a helicopter display with soldiers abseiling down to the main show ground while our own recruit soldiers from Templar barracks acted as guides, escorts for handicapped visitors and arranged for the erection and later clearing of tents, stalls and other temporary structures.

We were blessed with fine sunny weather on the day of the fête in early September. We opened doors at two p.m. and produced an action-packed programme until we had to ask some reluctant late visitors to leave at seven p.m. The fête was packed with crowds throughout those hours. All the car parks were full including the farmer's field. Everyone seemed to enjoy the afternoon and were motivated to help fill up our many collection boxes. Our soldiers then dismantled all the tents and stalls and the site was left in the same state we found it. The last main function was to await the result of the amount of money that had been collected throughout the day. At last, our bank manager committee member emerged. He announced that a net grand total of just over fifteen thousand pounds net had been amassed – this to be presented to the William Harvey hospital by the president of the Hospital League of Friends and publicised by the local press and TV network. Our final meeting of the committee was held the following week. All members attended. Everyone was thrilled by the success of the fête, enthused about the organisation and proud of the part they each had played. I reflected that sometimes straight forward military discipline can be very effective!

End of digression.

Carol and I were conscious that, although we were temporally accommodated in a military house, we did not own a home of our own. We found a suitable semi-detached house near the centre of Ashford and bought it with a maximum mortgage. We moved in directly the sale was completed. From then on, we would always have a home of our own.

While I thoroughly enjoyed the job in the UK, I hoped that I might get the chance to return to Germany again at the end of this Ashford posting. I had two ambitions. One was to improve my ability to speak the German language well. The second was to bid for one specific job which really attracted me. This was to be the head of intelligence and security for our main operational headquarters, First British Corps based in Bielefeld. This job was described in military terms as Chief G2, I (BR) Corps. During my second year in Ashford I discretely lobbied my seniors for this job and to my delight I received instructions that I would leave Ashford in early 1981, attend a German language course to linguist level in Mulheim, Ruhr then take over in September as Chief G2 – exactly as I had wished. My luck was in! In late December, I handed over my job in Ashford to another officer and in the first week of January, drove back to Germany.

xxx

Chapter Thirty

1981–1986

The next six years were some of the most fulfilling of my life. My work in the military was challenging and rewarding, my personal life with Carol was settled and amicable, we had good social contacts and no immediate financial or emotional concerns. As there were no major events which impacted on this study of "the meaning of life", I've summarised these years into a Wikipedia type format and then fast forward to the next part of my life where again I was faced with personal moral and spiritual dilemmas.

The main events were.

1981–84.

- Attended German language course to "linguist" level at Higher Education Centre, Mülheim, Ruhr. Achieved a degree of fluency in the language while accepting I would never make an accomplished "linguist"!
- Completed first full marathon, (42 kms), held in Enchede, Netherlands. "Hit the wall" at 35 Kms and staggered home in well over the three-hour target I had set myself. Vowed to study how to time the event better, to train harder and to learn how to improve my finishing time.
- September 1981. Carol joined me in Germany and we moved to a military house in Bielefeld. Started new job as Head of Intelligence and Security, HQ 1st British Corps. Carol was employed as a teacher in the military school in Gütersloh.
- Key political events influencing volatile time in East-West relations were:

. 1979. The Soviet invasion of Afghanistan

. 1979. Soviet deployment of SS20/RSD-10 theatre nuclear missiles and the NATO response with the deployment of Pershing 2 nuclear missiles.

. 1980–81. The Polish crisis which led to the imposition of martial law.

. 1981. The election of Ronald Regan as President of the US.

Note: The Polish crisis not only marked a new phase of Soviet domestic repression but also a sharp escalation of the "Cold War". Initially the Soviets were wary of Reagan's election and in late 1981, there was deep acrimony and hostility in NATO-Soviet relations

- Worked closely with British intelligence assets and those of other NATO Corps in Germany, integrated intelligence product and presented assessments in 1st British Corps studies, war gaming and field training exercises.
- Gave intelligence and security presentations to visiting senior military and politicians.
- Ran further marathons: London, Rotterdam, Verden and others, reducing finishing time to well under three hours. Gained status as "international veteran élite!" entitling those to line up in front group of city marathons!

1984–6.

- Back to Ashford, Kent. Promoted to full colonel as Commandant of Intelligence and Security School. Carol and I lived in a military house in Barracks then bought our own house in Brabourne Lees, Kent. Carol worked as a peripatetic music teacher.
- Gave presentations about the work of our Intelligence school to VIP visitors including all major "royals" and politicians such as Michael Heseltine, then Minister of Defence.
- Visited US, Canada, Hong Kong and Kenya on military assignments.
- Completed Open University. Attended award ceremony at Guildford, Kent

xxx

Chapter Thirty-One

NATO Defence College, Rome

Note: Back to the narrative of "one man's journey" when life gets complicated again, mainly due to my own stupidity!

I had barely completed two years at the Intelligence and Security School in Ashford when in June 1986 I was told that my tour there would be shortened as I was to be posted to NATO headquarters in Brussels in February the following year. Not just that but, as a prerequisite for this job, I was to attend a six-month course at the NATO defence college (NDC), based in Rome, this to commence in September. I contacted the admin staff of the NDC about accommodation and was told that an apartment that was rented by the college would be available from early August. They didn't like to leave such properties vacant due to squatter problems and asked me if it would be possible to move there in August. Would it possible? What a question! I immediately confirmed we would plan to arrive as they requested – i.e. a free summer holiday based in Rome!

Now having two dogs (and cat and a guinea pig!), Carol and I were no longer able to travel so freely. Our revised plan was to find good accommodation for our pets, then for Carol and I to drive down to Rome, stay three weeks together then for Carol to fly back, retrieve the pets and continue her teaching job until the end of that year. She would visit when possible then we would transfer as a complete family to Brussels the following February.

Carol and I left our house in Kent in mid-August 1986 and were able to enjoy our summer break in Rome. We alternated site-seeing days in the city with trips to the beach at Ostia, a thirty-minute drive away. Our allocated apartment was in the residential district of Mostacciano. The NATO defence college (NDC) was a short bus ride away in the business district of EUR. I was required to report there during the first week of September.

Extended digression – driving in Rome/Jolé

Driving in Rome was a unique experience, very demanding for northern Europeans used to strict protocols of rights of way, one-way streets etc. In Rome, such rules were very flexible. Typical were Roman drivers' reactions to traffic lights. At some lights, drivers would stop at red and correctly wait to move off until they changed to green, at some, red lights were totally ignored and at others, red lights seemed to be considered as advisory – maybe to stop, maybe not! During the first week that Carol was with me, I was hesitant and timid trying to drive on the streets of central Rome. I was so stressed that I wondered if it would sensible to limp the car back to our apartment, park it in the underground parking, then leave it there for most of the time and instead take the local buses and metro. But first I decided to study the Roman system and try to copy their driving techniques. I learnt a few tricks. First, wind down the driver's side window and stick your elbow on the door panel. Gesticulate regularly with your right hand, preferably while smoking. Line up the car at the compulsory red traffic lights, keep your foot on the clutch with the revs well fired up, then launch the car at full speed as soon as the green light appears so as to gain maximum advantage over the other drivers. The system seemed to work well and when I tried it, I seemed to blend far better into the flow of the traffic than by my former timid style. When Carol re-joined me after a few months she was horrified by how my driving had changed, accusing me of being reckless. I remember taking her to a crowded piazza in the city centre which was packed with parked cars, some double and some even triple parked. I challenged Carol to inspect the cars for damage. She found it difficult to find any that had even a scratch. Some sort of evidence that, though Romans drive fast, they drive safely – in their own style!

xxx

Carol flew back to UK as planned after our summer break together. Our course assembled in the first week of September, with fifty "students" from all of the NATO nations. The number of students per nation depended on the NATO budget contribution made by each: the US had eight students, Germany seven, the UK six and so on. Most students were military with an average rank of full colonel but a quarter were civilians, mostly working for their national foreign or defence ministries. The purpose of the course, introduced by General Eisenhower in the 1950s, was to bring together personnel who were to be posted to NATO establishments around the world. We worked in mixed nationality syndicates, received presentations from all NATO nations, travelled as a group to most of the participating countries, had written, oral and language assignments – allowing time to socialise among ourselves in order to get a full understanding of other national histories and present priorities.

Occasionally I drove from the apartment to the college but more often would take the number 504 bus which had a stop outside the apartment and another near the college. The bus was usually quite empty when I got on but filled up along the way to EUR. At one stop at the top of Viale del Carmelo, about a kilometre from my apartment, I noticed one lady regularly got on the same bus. I don't know what it was about her that I initially noticed. She was good looking but not beautiful, she was well dressed but not extravagantly, she was of average height for a woman, she was usually alone and I didn't hear her speak. Sometimes she found a seat in a different part of the bus and I was only aware of seeing her when she got on the bus and then got off again at a metro station a few blocks before the NDC stop. One day when the bus was crowded, I offered up my seat to an old gentleman who I could see was having difficulty keeping his balance. Then I found myself standing next to the same lady from Viale del Carmelo. We were squeezed close to each other due to the congestion of the others on the bus. We didn't speak. She was much shorter than my 182 cms and when I looked down at her I noticed she returned my gaze. We didn't acknowledge it but were aware of each other. I found myself slightly unsettled by her presence but I didn't know why.

The next week I didn't take the bus as our NDC course travelled up to the north of Italy to visit a parachute battalion based near Pisa. Then the following week, I again took the 504 bus. For a few days I didn't see the lady from Viale del Carmelo. Then on the Friday I saw her get on. For a while I was sitting on the inside of the two-seater banks with another gentleman on the outside seat. Later, the gentleman got off at his stop. His place was taken by the lady from Viale del Carmelo. I felt a sudden flutter of expectation. I did not know why. For a time we didn't speak, then almost as if it was an effort to get the words out she blurted:

"My name is Jolé Garratini, I work for El Al airlines but I'm not Jewish!"

This introduction was disconcerting. Why would she think I would care if she was or was not Jewish? I replied:

"I'm Mark. We have never spoken before, why do you speak to me in English?"

"Oh that's easy. You don't look Italian, an Italian would never wear shoes like yours, and nor would an Italian man offer his seat to an old gentleman the way you did the other week."

About the shoes, I usually came to the college wearing my standard uniform, less beret, with a zip up windcheater to cover it up to appear, so I thought, incognito. I hadn't realised my shoes were such a giveaway.

We said nothing more for a while. Then she said:

"Today is Friday. What are you doing this evening?"

In fact that evening, the college was hosting a reception for a group of former NDC students who had booked a reunion that weekend. I knew I was expected to attend but instead I said to José.

"Nothing special. Why do you ask?"

We were by now nearing her stop at the metro station. I could see that José realised this as she hurriedly searched in her bag for a notepad and pen and I saw her scribbling on the pad. In a rush she said:

"Because I would like to see you. If you like, why don't you phone me this evening? This is my number."

I took the note from her but didn't have time either to think about what she said or to give her a reply as she hurried to get off the bus.

That Friday, our course programme continued on schedule. We worked in the same mixed nations syndicates and I enjoyed the lectures, the company of my fellow students and the chance to practice the German language with our German students. But throughout the day, I kept thinking about my encounter with Jolé and her unexpected invitation. I knew I should attend the evening soirée at the college and contribute to the hosting duties but I couldn't help wondering about this little Italian lady and wanting to know more about her. After the final session of the day, the student classes dispersed. It was five p.m. We were expected to reconvene at eight p.m. to meet and host our visiting guests.

I took the bus back to my apartment in Mostacciano and, as usual, changed into running kit and went a for an hour's jog. Normally these sessions helped to clear my mind. But not today. My present dilemma was whether to do my duty at the college or to follow up with Jolé by calling the number she gave me. I returned to the apartment still undecided. I knew what was my duty and the sensible thing to do. But I felt the desire to learn more about Jolé. I knew I could either call her and tell her I was busy this evening and suggest that we could meet at some other time. Then I could carry out my duty at the college. Or I could not call her at all. Or I could call her and suggest we meet this evening. I realised I knew the minimum about her other than approximately where she lived, her name and that she told me she worked for El Al but wasn't Jewish! Was she married? Did she in fact intend to introduce me to her husband and family? Was she even serious that she wanted to see me, and if so, why? All these were questions to which at present I had no answers. But I wanted to find out.

By seven thirty p.m. I knew I could no longer put off the decision. If I was to go to the college, I needed to get changed into a smart suit and get moving now to be on time. If it was to follow up with Jolé I needed to phone her. I called her number!

Her first words were: "Hello Englishman, I hoped you would call. I was wondering if you might like to come to my apartment for a cocktail." By then, I knew I was committed. Jolé gave details of where she lived and we arranged to meet there at about eight p.m. I dressed casually, got in my car, found my way to Jolé's apartment block and parked outside.

She lived on the second floor of an undistinguished apartment building. She had given me the entry code to the building which buzzed me through when I stabbed in the numbers. Inside, stairs led to the upper floors. I couldn't see an elevator so I climbed to the second floor and found a door labelled Sig.na Garritina. I rang the bell.

Jolé opened the door straight away. She had changed out of her working clothes and now wore a stylish low-cut dress and high heeled shoes. Her jet black curled Italian hair glistened as if freshly washed. She was wearing make-up but had applied it lightly with subtilty. She looked great. She led me into her small sitting room and invited me to sit on the only settee in the room. I accepted her invitation for a cocktail, and while she busied herself mixing the drinks, I took the chance to look around her apartment. There wasn't much to see. The entrance hall led directly into this room which had an open American style kitchenette at one end. There seemed to be only two other rooms which I supposed were a bedroom and bathroom. That was all. My first deduction about her was that she lived alone here. There wasn't room for anyone else

Jolé came over to the settee and sat down next to me placing the drinks glasses on a small table in front of us. So began an evening I shall remember for the rest of my life. We toasted each other with the cocktails and straight away we knew there was something special happening. We had no hesitation, no awkwardness, no guarded inhibition. I told her straight away that I was married but my wife was in England at present but would occasionally join me here in Rome during my studies at the NDC which were to continue until February. Jolé told me she had been divorced for some time and had no present relationship. Having cleared these basic facts, we decided to enjoy each other's company for the evening, to talk, to laugh, just to see how things developed. I soon realised that Jolé had a mischievous sense of humour. After our second cocktail, Jolé suggested we go out to eat some pasta together. That sounded like a good idea although I realised I needed to drive carefully after the drinks. We took the road leading west, crossing over the GRA circular Rome city motorway and onto the road leading down to Ostia. It was a dry evening, mild for this time in early October. In Ostia, we found a small café by the beach, ate pasta of Jolé's choice washed down by an excellent chianti. We never stopped talking and joking and laughing. It was nearing midnight by the time we left. I remember coasting the car back with Jolé holding my arm. I was feeling I was in a dream. This was a perfect evening. When we got back, Jolé guided me into a reserved parking spot and together we returned to her apartment.

Jolé opened her front door and led me back into her apartment. She locked the door and we went through the living room and directly into her bedroom. There was no hesitation. I pulled her to me and we kissed. I have no idea how we undressed, all I do know was that I needed this woman and I needed her right there and then. What was this about? I didn't care to rationalise it. I just felt a surge, an outpouring of emotion, of passion, of a welling up of a craving need that had somehow been repressed until now. I had never before felt like this. It was basic, primeval, unstoppable. Jolé went with me, understood everything I was feeling, was an eager, energetic and willing partner.

There was no way I could leave that night. We clung to each other, were locked into an embrace that we only released to respond to further bursts of raw physical need. I felt free, uninhibited, totally fulfilled. At last, I have no idea when, we fell asleep entwined in each other's arms.

I was woken by a shaft of morning sunlight beaming through the curtain of Jolé's bedroom window. We were still holding each other but not in exactly the same position as I had remembered when finally, we had both drifted into a long, for me, dreamless sleep. I carefully extracted myself, discovered where her bathroom was and had a long satisfying pee. I got back into bed and looked down at Jolé. She was still sleeping, lying on her back, covered by a bedsheet but with one bare breast exposed outside the sheet. I thought back to what had happened last evening. I was still in a daze. I didn't understand how I could have been so totally swept away, how I had lost all control of my emotions, how I had felt such a desperate need for her, how my sense of values, of responsibility, of maturity had no meaning anymore. I had come to her apartment thinking – I don't know what. I had ended the night in a state of total fulfilment, an emotion I had never ever felt during the forty-six years of my life so far.

I should have been feeling guilty. The morning after the night before! When I had married Carol, I remember making a pledge to myself that I would not let her down as I always felt I had Gizèle by having the affair with the lady from Winchester. But this was now, some ten years later. Last evening, thoughts of Carol didn't even enter my head, as they should have done, as I got lost in a magical world, experiencing emotions I had never known before. Now, I realised I should have feelings of contrition, of guilt, of letting Carol down. I should have had. But I did not. I suppose I knew I must rationalise my feelings, get a grip and a sense of proportion. But not now, not yet.

I got back out of bed, found my underpants, trousers and shirt, pulled them on and went through to the kitchenette end of her living room. I was thirsty but not sure if the water from the tap was safe to drink. I rummaged around and unearthed cups, coffee and a percolator of the same type as I had in my own apartment. I made two cups of coffee. Perhaps it was the sound or the aroma of the coffee brewing that woke her, because when I came back to the bedroom, Jolé was sitting up in the bed. She had pulled the bedsheet up to her chin. I passed her a cup and sat down at the side of the bed.

For some time we didn't speak – just looked at each other as we sipped the hot coffee. In those moments I had absolutely no idea what to say. To try to fob off our situation as something light – just an evening's socialising by two adults? To begin to tell her what the night had genuinely meant to me? To suggest meeting again at some future date? None of these options made any sense at the moment.

I finished my coffee, got off the bed, pulled on my shoes and picked up my jacket. I went back to the bed, lent over to Jolé and kissed her lightly on her forehead. I went to the door, turned back and said, "I'll call you", let myself out of her apartment, found where I had parked my car and drove back to my own apartment.

xxx

I was relieved I had no commitments that Saturday. My mind was numb. I still couldn't think straight. I felt the need to move, to do something that might help me to work out what the hell was going on. I went back to my car and drove slowly back down to Ostia, not the area where we were last evening, but further along the coast. During the season, beach huts selling drinks and snacks were littered along this stretch of the coast but now most of these were closed for the season. I found one that was still open, bought a beer and settled down on a beach recliner. It was quiet and peaceful there. The early autumn sunshine was still warm and I stretched out facing the sea. I tried to get a perspective about last evening. What did I think I was doing? I was now married to a woman who suited me well, was sincere, conscientious, and had supported me well both socially and professionally. Yet here I was being unfaithful to her. My career in the military was going well, I was now a full colonel and had been selected for a prestigious NATO job. My future prospects were good. How could I even think of putting all this at risk by having an affair? And yet, why did I feel so unbelievably fulfilled when I had been with Jolé? I got up from the beach-recliner and walked for some kilometres along the now near deserted beach. I could resolve nothing. Still in a state of confusion and despair, I got back to my car and drove to my apartment in Mostacciano. The next day, Sunday, I had been invited to join a fellow NBC student, a naval officer called David Wood and his wife Hillary on a trip to visit the famous monastery at Monte Cassino, the site of one of the most famous battles of WWII. I hoped this would act as a distraction and perhaps clarify my jumbled thoughts.

xxx

David Wood had offered to drive us. He and Hilary were in their car ready to go when I joined them at nine a.m. the next morning. The weather was still fine. It was good to get out of Rome for a while, in my case just to clear my head. David drove onto the A1 Autostrada and via Frosinone we reached Cassino town by about eleven a.m. then headed up the tight winding bends from the flat fields of the Liri valley to the spectacular views at the top of the mountain. I had earlier studied the details of the Montecassino battles between the German defenders and the allied attackers that took place during the first five months of 1944. But it was only by actually being at the top of the Montecassino mountain that it was possible fully to appreciate its dominant position that was vital for the Germans to defend and for the allies to capture. It had taken four months of desperate fighting between January and May 1944 before the feature was finally captured. It had involved four separate major battles and several bombing raids on the monastery itself, the most devastating being in February when over two hundred heavy and medium bombers had dropped four hundred and fifty tons of bombs and reduced the monastery to a vast pile of rubble. Eventually it was Polish forces who finally captured the monastery and raised the Polish flag over its ruins. No visit to the mountain is complete without spending time to visit and respect the cemeteries of the various nations who were involved. In total there were estimated to be fifty-five thousand allied casualties and twenty thousand Germans killed or wounded. Particularly poignant was the ages listed on the gravestones of the fallen – so many either in their teens and early twenties – a truly sobering fact. And what about religion? Both the German High Command and the Allies believed that God was on their side! Over seventy thousand young lives were lost over the need to control one mountain top! I found the visit greatly helped to put my petty personal dilemma into perspective.

David, Hilary and I had a light lunch in a small trattoria in Cassino town centre then meandered back to Rome. Hilary insisted I join them for supper in their apartment. I was pleased to accept and we spent a pleasant relaxed evening discussing Montecassino, the impact of visiting the graves of so many thousands of young Allied and German soldiers, the NDC course, and how we all were benefitting from this six months away from our usual military jobs. Of course, I made no mention of my adventures on the previous Friday evening.

The next day, Monday, I caught the 504 bus as usual. I checked the passengers joining at Viale del Carmelo. Jolé wasn't there. Nor was she during the rest of the week. I had mixed feelings. I wasn't sure how we might be with each other but I suppose I was quite relieved I didn't have to find out – at least not just yet. During the week, evenings were filled with social commitments connected with the NDC. On Friday morning, again no Jolé. I was wondering if she might have had a bad conscience about our passionate evening. Or perhaps she was ill. Or even gone away. I had to find out. When I got back to my apartment, I realised that, if Jolé was still in her El Al job she wouldn't be back till at least seven p.m. I went for my usual run, then forced myself to wait. At seven forty-five p.m. I called her number. She picked up. She sounded fine if a little guarded and reserved. I couldn't help but ask her if I could come round to see her. All she answered was: "Yes please!"

She let me in to her apartment as soon as I rang her bell. We didn't say anything then – just held each other. We stayed like that for some time before talking. Finally I said: "I've been worrying about you all week. Why didn't you take the bus as usual?"

She took her time to reply and seemed to be more serious than I had seen her before. At last she said: "Mark, last Friday was a truly magical evening for me. I wanted it to continue, for us to be lovers, who knows, perhaps more. After you left last weekend, I had a good think as I wanted to be clear in my thoughts before we talked again. That's why all week I took a later bus. I wanted to be sure what to say to you when we next met. And I realised I was dreaming to think we might have any sort of long-term future together. Mark, you are married to a good woman, as you told me. You have a responsible and successful career which you must not put at risk. And you will only be in Rome until next February, that's just four months away! Of course I want to keep seeing you, you must know that. But we can't get too serious. It could end up badly for everyone involved. What do you think?"

I was feeling so much for this woman who had drawn out of me emotions I had never had before. I wanted her so intensely. But I knew what she said was right, particularly that my time in Rome was strictly limited. In February, I was to move to Brussels. From then, there would be nothing here for me in Rome if I were to stay to be with Jolé. I would have to give up on my military career and I had no transferable skills which I could draw on for income and I didn't speak good Italian. And for Jolé, this was her home, her life. She was Roman, she belonged here. I said:

"Yes, I know you're right but I suppose I just didn't want to admit it. But Jolé, we've just found each other. We can't just walk away and pretend we had never met."

"We don't have to. I would love for us to continue to be together when we can, when it's safe for you. But we must be realistic. Our relationship, such as it is, will have to end in February when you leave Rome. I accept that. I don't like it, but I accept it. So let's just live for the day, as you say – we only live once!"

Jolé took a step back from me, spread her arms out wide and smiled as if to say our problems were resolved. Her reply helped to reduce the tension between us, to lighten the mood. I knew she was right; for now at least. For the rest of the evening we stayed in Jolé's apartment, she cooked pasta, we drank some wine, we talked, we laughed, we teased each other, we made love, and we resolved, as she said, to live for the day.

End of Digression

xxx

Touring with NATO Defence College

We had a busy programme ahead of us at the NDC. In November, the whole college decamped from Rome and travelled on what was called "The Iberian, North Atlantic tour". We kicked off in Lisbon, then via the Azores to start the Americas tour in Quebec, Canada. Wives were encouraged to accompany the tour so Carol had arranged to extend her half-term school break, spend a few days in Rome, then travel with us.

I wondered if I would feel differently about Carol when I went to meet her at Fuimicino airport on her return to Rome in November. But no, we were pleased to greet each other again after our autumn separation. She was keen to update me about our domestic situation in Kent, the house we had just about moved into before leaving for Rome, how our two dogs and one cat had been settled into kennels, highlights of her school term and local happenings in Ashford. We reverted back into our normal relaxed relationship. I was inwardly conscious of my infidelity to her, of my still raw feelings, but I didn't tell Carol. She was excited by the prospect of our American tour. Nothing would have been achieved for anyone if I had confessed about Jolé. At least that is what I told myself.

There were a few key events before we left for our tour. The first highlight was an invitation to our college to attend a papal audience in the Vatican with the Pope, then John Paul II. No matter what our religion, it was a major event for us all. All those wives who were accompanying their husbands at that time were also invited. We ensured that those who had Catholic faith were in the front row. The Pope, accompanied by members of the papal household addressed us from a raised stage, then he came down to greet his audience in person. He had great presence and exuded a feeling of serenity. Our Catholic lady wives were transfixed and one or two seemed on the point of feinting. It was an unforgettable experience particularly for these Catholic ladies.

The second event was that the British members of the NDC were required to attend a Memorial service to commemorate November Armistice Day. This was held at the British War Cemetery in Via Nicola Zabaglia, alongside the Aurelian Walls. It fell to me to read the Act of Remembrance ending with the emotive words: "We will remember them." I have always found this short service, and particularly those final words truly meaningful. Apart from respecting the names of those British soldiers killed in the Italian campaign, it reminded me of those military colleagues I knew who had been killed in action. Also, having recently visited Montecassino, I mourned for the young soldiers who had perished during the battle to capture that historic mountain. Like most others, I always get emotional during those Memorial ceremonies. I get flashbacks of the various personal incidents I had been involved in and question why I had been spared the fate of these young men and was still in the land of the living and able to participate in the ceremony. On these occasions I felt hypocritical quoting words from the prepared Christian text that, in my heart, I did not believe. But that was my duty as a British army officer.

What an amazing experience to have been a part of our NATO Defence College tour! We had our own aircraft, courtesy of the Belgian government, which took off from Ciampino airport. Our first port of call was hosted by the Portuguese Minister of Defence in Lisbon. Then across the Atlantic first to Canada (Quebec, Montreal, Toronto, Ottawa) and then on to the US (North Dakota, the Carolinas, Florida – finally up the north coast to Washington, via Norfolk, Virginia). We made at least one night stop at all the above, were not only given briefings by senior political and military staffs, but also hosted to social events every evening. Professionally and socially rewarding.

Carol enjoyed herself thoroughly and made good friends with many of the other students' wives. We had only one night together back in our Rome apartment before she had to fly back to UK to resume her job in Ashford. The next day I took her to the airport, kissed her goodbye and drove slowly back to Mostacciano. I let myself back into my apartment, the first time I had been alone for several weeks. My mind was a jumble of mixed thoughts and emotions that went something like this:
- I'm so fortunate to be living through this international experience.
- My career is going well. I'm making great friends and contacts.
- I'm blessed with good health.
- I don't see enough of my sons
Carol and I enjoyed being together during this tour – a concentrated environment of constant travel and socialising. I can tell Carol has been motivated. She's a mature, efficient and well organised woman and I know I'm lucky to have her as my wife.

I'm looking forward to the challenge of my next job at NATO headquarters in Brussels

Despite all the above, I'm restless. I'm missing Jolé and had thought about her every day during our tour.

I realise I'm a total fucking hypocrite.

Digression – Jolé again

That was enough of self-analysis for one evening. I knew what I needed to do. I called José and was relieved to hear her voice. I asked her if she would be free the following week-end and suggested we might get away from Rome. She said she would try to fix something using her El Al contacts. She didn't disappoint.

When I picked her up on Friday evening, Jolé was mysterious. She told me to drive onto the GRA motorway and to pick up the autostrada, direction Naples. I had never been there but had heard of its high crime reputation and wasn't sure why we were going there. But that was only a staging point, as Jolé directed me to drive on from Naples towards the coast. The surprise she had for me was to have booked two nights in Sorrento, in the Grand Hotel Excelsior Vittoria, the most historic hotel in the town. Not only that but we were shown into what I guessed must be one of the best suites in the hotel. When the bell-boy had dropped off our bags and left, Jolé said:

"I wanted this weekend to be special. Does this suit you?"

I was incredulous. I pulled her to me and said:

"You are an amazing lady. How on earth did you manage this?"

"I'm pleased you like it. I do most of the travel arrangements for El Al's Rome office. This is one of the perks. Don't worry about the bill. Everything is taken care of."

That was the start of a magical weekend spent with Jolé. We had arrived late after the journey from Rome and we decided to postpone any exploring of Sorrento until the following day. As it was, we were content just to be together again and needed nothing more than to luxuriate in the comfort of this beautiful room. Being with Jolé seemed to be so absolutely right. I felt complete. Jolé was the woman of my dreams. All of my complexes disappeared. So I was a hypocrite, so I was being unfaithful to Carol, so I was putting my career at risk, so I should have had more sense, so I should not be here. But I didn't care. The night faded away in the warm glow of being together in each other's arms.

When I woke the next morning, Jolé was already up. I noticed she had showered as her hair was still damp and she had made up her face. She was dressed in a soft towelling dressing gown provided by the hotel. I got out of bed and put on the gown she had laid out for me. Together we went onto the balcony of our room which had a direct clear view out over the bay of Naples. The hotel was perched on a high outcrop providing a panoramic backdrop over the sea with distant views of what I learnt were the islands of Capri and Ischia. The weather was mild for late November and rays from the early morning sun were highlighting patches of the seascape. We could see small fishing boats and a ferry plying its way towards the islands.

During our two days in Sorrento, we didn't think about the future, we just enjoyed the easy relaxed time of being together – a couple happy and grateful that we had found each other. We followed some of the walks recommended by the hotel, we had long lunches but no plan other than to make the most of this precious time we had together. We didn't want think beyond this weekend.

When I dropped Jolé at her apartment late on Sunday evening, we knew we had lived a wonderful dream. We also knew it was what it was, no more, no less. The next day we would both resume our separate lives. But that was for tomorrow.

End of digression

xxx

Back at the college, we were preparing for our next tour – to the European capitals of NATO member countries: – Oslo, Copenhagen, London, Athens, Bonn ending in Paris. Again, we travelled with the complete course, and over the next two weeks we had meetings and discussions with the leading political and military officials from those countries. Carol didn't come on this tour but arrived back in Rome the day after the course had returned, when we all had a break for Christmas.

We spent that Christmas period based in our Rome apartment. I showed Carol places that I had discovered during the past four months and we met up socially with several of the course students and their wives that Carol had got to know during the America's tour. On Christmas Day, we went early to the Vatican and found a space amid the jostling crowds there to attend the Papal address, known as the Urbi. Although neither I or Carol were Catholics, the atmosphere was memorable.

I tried my best to be relaxed and conscientious being with Carol again and to ensure she enjoyed her last stay in Rome. During that time I was contacted by my future boss in NATO HQ, Brussels. He told me he wanted me in post immediately after the end of the NDC course as there was a major NATO exercise planned to start that week. He explained that my predecessor had to leave early and his job urgently needed to be filled for the exercise. I replied that I would come to Brussels as soon as practical and we agreed I would return to UK immediately at the end of the course, would pick up Carol and we would drive together directly to Brussels. This arrangement meant that we had a lot to do – including to try to rent out our house while we would be in Brussels, decide what to take and what to leave, and to organise our dogs and cat who, under UK rules, would again have to be quarantined for six months when later we came back to UK.

xxx

End of NDC Rome, back to UK then to Brussels

I took Carol back to Fuimicino airport on the afternoon of 2 January for her flight back to UK then drove slowly back towards my apartment. I knew it was wrong but all I was thinking about was being with Jolé again. And I knew that I absolutely should give time and space before thinking of seeing her again. I knew I should have but I didn't. Instead I drove directly to Jolé's apartment, parked, ran up the flight of stairs and rang her door bell. She opened straightaway. We clung to each other. I felt I was home.

The NDC course was to finish on 13 February, six weeks from now. Suddenly any time we might have together seemed impossibly short so we resolved to do all we could to spend as much time as possible together. There were regular social functions it was my duty to attend at the college and Jolé also had some evening work commitments. But we made it work as well as we could. We reserved one weekend to try to go away from Rome again. Jolé said she had an idea where we might go but wanted it to be another surprise. That Friday, we met as early as we could both get away. Jolé told me to drive to the airport and park up. In the departures hall, she led us through to the line for Venice, a city I had always wanted to visit. Jolé already had tickets and I later found she had also booked a hotel of similar standard to the one in Sorrento. Clearly, she had great contacts in El Al! As before, it was magical to be with this fascinating woman. I just adored every moment we were together. Venice was as enchanting as I had imagined though I would have been content to be anywhere with Jolé. The only negative was that I had no idea how cold it could be in Venice in the winter. On the Sunday afternoon, we visited the Glass Museum on Murano island and left it late to leave for the airport. As darkness began to fall, the water started to freeze over but our boatman guide just smiled and saw us safely to the mainland. We arrived back in Rome very late that day sobered by the realisation that this would be the last such trip outside Rome that we would make.

We reached the final days of the NDC course. During our time we had had presentations and studies of all the NATO member countries – at that time sixteen, and had visited most of them. We had learnt about the working procedures of the alliance, how it operated, its command structure, its communications and its assessments of the perceived current threats it faced. One main objective was for us to get to know closely our fellow students as we would be working together either directly or through our NATO communications as we were all leaving Rome to take up appointments in various NATO posts. We all felt this objective had been fully achieved. Our student colleagues had now become our close friends.

On 13 February, we all gathered in the main lecture theatre and our Commandant. German General Ule Wettler gave the farewell address. We said our final goodbyes and the course dispersed. It was time for us all to leave for our staff appointments, in my case at NATO headquarters, Brussels.

I had tidied and cleared my apartment, ready for its next occupant. My car was packed and I was ready to leave. I had lived through this final period in something of a dream. I was keen to discover my new job in Brussels but equally was dreading my departure. I told everyone I was leaving that evening. In fact I spent it with Jolé, our last time together. Next morning, we couldn't bear to drag out that moment. We knew we had both lived through a period of our lives we would treasure forever. But our relationship had to end that day. It had no future. Ironically it was 14 February – St Valentine's day!

XXX

I was in my car at about six thirty a.m. for the drive back to UK. I headed for the GRA ring road then onto the Autostrada heading north. I was driving too fast but I didn't care as my mind was totally filled with a miscellany of thoughts: the pain of leaving Jolé and the final realisation that I would probably never see her again. We had agreed it would be counter-productive to try to continue to keep in touch by mail. So that was that – over – finished. I knew it would take some time, if ever, for my feelings for her to diminish.

Now I had an epic drive ahead. I hadn't studied either my route back or the present February winter weather conditions as closely as I should and I cursed when the driving rain started to turn to sleet. I knew that the first leg, from Rome to Milan, was about six hundred kms. I had been told that normally this should take about five hours to drive but in this weather, who knows? I still hoped to do it in four. The map I had was small scale and I wasn't at all sure it showed up to date details of new motorways. I was driving my eight-year-old VW Passat, fully loaded with all the stuff Carol and I had brought to Rome, plus what we had acquired while there. I had filled up with diesel but that was all, I hadn't even checked the tyre pressures. I knew I should have prepared far better for this drive. Too late now!

My mind was also busy with wondering how it would be to try to pick up my marriage to Carol and reset it for our continuing life together. Almost as soon as I could get back to Ashford, we would have to reload my car, Carol also now had hers, a Mini, and set off for Brussels. We'd also had to pack in our two dogs and cat and declare them at both Dover and Calais customs, as per EU rules, on our way to Brussels.

And how would it be between Carol and me? Should I make a full confession to her about the relationship I had had with Jolé? Then we would have to face a major emotional disruption of our marriage together, even whether Carol would come to Brussels at all, just at a time when we would have to pack and leave Ashford straight away in order for me to honour my agreement with my new boss in NATO. I knew I would have to face this issue at the end of my drive back but there was no point in stressing about it now. Easy to say but…

The weather conditions didn't improve as I pushed on driving north. The sleety rain/wet snow continued. I had to keep the windscreen wipers at full pelt and found myself squinting through the screen. I reached the outskirts of Milan and made out a sign on the Milan ring for Como and Switzerland. I headed that way. There was another issue that became ever more pressing – I was bursting for a pee! I started bouncing up and down at the wheel until at last I saw the signs for a petrol station. I pulled off the autostrada, parked up and sprinted through the rain to the loo. What sweet relief! I then filled up the car with diesel and hit the road again.

At the Swiss border, I found the motorway pass sticker I had bought on the journey to Italy last summer was still valid so I didn't have to stop to buy a new one. By now I was "in the zone" and was determined to push on stopping only to pee and refill the tank. My mood improved slightly as the rain eased and now there were intermittent snow showers but not heavy enough to have to slow down. I remember passing by Lugarno, Bellingzona, Lucern and then reaching the German border at Basel. By then, it was just after six p.m. and was already dark again. I reckoned I was good for another couple of hours before I would need to stop through exhaustion. I passed by the signs for Freiburg and then, when I saw that the next town was Baden-Baden, I decided that was enough for one day. If weather conditions the next day were reasonable, I should be able easily to get to Calais, Dunkirk or Zeebrugge and catch the ferry to Dover. I pulled off the autobahn at the signs for Baden-Baden, drove towards the stadtmitte and saw the sign for hotels, followed that, pulled up at the first hotel I came to, parked up, took out my overnight bag, locked the car and made for reception. It was eight thirty p.m. I was relieved that there was a room available, I took it, found the room, stripped off, showered and got into bed. It was only when I was nodding off to sleep that I realised I was hungry as I hadn't eaten since a hurried snack with Jolé early that morning. Too late now!

Next morning, Sunday 15 February, I felt fresh, did my ablutions and was ready to go again. But first I had to eat something. I was in luck; a buffet breakfast was served from six thirty a.m. I was the first customer. By seven a.m., I left Baden-Baden and was back on the road. Now, I was in familiar German geography and roads that I knew from my earlier military days there. The weather had improved. It was still grey and cold but at least the road was dry. I made good time and by early afternoon I was approaching the channel ports. Zeebrugge was the closest but I didn't have a booking reservation and I reckoned my best bet was to push on to Calais as there were more frequent cross channel ferries and it should be easier to catch one at short notice. And so it was; I just managed to drive onto a ferry which left at three thirty p.m. meaning, with the hour's time difference, should dock in Dover at four p.m. UK time. I had only just pulled my car into the space indicated by the marshal when the ferry pulled away from its mooring. As I climbed the stairs to the upper deck, I could see we were already passing the Calais harbour wall and heading out to sea. When I stuck my head out onto the open deck to get some fresh air, all I got was a blast of freezing cold wind so I hurriedly closed the deck door and spent the rest of the crossing sitting on one of the inside bunk seats. I had another go at trying to decide what I should say to Carol. I contemplated coming completely clean, telling her straight away all about my affair and hoping she could find it in her to forgive and we could start over anew in our changed life in Brussels. But that could well cause a major crisis between us at the very time we need to be sharp, well organised and together. Better surely to act as normal, as if nothing irregular had occurred in Rome and we could get on with sorting ourselves out for our next move. When we were settled in Brussels and the circumstances were favourable, I would make my confession then. Decision made, I would greet Carol as normal and together we would make the trip to Brussels.

xxx

The ferry docked in Dover on time and one hour later I pulled up outside our house in Brabourne Lees, near Ashford. A couple of days before, I had phoned Carol to say I hoped to be home that evening and, true to her efficient nature, she was there: ready and welcoming! We embraced with the enthusiastic accompaniment of the wagging tails of our two dogs. But then Carol's welcoming attitude changed. She said:

"During the last weeks I tried to call you at the apartment, but you were never there. Where were you every time?" I hesitated and I could tell she was suspicious. Then she came right out and asked: "Were you having an affair?" There it was, a direct question. My decision not to tell her was blown. I simply couldn't lie. I told her "yes" and tried to tell her as it was. I suppose I could have said something like: "Yes I was lonely there in Rome but it didn`t mean anything." But although I knew I'm a hypocrite, I simply could not be that insincere to a woman I've lived with for ten years.

We had a terrible evening. Carol was quite rightly distressed and I didn't know what she might decide. Would she now come with me to Brussels at all? I couldn't blame her if she decided to leave me. I would have preferred to try to give her time for us to work things out but I was committed to go to Brussels not later than the next day. Carol had made us a "welcome home" supper but instead she went directly up to our bedroom. I left her alone and went to bed in a spare room. I suppose I had known deep down that Carol would find out about my affair with Jolé, that I should never have let happen. But I had been totally swept away, besotted with this beguiling Italian lady and wasn't prepared to recognise the inevitable outcome and the damage it would do to my marriage to Carol. I couldn't sleep that night and after several restless hours, decided to get up. I took our two dogs for a long walk then decided to load up our two cars. I would be ready to leave that day, hopefully together, but if it had to be, then alone.

Carol didn't appear until late morning. There was a natural stiffness between us, an attitude we had never had before. We talked and after a time Carol asked me to tell her how it had been with Jolé. So I told her the full story, Carol deserved nothing less. I ended by telling her that Jolé and I had resolved that we had no future together and that with the end of the NDC course in Rome, so would our relationship end. I said I would need to leave for Brussels that afternoon and would be reporting for my new duty at NATO HQ the following day. I hoped she would come too. Carol didn't reply.

xxx

The NATO HQ administration had written to tell me I had been allocated accommodation in a suburb of Brussels called Steerebeek and had sent directions with a key. I didn't know the city and I reckoned I couldn't leave later than mid-afternoon in order to get to Brussels, find the property and be ready for work the following day. We had a silent lunch together then I decided to take our dogs for another walk in the hope that we could then all be loaded up for the trip. When I came back, I was pleased to see Carol was busy checking the car loading and making sure that we had room for our own packing and our two dogs plus one cat. At least we would start together. I hoped it would stay that way.

We drove in convoy. I had the Passat, with our dog Suzi and our cat. Carol was behind in her mini with Gemma, our other dog. We had to contend with a period of heavy snow as we drove through northern France and into Belgium and it was late evening before we reached the Brussels ring road. Snow was piled up on the verges of the road which was icy but just about drivable. Twice I went the wrong way and had to double back and it was not until nearly midnight that we eventually found Sterrebeek and tracked down our new house. It was detached and as far as I could tell in the dark, it seemed to be old and have character. We parked up, I tried the key in the lock of the very old door. It worked. We had reached our new home. Inside the lights worked but it was freezing cold. I struggled with the antique boiler but couldn't get it to work. We would have to freeze tonight.

I was up early next morning. I tried again to fiddle with the boiler which eventually fired up. I took the dogs out in the still dark morning. I unearthed the one set of uniform that I had fastidiously kept in a good state. I was now ready to embark on another new chapter in my life.

Pause

During the last few days in Rome and while I was driving home to UK and then on again to Brussels, I had tried to rationalise about my life at that point; what was it about, where was I going? But my mind was just a jumbled mix of miscellaneous thoughts: missing my sons, Rome, the NDC course, feeling guilty about Carol, the mass graves of young soldiers buried in Montecasino, the opulence of the Vatican, meeting the Pope, the variety of experiences during our tours in North America and the European capitals, my military career so far and thoughts about the next job in Brussels: all the above but also trying to understand the deep, basic emotional desire I had felt for Jolé and the wrench of having to leave her and move on. That was my life as it was then. It was enough to live in the present. There seemed no place for deeper thoughts.

xxx

Chapter Thirty-Two

NATO Headquarters Brussels

Routinely, on the first day of joining any major international organisation, there is a mass of induction administration to sort out – introductory requirements such as: entry and security passes, allocation of car parking and office space. New arrivals would spend a day or more completing these procedures then attending orientation briefings about the geography of the premises and introductions to key staff before settling into the new post.

But not today as the HQ was gearing up for the start of a major training exercise. At nine a.m. sharp, I reported to my new boss, Rear Admiral Saco van Idsinga from the Netherlands. He was friendly and welcoming but also impatient for me to be a productive member of his division straight away. He told me:

"Glad you could make it on time for the start today of the first major training exercise to be conducted on a full NATO wide scale. Our Intelligence Division is to play a key role in providing twice daily intelligence assessments both to the military committee and to the political staffs of our NATO HQ. We are having to pit our wits against a full exercise planning and organising staff which has been set up by the US Pentagon staffs in Washington. All secure communications are in place and have been tested. We are to co-ordinate input from all our NATO commands Europe wide, and produce our integrated analysis. We are short of experienced staff particularly those with detailed knowledge of Warsaw Pact military tactics. I've read your CV and we need to use your knowledge. You are to head up a team jointly with Colonel Christian Uhr, our German army rep and you are to produce the ground forces input. The cells have already been set up and I need you to join in directly. Is that clear?"

I thought it was as clear as mud but didn't say so. I replied, "Certainly, Admiral – I'll go to find Christian and get started right away." The admiral nodded and rushed off to deal with some other priority.

My reply was bullshit but I wanted to make a good start. I asked around and eventually found my way to the "ground forces" cell and met up with Colonel Christian Uhr. I introduced myself and Christian seemed relieved to meet me. He explained his small team of supporting staff officers was very inexperienced and, until I had joined him, he had to carry a full twenty-four-hour responsibility for intelligence analysis of ground forces input. Now he could share these duties with me.

My instruction from the Admiral had been very clear. I was to get stuck into the new exercise and stay with it. I could tell that Christian was in dire need of support. I would have to put everything else aside and work with Christian until the end of this multi-national alert training exercise which was scheduled to last for two weeks. I had no prior knowledge of the exercise scenario or of this level of intelligence. Too bad, I had to get a grip and work.

I was very conscious that I had left Carol in the middle of a cold winter's night in a different house, which I hoped might by now be starting to warm up, and in a different country. Her husband had just confessed to having had a passionate affair and now she was stuck having to find her way around, sort out the house and look after two dogs and a cat! I wanted to call her to explain my situation here but we didn't yet have a phone connected in the new house. She would just have to cope!

I settled down and did a lot of reading. I realised I had several positives. Firstly all the material, both written and verbal was in the English language. Although there were many other staff officers here who were native English speakers – Americans, Brits, Canadians – the majority were not and, added to the complexity of the exercise material, they had to work in a second language. Secondly, as I read into the details of the exercise scenario, I realised that this was not dissimilar to the format and material used during the many exercises that I had participated in 1st British Corps in Bielefeld. What was different was the level. I needed to adjust to this.

After the initial baptism of fire at NATO HQ, I found it stimulating to be immersed in the intricacies of this work. I liked working with Christian who showed the same qualities of hard work, attention to detail and professionalism that I had learnt to respect in the German officers in the NDC, characteristics that I wished many of my fellow Brits would acquire. We made some early errors but as the exercise wore on, we settled down to working as a team and producing timely analysis and assessments which were judged to be accurate by the US led exercise organising staff.

It was not until the end of day two of the exercise that I managed to rush back to our house in Sterrebeek. I had been concerned for poor Carol. I need not have worried. As I entered the house, I noticed it was warm and tidy. Carol was there. I told her how I had been put to work immediately, had caught a few hours' sleep in a chair at my new workspace, and hadn't been able to call her to explain. Carol seemed calm, she told me she had explored the local area, found the shops and stocked up, she'd got to grips with the heating system, unpacked our bags and tried to make the house homely. She seemed calm and to have adjusted to this new situation. I admired how well she was coping.

We kept up our exercise "ground forces cell" duties for the stipulated two-week schedule until at last we heard the radio message "Endex", meaning that the exercise had now been completed, that we could dismantle our temporary "war" roles and revert back to normal peacetime duties. Personally, this gave me the chance to carry out all the induction processes that had to be put on hold for the duration of the exercise, to find my real office, to meet all the other members of the Intelligence Division, who had been fulfilling other roles during the exercise, and to work out what were my main duties and responsibilities. I found that my job required me to work closely with Admiral van Idsinga, to ensure his policies and directives were clearly passed down to those responsible and to ensure they were carried out to his specifications. I soon found him to be a delightfully easy person to get on with: professional and highly motivated but with an easy relaxed personality. He loved to laugh which he did often. Most days would begin with the two of us discussing our Intelligence Division's work priorities and how he needed them to be carried out. He was always open to and would accept advice. When he had made his decisions, it was my job to ensure they were implemented.

The Intelligence Division of NATO's international staff comprised officers and soldiers of all the NATO member nations. The rank of the Director was that of a one or two star general (in our case naval Rear Admiral) and the rest of us were either full or lieutenant-colonels from a mix of the sixteen member nations. This grouping could have been a recipe for rivalry and friction but largely due to Saco van Idsinga's personality, we all worked and socialised very well together.

During the years I worked in Brussels, our main focus was to follow, assess and report on the political and military developments of the Warsaw Pact countries in general and the Soviet Union in particular. It was a pivotal period of East-West relations. Following the years of tensions of the Brezhnev area until his death in 1982, there was the short period of drift under the ageing Andropov and Chernenko. In December 1984, the British Prime Minister Margaret Thatcher met Michael Gorbachev for the first time and early the following year Gorbachev was appointed General Secretary of the Soviet Communist Party. Early on, Gorbachev showed that he wanted to radically reform how the USSR was governed and how it operated. His term as leader of the Soviet Union coincided both with Margaret Thatcher period as PM and with the US Presidency of Ronald Reagan. Summits took place between Reagan and Gorbachev in Geneva in 1985 and in Reykjavik the following year to discuss arms control and the non-proliferation of nuclear weapons.

There was one major event that directly affected our Intelligence Division while I was there. On 7 December 1988 Gorbachev addressed the United Nations General Assembly. During this speech, he announced that Soviet Forces were unilaterally to withdraw fifty thousand troops and five thousand tanks from Eastern Europe. This was of major significance particularly as the following day, there was to be an already planned meeting of the leaders of the NATO nations to be held in our HQ building in Brussels. That evening, Admiral van Idsinga set his staff the task of analysing the detail of Gorbachev's speech, discussing our findings with the intelligence communities in the national capitals and producing an agreed assessment of the Gorbachev speech to be given to NATO leaders in order for their response to the Soviet leaders to be formulated.

Together with our two senior analysts (one US and one German) I worked late that evening. We reached an agreed conclusion that Gorbachev's speech was genuine and consistent with his earlier policy aims. However, when we contacted the intel staffs in the US, UK and German capitals, we found that only the German experts in Bonn agreed with our assessment. In London and Washington, there was deep scepticism about Gorbachev's announcement and concern that the west might be being duped. They sought much more collateral evidence before accepting his announcement of troop withdraws as genuine. Our problem then was to try to reconcile these conflicting views before our assessment was put before our leaders at the Summit of the National Heads of State the next day.

Comment. I leave this subject here as I wrote my novel "Verification" based on this Gorbachev speech and what flowed from it! End of hint to reader!

Our life in Brussels was good. Carol seemed to be contented and gradually our personal relationship improved and we resumed our relaxed attitude towards each other. She got a teaching post, first in Mons, a fifty-minute drive away, then in a private school located conveniently near to our house. We found Brussels to be a great city to live in, with excellent restaurants, theatres and cinemas all with easy driving access via the inner ring road. We regularly socialised with fellow NATO staff members, the majority of whom were of similar age and interests. My two sons came to spend holidays with us although there was a coolness between them and Carol. At least now I was able to spend more time with them and had a decent home for us all to stay in Brussels.

XXX

Digression – the Belgian lady

I would like to record that our tour in Brussels was harmonious throughout but that was not the case. Again I was the cause due to my own stupidity. One evening I was invited to an after-hours function given by members of the civilian staff at NATO to say goodbye to a well-liked gentleman who was retiring from our HQ. It had been my intention just to drop in for a drink, circulate for a short while, then leave. That was the intention but not the reality. There were also some work colleagues attending who I knew well and we started to chat and share reminiscences. We had a few drinks and music was played. Somehow, I found myself dancing with a petite and gamine Belgian lady who I had met casually on a few occasions in our staff canteen. The lady told me her car had broken down and asked if I could drive her home. I should have backed off and politely declined. I should have but I did not. Instead I drove her home – big mistake!

The next evening I was working late in my office, preparing a presentation for Admiral van Idsinga to give at the Military Committee meeting the next morning. It was not unusual for me to be the last to leave our division in the evenings, the only time when my phone stopped ringing. It was about seven thirty p.m. and as far as I knew, I was the only one left in our branch. Suddenly, the door opened as someone came in. I looked up to see the lady I had driven home the previous evening. I will call her Paulette Lecroix, though that was not her real name. She said, "Mark, I want to see you again. Will you run me home?"

I had nearly forgotten my indiscretion the previous evening and I didn't know how to react. I realised how stupid I had been to have driven her home. Now I had no wish to get involved further with her but here she was. I said something feeble like:

"I'm sorry Paulette, but I'm afraid I'll be tied up with my work for some time then I have to get straight home. I hope you can get a lift home with someone else."

That didn't cut it. Paulette firmly sat down in the chair opposite my desk and said:

“No, I want you to take me, like you did last night. I’ll wait.”

I was stuck. There was no one else in the branch office. Although our division was a restricted access area, Paulette had been a permanent NATO employee for many years and her pass gave her access to all parts of the HQ and to our room and phone numbers.

I tried to persuade her politely to leave but it was no use. She had made her intentions very clear. She wouldn’t move until I did as she wished. I couldn’t bring myself to physically throw this petite little lady out. There was nothing for it. I packed up my papers and secured them in my filing cabinet. When I went to leave my office. Paulette accompanied me. When I went down the corridor to our division access point, initiated the security protocol and left by the side exit point used by our division’s personnel, Paulette came too. When I went to my car, unlocked it and got in, Paulette got in beside me. I remembered where she lived, so I drove there, parked and walked the hundred metres to her door. She took out the entry pass key to her apartment block and inserted it into the outer door. I took that moment to act like a coward, to return hurried back to my car, got in, started the engine and drove off. As I drove home, I thought how pathetic I had been. I absolutely should have been more sensible and mature last evening and not have taken her home. I just hoped she would now back off and leave me alone in future.

Paulette did not back off. The next day, my phone rang soon after I got to my office. It was Paulette. She told me she was upset that I had left her the evening before and that she wanted to see me again. I told her, politely but firmly, that I was not interested to get involved and put the phone down. A few minutes later, she phoned again. And again. And again. It became impossible to do my work. I decided to disconnect my phone, although it was an essential tool for my work. It was no use as, a short while later, my colleague in the next office came to mine and told me that a lady had just called his office asking to speak to me. It was Paulette. Then I realised I had a serious problem caused by my own stupidity. She was now stalking me and I had to deal with this now as her phone calls prevented me from doing my work.

I searched through our staff directory, found the number of the Head of Personnel for the civilian staff, reconnected my phone, called that number and asked for an urgent meeting. Asked what was the subject, I said I would explain when I got there. I then disconnected the phone again and went to find the Head of Personnel's office. This was located in a part of the NATO building I was unfamiliar with. When I found the office, I knocked then went straight in. Behind the desk was a middle-aged lady, also Belgian, who was the Head of Personnel. Her name was Madame Picard. I apologised for my intrusion but explained that I was being stalked by Paulette Lecroix, a member of HQ NATO's civilian staff. I told her about her coming to my office the previous evening, refusing to leave until I drove her home, and that today she was constantly ringing my office making it impossible for me to work. Madame Picard heard me out. I could tell she was sceptical about what I had said. She then asked the obvious question.

"Why do you think she is doing this. Have you been encouraging her?"

I expected this question and knew I had to answer frankly so I told her I had been too friendly at the staff party, had driven her home, which I now regretted but had later told her I didn't want to have a further involvement. I feared Madame Picard would next ask the question, "Did you have sex with her" but fortunately, she did not. If she had, I would have truthfully told her I had not and had no intention to but I was not sure she would have believed me. She said she would speak to Paulette and tell her not to phone me anymore. I thanked her profusely and left feeling, or hoping, my action would have solved the problem. I also felt that, if there were to be some sort of jurisdiction, Madame Picard, herself a Belgian national who had known Paulette for many years would not take my side. I wouldn't blame her.

My meeting with Madame Picard did help for a while. Paulette did not phone my office again that day. Instead, when I went to the staff gym to change for my usual lunchtime run, she was there. She didn't say anything, just made sure that I knew she was there. When I left work in the evening, often she would be standing next to my car. She didn't try to block me, she just made sure I knew she was there. When I drove home, I wondered if I should tell Carol, admit I had been an idiot and hope she would be understanding. But after my affair in Rome, I feared this incident would stir up all the past recriminations. I decided not to tell her and hoped that Paulette would give up.

It was not to be. Shortly after I got home, our house phone rang. I answered. It was Paulette – she had found my house number. She said she wanted to see me and could I meet her. I put the phone down. Carol was there and asked who it was. I told her it was a wrong number. Bad decision – I should have told Carol then about Paulette. Soon after the phone call, I heard a loud banging noise outside the house. I went out to check the cause. There was Paulette! She was hitting a stick against our dustbin to attract attention. I asked her what she wanted but she just half smiled, got in her car that she'd parked outside our house, and drove off. I suppose she just wanted me to know that she could always find me and get at me wherever I was.

There was nothing else to do now than to tell Carol the full story. She was justifiably very upset and accused me of being unfaithful to her again. When we went to bed, I wasn't sure whether Carol would decide to leave me. Next morning, she said she had decided to stick with me, at least for now. I drove to work and went in to see Admiral van Idsingsa as soon as he arrived. I felt it my duty now for him to hear about this harassment before he would surely hear it from some other source. I told him about Paulette and how I had been stupidly over-friendly to her, that she had made constant phone calls in the office which totally disrupted my ability to work, how I had reported to Madame Picard, how the office calls had stopped for now. I also told him about her calls and visit to my house. The Admiral heard me out and, much to my relief, told me that my story was very similar to one of his own some years before when he was working in the Dutch Naval HQ. He said he would talk himself to Madame Picard. He was true to his word.

For some time, I had no further direct contact with Paulette but she regularly let me know she hadn`t given up, by again being at the gym at lunchtime, by standing next to my car when I left work and sometimes sitting in her car in the evening while parked directly outside our house. It was, to say the least, unsettling as I suppose she intended.

Then there was the incident near the Avenue Louise in central Brussels. I had enrolled in a course to try to improve my French by attending an evening class at the language school there. One evening, I had parked my car by having to squeeze into a small space with my bumper close up the car in front. When I returned to the car after the lesson, I found another car parked behind mine with its front bumper touching the rear of my car. It was wedged in and impossible to move. Paulette was sitting in the car behind mine. It was late and I was tired. I suppose I should have left my car where it was and taken a taxi home. But I was fed up with Paulette's constant harassment. I went over to her car, opened the driver's side and said sharply to Paulette:

"What do you think you are doing? Get out and talk." To my surprise, she did as I asked, got out of her car and stood next to me. I really didn't know how to handle this being very conscious of the reality that if I called the police, I was in Paulette's country, the police spoke her mother tongue whereas if I lodged a complaint against Paulette, the police would be unlikely to take my side. Here we were late at night in the middle of Brussels. Paulette was a petite woman whereas I, a Brit, am quite tall. I would have a hard job trying to get Paulette arrested for harassment! So I tried another tactic and invited her to come and have a drink in the nearest bar. Somewhat to my surprise she meekly agreed.

We found a small unpretentious bar nearby. I took a small beer, Paulette a glass of white wine. I told her calmly that I had never meant her harm but also I had no interest ever to have a relationship with her. She tried several approaches. Would I come home with her – just this once to say goodbye? I said "No!" She said she needed to go to the doctor the next day to have a mole removed from her back. She was frightened to go on her own. Would I help her by coming with her? I said "No!" She said she realised she had acted badly, would I come with her to explain to her personnel department? I said "No". From our seat at the bar, I could see where our cars were parked and to my relief I noticed that car that had been parked directly in front of mine had gone. This was my chance. I put down enough Belgium francs to cover the cost of our drinks, got up said a quick goodbye to Paulette, hurried over to my car and drove off. The last I saw of her was hurrying towards her car. I took side streets back to our house in Sterrebeek in case she had tried to follow. I don't know what was in her mind and why this last encounter had some effect to dissuade her. For a time, Paulette continued her stalking – sometimes she would still be at my car as I left the office, sometimes she would park outside our house and still she made the odd call, rarely speaking but I always knew it was her on the phone. Whatever, gradually the situation eased. It had been provoked by my own stupid indiscretion. I hoped I had learned my lesson!

End of digression

In the early autumn of 1989, I was informed of my next posting. I was to be promoted to Brigadier and would be Assistant Chief of Staff (ACOS) at Allied Forces Central Europe (AFCENT) in charge of Intelligence and Security. AFCENT was located in Brunssum, the Netherlands. Both Carol and I looked forward to our next move, one hour's drive down the motorway from Brussels.

My tour at HQ NATO taught me a great deal. I learnt, for example:

- To broaden my knowledge of Warsaw Pact capabilities to include all elements of their armed forces – army, rocket forces, navy, air, special forces – and how all these elements were co-ordinated by the Soviet High command.

- To understand the political element of NATO and the workings of the Summits of the national Heads of State which were held twice annually in the HQ in Brussels.

- To learn how best to harmonise the working relations of the, then, sixteen member nations of NATO.

- How fortunate I had been to have spent three years working and socialising with the so many intelligent and charming other members of the alliance.

- How lucky I was to have such a practical wife who had so far put up with my Roman affair and my stupidity with Paulette.

- **What a fucking idiot I can be!**

xxx

Chapter Thirty-Three

Headquarters, Allied Forces Central Europe (AFCENT)

Brunssum, The Netherlands

Below are some of the abbreviations used by the military, particularly as organisations evolve and adjust to reflect changing political events and priorities. During the time I worked for NATO, there were sixteen member nations. Since then, the Warsaw Pact collapsed and several eastern Europe nations have joined e.g. Poland, the Baltic states and, more recently, Finland and Sweden. The main military commands in 1989 were:

- SHAPE (Supreme Headquarters of Allied Powers in Europe), based in Casteau, Mons, Belgium. SHAPE operated under the political control of NATO HQ in Brussels. It commanded the three regional groupings of Allied Forces:
- AFCENT (Allied Forces Central Europe), based in Brunssum, the Netherlands – my new home!
- AFSOUTH, based in Naples, Italy.
- AFNORTH, based in Kolsas, near Oslo in Norway.

My lifestyle took quite a leap when I took up my appointment in AFCENT. For a start I was the head of the Intelligence Division, a multi-national group of some forty personnel, a mix of military officers and civilian analysts. My immediate boss was an American, Major General Rich Grifitts, the Chief of Staff, who in turn answered to our Commander in Chief, initially German General Heinz-Hennig von Sandrat. At the same level as my job (one star General) were the heads of Operations, an American, Policy (a German), Communications (Dutch) and Logistics (Canadian). I joined a well-established organisation whose main task was to follow and analyse the developments of the now disintegrating Soviet Union, the East German communist regime and the fast-moving changes in other east European countries. The role of my newly inherited Division was pivotal to this task. Other missions were to keep our HQ up to date concerning developments in the Kosovo/Bosnia conflict, the allocation and preparation of NATO forces intervention in the Balkans, security aspects resulting from the Iraq invasion of Kuwait (and the resulting Operation Desert Shield); and the security threat to our NATO forces.

My new job also came with such perks as the allocation of a house in the nearby Dutch town of Sittard. The location was excellent. Sittard is in the regional area of Limburg. It is a pretty town with all social amenities but in addition it has easy car access to Maastricht, also in Holland, to Aachen (in Germany) and to Liège (in Belgium). Each if these towns have their unique and charming characters. I was soon to be fifty years of age when we arrived at AFCENT. I appreciated how lucky I was to be here and, with Carol and our black Labrador Gemma, (our other dog had died when we were in Brussels). We settled down together to a period of quality domestic living.

One national duty I was tasked to perform was, as in when I was in Rome, to attend the annual Remembrance day commemoration on the closest Sunday to 11 November. This was held in Sittard cathedral. I respected how well this event was supported in the UK, but in the Netherlands, it was even more so. The day brought back the past memories experienced by the Dutch nation during the years of occupation by Nazi Germany, a period of major disruption, deaths and poverty for so many. On the commemoration day, the Cathedral was completely full so that many had to listen to the broadcast of the service from outside. After the service, the mayor and local dignitaries collected at the town war memorial when it was my duty to give the "we will remember them" quotation.

I wondered why, then nearly fifty years after the war, the Dutch population of Limburg should feel the need to be in a church and worship, considering that over half the population declared they had no religious denomination. Of those who did, some twenty-three per cent were catholic, fifteen per cent protestant (including Dutch reform church) and the remainder were mostly Muslim. I supposed that in times of stress, many people turn to religious symbols as a form of comfort rather than belief.

XXX

My life was, and I suppose still is, something of a roller coaster. If ever I were to get cocky or over confident, I would be quickly put back in my box – probably nature's way of teaching me something of the meaning of life – who knows? Towards the end of my second year at AFCENT, I was told by our UK Ministry of Defence (MOD) that I had been selected to be the Defence Attaché (DA) to Germany as my next job, initially based in Bonn. This was a particularly fascinating period of German history as the nation sought to assimilate an additional seventeen million people to its population from the now disintegrating East Germany. The capital city would revert back to Berlin as the country reunified. I was thrilled to be selected to be a part of this. I was told however that for the time being I was to keep this appointment confidential. I did of course tell Carol who was equally delighted and one weekend we took a trip to Bonn to familiarize ourselves with this city.

After the initial notification, I heard nothing more for some time. The date of the appointment was fast approaching and my successor in AFCENT had been selected. I started to make discreet enquiries to the MOD about the Bonn job but these were met with evasions. As the date became ever closer, I needed to get on with administrative planning. I was wondering why there was a mystery? Eventually, with only three weeks to go before the appointment was due to be implemented, I was curtly told that I would not after all be going to Bonn. Instead, another officer, an ex-guardsman, had been selected. I did some research including through my German contacts, and found out that the wife of the guards officer was a close personal friend of the British ambassador's wife and the job had been fixed for her husband. I made a token protest but found it was a fait-accompli and the decision was final. Frustrating but there you go! Life is not always straightforward. With Carol's agreement, I made a decision. I told the MOD that I would not take any of the alternative jobs that were offered but instead would leave the army.

In March 1993, I handed over my AFCENT job to another British officer, packed up our belongings, took our darling black Labrador and our cat, to quarantine kennels, where they would stay for six enforced months. Carol and I drove back to our house in Brabourne Lees, Kent. I had to adjust to being a civilian and to start from zero to try to find a new job. I was fifty-two years old.

xxx

Chapter Thirty-Four
Back to UK – A Civilian Again

In hindsight, I should have started to prepare for a second career much earlier. I had been absorbed in our lives in Holland and, until the withdrawal of the attaché job, I had expected to remain in uniform for at least a further three years until I would be fifty-five, when military officers below the rank of three-star general are required to retire. By deciding to leave when I did, I had done no detailed planning for work as a civilian. In fact, no planning at all. I was still feeling fit and very active. I had the prospect of another ten to fifteen years ahead before I could think about fully retiring from working. I realised I had to concentrate on studying the job market and trying to find a satisfying job to last me through until my mid-sixties.

I started my job hunting with false optimism, buoyed up by the remarks of several of my colleagues who told me that I should have no difficulty finding a suitable job in UK. It didn't happen. I searched all the usual channels of job advertisements and fired off applications for any of these that I thought I would be qualified to do. It wasn't long before having to face the harsh reality that my background had no particular relevance to civilian employment. I also learnt that not having been living and working in UK for several years, I had no contacts who might be prepared to act as referees. I was a job seeking loner. I was not overly concerned initially as I was pleased to have a break from working and spent much of the summer of 1993 renovating our house. It was a sound, well located property but it was built with plain red bricks and lacked character. I worked with a colleague who had far better building skills than me and together we overlaid the roof with authentic Kent peg tiles and painted the lower half white. What had been a rather ugly little house was now transformed into a charming character property.

There was another positive at that time. The mandatory six-month period of quarantine for our labrador dog Gemma and our cat expired and Carol and I rushed to the kennels to be reunited with them. We had a wonderful reunion. Gemma had put on a lot of weight during her six months confinement. I resolved to slim her down gently. Then as soon as she was fit again, we could resume our exercise schedules together. Our cat was his usual lofty self, living a life at a level far superior to us mere humans!

House renovation was merely a distraction from my need of full-time employment. My many applications failed to end up with a decent job offer. Either I would get an immediate rejection or be called for interview, then perhaps a second, sometimes even a third or more, often ending up being told I had come a strong second – which was to me as much use as being a hundred and second! The bottom line was I didn't get the job! The months passed by while I remained unemployed. We still had a mortgage to pay and our few savings were rapidly dwindling. Something had to done.

One day I saw an advertisement by a leading insurance company, Friends Provident, announcing they were recruiting applicants to be sales agents in the Kent area. I knew nothing about insurance but, what the heck? I was interviewed and at last was offered employment. Not at all what I had in mind but a job was a job! First, I had to attend various courses to be licenced to sell insurance. During these training courses I found myself with a group of men and women, from a range of different backgrounds and who were mostly far younger than me. I enjoyed their company and we managed to have a lot of laughs while still concentrating on the somewhat tedious but very necessary subject of insurance regulations and passing the required exams. By the end of 1993, I had qualified and was employed to work within a catchment area covering the south east sector of the county of Kent.

This was how it worked. One evening every week, our group of about eight people, gathered in the Kent office in Maidstone. We were given an initial list of "prospects" which we had to add to as our contacts developed. Then we would spend the evening, with a legal cut-off time of nine p.m., phoning our prospective customers, requesting their agreement to visit them with the objective of reviewing their finances and making recommendations which hopefully would result in sales for Friends Provident. Somehow, I found this method of "cold calling" somewhat uncongenial but that was the system, that was the only way we could get our initial contacts with potential clients. Once we had acquired enough agreed visits and had the agreement of our eager young manager, we were on our own for the rest of the week while we visited our clients in the neat little cars provided by the company.

Being an insurance salesman was something totally different from anything I had done before and I knew that my former work colleagues would view the job as a major comedown from being an army brigadier. But needs must. At least I had employment. I had a low basic salary but was paid a commission on all completed insurance policies sold; an incentive to be successful. We were taught how we were to conduct our meetings with customers. First, we were required to carry out a face-to-face interview with the client and, where relevant, his or her partner, a process which routinely took up to three hours. That was the first visit. Then we would prepare our recommendations for the customer regarding savings or life insurance, pension plans etc. We would then arrange a second visit where, we were very firmly told, we should close the deal by obtaining the customer's agreement, in writing, to purchase a policy from the company. We would then submit all our paperwork to our head office to ensure our proposals were suitable for the client's financial profile and complied with the government's legal requirements. Once this process was finalised, the transaction was completed. I respected that Friends Provident was scrupulously honest in ensuring that all policies were suitable and affordable by the client.

I had some memorable meetings with the "clients" who were good enough to allow me to visit them and I was lucky to meet many who had led really full and interesting lives. Our office manager pressed us to complete the sale on our second meeting and to keep it as short and business-like as possible. But often I found the "close the deal on the second visit" instruction often turned into a more social than business affair. I enjoyed being an "insurance salesman". During these evenings, I had long conversations with some "clients" who were Christians/Muslim of varying denominations (and others who were non-religious) and were keen to justify and expand on their beliefs. It was a pleasure to visit and discuss life with them. Some kind clients plied me with cups of coffee, which I accepted and gin and tonic or wine, which I regretfully had to decline. Sometimes, we had supper together and had extended chats which ranged way beyond the confines of their proposed insurance contract. I learnt a great deal about people's lives, politics, religions, habits and financial ambitions which were often very diverse. Because the initial point of such evenings was to discuss life planning, many of our conversations involved my "clients" views about the meaning of life and what happens after death. As the visitor to their homes it was my job to be a "good listener". It also gave me great material for writing this book!

Some "clients" were determined to make as much out of the investment element of savings, some were concerned mainly about safeguarding their inheritance for their children, others wanted to make as much as possible quickly to enable them to live their lives to the full in the short term. One such couple told me they had three children, who they had brought up well including paying for them all to attend private school and had subsided their university years. They felt they had done their stuff for their kids all of whom had now left home and had steady jobs. Now all they wanted was to have enough funds to be able to afford to continue maintaining their house, to sail their boat and to live well until they died. They told me. "We would be content if we could spend our last penny on the day we die!" I replied. "Fine – that can be arranged but can you tell me the exact date you will die?" Ah, that was the problem. Most lives are unpredictable and who knows how they will pan out. Some individuals may have a premature death through accident or ill health and, conversely others could live long and healthy lives into old age. I learnt to appreciate how important it was to be insured with a policy of sufficient flexibility to cover these unknown outcomes.

I did my best to take my new job seriously and did rather well financially; one month even topping the sales statistics for the company nationwide. I confess I was not as concerned about this top sales honour as I was by the healthy commission I earned from the sales and the wide range of opinion offered by my many "clients" about their views on life, what it meant to them and their loved ones, how they and their partners wished to live now, what their expectations were for the rest of their lives and what their expectations of might happen to them when they died. Some said they felt confident in their reliance that God would ensure their resurrection and life everlasting; others remained undecided about their personal expectations but anyway wanted to ensure their children would be well provided for financially when they died. Despite listening to many points of view, there was absolutely no consensus about this eternal question,

One of the down sides to the job was that many of the client meetings had to be held in the evenings after they got home from their work. I had known from the onset that, although Friends Provident gave me useful employment for which I was grateful and which taught me a great deal about a previously unknown area, I was still hopeful of getting a job which was more in line with my previous military experience. Another minus was that while I was committing to these arranged visits, I was no longer available for other interviews or work. After about six months of this routine, and by then having restored some of our flagging finances, I decided to leave this job much to the annoyance of my local manager who had invested time in my recruitment, training and most importantly, his share of my commission!

xxx

Chapter Thirty-Five

UK

Positives and negatives

About the time I left Friends Provident, the property market was forecasting that the price of housing was likely rise sharply in the near future. I thought it a good idea to try to sell our now pretty fully functional house and look for another as a hedge against future price rises. I discussed this with Carol who was not against the idea but less enthusiastic than I was, particularly while I no longer had a full-time job. She was probably right. I started checking out the local estate agents and we put our Brabourne Lees house up for sale.

Digression – "The Beeches"

Some of the insurance clients I had visited lived in Saltwood, a small village situated high on the cliffs above the seaside town of Hythe. I liked this village, it was small but had all the classic features of English rural life: a castle, a thousand-year-old church, village square and hall, surrounding farmland. It was relatively isolated yet still had easy access to Hythe, Folkstone, Ashford, and to shops, and good road and rail connections. I liked the idea of living there.

I would often come home with bundles of brochures with particulars of houses for sale and Carol and I would each read through them and began compiling a short list. Early on during this search I came across details of a house in Saltwood. I knew straightaway that in theory it would not be suitable. It was located in a private road, had six bedrooms and two acres of land. It was called "The Beeches". I couldn't resist putting it in my short list pile. When she saw it, Carol immediately discarded it – too big, too much land, and far too expensive. On our next search session, I again put The Beeches back on the short list. Again Carol rejected it. I couldn't justify why, but I couldn't help being attracted to it. One day, I decided to drive to Saltwood on my own to check it out. I discovered it had a private drive and it was not possible to see the house from the road. I parked and walked up the drive hoping the owner would allow me to view the property although I not made an appointment. When I got up to the front of the house it was obvious that no one was living there. The surrounding grass was long and the garden had clearly been untended for some time. My overall feeling was very positive. I liked the look of the house from the outside. I walked around the perimeter of the garden. It was beautiful, quiet and welcoming. I went to see the estate agent who took me to inspect the inside of the house. It was unfurnished and in need of some upgrading but I liked the feel of the rooms, the aspect, everything about it. There and then I fell in love with The Beeches though I shared Carol's down to earth view that it was too expensive and we absolutely couldn't afford it. But I couldn't give up on it. The local estate agent told me that the owner was a clever guy who had got a job working for a company in the US, had bought a house in California and had moved there permanently with his family. The Saltwood house had been on the market for some months. Through the estate agent, I put in an offer substantially below the asking price. I had never done such a reckless thing before and I certainly did not have the present means to support the offer. I was sure it would be rejected but what the heck? I didn't know how to tell Carol what I had done so I kept quiet about my crazy offer as I was sure the estate agent would tell me the owner was not interested in my low bid.

It was mid-summer 1993 when two events happened at about the same time. First, we received a firm offer on our present house at Brabourne Lees. We were told the prospective buyer had already sold his own house and was keen to complete on ours as soon as possible. He had agreed to our asking price. The second was a reply from the owner of The Beeches. He would not accept my offer, as I had expected, but instead said he would consider an offer below the advertised price. This was still much more than I could afford but it got me fired up as it was clear the owner really wanted to sell. Through the estate agent, we carried out a series of offers, rejections and counter offers eventually agreeing on a figure. I knew that, even with the net money from the sale of our present house, we would still be well short by several thousands of pounds. I didn't care. My heart was set on buying The Beeches and somehow we would find the funds. I still didn't tell Carol fearing she would insist that I back out of the deal.

There followed a scramble to raise the money. I managed to persuade our bank to give me a mortgage well above what my paltry army pension should merit, and the army agreed to commute some of that pension. These funds just allowed me to scrape together the agreed amount to buy The Beeches. I still kept stalling Carol, telling her we would have to rent somewhere until we bought another house. Our estate agent and solicitor arranged that we would complete both the sale of our present house and the purchase of the Beeches on the same day. On that agreed day, we had all our goods packed and did a final clean of the house. We had to await confirmation from the estate agent that all had been completed and we were free to pick up the house keys and take possession of The Beeches. Carol was not happy as she still thought we were to going to move into some temporary rented accommodation. I didn't disabuse her. There seemed to be some technical delay and it was not until late afternoon that I got the "all clear" from the solicitor to move. We then drove to the estate agent, collected the keys and went straight on to Saltwood. I drove up the drive. It was now late evening and the setting sun showed up The Beeches in all its glory. Carol assumed that this was a house I had rented on a temporary basis. I unlocked the front door and took Carol for a tour. We checked out the two large sitting rooms, the separate dining room, the spacious kitchen and the separate laundry room. We then went upstairs and saw the six bedrooms. The house was empty but I had managed to buy a double bed and have it installed in one of the bedrooms. This had a balcony from which we could see out onto the large rear garden. The rest of our inspection would have wait until tomorrow. I turned to Carol and then admitted to her that I had actually bought not just rented this house. I waited for her reaction fearing she would be upset and angry with me for taking such a rash decision. She was not angry. Instead she was as thrilled as I was. We had bought a beautiful new home. Now I had to find a way to pay for it.

End of digression

xxx

As more months passed, I was still following up on replies to my continuing job applications and still, no decent offer. Yet again, I was short listed but not finally selected. I consulted employment experts and sought advice about my interview technique as I realised I had to try to be better at putting myself across to prospective employers. I researched the background in as much detail as I could find about a prospective employers business and future aims, hoping this knowledge might impress them that I really was the right person for the job. It didn't work. I still had so much energy and desire to work but was unable to find a company willing to take me on. I was frustrated and depressed. I took late night walks with my darling dog Gemma, routinely stopping by a farm gate in the dark as I reflected that if I didn't find some new source of income shortly, I would have to put our new lovely house back on the market, sell it for the first decent offer and downsize back to a property we could then afford. Gemma seemed to understand and would nuzzle up against me in sympathy. Dogs have an amazing instinct to empathise.

Digression – WWF

There was one interview when I really blew it. I had been asked by the personnel department of the charity, World Wildlife Fund (WWF), to attend an interview at their main UK office building in Woking, Surrey. The job was to be the fundraising manager for the UK section. The interview would be at ten thirty. I had got used to getting up early and trudging up the M20 motorway, then to transfer to the M25 circular and on round the west side of London. I had made similar journeys for several such interviews before and knew it was possible to get there in two hours. But such was the rush hour traffic congestion, I had learnt it was prudent to allow an extra hour to be sure of arriving on time. No problem. That day I set off at seven thirty and was glad I had factored in the extra time as there were major traffic delays along the route and it was ten fifteen by the time I had found the WWF building in Woking, parked up and reported to reception for my interview. I was directed to a side room and told to wait to be called.

I waited, and waited. No update information, No coffee, Nothing. At last at about twelve fifteen, over one and a half hours after my scheduled appointment, I was called and asked to go to a room on the floor above. There was no guide. I found the room, opened the door and went in. In front of me was a table behind which four individuals were sitting. I need to describe them. On my left was a gentleman, I would guess in his late fifties. He had long hair tied up in a pony tail, and a straggly beard. He was wearing an open neck sports shirt. Next to him was a lady with a florid red face and a large protruding nose. I hesitate to use the world "fat" but struggle to find any other suitable adjective to describe her size. Her hair was of a mousey brown colour, curly but seemingly uncombed. Next again was another lady. She was slimmer, wore thick pebble glasses and had long dark lank straight hair stretching down to below her shoulders. On my far right was another gentleman. He was black skinned, his hair was fashioned in the "Rastafarian" style. He wore a T-shirt, a dangling neckless and large rings on the fingers of both hands.

The gentleman on my left looked up when I entered the room, and, gesturing to a chair positioned in front of this panel, said, "Take a seat!" That was all. I duly sat down and waited. The spokesman then went back to scribbling some unseen notes. The other three were having a quiet conversation between themselves. Again, I waited. I slowly started to boil with impatient anger. It was hard to believe that they could have been so discourteous. Or was their attitude some cunning interview ploy just to see how I, as a job applicant, would react? I soon concluded this was no ploy, they were just a lot of pathetic no-marks!

I had had enough. I asked myself what the hell was I doing here. In a moment of impetuousness, I jumped to my feet and said something like:

"Right you lot, put your pens down and listen in. I was asked to be here to meet with you at ten thirty this morning. It is now 12.20 and all you've told me is to "take a seat" while you carry on with your scribbling. The job you've advertised is to be fund raising manager for your UK section of the WWF. Having had to put up all morning with your total lack of politeness and courtesy, I have absolutely no wish to raise funds for such a pathetic bunch of people like you four. Good morning!"

I didn't wait for any of these worthy ladies and gentlemen to respond. I turned and walked out of the office, found my car and drove back to Saltwood. Another day wasted. On the drive home I realised my truculent outburst had achieved nothing. Perhaps if I had ever got to know these four, I would have found them to be charming people who I had totally underrated and the WWF could well be an excellent and efficient organisation. The only loser that day was me.

End of digression

xxx

There was another incident at about that time which added to my growing depression. During the past few years, my relationship with my two sons had much improved. They were then both in their twenties. A few years before they had both, independently from each other, travelled around the world, supporting themselves with any temporary work they could find. I was very proud of the way they had both matured and was pleased now to have an easy and relaxed relationship with them. Together they had decided to go to live in Indonesia and to try to make their living successfully there. They regularly returned to UK to visit both Gizèle and to stay with Carol and me. When I was in the midst of my gloom of no job and no income, they came on one of their visits. Of course I delighted to see them but, as I suppose being a proud father, I didn't want them to know how desperate our finances had become. They had followed my progression through the ranks of the military and saw how Carol and I were now living in this lovely house. I had told them vaguely that I was doing consultancy work and I suppose they assumed it was paying well. I didn't want to disillusion them. On this particular visit, they told me they had realised how the UK property market was beginning to escalate and of their plan to buy an apartment in Winchester and to rent it out while they were back in Indonesia. They needed capital and asked me if I could fund them thirty thousand pounds. This was the first time they had ever asked me for money, it was for both of them, was a sensible plan and I wanted to do all I could as their father to support them. But thirty thousand pounds! And at a time I was desperately in need of more money to be able to retain The Beeches. Ah! I said I would have to talk to Carol, as all our money was in a joint account and that I would give them a decision the following day. That evening I discussed my sons request with Carol saying there must be some way of raising this extra cash. I had one idea of going back to the MOD pension providers and requesting them to release all my future pension entitlement in order to commute more funds. But Carol was adamant. She reminded me that I had been reckless in buying The Beeches when we couldn't afford it and that I must try harder to get a job. There was no way she would agree to my giving my sons the money.

I was stuck. Carol's and my dwindling assets were in a joint account and I could not proceed in trying to raise the funds without her consent. There was no other option. The next day, I had to tell my sons that I was not able to provide them with the money they had requested. Naturally they were very upset. They had imagined their father would have reserve assets and that I was failing to support them. They were fully justified. I had let my sons down very badly.

What the hell had I done? I had totally overstretched our finances to buy a house we couldn't afford. Why? Was it some sort of protest or compensation because I had been so unsuccessful at gaining good employment after prematurely leaving the military? This had primarily been because I was piqued that I hadn't got the Attaché job in Germany. I could have stayed on in the army for a further three years but was too arrogant to accept a lesser job! And now, just when, for the first time ever, my sons had asked me to fund their very practical plan, I had let them down by having to decline their request. And this at a time when, after so many years, we had at last resumed a good father/son relationship. I still didn't understand the meaning of life but I did know that it shouldn't have been like this – mainly caused by my own stupidity!

xxx

Chapter Thirty-Six

UK: Work Again at Last!

I had another idea to fill my time between job interviews that might make some money. I had always enjoyed writing though until now it had primarily been producing military, political and analytical papers. But why not have a crack at writing a fictional novel? I sat down behind my computer. I drafted out a framework, wrote the introduction and the conclusion then spent a month, often writing from well before dawn until late at night, hacking away on what I hoped might be my "master piece"! I got to the end, did a thorough check of the draft and started approaching publishers. My book was called *Eight Days*. Of this more later.

Another initiative was to join a professional body called SCIP (The Society of Competitive Intelligence Professionals). This was a US organisation which had a UK affiliate society. Members primarily had a professional interest in researching how intelligence methodology could enhance business competitiveness. SCIP held monthly meetings and one day invited me to give an evening presentation in London. I was asked to give a resume of military sources and agencies and how these might best be harnessed for business success. I gave the lecture which developed into a lively Q and A session with SCIP members. After the lecture, we had an informal discussion session. At this, I met a New Zealand gentleman called Gary Bones. Gary told me he worked for a Reading based organisation with the holding tittle of DESC Ltd. The company was an ICL Plc spin-off company operating in conjunction with Fujitzu, the Japanese computer company. It was involved in many sensitive UK defence projects as well as purely commercial enterprises. He told me his company had a problem. They had been offered by Delfin Systems, a US company, to have the European franchise to promote and sell a new intelligence processing system. Although an attractive deal in principle, DESC was undecided principally as they did not have sufficient expertise in this area. Gary asked if I would be willing to come to their Reading office the next day to be introduced to the system and to give my opinion about whether it would be an attractive tool for businesses. I would be paid a day's consultancy fee. I readily accepted, anything for a few extra quid in the bank!

The next day, I drove to Reading and found the DESC Ltd offices. After an initial introduction to the company, I was given the briefing on the system which was called "Infopower". As the briefing proceeded, I realised that what he was explaining about this real manufactured product was almost identical to a system I had invented as part of the fictional book I had just completed. I was inwardly excited but tried not to let it show. After the briefing, the managing director asked if I thought there would be practical uses for the system here in Europe. I replied that I thought there certainly would be and proposed that I write him a formal Application Note and send it for his consideration. He agreed but said the company needed to decide quickly whether or not to proceed. I assured him I would get onto it directly.

I drove home and told Carol I would be busy for the rest of the evening. I got out my book, *Eight Days* and found the relevant chapter. This was where I had described, as a figment of my imagination, a new Intelligence integration system to counter international organised crime being inaugurated by a specialist team in Germany. I compared this imaginary system with the prospectus of the real "Infopower" system I had just been briefed on at DESC. They were almost identical! I gave a deep sigh as I felt at last I might have chanced on something that might lead to a worthwhile job! I spent the rest of the evening writing the formal Application Note, outlining how best the DESC proposed system could be exploited and what might be its most likely markets. I took most of this from the fictitious events from my book. This was at a time when email was in its infancy but fortunately, I had learned how to use it. Before I went to bed, I sent emails to the DESC managing director, to his line managers and to Gary Bones attaching copies of my proposals.

Shortly after I woke up the next morning, our phone rang. It was the DESC MD. He had received and read my Application Note. Could I come back to

Reading that day to discuss the Note in more detail? I told him I was on my way. At DESC, the MD, Gary Bones and the line managers and I discussed the "Infopower" system and I expanded on areas I had written in the email. This ended with the MD making two decisions. DESC Ltd would acquire the European rights of "Infopower" and I would be offered a full-time job to assist Gary to sell it Europe wide. I would be sent an employment contract straightaway. I found that the salary was more than satisfactory!

As I drove home that evening, I hoped that the decisions taken that day marked the end of a long hard struggle. At last, after three barren years, I would be in full time employment again. I hoped I would now be able to afford to keep up my mortgage payments for The Beeches, and begin to restore our flagging finances. I thanked my book. It hadn't yet even been published but it had got me a well-paid job!

Note: An updated and revised version of this book was later published under the title *The Warehouse*!

Gary and I then developed the detail of how best to exploit the system. He was equally enthusiastic and together we built up a presentation for us jointly to give to prospective clients. We then compiled a list of these prospects which included police and other law enforcement agencies and a range of corporate businesses. Our initial list spanned most of Western Europe. I didn't tell him about my book! Gary and I then hit the road. At last both my spirits and motivation were revived. Our role was to promote our "Infopower" package, tailoring its benefits to each individual potential customer. During this concentrated period travelling to most European countries, Gary and I got on very well both professionally and personally. I owe him a great deal for helping me bounce back after the previous lean years.

Those years of having no regular job were, in some perverse way, a "blessing in disguise". I had learnt that life can have downsides as well as upsides. I learnt never to be too over confident or cocky. Prolonged unemployment had taught me never to give up, never to stop trying and to be inventive. To take life as it is and not what you think it should be. If indeed there is a God, an all-knowing creator, I think that he/she would agree!

xxx

Our confidence was shared by many of our prospects and often we felt we had given a strong pitch which the DESC commercial department were tasked to follow up. By the end of the year 1996, Gary and I broke for Christmas, with plans to renew our joint presentations in the New Year. It was not to be. I had my first introduction to how ruthless some commercial companies could be. On 2 January 1997, I arrived back at the office at DESC Ltd, Reading that I shared with Gary. I found him clearing his desk. He told me he had just been summoned by the MD, told that our franchise agreement with Delfin Systems had been terminated and that DESC now had no further need for Gary's services. He was dismissed. My first reaction was of anger that the company should treat such a high grade guy in this manner. I also had to presume I would equally be out of a job. After sympathising with Gary, I went directly to the MD's office and asked what was going on. The MD told me that not sufficient sales had resulted from our presentations, that DESC's technical department had identified several defects in the Infopower system, that he had ended all contact with Delfin systems and had no further place for Gary. That was the way it was! Before I could ask the next obvious question, the MD told me the company wished me to stay on, change departments, and be the lead spokesman for the many clients visiting our DESC office in Reading. I left the MD's office with mixed views. I was really sorry about Gary but I still had a job myself – at least for now!

The next few months working at DESC Ltd went well. The company hosted a wide range of visitors to our Reading office – politicians, scientists, senior civil servants and military officers. My new job was to familiarize myself with the background of each visitor, concentrating on his or her specific area of interest and to produce a tailored briefing. I always kept my part general and then brought in technical experts as required. I enjoyed these sessions and during the year got to meet some high-grade interesting people.

There was a downside to the job. The DESC office was located in Reading, Berkshire and now all my work time was based there. Most of our visitors' presentations were scheduled for nine thirty each morning. For these to run smoothly, I needed to be at the office at least one hour before the visitors arrived. To be on time, I had to leave my house on the Kent coast not later than six thirty each day as traffic on M20/M25 motorways at rush hour never got less: the alternative was to stay at my own expense in the Reading area during most week nights. Not a cheap option. I tried to experiment between these two options. Neither was satisfactory. I even considered selling our Kent house and moving closer to Reading. But at last, we had a settled home and I was also reminded of the way the company had treated Gary Bones. I had no confidence the same might not happen to me.

At the end of 1997, the DESC MD made a sudden announcement. The company was to leave our Reading office and move to Basingstoke, Hampshire, a town situated even further away from our home in Kent. That was my signal to leave. The company had given me my first decent employment in corporate business for which I was very grateful. I told the MD of my decision. By I was fifty-nine years old, still relatively fit, energetic and hopeful that I could get further employment to last until my final retirement.

Again, I was back in the ranks of the unemployed and trawling through the papers looking at the job adverts. At least, I now had recent work experience, the MD of DESC had given me a good reference and I had a pool of good contacts who I felt I could call upon for support if I needed further references. The problem now seemed to be my age. Most of the job vacancies being advertised were for people in their thirties and early forties. This was a younger man's world. At fifty-nine, it seemed I had been written out of contention for many of the jobs I applied for. I wasn't specifically told as much but I found that was the implication. As the weeks of being unemployed again turned to months, I wondered if I would ever again find a worthwhile job.

xxx

I was in luck but, as had so often been the case throughout my life, not in a straight forward way. A couple of months after leaving DESC, I had a phone call from a gentleman called Robert Green who worked for a "head hunter" company called Russell Reynolds. He said he had attended one of my presentations and would like my advice. An American company, Brink's Ltd, was seeking to appoint a Director of Security for their business in Europe, the Middle East and Africa (EMEA). The profile they were looking for was someone in their late thirties/early forties with some international security experience. Robert asked if I know of anyone fitting this criteria who I could recommend? By chance, I did. During a DESC presentation in the Netherlands, I had met and been impressed with a young Dutch security executive. I had retained contact with him and knew that he was at present working for a German bank. He had earlier told me he was not settled in this job so I called him and told him about Robert's request. The Dutchman was enthusiastic so I phoned Robert back, gave him the man's details and that he wanted to be considered for the job. I felt I had done a good deed for a fellow security executive and hoped he would be successful.

A week later, Robert Green called me again. He said his company had interviewed the Dutchman but did not consider him to be suitable for the Brink's appointment. They had also eliminated several other potential candidates. They now wondered if I would be interested in this job myself! I hadn't even considered it earlier as I had been told the age requirement was late thirties/early forties. I queried this age differential and Robert replied that a suitable candidate of that age range had not been found so now the employer had specified that experience was the main criteria. Suddenly I became very interested. I was first interviewed in London by Robert and members of the Russel Reynolds team, then had two phone interviews by Brink's executives in the US, and finally by the MD of the EMEA group in Brussels, an American gentleman called Buck Crebs. The last of these interviews was in mid-September and I was told that I could expect a decision shortly.

Brink's is the global leader in total cash management, including cash in transit, ATM services and the international transportation of valuables. Everyday, Brink's transports millions of bank notes of all currencies and denominations. It therefore attracts high level attempts at theft and hence the vital need for strong and effective security procedures to counter this threat. Brink's EMEA had companies throughout Europe, and included Israel and South Africa. I read there were plans for new outlets in Poland, Czech Republic and Hungary. Each company was run independently but under the direction of the regional headquarters in Brussels. That was just the EMEA region. Globally, Brink's owned companies in fifty-three countries in six continents, fifty-thousand employees and seven thousand two hundred armoured trucks.

After a somewhat tortuous delay, I was eventually offered the job and started my employment with Brink's in November 1998.

Was this another of the Laws of Karma? The Law of Creation: "To make things happen in your life, you need to take action, instead of waiting for something to magically come your way!"

xxx

Chapter Thirty-Seven

Brink's

Europe, Middle East, Africa (EMEA)

I had my first business meeting with Buck Crebs, Managing Director of Brinks EMEA at our headquarters in Brussels. His initial briefing was short and to the point. He told me my appointment had been newly established as robbery attacks against our group's activities were high and recoveries and arrests were low. The main threats to the company were branch invasions and attacks on our trucks, during replenishment of ATM machines and through internal theft. This must be countered and corrected if the company was to remain viable. I had been selected to sort it out. I asked Buck one question. "What is my expense budget?" His reply "Expenses unlimited, Now get to it!" End of meeting! In other words, he gave me a free hand to do what I thought was best, no expense spared.

What a complete turnaround from all those barren years after leaving the army! The job was well paid and I had been given total freedom to sort out Brinks EMEA security problems. I had never before known such professional independence. But I'd better produce results!

My first priority was to understand the background to our losses to thefts throughout the EMEA group and to work out a long-term security strategy. I needed to establish how, where, how much had been stolen and how much recovered. The initial figure I learnt was losses of over thirty million US dollars during the year 1998. All European countries had been affected by the robberies which had included eight employees killed and other serious injuries sustained.

The national regulations regarding the use of weapons for our armoured vehicle crews varied in each country. In France, Belgium, Germany and Israel, our employees were permitted to carry weapons. In other countries, e.g. UK and The Netherlands, carrying weapons was strictly prohibited. We had to work within these disparate national rules. There were also wide differences in crew training. Many of the German crew employees had previously served in the army or police and knew how to handle their weapons, whereas some of the crews in, for example, France and Belgium had had minimum training in weapons handling, and live firing practice. We needed to improve training standards not merely regarding weapons but in general awareness and response to the threat of criminal attacks.

One particularly alarming aspect was the threat posed by what was termed "Tiger kidnaps". In such cases, armed robbers would break into the house of the key holder, usually the manager, from a branch and take his wife and/or children hostage. The manager would be told to go to the branch, open up the doors to the entry and to the vault. If he refused, the robbers would threaten to kill his family. I was determined to ensure that such attacks in future would be futile by installing all branches with remotely controlled interlock systems which could never be opened by one individual alone.

The easy part of my new job was to identify our main weaknesses and to set out our programme to rectify them. The difficult part was implementation. Nothing happens immediately. Making structural reinforcement to our branches (there were one hundred and eighty in Brink's EMEA region), implementing an electronic "overwatch" system of opening/closing our branches, improving the armouring of our trucks (there were more than three thousand), ensuring the "smoke boxes" carried by our ATM teams on the pavement were "robber proof", up grading crew training. All these aspects took time and money.

Initially our Brinks Europe headquarters was based in Brussels and Carol and I had intended that we would move there, a city we knew well from my earlier posting to NATO headquarters. However, the US corporate headquarters decided to move us firstly to London where we were based for two years, then in 2003 to co-reside with Brink's France head office in central Paris.

This final move suited me very well. My time was spent travelling between our country branches, or working from my home in Saltwood or commuting from there to Paris via the highly convenient Eurostar between Ashford and Paris Gare de Nord. To summarise this part of my life, for the next six and a half years with Brink's EMEA was one of the most enjoyable and rewarding times of my working life.

xxx

My relationship with our two sons was by now much improved. This meant a great deal to me. Anthony had married in 1999 and had brought Enny, his Indonesian wife back to live in UK. He was struggling to find good work but both he and Enny are clever innovative people and I hoped their circumstances would improve (as indeed it eventually did brilliantly!). In August 2000, Enny returned to Jakarta to be with her mother when she gave birth to her daughter. I flew over to be there just after the birth and, jointly with Enny's mother, gave our granddaughter her first bath! We marvelled at the new birth. Our younger son William remained in Jakarta. I twice went to stay with him and together we had great trips, to Bali, and a trekking down the west coast of Java. Our sons and I were now back in good and regular contact. It had taken many years of anguish but at last we were closely bonded back as father and sons! This renewed father-sons relationship, even more pronounced after so many barren years, was a major plus point to my "meaning of life."

Until now, Carol and I had been fortunate to have enjoyed good health but we both had problems during this period of our lives. Firstly, I had heart arrhythmia which was treated by a procedure called "cardioversion" where the heart is temporary stopped then jump started again. A simple one-day event. The same year poor Carol who, after what she hoped was a routine mammary test, was informed she had breast cancer. She had to undergo surgery and this led to her contracting a form of pneumonia. She became very sick and for a while her condition was grave and our doctors became seriously worried about her condition. Fortunately she recovered well and her cancer was cleared. These scares reminded us of the frailty of life and how important it is to appreciate the time we have on this planet!

Some years earlier my grandmother had died at the fine age of 102. Her daughter, Eileen, often said she intended to surpass the age of her mother. I had Power of Attorney over my aunt's affairs and for many years did all I could to visit and support her whenever possible. We always enjoyed our time together when I took her for a drive and had lunch at a local restaurant near to her base in Surrey. This was a challenge as I was so often out of UK. Eileen went through various stages of her life from total independence through to living for many years in serviced accommodation where she still retained her personal freedom but always had on medical and welfare support on call. Then, as she became more frail, she lived in a senior citizens' home with full time care. This is where eventually she died. She achieved her aim. She died aged 103, one year older than her mother. We arranged a church service for her funeral day particularly as she was a devout Christian. She and I regularly discussed her religion and her views on the afterlife. It was my honour to give the eulogy of her extraordinary life. More on her faith later.

XXX

There were weeks when, due to the priorities of the Brink's work, I would be away from home all the working week. During this period, I would socialise most evenings with the managers of the various EMEA countries where our company had business. They often introduced me to their contacts in government, police and the military. Frequently the subject of the threat of death to our crews was discussed and I listened to their views of the meaning of life and whether there is an afterlife. This background gave me further good qualifications for writing this book!

My weekly programme reflected the priorities of the job often dictated by robberies and other attacks on Brink's assets. On Monday mornings, I would drive to Gatwick airport, park up, fly to one country, visit the staff and carry out training with the crews and/or conduct security audits, investigation updates etc. Depending on the work requirements, I would either stay overnight or fly to the next country visit. Although Brink's business was essentially the same in all the EMEA countries, the emphasis, culture and way of operating varied greatly. Each had their unique security issues.

My Brink's job required me to visit and often stay for extended periods in all the countries where the company had offices and branches – France, Belgium, Netherlands, UK, Germany, Switzerland, Israel, South Africa, Hong Kong and the US and also detailed planning to open new facilities in Poland, Hungary and the Czech Republic.

I regularly visiting Brink's company in Israel. The country manager was a very cultured gentleman named Michael Kaharnov. His office was located in Tel-Aviv but he also ran branches in Jerusalem, Haifa and Be'er Sheva, all of which I visited and stayed for several days. His truck crews were all armed with USI sub machine guns which they handled with the professionalism acquired through their former military service. I found the Isreali security was very professional and disciplined and they sustained fewer robberies than the other Brink's EMEA countries.

Micheal Karharov used me, as I am not Jewish, to act as a go between with the Palestinian banking companies and west bank territories in Ramallah and Jericho. This Isreali/Palestinian liaison enhanced Brink's Israel's business and also gave me a fuller understanding of some of the deeply ingrained political and religious issues in this country. Note: I describe this experience in Part One above

xxx

By the end of 2004, our improvements to our procedures, equipment and overall security awareness was at last beginning to pay off. Our losses had radically reduced as had the number of attacks against our assets. Our analysis showed that the overall numbers of attempted robberies against security companies in general had not reduced overall, but robbers now favoured other companies to attack rather than Brink's. We hoped that was a true indication that, due to our improved state of security, we had acquired a reputation within the criminal community that others were considered more attractive targets to rob.

By early 2005, I started to think seriously about when I should retire. I had reached my sixty-fifth birthday the previous year and, apart from the frustrating years in my mid-fifties when I couldn't get permanent employment, I had been continuously working since the age of eighteen – approaching fifty years. Time to think of a life outside work. I decided a good time to leave Brink's would be on my sixty-sixth birthday. I had two objectives. Firstly I wanted leave on a high – hopefully with the security of Brink's EMEA in 2005 in a far better state than when I joined the company in 1999. It was agreed that our next General Manager's meeting scheduled for 20/21 April was to be my last appearance. My second objective was to spend some good time with William, who was still living and working in Jakarta. We were in regular e-mail contact and planned to spend some time together to go travelling in the islands of the Indonesian archipelago. I booked my flight to Jakarta and was excited by the prospect of spending a few weeks with William. Unfortunately, he later contacted me to say that the dates of our planned trip clashed with the final preparations and exams for his "Teaching English as a foreign language" course and that as a result he would have to cancel coming with me. I was sorry he couldn't come but decided I wanted to go anyway. Through William's contacts and those of my daughter-in-law, it was arranged for me to employ the services of an Indonesian national to act as guide and interpreter and to accompany me for the duration of the trip. I had booked into a hotel in Jakarta for the first night of my arrival. My guide would meet me there on Monday 25 April and together we would fly to the island of Lombok for the first phase of our trip. The guide's name was Cindy Franz. I didn't tell Carol about this arrangement.

xxx

My last working day was held in Cannes, based in the Hotel Barrière Le Majestic, the famous hotel facing the Palais des Festivals de Cannes. Carol flew over to join us and it was good to have the chance to spend time in these wonderful surroundings with her after so many years of us having to live separate individual weekday lives. We were able to explore Cannes and its surroundings and for Carol to meet all the country managers with whom I had shared so much of my working life during the past few years. In the morning, I gave my last security presentation to the country managers. In this I included a review of the "before and after years" that I had worked for Brink's. I ended by introducing my successor, Sjouke De Graaf from The Netherlands. I then turned and left. The next morning Carol and I had an early breakfast, took a taxi to the airport, caught our flight back to Lydd and were home in Saltwood by early afternoon. The next day, Friday, I took a taxi to Heathrow airport to catch a plane to Jakarta – the start of my life in retirement.

xxx

Chapter Thirty-Eight

Indonesia

Jakarta, Java

I was sitting in the lounge at Heathrow airport waiting to be called for the Emirates flight to Jakarta. I don't know why I was feeling unsettled and nervous yet excited to be embarking on this new adventure. I had spent endless hours during the past few years waiting at airports and flying around the world. That part was nothing new. Nor was flying to Jakarta, I had been there several times before when visiting our sons. But this time it was somehow different. This was personal. I was in my own free time, Brink's was still paying me for the next month yet I was completely free to decide where I went, what I did, accountable to no one. I wondered why I was inwardly content that Carol was not with me. We had discussed the trip. I remember I had told her I hoped to include scuba diving and snorkelling – she couldn't swim. I said I hoped to do some jungle trekking – she didn't like long walks. I said we would need to get used to the hot humid climate – she didn't like the heat. Perhaps I had overemphasised these aspects as secretly I preferred for her not to be with me on this particular trip. I had hoped to have shared the Indonesian travel experience with both Anthony and William, father and sons. But Anthony was busy with his work in UK. So it would be William, just the two of us. He also enjoyed all the same activities. He was an excellent swimmer, was already fully acclimatised to the heat, was totally fluent in the Indonesian language and was keen for us to explore parts of Indonesia that would be new to both of us. Now he had to drop out of the trip but at least I would be seeing him in Jakarta both before setting off for my adventure and again when routing back on my return.

It was late on Saturday evening when eventually I got to the hotel that William had booked for me. This was after the long flight which had included a three hour stop over at Dubai, then the scrum at the immigration hall at Jakarta's Soekarno-Hatta airport and the taxi's fight through the city's then permanent traffic jams.

The next day, I met my daughter-in-law Enny's father and her sister for lunch, had the chance to update them about Enny's world in the UK and in the evening spent an excellent few hours with William. We both regretted that he couldn't join me for the start of my adventure the following day.

I had only had a brief contact by email with Cindy Franz, who was to be my guide. I had told her that I wanted to travel widely in Indonesia for one month, that I wanted to swim, jungle trek, enjoy Indonesian cooking, culture and religion (s), relax and get fit. I said I needed her to assist in arranging travel and accommodation and to act as interpreter when needed. She had replied that was fine with her. We agreed on the fee I would pay her for the four weeks she would spend with me. I had told her my age so that she wouldn't have too much of a shock when she met this old man! She told me she was forty-one. I told her our first stop was to be in Lombok and that I had already booked the flight and first hotel there. We would decide our further program later. We had arranged to meet in the hotel's lobby at eight a.m on Monday 25 April, ready to travel.

She was there on time. The lobby was crowded with many guests in the process of checking out as I was. When I saw a young Indonesian woman standing nervously on her own with a backpack and small extra carry-on bag, I felt it must be Cindy. She was wearing jeans, flat practical shoes and a floral blouse. Her hair was cut short giving her a rather boyish look. We introduced ourselves and as soon as I had checked out, we left the hotel, found a taxi and together we headed to the airport. This was the start of a time when our two lives came together for four concentrated weeks.

We got to the airport in good time. Cindy's early reserve slowly eased and I discovered she was an intelligent and perceptive woman. She had a lively sense of humour and an easy laugh. By the time we boarded our plane for Lombok, I felt we were already friends.

xxx

Lombok

I couldn't have wished for a more enjoyable tour of a small part of the vast country that is Indonesia; diverse both in geography and in religion, Muslim, Christian and ethnic (more on this later). Our first stop was a three-night stay in the one hotel I had pre-booked near Mataran, the capital city of Lombok. I set Cindy her first task. She was to find and hire a car with a driver, to research a hotel which would give easy access to the Gili islands. I had read these islands were superb for snorkelling. She did a good job, returning on day two to tell me all was fixed. She had bargained for and got a good price which she had achieved by not saying the booking was for a British tourist. By the end of our first hotel stay, I was already appreciating that hiring Cindy was not only a good financial investment but also that she was turning out to be a lively and pleasant companion.

I found the Gili islands were everything I had hoped for and more. The snorkelling was spectacular. I had never before experienced anything so beautiful and natural as the under-sea world. I was mesmerised. After a full day in and out of the sea, I returned back to our hotel tired but fulfilled.

Cindy had hired a driver and his four-by-four vehicle. The next morning the driver, his name was Basuki, and his vehicle arrived. I found the car comfortable and in a good state so I decided to hire him for the rest of our stay in Lombok. I spent the next day exposing my winter white skin to the tropical sun by the hotel pool while I sent Cindy and Basuki off to research our next venue.

Digression – the jungle edge.

That evening Cindy reported back. She said that she had learnt that about an hour's drive north of Mataran was a village from where it was possible to trek through a trail of natural jungle. This led to a steep cliff from which cascaded a dramatic waterfall. She understood that the trail was quite tough going but we could hire a local villager to guide us. Cindy said, "Well you did ask to do some jungle trekking – but it might be a bit too tough. What do you think?" I took this as personal challenge to prove something to myself or whatever.

The drive to the village started on a good metalled road and ended in a rough track. Basuki found the village and linked up with our local guide, a young fit guy whose name was Rimba. He was dressed only in T-shirt and shorts but carried a long cane stick and a shoulder bag. He spoke no English but Cindy acted as our go-between. We could see that our route was through a steep jungle clad mountain range. We had barely cleared the edge of the village before the trail narrowed and we found ourselves pressing our way through thick undergrowth. After about an hour's walk Rimba told us to take care negotiating the next part of the trail. For the next twenty metres our route was reduced to a narrow track along the right edge of the cliffside. On the right was a sheer vertical drop into a valley far below. The track was wet and slippery from recent rains. I hesitated. Although years before I had walked such trails, for example in Borneo, and had not been troubled by vertigo, this was different. There were roots of trees above us that we could use as hand holds along this narrow passage but I wondered what the hell I was trying to prove here. We were completely isolated. Only Basuki back in the village knew where we had gone and I couldn't rely on him to summon help if any one of us should slip off the edge of this highly dangerous track. If we did fall it would almost certainly be fatal and rescue would become irrelevant.

I turned to check Cindy's reaction. She returned my gaze and said nothing. I couldn't read her thoughts. I weighed up the options. If we went ahead and made it safely, we would have proved – what? I had the fleeting thought that if I were to slip and fall to my death it would in some strange way be a fitting end point to my until then full and active life. What a dramatic way to go! Then I thought of Cindy. What if I made it but she fell. I would have been responsible for this lady still in the prime of her life. Then again, I thought how pathetic it would be if I were to turn back here at the first challenge we had faced during this trip where I was seeking adventure. Decision made – we go on! I signalled to Rimba to go ahead. He edged steadily on using the roots as hand holds to support him. He seemed unconcerned by the sheer drop on his immediate right side. When he reached a part where the track widened, he beckoned me forward. Cindy seemed positive and indicated I should follow on behind Rimba. It was my turn now. As I started along this passage, I could feel my feet slipping on the wet muddy surface. I held firmly to the roots above and edged forward. I forced myself not to look down. At last, I reached the end of this dangerous section intact. I was now again on firmer ground and the hillside jutted up on the right to protect against falling. I wondered about Cindy. She was already half way along the passage. I waited till she was close and I could reach for her hand. She was there, we had all made it.

It took another hour's walking before we reached the waterfall. The route had been tough but there were no other precipitous parts like the one we had negotiated earlier. It had been hot and sticky and I found I was sweating profusely. We heard the rumble of rushing water well before we saw it. We turned a corner and came face to face with the cascading water falling from a cliff so high above us it was hard to make out where was the top through the sheen of mist as the water tumbled off the cliff top. Immediately ahead was a large pool of clear, fresh, cool water. We had reached the end point of our trek.

Rimba didn't hesitate. He immediately stripped off his T-shirt and plunged into the water. I followed him. After our long hot sweaty trek, I cannot remember ever feeling so refreshed. The water was cool and the perfect antidote to the jungle's heat. I wondered about Cindy and how she would react but I need not had been concerned as her head bobbed up out of water beside me.

After our swim, Rimba opened his backpack and produced bananas and passion fruit which he generously shared with us. We then set off to retrace our tracks back to the village. Crossing the narrow passage was again daunting but we took our time and used the same root holds that had helped to see us safely across before. Dusk was beginning to form as we found

Basuki waiting for us with the vehicle. When we eventually got back to our hotel we took a quick shower, had supper and went straight to bed. No bad dreams that night!

End of digression

The next day Cindy said she had learned of an excellent resort down in the south of the island She had arranged for Basuki to drive us and said that adequate nearby accommodation was available for him. I agreed we would spend two days there with a reserve that we might stay longer if I chose. By now I had got to know Basuki well and to like and trust him. I asked him, via Cindy's translation, if he was comfortable with staying with us as our driver for some days. He said he was but that, as a Muslim, he had the need to pray at stipulated times of the day. I respected his devotion and agreed he could stop when his faith required. I learnt he was married and had a young daughter. I suggested he could bring them with us so that they could use the trip to have a short family holiday together. By seeing Basuki's positive reaction, I felt we were all gelling into a little team.

Cindy had told Basuki to meet us at the hotel the next morning and we found him waiting for us in the hotel car park ready to go. As agreed, his wife and little daughter were installed and Basuki formally introduced us. The drive was on a decent jungle lined metalled road meandering through to the southern tip of the island. It took about four hours to arrive at Kuta. Here we found a small but clean guest house for Basuki and his family. Basuki dropped us at our hotel. I told him we would call him when we needed him to drive us again.

The hotel was situated in the centre of a small u-shaped curved bay with a beach of fine sand. It was shielded by small hills. It comprised a central building housing the administration, an open bar and an atmospheric restaurant. Around these buildings were clustered several small but well-proportioned separate chalets for the guests. All were located a few metres from the edge of the bay. Inside, the chalets were well equipped with a part open roofed bathroom, had a main bed and a second smaller one. Cindy and I could lodge together but each with our own privacy.

That evening Cindy and I climbed to the top of one of the hills that framed the bay, judging our arrival just in time to watch the sunset as it slowly disappeared below the sea line – a majestic glowing wonder of nature! Later we enjoyed a fresh fish supper in the hotel restaurant.

The next day we called up Basuki and decided to have an adventure tour to a part of the island of Lombok which appeared to be largely uninhabited, at least very few roads and villages were shown on our map. At one point we seemed to have lost our way when we came across a small village. We saw a gentleman, stopped and Cindy asked for directions back towards Kuta. To our surprise this gentleman spoke some English. He told us his name was Father Ahmed. He said he was teaching local children from this village and invited us to meet some of his pupils. He escorted us to a building used as the children's classroom. Father Ahmed provided chairs for us and asked us to wait. When he reappeared, he was escorted by some thirty children whose ages, I guessed, ranged from three or four up to mid teenagers. They all greeted us with smiles and laughter. Father Ahmed had them line up and proposed that they sing and play for us. The children then performed a series of short songs, some playing instruments I had never seen before, some drumming and all the while heartedly singing songs which I supposed came from the traditions of the local area. All the children seemed happy and enthusiastic. They were very poorly dressed but I was moved by their positive and delightful attitude.

After the children had performed for about half an hour, Father Ahmed called for them to stop and to say goodbye to us. The children came forward to us, smiled and shook our hands before they left. After the children had gone, Father Ahmed explained that there were no state schools in the area. The children usually grew up without any formal education and worked on the land with their parents from an early age as had been the custom for generations. Father Ahmed had managed to gather these children together when they were freed by their parents and was teaching them as well as he could but was restricted by lack of funds to buy books. The children's learning was progressing well within the obvious financial limitations. We could see for ourselves how keen and motivated these little children were.

Inwardly, I felt somehow that I was meant to have come here today to this little village in the "middle of nowhere" in south Lombok. I had no idea how I was going to spend my retirement. I knew how lucky I had been to have been born and brought up in a country which provided me with a decent education and the opportunity to work, to make money, to live well. Here, today, seeing these children who had nothing but a good spirit to help them in life – perhaps I could do something positive to help them. Perhaps I could buy them decent books and provide the chance for them to get future education and opportunities. Perhaps I could do more than that. These were just initial thoughts and I said nothing about this to Father Ahmed, only to thank him for introducing us to the children and to praise him for all that he was doing for them. I made a note of his personal details and those of this village. All the way back to our Kuta hotel I was trying to think how best I might be able to assist Father Ahmed in the wonderful work he was doing for these children.

There was another thing; the co-existence of the different religions. In the "western" world, the predominant religion is Christian, while in the Middle East Islam dominates. In Lombok, in my first few days here, I witnessed easy tolerance between these two religions. Basuki was a Muslim, who devoutly prayed at fixed times every day. Father Ahmed was an equally devout Christian. Each faith here seemed easily to tolerate each other. How refreshing! Yet the essence of each religion, Christian and Muslim, taught that each was the one and only faith – Christians to follow "the Lord Jesus, the son of God and his commandments", Muslims to follow "the noble Qur'an, which acts as a proof for the prophethood of Muhammad, "peace be upon him!" Surely both cannot be exclusively correct!

xxx

Whenever it had been possible to get an internet connection, I had been exchanging messages with Carol, sending highlights of my activities here and checking on how things were back in Saltwood. When we got back to our hotel in Kuta, I went to the administrative building and checked my email box. There was a message from Carol. It was about one subject only.

Carol wrote that she had just found out from Enny, our daughter in law, that I was travelling with a woman companion. Her mail was full of invective. She accused me of being disloyal to her and to having an affair behind her back. She insisted I should return home immediately. I read through all that Carol had written. There was a lot, all on the same subject. I closed my laptop without acknowledging Carol's mail. I had to think. I didn't know how to react. I went to the bar at the hotel, bought a beer, took it over to the beach and sat down on one of the beach chairs. I tried to make sense of where I was in my life.

I tried to see things from Carol's point of view. During our twenty-eight years together I had been involved with another woman twice – once in Rome and once in Brussels. The first had been a serious affair. The second was one stupid act eighteen years ago, when I drove a Belgium lady home and must have given her the impression I wanted more. Each time Carol and I had been reconciled and our lives had moved on together. Now she was accusing me of having an affair when there was absolutely nothing sexual in the relationship I had with Cindy. I had to admit that, when William had dropped out, I should have told Carol. For some reason that I couldn't clearly rationalize I had chosen not to. I wondered why not. I suppose that I wanted to have this month away from my home and away from Carol. My failure to tell her that I had hired a female guide in the first place had been unwise. Not openly referring to Cindy in my recent emails had made Carol suspect me of being unfaithful to her. Understandable I supposed – although it had no basis in fact.

Carol's email was not just an expression of concern. It was an outright accusation and an insistence I should return home. Yet here I was in south Lombok having been away for only one week of my planned month-long tour. My relationship with Cindy had been correct and respectful. Why should I give up this one time in my life that I was feeling truly independent and free, just because of Carol's false accusation? I decided to delay replying to Carol until the next day. I did not tell Cindy about the email.

I struggled with this dilemma during the night. I had not been a faithful husband to either of my wives and for the umpteenth time I went through the reasons why. Each time I knew there had been strong solid reasons behind what I had done in my life. I would come through the thought process feeling I could excuse myself that I really had done my best to please and satisfy both of these ladies and that I shouldn't keep beating myself up. Then again, I felt that I was just making excuses, that I should have cared more about both Gizèle and Carol and that I should have been more responsible. I kept repeating this thought cycle of excuses and guilt and never coming cleanly out the other end.

Eventually I got some sleep and woke up to another beautiful sunny morning in south Lombok. Cindy wasn't there but then she soon returned to tell me she had found out that there was a village quite close by where a boat could be hired that took passengers out to sea on snorkelling trips. Would I like to go? Sounded just what I needed to clear my head about all my guilt feelings. I readily agreed. There was another thing. We could either call Basuki to come or we could hire a local motorbike and take that to the village. I hadn't driven on two wheels since I was in Cyprus all those years ago but it sounded fun. Let's do it!

Digression – to perish at sea – again!

It took me some time to get used to riding a motorbike again and I made a few practice runs around the hotel grounds to get used to the balance. I had asked at the hotel reception if they knew about this village boat trip business but drew a blank there. The receptionist who was a local resident not only didn't know about the boat hire business but didn't even know of such a village in that area. Our only source was the young local man that Cindy had spoken to. He said he would lead us to the village. Sounded intriguing so off we went, with our new young guide on the lead motorbike and us following on, me at the controls and Cindy riding pillion. The young man set off at speed and I found it difficult to keep up at first while I familiarized myself to the joys of riding on two wheels. It brought back memories of both my teenage years. I wondered if by agreeing to this escapade I was somehow just trying to recapture my youth. I also wondered what this silly sixty-six-year-old man thought he was doing!

That was just the start. Our young guide found his way to the mysterious village, drove on down to the seafront and pulled up at a small jetty. He pointed to this then turned his bike round, gave us a wave and drove off. At the jetty was a long but very narrow boat. At one end was a Mitsubishi engine and there were wide wooden outriggers on each side. We were examining the boat when two young men appeared and, with Cindy's interpretation, offered to provide masks and flippers and to take us out to sea. Lifejackets were not provided. They explained that the sea here always had a stiff cross current and the best way to enjoy the experience was this. The swimmer would be dropped off at one point, go with the current while the boat roared on ahead then turned facing the swimmer who would then grab hold of the outrigger as he was swept past. The young man gave this description as if was the simplest procedure. I could tell Cindy was now regretting this whole idea as she made it clear there was no way she would participate. She suggested we just thank the young men and drive back to the hotel. She was right but this was supposed to be an adventure month, I was a strong swimmer, so let's do it!

Our boat consisted of the two young guys, me and a well-worn set of mask and flippers. We chugged out to sea and it soon became apparent how strong the current was. When the boat was steered into the current's flow we were roaring along, but when we turned to face the current, the engine struggled to make progress. After we had been at sea for about twenty minutes, the young man doing the steering, indicated that this was good place to jump overboard and start the snorkelling experience. I knew that if I hesitated, I might chicken out. Before I had time to think it through, I put on mask and flippers and jumped over the side. As soon as I turned face down, I was thrilled to have gone along with this crazy venture. Beneath the surface, I was seduced by the scene below, everything I had experienced before at the Gilli islands but multiplied several times. There was a whole maritime world down there which I found intoxicating. I was passing by at seemingly breakneck speed – not only fish of all descriptions but turtles, rays and other sea creatures I had never seen before. It was mind blowing. I stayed mesmerised by this scene for some long time before I had to tell myself I must tear myself away to orientate back to the world above the sea depths. I forced myself to turn and look up. I could tell I was still being carried along at speed with the current. To my left, I could just make out the coast. It seemed a long way away. I turned to my right looking for the boat. There was no sign of it. I realised that my life was entirely in the hands of the two young men who were driving the boat. I had never met them before. I didn't know their names; I couldn't speak their language. But in some strange way, I didn't care. A whole kaleidoscope of thoughts and images flashed through my mind. I had lived a wonderful life and had been blessed with good fortune. I had come through operational situations while in the military without a scratch, I had travelled the world and had a wealth of different experiences. What if the boat never came to pick me up? I could remain in this sea paradise and perish right here, right now. If that is the way it has to be, then so be it. Let it happen. I was still in this state of philosophical acceptance when I looked up and there was the boat. It seemed to be stationary but the current was driving me towards it. I came closer and as I was being pushed past it, I stretched out and just managed to clutch hold of the wooden outrigger. Then hand over hand, I made it to the side of the boat. One of the two young guys, took my arm and helped me into the boat. Together we made our way back to the shore and to the jetty where Cindy was waiting. As we climbed ashore, she called out: "How was it?" I replied. "Fine, very exciting!" I didn't tell her the thoughts I had just had.

End of digression

I drove the motorbike back to the hotel more slowly than we had come. We had no hurry. It was a good feeling. I was still wet after the swimming but quickly dried out as we drove along this little jungle lined road. The temperature was as always in the middle of the day around thirty degrees and the air rushing by was cool and bracing. I felt good. So far, this trip had more than met my hopes. I had already had great physical exercise and could feel I was losing some of the weight I had put on through all those Brink's business lunches and suppers. I had already faced some stiff physical challenges. And I was enjoying the company of this charming young Indonesian lady who was clinging on to my waist. As we neared the hotel, I realised I must reply to Carol's email. I still didn't know how to respond.

At the hotel administration building, I sat in front of the computer and typed in the code protocols to access Carol's email box. I had decided to be conciliatory and apologetic. I still didn't know whether I should abort my plans for the rest of the month. I pressed enter, ready to type out my mail. But there was another message from Carol. This was a repeat of the one the previous day and was full of accusations and criticism not just about me not telling her about hiring Cindy but a further list of other misdemeanours I was supposed to have committed. I read carefully through Carol's mail, twice. Then I closed down the computer. I had to think. In many ways Carol was correct. I had been self-centred and probably should have talked to her more about this trip to Indonesia and included her wishes by arranging a program where we could spend at least part of our time together here. But I had just gone ahead doing what suited me without considering Carol. I opened up the computer again, logged on to Carol's email and wrote that I could understand that she was upset, but that there was nothing sexual in my relationship with Cindy, that I was not coming back until the end of my planned month, then we could talk about all her concerns. Short and to the point.

XXX

We stayed two more days in this hotel then started to plan our next move. I ruled out Bali as I'd already explored that beautiful Hindu island with William. I had heard about Sulawesi and asked Cindy to do some research. I was having supper alone in the hotel restaurant when she rushed in and excitedly told me she needed my confirmation for the provisional bookings she had made for the next stage of our tour. This was her proposal. Basuki would drive us back to Mataran the next morning where we would take the afternoon flight to Makassar in the south of Sulawesi. We would stay two nights there before driving to Toraja. Another two nights then a long all-day drive to Palau, a port town midway up the west coast of Sulawesi. From Palau we could fly the next day on to Manado at the northern tip of the island, famous among other things for its scuba diving. That itinerary would mean that we could gain a real insight into this fascinating part of the Indonesian archipelago. Cindy described what she had researched about

Toraja and the individual culture of its people. I had been looking at Cindy as she had been speaking and realised that we had now developed an easy relationship between us. Back in Jakarta, we had started out in the reserved and formal manner of a strict employer/employee relationship but here we now were as two people enjoying our time together and equally motivated to gain the maximum experience from these few weeks. I found I was infected by Cindy's fresh enthusiasm. My thoughts went back to my earlier emails with Carol and all the bitter words she had written. I decided that I would do my best to straighten things out with her but that would have to wait. Perhaps I was wrong but too bad, I was as excited as Cindy about the next phase of our tour.

The next day, we found Basuki and his family ready and waiting in the car. He told us, via Cindy, that they had very much enjoyed their time in Kuta and confessed it had been the first time he and his family had ever stayed away from their home in Mataran. Basuki then solemnly gave me back the balance of the money left over from the float I had given him to cover the costs of their stay. He had kept a detailed record of every rupiah they had spent. I was amazed how little they had used and Basuki's honesty. It was humbling.

Basuki took us back to Mataran airport and we had an emotional parting with him and his sweet wife and daughter. It's amazing how perfect strangers can become so close in such a short time. Basuki had no great education: he was trying to sustain his family on the uncertain wages of taxi driving. By pure chance Cindy had chosen him to be our driver. I had come to like and respect him. Years later when I picture his face, I have a warm feeling of affection for that gentleman.

xxx

Makassar, Sulawesi

We landed at Makassar airport in the late evening, took a taxi through to the city centre and checked into the hotel Cindy had booked for us. By then it was too late for sightseeing and in any case we were too tired. Next day, Cindy went off to do more route planning while I explored some of Makassar's history by taking a guided tour. I know I didn't do justice to gaining a full appreciation of this city's long and varied Bugis peoples history; from its Portuguese and Dutch colonial past during the spice trade wars era up until its conquest by the Japanese and later its development as an integrated part of Indonesia. I visited the seventeenth century Fort Rotterdam with its comprehensive museum, the majestic Great Mosque and the Museum Kota Makassar. This tour took up the whole day and it was evening when I met up again with Cindy to find out what she had uncovered for the next part of our tour.

Cindy had used the internet and a local agent to plot our next stop. This was to Tana Toraja, known colloquially as "The land of the dead". This sounded totally unlike anything I had experienced or even previously read about before. I'd learnt it's a region situated inland some eight hours drive from Makassar. Although I found the hot bustling city of Makassar interesting enough, I was keen to move on to Toraja. Cindy had hired us a car and driver. The next morning we left early for the long drive to Toraja which we reached in early evening after two meal/comfort stops along the way.

Toraja, Sulawesi – the land of the dead

Toraja is an inland regency of South Sulawesi, home to the Tana Toraja ethnic group. Although it is now absorbed politically by Indonesia, it retains a totally individual culture and set of traditions which have survived the best efforts of both Portuguese and Dutch missionaries during colonial years to convert the Toraja people to the Christian faith. Some of the local people I spoke to claimed their religion was Christian but if so it was the strangest version I had ever known. The unique custom of the Toraja people is to preserve their dead with herbal treatments and keep them in their homes, sometimes for years, until the family can afford a formal funeral.

The family members visit and talk to the dead bodies each day as if they were still alive. The bodies are kept in open coffins and Cindy and I were able to visit some homes to see this custom for ourselves. We found the local people to be completely open and willing to explain their customs to us, though Cindy had some problems with translation as their version of the Indonesian language was as different as were their other traditions. We were also able to visit areas around the village where both complete mummified bodies and hundreds of human skulls were stored. Our Torajan guide took us to caves filled with skulls explaining that individual families retained caves and could identify skulls, placed side by side, that had belonged to generations of the same family.

Our visit did not coincide with a formal funeral ceremony which took place from time to time when the deceased family had raised sufficient money to fund the event. However we were told that it took the following form. First, there would be the slaughter of a number of pigs and water buffalos as a sacrifice so that "the human souls may be freed and begin their journey to the afterlife". The mourners would then feast next to the bodies of the dead before putting them into death caves or in rows along the edges of cliffs. There followed what was described to us as a walking death festival when several other bodies that had been left in caves for long periods were taken down into the centre of the village, identified, uncovered to examine the state of their decomposition and celebrated during what was described as a day of happiness, joy and reunion with their dead relatives.

This was a culture totally alien to anything I had known before. But I found the local Toraja people to be open, friendly, well balanced and following a style of living which had been constant for hundreds of years. I felt their proud lifestyle needed to be respected and shown as much tolerance as any of the mainstream religions in the world. They had firm beliefs as to the meaning of life and the afterlife. They could well be right.

xxx

Manado, Sulawesi

The last stop of our tour was to Manado in the north east tip of Sulawesi island. I was attracted to go there for two reasons; firstly I'd read there was some of the best scuba diving spots in world in the Buneken Marine Park, which was renowned as the centre of the "coral triangle" and also that there were good mountain and jungle trekking routes. Both activities filled my last part of my stay in Indonesia. Concerning scuba, I had been warned that I should not dive below ten metres due to my earlier heart arrhythmia problem and I had resolved to stick to this medical advice. But when I took the first dive in Buneken, I threw caution to the wind particularly as the other divers around me were descending down to much lower depths. The sea world below was absolutely stunning – vast fields of varying species of coral and fish, molluscs and marine life. I had earlier been seduced by the snorkelling in Lombok but here with scuba kit there was the opportunity to dive down deep and explore in detail. For me it was a once in a lifetime experience. I was relieved that I had no heart after-effects.

I interspersed the days between scuba diving and travelling inland either to trek up volcanic mountains, one of the most memorable being Soputan, or to explore the jungle mostly in the area of Tangkoko national park. When it was possible I took a local guide to lesser-known regions and during this time was able to see such rare birds as hornbills together with lizards, snakes, macaques and the endearing little bug-eyed tarsiers.

My contract with Cindy ended after the four weeks she had been with me. I decided to stay on in Manado for a few extra days to complete my full month tour. Cindy had made my outstanding tour possible through her efficient research, organisation and interpreting. It had been a pleasure to have had her with me and we had progressed well beyond a formal employer/employee relationship. We had become good friends. I got up early to see her off when she left our hotel to catch her flight back to Jakarta. We discussed my aim to do some charitable work to aid the children we had met in South Lombok and that we would keep in email contact about that venture. I hoped that Cindy could act as our go-between with Father Ahmed.

xxx

A few days later I also flew back to Jakarta, staying one night so that William and I could catch up. I tantalised him with the stories of all my adventures and what he had missed and we vowed that next time we could try to do a similar tour together. William told me I looked very different from when I had first arrived in Jakarta from UK one month before. He said I had lost a lot of weight and looked in much better shape. He was right. I had not felt so fit and well for many years. My Indonesian tour had done wonders for my health!

As I flew back to UK, I wondered how it would be with Carol. Our emails had become less frequent after her first vitriolic attacks against me and her accusations about my supposed affair with Cindy. There was really no point in continuing to try to correct her as her mind was made up. I hoped we could be reconciled when I got home and was determined to try my best. If not, maybe we should reconsider our lives together.

xxx

Chapter Thirty-Nine

Life in Retirement

UK

My homecoming didn't go well. As I walked back through our front door, my two darling dogs were ecstatic. It was a joy to be reunited with them. But it was very different with Carol. She was polite but stiff. No welcoming embrace and my own gestures of affection were rebuffed. I knew I was in for long uphill struggle if we were ever to be fully reconciled.

Now, aged sixty-six, it felt strange to be back in my own home in Saltwood and to have no fixed work to do – difficult to adjust to being completely retired. My work colleagues had spoken of wanting me to do consultancy work for them on a part time basis but none followed through. I had no work programme, no office to go to, my phone didn't ring constantly as I had become used to for so many years, the inflow of emails ceased. I felt disjointed, unwanted, thrown out with the rubbish, on the scrapheap. I set myself tasks to do, home improvements both in the house and the garden. This kept me physically busy but still mentally frustrated. I thought about the idea of pursuing the idea of setting up a charity for the Lombok children that I had discussed with Cindy and wanted to develop that idea. Not only was I motivated to help these children but thanks to the Brink's salary I had enjoyed over the past few years, I had the finances to be able to contribute to improving their lives. But I knew that if I pursued this, it would only alienate Carol further.

My relationship with Carol reached a sort of plateau. We coexisted politely but there was no warmth on either side. Often, we would get along quite well during most of the day but usually during our evening supper, Carol would again start up her accusations of me having had an affair with Cindy.

She rejected my denials and often we would go to bed in this state of bitterness towards each other. I spent many nights awake in the small hours just wondering how it had gone so wrong. Our early years together had been very close and intimate and I recalled so many good times we had shared together – our best being when we were in Germany, both of us with demanding jobs and fully supporting each other. I had a deep respect for Carol, how she had adjusted to each of the different postings and countries we moved to together. She had never complained when most on our moves entailed her leaving her own job to accommodate my new posting and often, again getting another teaching job in the new location. She was a neat and efficient person and always ensured our home was well run wherever we were. From a practical viewpoint, she had been a very good wife, partner and hostess, better than I deserved. So why had it been that I had had that affair in Rome all those years ago? And why had I been so keen to have the Indonesian adventure without Carol?

European Tour

I tried to think of what I could now do to repair our marriage and vowed to do my best. I contacted several of our former colleagues from the different places around Europe where we had lived during the past several years and found they were keen for us to meet up again. I devised a trip to revisit some of these locations and suggested to Carol that we take what I described as a "trip down memory lane". I was pleased that she agreed. We drove back to Germany, visited Goslar in the Harz mountains where years before we had often spent happy weekends, then to Bielefeld staying for a night near the house we had lived in for three years. In Bonn, we stayed with some of our former NATO Defence College friends and took a trip with them down the Mosel river. In Holland, we stayed with both former colleagues from our days in NATO HQ, Brussels and in AFCENT. On each of these days we routed via the houses where we had lived. Carol seemed to enjoy this reminiscence trip but throughout she continually returned to her accusing bitter tone.

I began to feel that our marriage was broken. There was another thing. When we had both been working, we would spend each day involved with our own professional issues and would only be together in the evening when we could relax, leave work issues behind and enjoy just being in each other's company. It was very different now that we were both retired and were together all the time. I knew that this is common to many couples who previously had busy committed jobs then suddenly found their lives and particularly their relationship with their partner changes – sometimes for the better, sometimes for the worse – regrettably in our case it was for the worse!

Egypt

Our trip down memory lane hadn't been successful. I hoped my next plan might be. I booked a tour of Egypt to include visiting Cairo and its pyramids and then a journey down the Nile as far as the Aswan dam, stopping at all the main historical attractions along that famous river. We went in November when the temperature was perfect for tourism. I knew Carol had always taken a great interest in Egyptology and seemed to enjoy herself. She enjoyed the trip but it didn't change her attitude towards her husband!

By then, I seriously thought it might be best for Carol and I to separate as we seemed, perhaps forever, to have lost the affection we used to have for each other. And what about love? Did we ever truly love each other? I wasn't sure. We were both now in our middle sixties, our finances were sufficient for us to split evenly and we could survive as both of us also had pensions. We still had time to move on and find new challenges. In hindsight it probably would have been the right thing to separate there and then and both gone our separate ways. But we didn't. Instead I thought perhaps our marriage would improve if we totally changed our life style. Both of us had always enjoyed taking holidays in France, we both spoke the language well enough to start out and the will to improve it further. When I suggested this idea to Carol, her response was very positive.

xxx

South West France

Early in 2006, after some weeks searching, we found what we were looking for. It was a property in a small hamlet called Gindou, located in the beautiful countryside of the Department of the Lot in south west France. It had thirteen hectares of partly wooded land and belonged to a gentleman who had been a sheep farmer but was now planning to retire to Brittany. The house was constructed from the attractive local white/yellow stone that characterised the region. It was set in grounds with far reaching views in a quiet and peaceful setting but with the closest shops in Cazals, a small town a few kilometres away. I liked the idea of learning a set of new skills – tractor driving, setting up my own fruit and vegetable plots, using a chainsaw to coppice the oak woods and to provide our own fuel for heating. In summary, to learn to live the French rural lifestyle. Carol seemed to warm to the idea and was enthusiastic about this change of our lives. So we bought this property and put The Beeches in Saltwood up for sale: the beautiful house I had struggled so hard to afford and which we had enjoyed now for thirteen years. But if by moving now we might save our fading marriage, so be it! We completed all the paperwork to become residents in France and by mid-2006, we were ready to start another new chapter.

When we finally left to start our new life in France, I knew this had to be a firm decision. Our house in Saltwood had still not then been sold which meant having to take out a second mortgage, leave the sale to our estate agent and hope for the best. We were committed. I hoped we had made the right decision but there were still some nagging doubts. Such is human nature – at least mine!

For some time, we settled in together really well in our new home. I struggled to master some of the country skills and together Carol and I furnished and oversaw renovations to the house. Carol's musical abilities were welcomed by the local community. She was invited to sing with a popular choir, often as the soloist and to play piano to accompany others. I was pleased to see her so motivated and hoped our new environment would rekindle our feelings for each other. From my side, I loved discovering how to optimise all the capabilities of handling a tractor with all its add-ons –

mower, load carrier, raking soil preparation device etc. I spent many days working in my woods, felling old trees, cutting them into logs, loading them onto a trailer, bringing them back to my log store and piling them ready for the winter's use. I revelled in coming back home to our property in the evening on my tractor comparing this country life with the years of commuting long distances back home to Saltwood from London, Paris or elsewhere in Europe. I felt liberated.

Our pets settled in famously. The two labradors immediately took to their new life with so much to explore. Every morning, they made sure I was awake and up early and we spent the first hour of the day walking the lanes and fields around our house and enjoying the fresh pure air of the region – no factories, very few houses, no pollution.

Carol was much quicker to socialise than me. She was regularly involved either with choral rehearsals or with the concerts which were very well attended and led to her quickly developing social contacts. Meanwhile, I had confined myself to my own world of tending to my land. That hobby was fulfilling and was necessary to maintain the property but I realised I also needed to have some other outlet. About the only time I ventured out was to drive down to Cazals, our nearest small town, to buy a baguette at the local boulangerie. Apart from producing delicious fresh bread, a further attraction was the lady who sold it. She was very popular with the local male population particularly as she had a majestic pair of breasts that she was not shy in exhibiting. They were just contained within an enormous blouse which proudly bore the logo, *"Moi aussi j'ai des yeux!* (I also have eyes!)" One day while in the town square I noticed a sign announcing the next meeting of the local walking club, known as *"La randonnée de Cazals."* It read that the club would meet at the square the next Wednesday at ten thirty. I loved walking and thought that perhaps this could be not only good exercise but also a chance to meet some like-minded local people and to learn more about the area where we had chosen to live. I decided to go there, introduce myself and, if they invited me, to walk with them.

Cazals Rando: *Department du Lot,* SW France

The following Wednesday, I arrived on time. Already there was a group of people dressed in walking kit. I asked the first group I came to if I could walk with them. They promptly directed me to a lady in the middle of the group and told me that she was the President and I should first speak to her. This was my introduction to Olga, a lady who was smart, efficient and very much aware of her responsibilities as the club's President. Olga was immediately welcoming and introduced me to other *Cazals Randonnée* members. Olga asked me if I had brought my car and when I said I had, she immediately allocated three French ladies to join me in my car. The ladies involved had no choice but to do as Olga instructed. She then told me to follow on with other vehicles behind the lead car. In this formation, we drove to the starting point of that week's walk, parked up and off we went. During this and subsequent walks I learnt about my fellow "randonners", and gradually got to know them firstly by identity and gradually they became a group of charming social friends. I found that an average numbers of walkers each week was about twenty-five, though this figure varied every week depending on individual commitments and inclinations. Total membership was about sixty. Ninety plus percent were French, the remainder being ex-pats mostly Brits and Dutch. Olga was the undisputed boss.

Of the French membership, the majority were ladies who mainly had been born and had grown up in the Department du Lot. They had a wealth of local knowledge about the region's history and culture. I found it easy to learn their names as, apart from Olga, nearly all the rest had names ending with "ette". There was Paullette, Annette, Josette, Claudette, Collette, Jeanette, Huegette, etc. All I needed to do was slightly blur the start of the name but end with a confident sounding "ette". That seemed to work!

The club had a weekly walking programme spanning every week of the year. Olga also arranged several excursions to various part of France where we could combine daily walks with cultural visits to local special points of interest. I found I fitted easily into this atmosphere and signed up to be a regular member. I enjoyed the friendly personalities of the fellow walkers, learnt much of the detailed geography of the Department du Lot and found it a pleasant and productive way to keep fit and improve my French. I asked Carol to walk with us but she declined saying she preferred to stick to her musical interests.

Apart from the obvious attractions of learning about the local countryside and keeping fit, another positive was having the chance to socialise. Most of the walks lasted several hours, allowing ample time to circulate, talk and get to know the characters, likes and dislikes of our fellow walkers. The common denominator with us all was our love of nature and enjoyment of the beauty of the countryside. The majority of our group were born and bred in the local area. It was fascinating listening to the stories of those whose families had been involved in the resistance during the last war. *Le Department du Lot* had been used for many air supply drops and the insertion of members of the allied forces to link up with the indigenous resistance fighters who operated in this area. On some walks, our guide would take us to areas where there had been actions involving armed confrontations between the German army and Resistance fighters. Our guide would bring the scenes to life by describing such incidents which had involved their own family, several of whom had been killed there. There were others who had very different backgrounds but had come to retire in this area. One such was Olga, our President. Her background was Spanish Catalonian. Olga told how her father, a doctor, had escaped from the Franco regime with his family by crossing on foot through the Pyrenees and had then settled in France. Perhaps due to her parents' background, Olga was a confirmed communist and regularly took part in local political protest marches. Conversely, many of our fellow walkers were strong Christians. Sometimes, we discussed religion and politics but I was never aware of any major frictions within our group. Our mutual love of the countryside, of nature and our good fortune to be healthy enough to enjoy the rural life was more than enough to sustain us. Both politics and religion were relegated to being of minor significance compared to the beauties of the natural world we were so lucky to enjoy.

xxx

Danièle

Danièle Gourdon joined our walking club in mid-2007. Danièle was French but, unlike the rest of the French members, she also spoke English, having lived for many years in ex British colonial Africa. We got on very well as we had many things in common. We had both lived in Nigeria at about the same time. Although we never met there, we were both about the same age and we both had strong memories of our time in Africa. We had also both experienced divorces in our lives and shared a common feeling of guilt that we hadn't done more to preserve our marriages. I was pleased to introduce Danièle to Carol and met and liked her Dutch partner, Richard who, like Carol, didn't choose to walk with our club. Danièle and Richard had that year bought a house in Cazals, and intended to spend each summer there. They stayed until October when they returned to their main residence in Utrecht. Danièle was still teaching French to business students and her classes in Holland lasted from October through till May. I found her to be good company and, when she and Richard left for Holland in the autumn, I looked forward to seeing them again the following year.

Digression – Split loyalties

The first excursion I went on with our club was to Matemale in the Pyrenees in June 2008. I asked Carol to come as well as I thought this would be an interesting trip for us to an area that was new to us both. Olga had told us that the area not only had good walking trails but there were also several cultural points of interest. Carol agreed to come but said she didn't wish to participate in the walks. Olga gave us the location coordinates and detailed me, in addition to driving with Carol, to take two of our lady members as back seat passengers. Fine by me but Carol was less than enthusiastic.

On the day of our departure, I stopped to pick up the two allocated ladies. They were both on time and were well organised with their luggage neatly packed. We had a pleasant drive and by early evening we reached the accommodation that Olga had arranged. I checked in with Olga, who had arrived some time earlier, offloaded the two ladies then Carol and I went to find our own room. Here we hit a problem. Olga had booked us all into a hostel complex designed to accommodate walkers (and skiers in the winter) who needed a clean, warm, dry environment to sleep and eat between the times spent out walking or skiing. It had basic utilities but no luxuries. Perhaps I should have found out more about this before asking Carol to come but now here we were. Carol looked around our allotted room and immediately objected to its basic facilities. There was only one small towel and one bar of soap. The bed had a paillasse type hard mattress. I explained that we were on a walking trip, not a private tour and that was the way it was. Also that the accommodation was inexpensive and some of our members could not afford more. In any case I was perfectly content with the room as it was. But Carol was adamant, she either had to have a better serviced room or she wanted us to leave and go back home. After her complaints, I asked her to wait while I talked to Olga to see if we could find a solution. Olga confirmed only what I had felt. We were on a walking trip, not an expensive holiday. She said that everyone else here was satisfied with their accommodation. I found myself in the difficult position of having to defend my wife's concerns to Olga while personally feeling unsympathetic to them. I was honour bound as her husband to support her position. There was another thing. Even if I were to tell Olga that we would now have to leave and return home, this wouldn't solve the problem as I had also brought the other two lady passengers and was responsible for their transportation during the trip. They were both content with their accommodation and wanted to stay for the whole duration.

I had no option. I went back to our room and told Carol that everyone else was satisfied with their room and that she would have to put up with it. I feared this would be the cause of our first serious row in France and so it was. The news of Carol's attitude quickly spread throughout the other walkers and my attempts to act as the apologist for her seemed were unsuccessful. During the few days of our time based in this hostel location, I arranged for Carol to be taken out on visits to the various cultural sites being advertised while the rest of us were hiking. Although I think she quite enjoyed these outings (and I certainly enjoyed the mountain hiking) there remained a tension between us and I was pleased when the time came for us all to return to our homes. I decided not to ask Carol to come on other similar trips organised by our walking club. It was better for each of us to have our own hobbies.

End of digression

Our weekly walks continued through the winter of 2007/8 as did Carol's regular concerts. Our social life developed from these two activities. I supported Carol's concerts, was pleased that she was so successful and popular with her fellow choristers and that her musical talents were so well appreciated. Most of the concerts were held in local churches. Although I always tried to be positive during these events which usually were followed with a "*vin d'honneur*" social drinks function, inwardly I felt that I was doing my duty to try to be a supportive husband. I appreciated Carol's ability, but most of the music was of a religious classical style that I found somewhat turgid. However Carol's fellow choristers were pleasant enough and the least I could do was to be there to support my wife. Inwardly though I came to accept that, although I was generally very content with our life in rural France and found it a great environment to retire to, my relationship with Carol was slipping back to the bad state it was in Saltwood. I began seriously to wonder if it would ever improve.

Our next trip with Cazalrando was a five-day visit in September 2008, based on Alquézar in Aragon, Spain. As with the previous away trip, this was interesting, informative and physically quite challenging. We all enjoyed the experience and the pleasure of each other's company, this time without Carol.

This was my second full year as a member of the club and I had integrated well with this charming group. I had been pleased when Danièle and Richard had again returned back from Holland to spend all summer with us in Cazals though Richard still declined to walk himself. On our last evening in Alquézar, Olga had arranged for us to meet in the town square for an evening drink together and the chance to thank our Spanish guide. I remember being late to leave our hotel for the ten minutes' walk to the square due to an update phone call to Carol. As I was hurrying to leave, I met Danièle who was also late. We walked together through the little cobbled streets of the town, and I remember a strong feeling that I was enjoying being with this lady and that I would have liked to have continued walking like this with her further than just to the Alquézar's village square. It was a passing thought which I soon pushed to the back of my mind as together we re-joined our colleagues.

Despite our clash over the earlier hostel accommodation incident, Carol and I continued in our separate ways, to enjoy the many positives in our lives living in south west France – the charming people, the beautiful countryside, good country food, the healthy standard of living. The one negative we experienced was the climate in the winter. The spring was as full of life's renewal as everywhere in northern Europe and by mid-May the summer season began with open air living, fresh but invigorating early mornings, vegetables beginning to ripen, trees and shrubs now in full bloom, lunches spent out of doors and long lazy evenings stretching until late. The summers seemed to go on well into October and it was not until the end of that month before people started to wear a light sweater. But then, around the turn of the month into "*tous saints*" commemorations on the first of November, the temperature could change, suddenly and dramatically. Winter could come seemingly overnight. The holiday season abruptly ended, many of the bustling markets closed, restaurants shut their doors, many streets were either deserted or frequented by people now wrapped up in thick coats. Personally I had no problem with this climate change for the winter. When the trees had shed their leaves was the best time for doing most of the tree felling. After such heavy manual work, I would return home feeling fit despite by now being well into my late sixties. I appreciated that it was not the same for Carol who felt the cold much more acutely than me. Our house had large rooms with high ceilings – excellent for cooling and ventilation in the summer but difficult to keep well heated in the winter. During these months, our house was never as warm as Carol would have liked no matter how high I adjusted the thermostat on the boiler.

Some British friends who lived nearby had decided they wanted to be warmer during these harsh winter months and in 2007 they returned from a trip to Spain and told us they had bought a property there and intended to decamp south each winter. They showed us photos of the property, marvelled at its low cost and said how they had enjoyed the change of scenery, and particularly of the mild winter climate. Their enthusiasm for spending their winters in Spain was attractive and I could tell that Carol was seriously interested.

Chapter Forty

France and Spain

In the spring of 2008. Carol and I drove down to the Costa Blanca region of Spain. I had done no research about where best to look for property in Spain so we decided to follow the route taken by our British Friends. We stayed in a local hotel near Alicante for a week while being shown around a wide selection of properties and eventually settled on a charming well-presented bungalow. It was located in a quiet road, was semi-detached and had friendly Norwegian neighbours. It seemed ideal for our use during the winter. What I had failed to appreciate was that in the winter season in Spain, sunshine and shade are the all-important features. Even on days with relatively low temperatures, it can be delightfully warm in the sunshine but cold in the shaded areas. The low angle of the sun in winter enlarges the shaded areas during the mid-winter months. This is all obvious stuff but I had been so seduced by the look and facilities of the property that I had overlooked such an obviously necessary sun/shade consideration.

We enjoyed our first winter (2008/9), being primarily interested to discover this area of Spain and to begin to understand and appreciate its rich history and culture. Carol seemed very contented to be there. Together we enjoyed this new situation and I hoped that at last we might settle back into a relaxed and easy relationship. Carol approached one of the leading international choirs in the area and not surprisingly was soon invited to be a lead soloist.

Digression: ***Le Tour du Lot***

Back in France the next spring, Olga announced that our Cazalrando club, in addition to our weekly walks and occasional week-long trips, was to embark on a project called *Le Tour du Lot*. She explained that the aim was to walk the total circumference of our department commencing at the most northern part and gradually covering the whole perimeter which we would take in two day stages. Each stage would comprise walking for a distance of about twenty kilometres on the first day, staying locally overnight, then walking another twenty kilometres on the second day before returning back to Cazals. The next stage would commence two or three months later with a further forty kilometres over two days commencing at the point we had finished the previous stage. We would continue with two consecutive days of walking until we had completed the circumference of the Department which totalled five hundred and fifty kilometres. The walks would follow mainly tracks and trails, and be on the road only when essential. The route should follow as closely as possible to the Departmental boundary.

The first two stages of the Tour were held during the next winter (2008/9) while Carol and I were still in Spain. These walks set the early markers and from then on, the Tour took on a momentum as each sector of the Department's circumference was successfully walked. Shortly after our return to France in March, Olga held a meeting to plan the next stages of the Tour for the remainder of the year. I was "instructed" to attend. Olga outlined her overall master plan and, with the clipped efficiency of a military general, she delegated each stage to a named individual who, she said, was to be responsible for organising the route, transport, accommodation and all other administration. Olga allocated to me a sector from Faycelles to Limogne-en-Quercy. This was to be held on 21/22 September and was designated Tour de Lot stage 5. The start point was about two hour's drive from Cazals. Olga was not the sort of lady to argue with. I had had my orders! I realised there were still several months to get the stage organised but I had better do a good job – or else!

As soon as I could free up my time at home, I set off to reconnoitre my allocated sector sticking as closely as possible to the line of the Departmental boundary. I found that part of this route was along of one of the original French trails of the Pilgrims Way. Mid way between my start and end point was the small town of Carjac and here I found a very adequate small hotel where our group could stay overnight. Each days walk would be about twenty-three kilometres and although there were a few hills to negotiate, most of the route followed was along lightly undulating tracks, part open, part wooded. During my several visits to this sector I appreciated the beautiful countryside we would be passing through. I blessed Olga for her inspired thinking to organise this tour and my good luck to have been allocated this particular sector. I thoroughly enjoyed these days spent on my own researching this magical area.

How strange it was that after all my time in the British army and the pressures of life at Brink's, here now I should become so engrossed and take such pleasure in a seemingly simple project as walking in the Lot. Such is the evolution of the values of life!

End of Digression

In June 2009, our *Tour du Lot* route ran from the village of Bagnac sur Céle ́ to Faycelles. By this time, the weather in the Lot had warmed into summer. The first day ended at Capdenac le Haut, a small town that overlooked the historic city of *Figeac*. The walk had been hot and demanding and we were all relieved when, after walking some twenty-five kilometres, we finally reached the hotel where we would be lodging overnight before resuming the walk the following day. After supper, Olga insisted we all had an evening stroll together to visit the old town of Capdenac. I found myself walking next to Danièle Gourdon. Later the group returned to the hotel and ended the evening with a final nightcap drink. Gradually people drifted away, saying their goodnights as they retired to their rooms. Eventually I found that only Danièle and were left. I sensed that it had been by design that we were alone together. So did Danièle. I realised that we were starting to become more to each other than just casual friends. We didn't pretend or try to put our feelings into words. We just knew that there was a mutual attraction. That evening I struggled to try to make sense of this feeling. We were both mature individuals, surely we should have been well past these sensitivities at our stage of life. Both of us were in long term relationships – me to Carol and Danièle to Richard. I liked Richard and knew it was wrong to have such personal feelings for his long-time partner. I felt it best not to try to speculate whether our attraction was merely due to the circumstances of the moment – the end of a long magical day or maybe it was something deeper. I tried to tell myself not to be so immature and to remember my social responsibilities and obligations. It was difficult to say goodnight to each other and I think we both knew there would be more to come.

The following day, our group completed the fourth phase, ending in Faycelles. From the point we ended this walk, we would resume in September when I would be the guide.

During July and August, Danièle and I met regularly. We walked with *Cazalsrando* and we socialised with Carol, Richard and other friends. Danièle and I made no attempt to have any relationship other than purely social, mostly together with our partners. Despite this, our attraction to each other persisted. I knew it. Danièle knew it but nothing passed between us. Nothing was said. What was going on? As the September date for our next *Tour de Lot* stage approached, I felt we needed to clear up what it was that we had between us, to rationalise our feelings, to know what this was all about. I suggested to Daniéle that we should find an excuse to leave the next walk early, to go somewhere, anywhere where we could be alone, to talk openly and honestly. Danièle agreed.

The walk the next week was centred on a small village some ten kilometres from Cazals. The walk intentionally coincided with the village's annual fête which included an outdoor lunch, an event which traditionally lasts for several hours; typical of deep rural France! Our club had signed up to participate but when we ended the walk, Danièle and I excused ourselves and discreetly left our colleagues to enjoy their boozy lunch. We drove to a quiet, private place, parked and, for the first time since our evening on the Tour de Lot were alone together. I can't remember what I said besides admitting that I was confused, I knew there was a strong attraction that was pulling us together but I didn't know where it was leading. Danièle was more direct. I remember her precise words. She told me: "I'm not asking anything from you Mark, but I have to tell you that I'm in love with you!" I was stunned that she should be so assertive and assured. I didn't know how to respond. Later, I drove her back to her house and we returned to our respective partners.

Two weeks later, it was my turn to guide the club on our next phase of the *Tour de Lot*. The weather was again fine and sunny and, after my previous reconnoitres, I had no difficulty taking the correct route. It was also my responsibility to allocate rooms in our overnight hotel. I ensured Danièle's room was located where I could visit her after everyone had retired. So it was that we discovered each other. It was as we had expected.

This was the last walk for Danièle before she and Richard returned to Holland for the winter months. We made no promises to each other. No firm plans about anything. Perhaps we both thought that our summer's attraction to each other was a passing phase and that the intervening months of no contact would dissipate our feelings. Time would tell.

xxx

When Carol and I had left Spain to return again to France in mid-March 2010, I had mentioned to the same estate agent who had sold us the house that should someone want to buy it we would be interested and then would look for another property with better orientation. To my surprise, we had only been back in France for about one month when the estate agent called me. He said a client liked our house and would we be prepared to sell it? I agreed and we settled on a price which, after fees and taxes, was roughly equivalent to what I had paid. Carol and I returned directly to Spain and began a fresh property search, determined this time to find a property with the right orientation and location. We visited over twenty houses in our price range during this two week's visit. One stood out well ahead of all the rest: location, orientation (not perfect but acceptable), privacy, proximity to amenities, state of maintenance, included furnishings etcetera. It ticked all the boxes, as they say! We negotiated the price and ended with a good deal. At last, I hoped we had found the right balance of living in the French countryside during the bulk of the year then retreating to a (now better researched) house in Spain for the winter.

In mid-May 2010, Danièle and Richard returned to Cazals to spend another summer. We first met up while shopping. I was with Carol, Danièle was with Richard. We greeted each other after the months apart and after our shopping, had a drink together, the four of us. But nothing had changed. I could feel it and I knew Danièle could as well. Another winter of months of no contact had made no difference.

Olga had organised a trip to the Pyrenees for a few days walking in the mountains. I signed up to for the trip, so did Danièle. During this week, Danièle and I fully participated in all the walking and evening social events. But there was one difference. We came together each night. We knew we were being unfaithful to our partners and we were acting in a crazy immature way. We knew all this but still we did not resist the strong drive that continued to draw us together. But within the club we acted as usual and participated in all the physical and social activities. There was no suggestion that anyone else was aware of our secret liaison.

XXX

The summer of 2010 passed for us as other summer's had before. I continued to cultivate the land on my property, Carol was busy with her singing rehearsals and concerts, we socialised with our, by now, extensive group of friends which sometimes included Richard and Danièle. Danièle and I only saw each other while with others, either during our weekly walks with the club or socially with our partners. Although we were both well aware of our continued attraction for each other, I suppose neither of us felt we could or dared do anything to upset the status quo of our established lives either with our partners or within the framework of our families and friends. Danièle had two children and four grandchildren to whom she was very close. They all visited her and Richard during the summer. Anthony, Enny, my granddaughter Alethea and William also came to stay with Carol and me. Outwardly, we continued to play our parts as accepted settled couples, parents and grandparents. We could see no other possible set of relationships, nor to do anything which might upset the love we had for our children and grandchildren. Yet, beneath the surface, our by now deep attraction for each other persisted.

As the end of the summer season approached, we were both concerned that yet another period of several months was approaching when again we would be separated with no contact. Danièle and Richard would be back in Holland while Carol and I were in our newly bought house in Spain. We had very few chances to talk together in private. Our last opportunity came with our next walking tour which was in Egletons in the Correze Department to the north of Le Lot. Unlike earlier walks, most days during this trip were wet and quite cold but, as ever, our intrepid walkers carried on regardless with no complaints. Our accommodation was quite basic and although Danièle and I had been allocated single rooms, these were all in close proximity to other walkers with little space between the rooms. We both were aware that the winter season was fast approaching and still we were searching for answers to our situation. We were not prepared to try yet again to let our feelings dissipate throughout the next long winter months. Still we had no idea of what we could do to change our present life's routine. Danièle suggested we should keep in regular email contact during the winter. I was not convinced, wondering what was there to tell each other that we didn't already now. But Danièle insisted saying that regular writing would be both a chance to keep contact even though we would be far apart physically and would be a means for us to discover more about each other and fully express our feelings. With some reluctance I agreed. The next few months proved that Danièle was right as very few days passed when we didn't write at last once to each other, sometimes twice, sometimes more!

There was an emptiness within me when in early October 2010, Danièle left again for Holland. I continued with the routine of my life. I prepared my garden for the winter and walked with our club on the year's final stage of the Tour de Lot which ended at Rocamadour, the small hillside village known as the *Citée Réligieuse*, where we jostled among the many pilgrims who worship and display their Christian devotion there every year. It was a fascinating route and I tried my best to remain sociable to my fellow walkers. But somehow, without Danièle, it didn't seem the same. As the end of October approached, Carol and I made our plans to leave for Spain. I had promised the lady mayor of Gindou that I would stay until the eleventh of November when we gathered at our village memorial to honour the fallen in the two world wars. Side by side we spoke the famous words of "We will remember them" in both the French and English languages. After this ceremony, well attended by local villagers, many of whom still had poignant memories of the last war, we had a *vin d'honneur* and luncheon with toasts offered to our French and British allegiance. The following day, Carol and I drove down to Spain with our two dogs and cat. We appreciated our change of house and being again in Spain with its mild climate. We found it easy to slot back into life on the Costa Blanca.

I realised how very lucky I was. Now we had two good properties which we alternated to optimise the climate between summer and winter and our finances were now sufficient for us to be able to live quite comfortably. Both Carol and I were in reasonably good health. Carol was blessed with having excellent musical skills, particularly her singing which always made her many social contacts. I supported Carol in her musical endeavours and together we coexisted efficiently. I was now in great regular contact with my two sons who were both healthy and settled in their lives. I was into my early seventies and knew it was time to settle down completely and count my blessings. What more could I wish for in life? And yet! I couldn't shake off a burning feeling of emptiness.

During my life I'd always needed little sleep, maybe four hours would be all my system seemed to need. It was no different now. During the few short hours that I slept, I always seemed to dream – long, disturbing affairs where I could never achieve what I was seeking. I would wake up feeling unfulfilled but relieved that the dream had been just that, only a dream.

Then I would lie awake for hours searching in my mind for something I found hard to identify. Throughout my professional life, I used to fill these hours by planning my next day's work, or get up and write a Tutor Marked Assignment for the Open University or even go early to my office. Back then there never seemed a problem with having so many waking hours. I always found a productive way to fill them. But now, in retirement, my focus was more concentrated on domestic life. There was a gap in my life, an emptiness, a void. And more and more I realised that it was due to living in an empty marriage. I felt dirty and disloyal to come to this conclusion. Carol and I had now been together for over thirty years. She had always been a straight and honest person. I recognised that she had supported me very well during my working life, particularly when I was in the military. Time and time again I asked myself why I was not more content? What was missing that was so important that I felt so depressed and unfulfilled?

Then I would always come to the same conclusion. My present life lacked a passion and vitality that I craved. I knew that I should put these desires aside and be content with all the good fortune that I had. But we only live once. As they say, "Life is not just a dress rehearsal". There is no second chance. This is it. In my early waking hours I came to the realisation that my relationship with Danièle was the root cause that had triggered all my thoughts of emptiness now. Our email letters continued to flow between us. Danièle always wrote in French, I wrote in English. That was the best way for us to express ourselves. There was no point in trying to hide our feelings and emotions in the letters we wrote to each other. I knew that I had always had respect for Carol but had never loved her. I also knew that Carol did not love me. Our lives together had turned into a sort of mechanical ritual.

This sort of zombie existence continued throughout the winter of 2010/11. My restlessness continued and I was anxious to be with Danièle again. I felt I had to know if what I was feeling was a real genuine desire for us somehow to be together, to live together or was my emotional feeling just some fantasy that I would grow out of. I had to know and to find some way to get together, to talk absolutely freely, to know, really know what it was that was driving this impulsion. Danièle told me she owned her own apartment in Paris that she had bought with the earnings that she made from her business in Holland. She wrote that she had reasons occasionally to go there to sort out legal issues. We decided to meet there for a weekend in early March. We felt guilty about our deceit to our partners. But I was driven by what to me was the primacy of trying to come to terms with the emotions that were dominating my life.

Danièle and I made the most of our short time together in Paris. We talked and talked and talked. We laughed together. We teased each other. We made love. We walked in the nearby Bois de Boulogne, sometimes we went out to eat, mostly we stayed in. We spent every part of everyday together. Those few precious days passed all too quickly, but they achieved their main objective. We stopped any further questioning. We had made up our minds. Despite the disruption and disloyalty it would surely cause, we decided that our love for each other was genuine and deep. We resolved that somehow we would reorganise our lives to be together. Of that we were sure.

xxx

Chapter Forty-One

A New Life

Gindou/Alicante/Paris

From then on, it was not if but when. From my side, no matter how empty my marriage to Carol was, we had been together for over thirty years. She, as Danièle and I, was now in her early seventies. How would she cope if/when we split up? My sense of guilt was unremitting. Was I just trying to make excuses when I considered that perhaps our relationship, Carol's and mine, was not totally one sided. We had travelled widely and lived in various different countries which Carol had enjoyed as much as me. She had been keen for us to move to France, and then to Spain for the winters, and, due to her musical talent had integrated better than me, certainly in Spain. We had been a close and efficient team throughout our working lives together but in retirement we had very little in common. So perhaps there was some blame on both sides or even no blame at all – or was I just using this line of thought as a means of trying to reduce my sense of guilt? My thought cycle continued to rotate.

After our weekend together, Danièle returned to Holland to continue her life with Richard and teaching French to her Dutch students. I flew to UK to spend a couple of days with Anthony and Enny. Without being able fully to rationalise my thoughts, I felt the need to spend some time with my son and daughter in law. I didn't tell them about Danièle but rather pathetically hinted that my life might soon change. All my remarks seemed to do was for them to wonder what their silly, old father was up to. I then flew back to Spain to continue the rest of our season there.

There were times when I thought that Danièle and I were a crazy, old couple. I had never heard of two people in their seventies falling in love and putting themselves through the emotions and turmoil that we were doing. There probably are such couples but I didn't personally know any. We were "senior citizens" with well-established lives, homes, families and friends. Yet here we were. I should be a responsible father and grandfather, the head of my little family, guiding and counselling my children and grandchildren as I handed down the benefits of my years of experience. Yet I was feeling like a love-stricken adolescent. It was crazy!

Digression – theft

The next few months were traumatic both for Danièle and me and for our partners. The implications of the disruption to our routine established life pattern was exacerbated by a myriad of outside events – the first of which occurred during Carol and my return trip from Spain back to Gindou. I had stopped the car for a "comfort" break after the first three hours of our drive. We were still in Spain. By then it was late Sunday morning. I took our dogs for a leg stretch walk around the perimeter of the parking area, returned and left them with Carol while I went for a pee. When I returned, I noticed a gentleman walking away from our car, getting into a vehicle which immediately drove off. I did not note the vehicle number. I asked Carol who he was and she said he was just someone who had seen our dogs and had come over to admire them. I felt suspicious and asked Carol to check her bag. It was missing. It had been very cleverly stolen by a nimble thief while Carol was distracted by the man I had seen. We did a quick inventory check. Carol's bag had contained both of our passports, all our credit and debit cards, driving licenses, health cards and two hundred euros in cash. Also in her bag had been a notebook in which she admitted she had written the pin codes of the cards. Of course the pin codes should never have been written down and certainly never held in the same place as the cards. We also should not have kept all our valuable documents in one place. Carol should have been more alert. All obvious and easy to say – in hindsight, but in the real world these things happen! I didn't blame Carol. There was no point.

I went straight to the administration office of the parking station and reported the theft as I knew that it was mandatory to report a theft to the police immediately if our insurance was to reimburse us. It took several hours before a local policeman arrived on this hot Sunday and listened to our report of the theft. I had to press him to write out a formal statement which we both signed and he gave me a copy. By this time it was late afternoon and we still had nine hours still to drive. We eventually got home after two o'clock the next morning. There then was the laborious process of reporting the loss to the police authorities in France, to the insurance companies and the banks involved. It was later established that over two thousand euros had been extracted from ATMs using our cards before they were blocked by the banks. Eventually we were able to get updated UK passports, replacement cards, driving licenses, health certificates and even our stolen money was reimbursed. All was restored but this process took many hours of visits, phone calls, letters and waiting in queues in the offices of the various government agencies and companies involved.

End of digression

Danièle and Richard returned to France from Holland at the end of April. We were naturally anxious to see each other again and we managed to do so but were rarely able to be alone. Either we would meet with our partners at some social occasion, or during our Wednesday walks with Olga and the club. Our main means of communication remained via our discreetly written emails.

I tried my best to continue to maintain a good relationship with Carol but I knew if Danièle and I were ever to be together, at some point we would have to make the move and tell our partners, our families and our friends. Via our emails, Danièle and I agonised about this – when and how – and about our guilt and the effect it would have on others around us. We realised the massive disruption it would cause to all our lives, where to live, the effect on our children, our finances, the many friends we had between us, knowing that many might be judgemental and end further contact with us but some hopefully would remain our friends – all this in addition to the emotion and hurt that leaving our present partners would be bound to cause. All this self-inflicted aggravation – but such was the price of love!

I had somehow hoped an opportunity might arise where Carol and I could discuss living separate lives without there being rancour or a bad emotional outcome but realised this was a vain hope. Then one conversation in mid-May triggered the beginning of the process. During our supper I had mentioned to Carol that I hoped that both of my sons would be able to visit and stay with us at some stage during that summer. Carol said nothing at that time but later we took a stroll with our dogs before bedtime. I suppose Carol had been thinking about our earlier conversation as she suddenly said: "I have to tell you that I don't love you anymore and I don't like your sons. I don't want them to come and stay here this summer. Do you think we should separate?" Her unusual abruptness took me by surprise. She had never spoken like that before. I took my time to respond but realised that her comment perhaps at last might lead to a positive way forward for us both. Or perhaps she had said that merely to try to hurt me. I didn't know. After a pause, I replied, "I know you have never taken to Anthony and William but they are my sons, I love them dearly and want to see them whenever I can. About your question, "should we separate?" Yes, I think we should!" That ended our conversation. We returned to our house and went to bed.

The next morning, Carol said, "Did you really mean it when you said we should separate?" I replied, "Yes, I did!" That was not what Carol was expecting to hear. I suppose she had made her comment the previous evening when she was in a mood of the moment – the sort of ill tempered, unthought through remark that sometimes married couples are apt to make to each other, all to be forgotten the next day. But from my side I knew I had to stick with my earlier reply which, in one phrase: "Yes I think we should separate" had started a process that would change our lives together. There could be no retraction now! When Carol realised I had meant what I had said, she became belligerent, she screamed, she swore at me. I realised that any mutually agreed separation that I hoped for would not happen. We were now locked into a world of recrimination, of accusation, of mistrust. What had I done? I had ruptured over thirty years of marriage, of joint achievement and mutual respect. But I knew deep down that this was the way it had to be.

Digression – the concert

There was another thing. Before we had left Spain the previous month, Carol had agreed to be the soloist in an international concert in Alicante in the first week of June which was the week after our "separation" conversation. At the time, I had my misgivings about this trip as it entailed driving a minimum twelve hours back again to Spain as flying was not a practical option. But the invitation for Carol to sing was a major compliment to her. Now, I felt duty bound to honour my earlier offer to support her and drive down again to Spain. It was not an easy trip. We drove back to Spain arriving in good time for Carol to rest before her rehearsals. On the day of the concert, Carol travelled with the rest of her choir while separately, I caught one of the busses that had been hired to take supporters to the concert venue in Alicante. I found a seat somewhere in the midst of the auditorium.

The concert hall was full. The performance was formally introduced by a distinguished Spanish lady and the choristers came on stage and took their places next to the orchestra. I could see Carol in the centre of the choir. She looked composed and well prepared. After the first few choral numbers, Carol sang her solo pieces. One was from the famous musical "Porgy and Bess", called "The man I love". Carol sang this piece with the great feeling and emotional sensitivity that haunting Gershwin song deserves. I listened to her voice which seemed to be focused directly at me. I couldn't help it. I was so moved by this song and the way that Carol sang it that I openly sobbed. I cried for the time we had spent together, for the mutual support we had given each other during the many years, experiences and places we had shared, I cried for the way our lives had fallen apart, I cried that now we could hardly speak civilly to each other anymore. I cried that I was now letting her down. But then, despite all this tearful sadness within me, I knew, absolutely knew that there was no turning back, that this was a sad, traumatic process that I had to pursue, just hoping that my instinct and judgement were correct and that the lives of all of us affected – Carol, Danièle, Richard, me and all our children would in time readjust. I looked around and was relieved that no one seemed to notice my tears. I was anonymous. No one here knew I was the man who had been unfaithful to the lady up there on the stage singing with such magnetic emotion.

After the concert, I joined the reception that the Alicante officials had laid on for the performers. I was introduced as Carol's husband and complimented on having such a talented wife. I could only appear proud and loving. When we were later alone, I praised Carol for her excellent performance. She merely smiled and shrugged. The next day we drove the twelve hours back to Gindou. The atmosphere between us was polite, but cold and frosty.

End of digression

Our trip back to Spain had been only a brief interlude in my efforts to arrange our affairs as tidily as I could. It took some time for Carol even to discuss our future, or lack of it. A prime decision was where we would both live as we now had the option of our two houses. I told Carol she could choose which of these properties she preferred, or neither, and I would take the other. After our upgrading of the Spanish house, its easier maintenance, the mild winter climate, the closer proximity of shopping etc and the many friends she had made there, I thought she would prefer Spain. But no, she said she wanted to stay in Gindou but hoped to find a smaller, more suitable house for her to manage.

By now, Carol seemed to accept that our separation was irreversible but was convinced that the main cause was that I was having an affair. My inclination was to be open and honest and tell her about Danièle – to bring the whole story out into the open. But that was not yet feasible as Danièle's partner Richard was still unaware that Danièle would soon be leaving him. He was a sensitive man and Danièle was struggling to find the best way to handle the delicate and difficult decision to tell him. Until then, I had to be evasive to Carol when she continually pressed me about this. In the end, as I suppose was inevitable, she suspected my lover was Danièle. She asked me if this was true. When I was again evasive, she rushed round to Danièle's house in Cazals and confronted her. Danièle had no option but to admit to our affair. Somehow, she managed to persuade Carol not at that time to tell Richard as she needed to do this herself.

The pressure continued to mount during June. Carol's tirades against me became more frequent and more aggressive. In our early discussions, Danièle and I had thought it might be best to plan to leave our partners and live together sometime the next year, 2012, when we hoped we might achieve an amicable arrangement with Carol and Richard. Now I knew this would never be possible, at least between Carol and me. Now that Carol had decided she wished to stay in Gindou and our affairs were as orderly as I could make then, I decided there was no point to delay further. It was time to leave.

After much deliberation, this is what Danièle and I decided. On the evening of 5 July, I would drive to Spain. Danièle needed to stay a few days longer, but would leave Casals by train to go initially to her apartment in Paris. When I told Carol of my decision to leave Gindou, she seemed quite calm and said she would stay overnight that day with friends as she did not want to be around when I left.

xxx

On my final evening, I loaded my car with a few necessary belongings and, with very mixed emotions, prepared to leave the house in Gindou that I had found, bought and enjoyed for the past five years. I wasn't just leaving Carol, the house and this beautiful part of France. There were also our two dogs that Carol insisted should stay with her. I was in no place to object. Before I left, I took them for a last walk, along one of our favourite trails. I was alone as Carol had already gone to stay with our friends. It was about ten p.m. when our dogs and I got back. I knew the time had come. I should now get in my car and drive off. But I wasn't yet ready. I also knew I should not drink any alcohol as I was about to drive for twelve hours. I didn't care. I poured myself a full glass of whiskey and took a long slow swig. Our dogs came up close and I stroked and cuddled them. Dogs are very sensitive animals, they both seemed to know my feelings and pressed themselves into me. I thought this was probably the last time we would be together. The older one was now thirteen, the average natural life span for a labrador. He was already beginning to slow down. The younger one was only nine. I got off the chair and lay down on the floor. The two darling dogs came and lay down close to me while I continued to caress them. I could feel my tears beginning to well up as we lay together. We stayed like that for some lingering moments but I knew I had to say goodbye. Eventually I tore myself away, got up, closed and locked the door, left the key where we always hid it, got into my car and drove through the night to Spain.

I had a couple of refuelling stops on the way, otherwise drove straight through to the Spanish Costa Blanca, arriving the next afternoon. I should have been clapped out when I let myself into the house but I was too restless to be tired. My first priority was to set up my laptop and wham off an email to Danièle to check how she was and to let her know my situation. I got a quick reply. She told me she had bought the ticket for her train to Paris in three days' time. I still felt a mix of guilt about Carol, sadness, frustration but an overall sense of relief that the final break had now been made and she and I could get on with the rest of our lives. I sent Carol a quick mail, hoping I hit the right tone but I thought it would probably be some long time before she replied, if at all. I looked around the Spanish house and was still pleased I had made the decision last year to sell the first house we bought and to buy this one. At the least it would be a good base to start a new phase with Danièle. I hoped she would like it here. If and when our Gindou house sold and Carol and I split the proceeds, Danièle and I could explore other options, perhaps an apartment in the south of France, perhaps to the Malaga area in Spain's Andalucía region. I was excited that soon we should be living together. But all that was for the future.

With all the recent turbulence, it hadn't dawned on me that I had never been in Spain before during the summer. Now it was early July in the midst of Spain's long summer season. As I began to unwind, I appreciated that we had our own pool. I checked the water temperature; 29 degrees, close to the air temperature which during the middle of the day was nudging up to the mid-thirties. After long swims in the pool, plus a couple of visits to the nearby beach to swim and sunbathe, I felt refreshed, renewed. What a contrast to the days of struggling to resolve and organise our lives back in

France. I was still feeling all the guilt pangs about both Carol and Richard and knew those would always endure but what was done was done. The best I could do concerning Carol was to tell myself that there are always two people in a marriage. I was the one principally at fault but Carol hadn't been blameless either. At least I knew that I had left her with exactly half of all our assets – properties in joint names and an exact division of our finances. That amount, together with her own pensions should ensure she would always be financially secure. I had deferred to her choice to stay in France rather than Spain. She was well established socially, had many local friends and was much respected for the musical contribution she brought to the local community. Perhaps I could learn not always to keep beating myself about this issue.

Two days after I had arrived in Spain, Danièle phoned. She told me she was on the train on route to Paris, having left Richard at Gourdon station. She said she was feeling dirty (her words) and that it had been so difficult for her to tell Richard she was going to leave him. I knew it would take a long time, if ever, fully to come to terms with our actions. But during our short talk, we both reconfirmed that, deep down, we knew we had done the right thing. We both knew we had made the decisive move. There was no going back.

At last it was Wednesday, 13 July, the day we had planned to be together! I made sure the house was clean and tidy. I wanted to present it well to Danièle when we at last would be back here together. I felt I was floating along on a dream wave as I drove to Alicante airport, parked up in the "long stay" and passed through ticket and security controls. The Vueling flight was on time and two and a half hours later I was in a taxi at Paris Orly. I told the driver: "Boulevard Suchet" and sat back and watched the Paris skyline flash by as he negotiated his way around the *peripherique*, exiting at Porte d'Auteuil. A few minutes later, I told the driver where to stop, paid his fare and got out. I stood in front of the fine old 1930s building where Danièle had her apartment. I knew the security code at the front door which allowed access to the main entry vestibule. I got out the two keys that Danièle had given me. The first opened a door to the passageway which led directly to her own door. I took out the second key and inserted it in the lock. It turned and the door opened. Danièle was standing there waiting for me. As I stepped across the threshold of her apartment I told her, "From this moment, our life together begins!" I then took her my arms and kissed her.

XXX

Chapter Forty-Two

Alicante

Fourteen years have passed and here we are, Danièle and I, still alive and kicking although beginning to creak! We are still living in the same house in Spain. Our decision all those years ago has been fully vindicated as now we move towards the end game of our lives. I get on very well with Danièle's children and grandchildren: Anthony and William adore Danièle. They all regularly come to stay with us. We spend most of our time in Spain with stays in Paris twice each year. Despite some hiccups we are blessed still to be in quite good health. We spend all our time together and are still keen walkers though we now we find the same slopes seem to be steeper and longer than they used to be!

Our life style here in Spain is simple, relaxed and straightforward. At last we both found the right partner with whom to spend the rest of our lives. Danièle and I are at ease with each other. Our restlessness, our frustrations, our searching have long since subsided. We have peace and belonging with each other. We at last have found our true home! Such is the chance of life. Some find the ideal match for a partner early in their lives and never query or even think of other alternatives. One of my oldest friends is exactly in that situation. He met the girl who later became his wife when they both were in their late teens, got married, had three fine and healthy children, several grandchildren and never had the slightest doubt about their long and enduring relationship. That didn't happen to Danièle and me. Throughout most of our adult lives we were both living with good honest partners, but not the right ones. That was until so late in our lives. Fate, chance, poor judgement. Who knows?

We are also both now published authors, I write in English, Danièle in French just as we used to with our constant emails to each other all those years ago. We both encourage and are objective critics of each other's work. Danièle's fourth book has now been published (initially only in French but now also in English). It's brilliantly researched and written. Meantime, I struggle to complete this story, now my fifth book.

We never cease to marvel at the diverse culture of Spain, a country that has experienced periods of extremes of the different civilizations that have gone into shaping its history: those of the Castillians, Catalonians, Lusitanians, Galicians, Basques, Romans, Visigoths, Arabs, Jews; each renowned for their varied religions, customs and languages which have contributed to the rich tapestry that makes up modern Spain today. The Carthaginians and the Romans fought over it, the Visigoths occupied it then the Moors conquered and ruled it for more than seven hundred years, leaving behind a legacy of fine architecture, lyrical poetry and the most advanced science and medicine of the time. It was then "reconquered" by the Spanish under King Philip II who presided over the richest period of Spanish history. Danièle and I have toured and stayed in most regions of the country. In our opinion, no city typifies this country more than Toledo which still retains the evidence of much of its diverse history. In one short narrow street, there still are a Moorish church, a Visigoth cathedral and a Jewish temple, all still standing and located right next to each other. Toledo also boasts its Catholic cathedral, a quintessential example of the Gothic style with its flying buttresses, internal chapels and unique roof design. Another is at Burgos, a city which combines both the Christian heart of the Saint James Way – the route of the Camino de Santiago de Campostela and the rich archaeological discoveries of the origins of man at the nearby Sierra de Atapuerca. Spanish cathedrals are still laden with gold fixtures, demonstrating the period of enormous riches accrued by the Catholic church. One can wonder at this opulence. To some it is a magnificent and glorious tribute to God; but to others it is evidence of the obscenity that the church coveted such enormous wealth while its inhabitants were so impoverished! As Garcia Lorca is quoted to have remarked, "In Spain, the dead are more alive than the dead of any other country in the world."

xxx

Part Three

Reflections

Chapter Forty-Three

"*After the Earth dies some five billion years from now, after it's burned to a crisp or even swallowed by the sun, there will be other worlds and stars coming into being – and they will know nothing of a place once called Earth.*" – Carl Sagan

Two thousand years after the death of Jesus Christ, his legacy lives on: the many magnificent cathedrals, churches, artefacts, statues, paintings, and the prolific volume of literature produced about the Christian faith, are all testament to the enduring appeal of Christianity.

The funeral services held following the death Queen Elizabeth in September 2022 were revered by the crowds who queued in their thousands to visit her lying in State, lined the routes to witness the processions through Edinburgh, London and Windsor and by the many millions around the world who watched the services on television. Queen Elizabeth was a devout Christian, a faith which guided her throughout her long life. The Christian clergy were at the centre of the funeral service, part of the fabric of the traditional custom of bringing people together to unite in reflective thought. The magnificent historic architecture, the words of the hymns and psalms, the stirring music, the pageantry, the traditional uniforms of the participants, the discipline of the military escorts, the stirring and emotional music, all combined to inspire.

Religious faith provides a great source of comfort and peace for the billions of the world's population who identify as believers of one faith or another; but as well as positives there are also negatives. Man's belief in a religious faith can also be destructive and has often been the cause of division and bloodshed: in Nigeria (Christian versus Muslim), Middle east (Sunni versus Shi'a), Cyprus (Christian versus Muslim), Ireland (Christian Catholic versus Christian Protestant), India-Pakistan-Bangladesh (Muslim, Hindu, Buddhist), Palestine (Jewish versus Muslim) and many more. Yet still religious leaders cling to their belief not only in the existence of God but that their particular interpretation of God is the only true faith!

xxx

For much of my life, I gave little serious thought about death and the possibility of an afterlife. Although I had several times faced near death or had to deal with the deaths of others, including my own family, I was always selfishly relieved it was someone else who died, not me, and I moved on to other issues in my life. No single event prompted my research into this subject. It might have been having experienced both heart and cancer problems in my seventies, both thankfully recovered (for now at least!). I realised that in my advancing years no matter how hard I try to keep fit and trim, there is no way of preventing the ever-increasing spread of wrinkles and other signs of the gradual but unstoppable growth of the aging process. Medical science has made amazing progress in helping us to survive major illnesses and to prolong our life span, but this helps only to delay the inevitable. In end we all die, all the estimated eight billion of us currently living on Planet Earth.

During the past few years, I have been studying and researching all I could find about this fundamental subject and have waded through the wide variation of opinions about who we are, why we are here, what is the meaning of everyone's life, and what happens when we die. The reality is that when we die, our physical bodies are either buried or cremated – or are left on some remote battlefield/besieged city such as Flanders, Monte Casino, Dresden, Mariopol or Bakhmut! Is that all there is? Or is there something else? Do all individuals really have souls and proceed to some other place in an afterlife? Christians believe they do and this belief gives them hope that their souls may be resurrected and sent to heaven. That is of course providing they believe in their interpretation of "God, the saviour", that they follow the Bible's teachings and obey its commandments. We refer to terms such as "our souls, our spirits, redemption." Is it possible that some version of an "afterlife" might apply to all humans who have ever, and will ever, exist on this earth? Could the souls of Abraham, Moses, Socrates, Shakespeare, Einstein and the trillions of other humans who have ever lived, still be out there somewhere, sharing an afterlife forever? According to the New Statesman (20 November 2019) "Most people hold curiously similar views about life after death suggesting there is no more to it than religion, fear or an inability to imagine not existing – confronted with the finality of death, the majority of us, dogged rationalists included, cling to the belief that it is not the end."

In Part One of this book, I examined the beliefs of the main religions of the world, their similarities, their differences and how thinking and interpreting of faiths has evolved over the years, mostly in recent times due to our advancing knowledge of science. I also described the thinking of some of the prominent non-believers, particularly the theories of Darwin. I quoted from Richard Dawkins and his fellow atheist "Horsemen". I recorded that some philosophers and thinkers use the term "consciousness", a function that is quite separate from our physical bodies. This term is particularly relevant to the study of near-death experiences, to reincarnation and to child prodigies.

In Part Two, I gave a detailed description of a life. As I described in the introduction, I had to use my own as it's not possible to dig deep down beneath the surface of anyone else's. I showed both that part of life that is overtly on display for others to observe but also many of the inner thoughts, desires, activities, dreams and, particularly, the many mistakes made.

xxx

Below are some observations relating to my personal experiences about the main religions.

Christianity

When I was still serving in the military, church services were events I often felt I had to attend when instructed – military services, remembrance Sundays etc. I found such ceremonies meaningful as a time to remember and mourn those whose lives had touched my own, of my own family and also those in the military who had died on operations both on my own side and those of my "enemies" at the time.

While in Africa, I was exposed to both positives and negatives concerning the Christian faith – with the caveat that my experiences were restricted to the period when I was in Nigeria, the Cameroons and the Congo in the 1960s. The positives included the exemplary work done by Christian mission hospitals in caring for the sick and malnourished. Most of this selfless work was carried out mainly by Belgian, Irish and French nuns whose mission was caring and not preaching. The negative was witnessing the adverse effects of some Christian priests who felt it was their duty to bring the word of God to the infidel by preaching the Gospel and trying to convert the "poor ignorant African people to Christianity." Often these "men of the cloth" lacked an understanding of the traditional culture of many proud African tribes who had been living in harmony for many generations with their own traditions and spirituality. The intervention of Christian priests resulted in needless and often harmful disruption of the African's way of life.

I spent time in Northern Ireland during the period of "the troubles". Religion and politics were intermeshed particularly with the political exploits of The Reverend Ian Paisley. In 1969, Paisley founded the Martyrs Memorial Free Presbyterian Church in Belfast and promoted a highly conservative form of Biblical literalism. He used his church to denounce the Roman Catholic church which he accused of deviating from the Bible and thus from true Christianity and to promote his political career initially within the Ulster Unionist Party. He was elected the Member of Parliament for North Antrim and later formed the Democratic Unionist party (DUP) which became the leading protestant voice in Northern Ireland. Throughout his joint religious/political career, Paisley was staunchly opposed to accommodating the aspirations of the nationalist community in Northern Ireland. Conversely, from the Catholic side, the formation of the IRA with their vicious uncompromising attacks on Protestant individuals and properties – the bombings, assassinations, kneecapping etc carried out in the name of Catholic faith, again highlighted the danger of mixing religion with politics.

The audience given by the Pope, then John Paul II, in 1987 while I was a student at the NATO Defence College in Rome was deeply moving – details in Part Two. The whole ceremony was carried out with great professional polish, honed by many years of organising such audiences. After the formal speeches, Pope John came down from his stage to mingle with his audience. Particularly memorable was the effect that he had on the catholic wives of our college members. They were overcome, looking in total devotion and awe at the pontiff, almost to the point of swooning away. John Paul had a commanding presence which reinforced the faiths of those ladies who had been brought up in the Catholic faith.

Personally, I had to struggle with the issue of the education of our two sons. To summarise what I wrote in Part Two, despite my many misgivings, I gave way to Gizèle's wishes for our sons to be educated in private Catholic boarding schools. Throughout their years at these schools I was always uneasy about leaving them for the many months of the schools' term-time in the sole care of Catholic priests although I had no justifiable grounds for complaint. In recent years, there has been much adverse publicity about illegal, inappropriate behaviour and hypocrisy of some Catholic establishments. I have no entitlement to add further to this subject other than feeling it is not healthy or moral for young priests to have to remain celibate during their years in the priesthood, particularly those who have younger children in their care.

As my grandmother and later my aunt grew old, I had legal Power of Attorney for their affairs. When they neared the end of their lives, they both moved to retirement nursing homes in England. I visited each of them whenever I was able to, restricted by my overseas postings. I have referred to these fine ladies in Part Two above. My grandmother was a strong-willed lady who liked to reminisce at length about her youth which stretched back well into Victorian days. Her highly articulate stories were full of events she had attended and people she knew. She expressed no fear of her impending death and I never once heard her talk about religion, or God. She died at age 102. My aunt was very different. Usually the first thing she would say when I visited was "Could you pray with me?" Of course I did. These prayer sessions had little meaning to me but they meant a great deal to my aunt. In her later years, her faith in Christianity was a strength that sustained her and gave her much comfort. She just out-did her mother, dying at the age of 103.

I like to stroll around graveyards wondering about the lives recorded on the gravestones, some having been lying there for hundreds of years. I also love to sing hymns lustily, remembering the words of the old favourites that I learnt back in Bath abbey all those years ago. I admire the story of the person of Jesus, of his disciples and of all the parables narrated in the New Testament. I have no idea whether or not such a person as Jesus actually existed but I accept that he may have and was a charismatic character, teacher and role model. I have respect for the many millions of Christians who do indeed believe that Jesus was the son of God, who follow the teachings of the Bible and find comfort and peace in this belief. But was he the son of God and was he resurrected? For me, there's the big doubt!

When I was staying in Paris a few years ago, I decided on a whim to visit the Notre Dame Cathedral, to find a quiet area, and just sit and think. (This was in 2018; the following year, the cathedral caught fire with devastating destruction). I sat there for some hours losing track of the time. I tried to concentrate my thoughts about life and to keep my mind open to any influence that might occur in this majestic ambiance. I wondered how people like Justin Welby, the present Archbishop of Canterbury, while living the life of a business executive in the oil industry, should give it up when in his middle age then to train to be a clergyman. I wondered how it is that some distinguished academics, who have been exposed to the highest levels of science became believers in Christianity, a faith which stems from unproven events of two thousand years ago and which are recorded in a book of highly questionable provenance; while others, of equal academic distinction find that science has convinced them that there is no evidence that there is a God, a creator, an afterlife. I wondered why it is that some followers of Islam feel so passionately about their Muslim faith that they would kill those who are non-believers. I wondered why some atheists can be as dismissive and condemning of spiritualists who do not share their own convictions.

I felt very moved emotionally while sitting there in the Notre Dame. There was an atmosphere of calm, of history, of continuity, of majesty. But did it bring any form of inspiration, of something greater than a deep admiration for the construction of this wonderful building and the atmosphere that it created. For many, perhaps it did. Unfortunately, all I felt was the satisfaction of taking time for reflection here. Nothing more.

When I'm in Paris another compelling visit is to Les Invalides. Here is one of the best presented and comprehensive exhibitions of the events of WWII: the war in Europe, in north Africa, in the Far East – at sea, on land and in the air. I find it sobering, as a retired professional soldier, to reflect on the fact that during the period 1939–45, an estimated 70–85 million people perished, that is about three per cent of the 2.3 billion people on earth in 1940. Is it possible that there is a God who ensured an afterlife for all those "souls" who perished?

xxx

Islam

In Part Two I relate my personal experience of interactions with the Islamic faith during the years I spent in Nigeria, Malaysian Borneo, Bahrain and Indonesia.

Nigeria. The majority of soldiers I served with in the Nigerian Armed Forces were Hausas from the northern regions of the country. As far as I can recall all Hausas were Islam followers though they always described themselves as Muhammadans. I never heard them use the terms Muslim or Islam. They openly talked about their religion and even during our arduous operational periods, they always managed to pray and to fast during Ramadan. They were model examples of how to follow a faith yet not to allow it to dominate their lives or be prejudiced against other religious beliefs. My tutor in "Muhammadism" at that time was our company sergeant major (CSM) Kabala who also taught me to speak the Hausa language. Kabala was a sincere believer in his faith, an exemplary soldier, brave, loyal and patient (especially with his British pupil!)

Brunei. This is now a strongly Islamic state. Times have changed radically since I was there in 1964–5 when Sultan Omar Ali Saifuddien was tolerant towards us non-Muslims. So should he have been as British troops (especially the Royal Marines) were responsible for putting down a coup against him and restoring him to his throne! He abdicated in October 1967. His successor, Hassanal Bolkiah has progressively installed a regime of strict Islamic principles including Sharia law. The opulent Jame'Asr Hassani Bolkiah mosque in central Brunei town is a testament to the Sultan's devotion to his faith.

Bahrain. I lived in Bahrain from 1967 to 1970 (details in Part Two) in what was, and still is, an Islamic state. In total contrast to Brunei, which was relaxed but is now governed under strict Islamic rules, Bahrain was then a very conservative state with the local population observing such practices as all women being required to wear the full bourka when in public places. Nowadays I read that the capital, Manama, is described as "a strikingly cosmopolitan city". This change probably occurred after the opening of the King Fawd causeway which now links Bahrain to Saudi Arabia.

This island nation has been ruled by the Al Khalifah family since the late eighteenth century and is notable in that the Khalifahs and most of the wealthy Bahrainis are Sunnis but the remaining majority are Shi'as. This is one example of where both variants of Islam co-exist peacefully together. I was fortunate to be invited socially into the homes of some of the leading Bahraini families. I was struck by their hypocritical habit of acting one way in public and quite another in private. For example, (to quote from Part Two), though the ladies dressed and acted with full Islamic modesty when out of doors, at home they stripped off their robes, dressed in smart western clothes, used make up and many of them smoked. Their menfolk freely helped themselves from their well-stocked cellars of wines and spirits – in a country where, in law, alcohol was forbidden!

My other close encounter with the Islamic faith in Bahrain was observing the Shi'a practice of self-flagellation by young men – details in Part Two. I admired the courage and devotion of the poor participants but I could not relate it to having any relevance to what a God, if there is one, would have prescribed or to my quest to discover the meaning of life!

Oman. In Part Two, I described my mission when with the STANOC centre of laying sensors on wadi trails during operations in the Dhofar region of the Oman. During this time (1974), my trials team was hosted by Dhofar soldiers with whom we shared our lives. They and our rebel enemy were all Muslims. Despite being involved in a shooting war, both sides observed basic Muslim practices of prayer. I was not there during the Ramadan period so I don't know how well they observed the fasting rules. I left the Dhofar feeling respect for those who believed in the Muslim faith but with no personal pull or attraction towards it.

Indonesia. My experiences in different parts of the vast country of Indonesia are from adventures with my sons (William still lives in Bali) and during my travels with my Indonesian guide as described in Part Two. Indonesia, which comprises over seventeen thousand islands, has a population of two hundred and seventy million. Its largest religion is Muslim with an estimated two hundred and thirty-one million followers, the world's most populous Muslim majority country. The country is a Presidential Republic which describes its religious pluralism as "Unity through Diversity – Bhinneka Tunggal Ika", officially recognising: Islam, Protestantism, Roman Catholicism, Hinduism, Buddhism and Confucianism.

Although the Muslim religion dominates in Indonesia, Islamic parties do not control the political agenda. In the 2019 national elections they took a moderate and pragmatic approach, not making religious ideological issues the main narrative of their policies. The results of that election produced victory for the Indonesian Democratic Party of Struggle (PDI-P) and the Indonesian People's Movement party (Gerinda), neither of which are Islamic parties. Joko Widodo has now (2024) just completed his second term as President during which he led a pragmatic non-religious government.

xxx

Judaism

Note: I wrote the draft of this book prior to the 7 October 2023 Hamas attack on Israeli settlement and the subsequent turmoil in the middle east.

I frequently stayed in Israel during my years working for Brinks on visits to our branches in Tel Aviv, Jerusalem, Haifa and Beersheba. In the evenings I spent many hours socialising with Brinks Israel managers and the contacts they introduced me to, which enabled me to gain a good understanding of their religion, their politics and the priorities of their lives. Because of my military background, I was invited to commemorative services held at the most impressive Yad La-Shiryon memorial site and museum at Latrun. There, I toured the memorial for fallen soldiers from the armoured corps. These ceremonial days included historical briefings recounting the main tactical moves made by Israeli forces during their 1967 and 1974 wars against Arab troops. I was invited to attend religious services to thank God for protecting HIS Jewish followers and enabling them to defeat their "infidel" enemies. From these visits to Latrun I gained a fuller understanding of the passion that drives committed Israelis to preserve their hard-fought efforts to hold and retain political sovereignty of the State of Israel, their strongly held faith of Judaism and their self-belief and motivation.

When working with Brinks Israel, as I was neither Jewish nor Arabic and was considered by both sides to be an acceptable neutral go-between, I acted as a mediator in their negotiations. My work required me to spend many hours north of Jericho dealing with the Arab side of the Brink`s business and, inevitably, hearing the Arab arguments about the oppression and divisiveness they received from the Jewish Israeli authorities and the resentment this caused among the Israeli Arabs. These discussions reminded me of other times in my life when there has been constant friction between different interpretations of "God" and the mix of religion, ethnic background and politics which so often hinders social, business and political harmony.

Besides those in Israel, I have many Jewish friends, some who follow their faith as strongly as those I met at Latrun but others, while remaining true to their birth heritage, are less fervent and passionate about the demands of the strict rules of the Jewish faith. I have learned to respect the Jewish faith and how its beliefs by many are still strongly entrenched. But not being a Jew myself, I find the strong rules, the six hundred and thirteen Jewish "commandments", examples such wearing of the Yarmulke and the "payos" side-curls are all far too controlling and contrary to what I see as living a balanced life.

XXX

Hinduism and Buddhism

My personal knowledge of both these religions is limited to having been acquired during my many visits to Indonesia, in particular the island of Bali where the Hindu religion dominates. I understand the enormity of both religions and their root establishment on the Indian continent – Hindu is the world's third largest religion with more than 1.2 billion followers worldwide while Buddhism has an alleged three hundred and seventy-six million followers worldwide, seven per cent of the world's population. What I have learnt is that Hindus believe in a God who has many manifestations, deities and images. They believe that existence is a cycle of birth, death and rebirth, governed by Karma – a complex belief in cause and effect. Karma, a Sanskrit word that roughly translates to "action, work or deed", is a core concept in several Asian religions including Hinduism and Buddhism.

Due to my limited experience of both religions, I am not qualified to comment on their spiritual values, for example in relation to the western religions of Christianity, Islam and Judaism. However, the more I have learnt about Karma and its Laws, the more relevant I believe they are to the lives we live today; at least the world where I have lived. Although they are referred to as "Laws", in reality they are a set of what I consider to be sensible life principles which denote the cycle of cause and effect – that actions have consequences, each action a person takes will affect him or her at some time in the future. I found this philosophy particularly relevant to my own life, the actions I took, some good, some bad and the consequences that these actions had. I can certainly relate to the "Great Law" – you reap what you sow: whatever you put into life is what comes back to you. The other laws also ring true regarding the actions and mistakes I have made in my life.

xxx

There are some similarities between Karma and the "Commandments" of both Christianity and Islam, but whereas Christianity/Islam demand actions and adherence e.g. "Thou shall not!" Karma guides and explains. It neither believes in one all-powerful Almighty creator (Christian God, Islam Allah) nor does it denounce the idea of a God (Atheism). Karma merely proposes a set of actions and spells out their consequences. Christian Prayers require us humans to worship and serve God, such as the Lord's Prayer which begins "Our Farther in Heaven, hallowed by your name etc". The closest I can find to Christians expressing similar sentiments to Karma is the Anglican Cristian prayer: (Source: Book of Common Prayer, 1892, 1928, modified.)

"Go forth into the world in peace,
Be of good courage
Hold fast that which is good
Render to no one evil
Strengthen the faint hearted
Support the weak
Help the afflicted
Honour all people"

So far, so good, all sound lifestyle advice merely counselling its followers to live as good citizens of the world. But then this Prayer ends with the exhortation:

"Love and Serve the Lord, rejoicing in the power of the Holy Spirit, and the belief on God Almighty, the Father, the Son and the Holy Ghost, be amongst you and remain with you always. Amen."
It's this last part that I cannot subscribe to!

xxx

The pace of scientific invention which was so prolific during the eighteenth century has continued at pace during my lifetime. It was only during my final years in the military that typewriters were discarded in favour of word-processors then rapidly by the early versions of computers. These at first were only used for data storage until first webmail then email were introduced in offices in the early 1990s. Now computers have gained ubiquitous status. It was not until I started working for Brinks (1998) that I was very proud to be issued with a "brand new technical device" called a Blackberry! Now a mere thirty years later, almost everyone owns its successor, the cell/smart phone. Apple launched their latest update with iPhone 16 (2024). We now have no need to use maps in our cars as we can programme our GPS to guide us to our destination. We can only imagine what new inventions and gadgets will be produced in the years ahead. Already society is grappling with AI and its vast potential for both good and evil.

New technical advances have also impacted religion. The Bible in Genesis describes God as having created earth, then Adam, at a date estimated by Archbishop James Usher as 4004 BC and by other Christians as about 6000 BC. Yet scientists have now shown that the formation of our universe was many billions of years earlier. In July 2022, the first pictures were presented to the world to mark the NASA James Webb Telescope's readiness to begin further exploration of space. The telescope has been specially tuned to see the sky in infrared – that is light at longer wavelengths than can be sensed by our eyes. This will give it the ability to look deeper into the universe and, as a consequence, detect events occurring further back in time – more than 13.5 billion years ago. So much for Archbishop Usher's estimate of God's creation in 4004 BC! Yet he was merely the product of his times. Understanding of our world has since moved on multiple times. As a NASA spokesman put it "Prepare for a new way to see the universe beyond where we've been before, beyond what we know, beyond time itself." (Quote from the Times newspaper 13 July 2022).

Diverse bloggers commented following this Times report. Here are two, which are in total contrast.

"If you are not moved then you must have a heart of stone. We are remarkable to be able to self-reflect on our own beginnings. So much better and wondrous and beautiful than any delusions of creational myths could offer. Science, discovery, human ingenuity and invention gives hope that religion could never emulate." Geena, Times 13 July 2022

Then

"Weird, I looked at the photos and became more awestruck at God's creation. Funny how we get to different conclusions but as long as we both tolerate each other and with respect for one another, I don't see a problem." EMI, Times 13 July 2022.

I have also highlighted the archaeological discoveries at the Sierra de Atapuerca, near Burgos, northern Spain, which contain a rich fossil record of the earliest human beings in Europe, from nearly one million years ago.

xxx

I'm certainly not alone in trying to relate events in my own long life, with all its mistakes and inconsistences, to my research into the world's main religions and other influences affecting the meaning of life. Here are some relevant quotes from distinguished individuals who have been on the same mission.

Stephen Hawking 2011. "We are each free to believe what we want and it is my view that the simplest explanation is there is no God. No one created the universe and no one directs our fate. This leads me to a profound realisation. There is probably no heaven and no afterlife either. We have this one life to appreciate the grand design of the universe, and for that, I am extremely grateful."

Steve Jobs. "Your time is limited, so don't waste it living someone else's life."

Abraham Lincoln. “In the end, it’s not the years in your life that count. It’s the life in your years.”
Nelson Mandela. “The greatest glory in living lies not in never falling, but in rising every time we fall”
Albert Einstein. “Look deep into nature, then you will understand everything better.”
George Alagiah, the much-loved newsreader and television presenter died of bowel cancer in July 2023 at the age of sixty-seven. In a video montage, Alagiah admitted it had taken him time to process when he was first diagnosed with cancer in 2014. He is quoted as saying:
“I wish I hadn’t had cancer, obviously. But I’m glad of the things I’ve learned about myself and about my community, my friends and my family as a result. I’ve gotten to a place to see life as a gift. Rather than kind of worrying about when it’s going to end and how it’s going to end, I’ve got to a place where I can see it for the gift it is, I feel that gift keenly every morning.” (Daily Telegraph 24 July 2023).

xxx

Part Four

Conclusion

Chapter Forty-Four

How many people have ever lived on earth? No demographic data exists for more than ninety-nine per cent of the span of human existence, but with assumptions about population size throughout human history, some analysts have made an approximation of this number and concluded that about one hundred and seventeen billion members of our species have ever existed on Earth. (Reference: PRB). Such a figure puts the span and importance of the individual lives of humans into perspective!

Facing the end of one's life is intimidating. Most humans fear the idea of dying and then just ceasing to exist. Theists believe in a God and an afterlife. Many who follow such faiths, and observe their commandments, have the confidence, stability and conviction that they will enjoy some form of "afterlife in heaven" when they die. Some have been taught such beliefs as children and have not felt sufficiently strongly to reject them when they are older. Others consider it best to adhere to the concept as an insurance when they die.

Advances in science have led many to disbelieve the concept of a God, a creator, as it is not supported by empirical evidence. They argue that many billion years ago, time, energy and matter came together in what has been called "the Big Bang". The Darwinian theory of evolution by natural selection has led many to conclude that we humans have evolved as a species from this origin on the planet we call Earth. This theory is supported by factual evidence of archaeological discoveries made, for example, in Atapuerca, Spain. Atheists argue that religion was born specifically from the fear of death, that it is just a fanciful way to deal with its inevitability: an individual's inability to cope with the concept of oblivion. As atheists don't believe in God, most don't either believe in an afterlife. Instead of being part of the creation of a god or supreme being, most atheists see themselves as a part of nature. With death comes a return to that nature; they are guided by the natural world and hope to find peace in the cycle of life, that death is a return to nature, the only things that endure after death are the memories that those living have of the individual and the legacy of the life now gone. To quote Stephen Hawking: "I regard the brain as a computer which will stop working when all the components fail… There is no heaven or afterlife for broken down computers; that is a fairy story for people afraid of the dark."

Many mysteries remain which for me do not readily fit with either theist or atheist beliefs. In this book, I have highlighted stories of those who have undergone near death experiences which no scientific logic can yet explain. Likewise, examples of reincarnation and of those who were child prodigies defy any rational explanation.

While hoping my research would bring me to reach some conclusion as to who, why and what we are and what happens when we die, alas, like all before me, I have found no definitive explanation. People have faiths, beliefs or theories. There is no consensus and no proof. Over three hundred years ago, Descartes is quoted as saying, "*Je pense, donc je suis*: I think, therefore I am." I know of no one before or since who has had a better idea. Equally, during the same seventeenth century, Baruch Spinoza wrote in his book *Ethics*: "There is no one to hear your prayers." Two brilliant men who were way ahead of their time!

We live within our own individual bodies and think we see the world around us in a unique and personal way. We think that we are someone, something special, somehow uniquely separate from all other mortals, that our thoughts, feelings, actions are individual and exclusive to us alone. Yet we must accept, at least I do, that in reality we exist in the same world as all of those who have lived and died before us and with the eight billion who share our world today and who, like us, all will one day die.

My many years of life have taught me that we are who we are. We have no control or influence about our heritage. We have feelings, we have emotions, we live the life that is in front of us and use the abilities we have been born with to grow and evolve throughout our lives. We form opinions, we progress, we develop. We take decisions, some wise, some stupid. Sometimes we do things which we later regret. We will live on earth for a maximum of one century, probably much less. We only have one shot at life; there is, as often quoted, no dress-rehearsal!

Some recurring spiritual themes that have been expressed over the past eight hundred years with differing emphasis and context but nonetheless with much the same underlying idea. "Understand the power of reason and that all life is part of and is from nature." This theme is common, for example to Aquinas, a thirteenth century Catholic, Spinosa, a seventeenth century Jew, Darwin, a nineteenth century atheist and to the laws of Karma (ancient Muslim/Buddhist).

I've learnt not to overcomplicate life. These few simple principles work best for me.

To understand:

- **Who is looking out from behind your eyes.**
- **The circumstances of your life; your birthplace, heritage, character, ambitions, capabilities, limitations.**
- **There's only one person to whom you are accountable – yourself.**
- **The importance of learning from making mistakes and taking responsibility for your own actions.**
- **Karma's Great Law, "You reap what you sow!"**

What happens to us at the end of our lives still remains a tantalising mystery. Only one thing is certain; every one of us will know the answer one day. I would like to have ended this book with a firm conclusion: but there is a problem. When I will know for sure and certain, it will be too late to tell!

xxx

Books cited, read or recommended

The list below shows the main influencers I consulted relating to this book. I have listed only one of their works but many have also written others on similar subjects. I have not read all (that would take forever!) but I have read some in their entirety and have dipped into others often via Kindle and/or YouTube. Most of these works are available via Amazon with the year of the latest print shown.

Ahmad S (2021) Morality, Nature and Evolution
Aslan R (2005) No God but God
Atkins P (2009) Physical Chemistry
Aquinas T (2012) Summa Theologica
Atherstone A (2021) Repackaging Christianity: Alpha and the building of a Global Brand
Barnes and Noble (2010) The Complete Works of William Shakespeare
Bell B (2018) The Priestly Way: A Spiritual Retreat for Priests
Beveridge H (2011) John Calvin: The Institutes of the Christian Religion
Bromily G (1953) Zwingli and Bullinger
Butler-Bowdon T (2020) Tao Te Ching, The Ancient Classic
Carbonell E (2003) Los sueños de la evolución
Cole R (2011) SAS Operation Storm (Dhofar)
Chrystal P (2018) British Army of the Rhine (BAOR) 1945–93
Churchill W (2010) Their Finest Hour
Dante A (1995) The Divine Comedy
Darwin C (2003) The Origin of Species
Dawkins R (2016) The God Delusion
Deleuze G (2002) Spinoza. Practical Philosophy
Delphi (2015) Collected Works of Voltaire
Dostoevsky F (2002) The Brothers Karamazov
Durman M (2020) Adsum: Mission and Passion
Einstein A (2010) Relativity: The Special and General Theory
Ehrman B (2018) The Triumph of Christianity
Frankl V (2018) Man's Search for Meaning
French D (2010) The British counter-insurgency campaign of Cyprus 1955–59

Freud S (2010) Interpretation of Dreams
Ganeri (2003) The Tipitaka and Buddhist Sacred Texts
Geothe J (2019) Faust
Graham B (2018) Just as I am
Greenblatt S (2010) How Shakespeare became Shakespeare
Greene B (2020) Until the end of Time
Guthrie W (2013) The Greek Philosophers from Thales to Aristotle
Harari Y N (2015) Sapiens: A Brief History of Humankind
Harris R (2022) Act of Oblivion
Harris S (2004) The End of Faith: Religion, Terror and the Future of Reason
Hawking S (1988) A Brief History of Time
Hitchens C (1995) The Missionary Position: Mother Theresa in Theory and Practice
Holy Vedas (2006) Hindu Ancient Texts
Hume D (2019) The Complete Works
Huxley T (2003) Man's Place in Nature
Hutner G (2019) Selected speeches and writings of Theodore Roosevelt
Ingersole R (2013) Why I am an Agnostic
Islam Publications Ltd (2021) The Holy Qur'an: Arabic Text and English Translation
Kant I (1993) Grounding of the Metaphysics of Morals
Kreeft P (1990) Thomas Aquinas: Essential Philosophical Passages of Summa Theologica
King M (2022) "I have a dream" speech
Larousse (2004/2008) Napoléon Bonaparte
Legge J (2007) Soekarno: A political biography
Lennox J (2009) God's Undertaker: Has Science buried God?
Lewis C (2009) Mere Christianity, The Screwtape Letters
Lightman A (2011) Einstein's Dreams
MacArthur J (2022) The Heart of the Bible
Mango A (2002) The Bibliography of the Founder of Modern Turkey
Marx K and Engels F (2014) The Communist Manifesto
McGrath A (2004) Theology. The Basics
Mishra P (2010) An End to Suffering: The Buddha in the World
Moody R (2003) Life after Life
Moriarty M (2011) René Descartes. The Passions of the Soul

Paisley I (1997) Christian Foundations
Ricard M (2002) L'infiniti dans la paume de la main.
Ross A (2012) Summary: Who moved the Stone
Russell B (1957) Why I am not a Christian
Russell W (2017) Martin Luther: The Ninety-Five Theses and other writings
Sagan C (2002) Cosmos
Sellars J (2020) Lessons in Stoicism: What Ancient Philosophers Teach us.
Seneca A (2022) Beginners Guide to Stoicism
Sheldrake R (2012) The Science Delusion
Sproul R (1998) Essential Truths of the Christian Faith
Stevenson I (1980) Twenty Cases Suggestive of Reincarnation
Strobel L (2004) The Case for – Christ, Heaven, Creator, Faith
Surhone L (2011) Operation Claret: Borneo Operations 1964–5
Swinburne R (1996) Is There a God?
Thamour S (2018) Why I am a Hindu
Thatcher M (1995) The Path to Power
The Holy Bible – (No references required!)
Thera N (2010) The World of the Buddha
Tucker J (2008) Life before Life: Children's Memories of Previous Lives
Tutu D (2016) The Book of Joy
van Lommel P (2011) Consciousness beyond Life
Welby J (2022) The Power of Reconciliation
Wells H (2018) The War of the Worlds
Wolfe T (2018) The Kingdom of Space